Praise for GRANDMOTHERS' WISDOM

"After reading this beautiful book, I could not help wondering, as I have so many times over the years, what the world would be like if the grandmothers had been in charge, women in every culture who alone know what it means to give birth, mothers everywhere who sacrifice their own bodies for the sake of new life, and do so with such courage, dignity, and stoic resolve. The word sacrifice means to make sacred, and every time a child is born, the luminosity of the divine is affirmed. Men make war. Women make life."

—Wade Davis, professor of anthropology, University of British Columbia, and author of *Beneath the Surface of Things*

"The birth of the Council of Thirteen Grandmothers was a blessing for many of us. It inspired many wom-en who want to protect and defend Mother Earth and her sacred system of life to step forward in more powerful ways. The Thirteen Grandmothers and all of those who have been working diligently for the next seven generations have emphasized the power of women, and especially grandmother-aged women who embody authority and wisdom. May this book inspire many more women to act to create a safe, healthy, sustainable, equitable world for generations to come."

—Pennie Opal Plant, Yaqui and undocumented Choctaw/Cherokee, founder of the Society of Fearless Grandmothers and cofounder of Idle No More SF Bay and Movement Rights

"Reading this book is like sitting at the feet of your aunties' aunties and realizing you have come home."

—Tyson Yunkaporta, author of *Sand Talk: How Indigenous Thinking Can Change the World*

"*Grandmothers' Wisdom* is a treasure trove of personal stories and insightful teachings from those who have experienced trauma but emerged stronger and more aligned with the cosmos. Each account gives us a glimpse into a unique journey and its challenges when reaching a deeper purpose, inspiring the reader too to stay the course to reach their own singular calling. These humble and courageous grandmothers and others like them are guardians of our future, whatever it may be. Their voices strengthen my spiritual bones, expand my heart energy, and prepare me to carry on despite fear or uncertainty in order to help bring about healing and a Life-enhancing future."

—Darcia Narvaez, professor emerita of psychology, University of Notre Dame and founder-host of EvolvedNest.org

"*Grandmothers' Wisdom* offers readers privileged glimpses into the lands and cultural contexts that shaped the beloved elders of the Thirteen Indigenous Grandmothers Council. Through the telling of their unique stories, contributors of *Grandmothers' Wisdom* weave a colorful tapestry of wisdom and sense for this aching world. A treasure of a little book, and a gift to generations to come."

—Sophia Rokhlin, coauthor of *When Plants Dream: Ayahuasca, Amazonian Shamanism, and the Global Psychedelic Renaissance*

"This beautiful book is needed now more than ever! The world is suffering from ego, arrogance, and ignorance due to lack of wisdom. The feminine voices of wisdom woven together here, in this timeless book, will guide us how we can recover our humanity and our love for one another. This book will prove to be a key to open our hearts and enter the house of happiness."

—Satish Kumar, president emeritus and founder of Schumacher College

"In a world that is heavy with the consequences of human rights abuses, the violent extraction of Mother Earth, and rampant colonialism, we need stories that remind us of our connection to ourselves and Mother Earth, stories that keep us tethered to the beauty of cultural experiences from around the world. This book of Indigenous Grandmother wisdom will inspire us right now and for generations to come. We are so incredibly lucky to have a chance to learn from the wisdom-wells of Grandmothers from across the globe, who leave a lasting legacy of love, care, and solidarity for us to embrace. I encourage you to buy this book, sit with the wisdom in it, and let it change the way you live your life and explore The Sacred around you."

—Kaitlin B. Curtice, citizen of the Potawatomi Nation and award-winning author of *Native, Living Resistance,* and *An Indigenous Celebration of Nature* series

"*Grandmothers' Wisdom: Living Portrayals from the International Council of Thirteen Indigenous Grandmothers* is not just a book; it's a profound testament to the resilience, wisdom, and guidance of Indigenous women throughout history. In a world where ancestral knowledge is often overlooked, this book stands as a beacon, reminding us of the invaluable teachings passed down through generations. This book is not merely a collection of stories; it's a roadmap for rematriating entheogens, preserving ancestral wisdom, and taking tangible steps towards liberation. Through the songs of our grandmothers, we find direct guidance on how to heal the wounds of our world and forge a path towards a more harmonious existence."

—Mikaela de la Myco, Mothers of the Mushroom

GRANDMOTHERS' WISDOM

Living Portrayals from the
International Council of Thirteen Indigenous Grandmothers

SYNERGETIC PRESS
SANTA FE • LONDON

A full list of image credits appears on page 478.

Published by Synergetic Press
1 Blue Bird Court, Santa Fe, New Mexico 87508
& 24 Old Gloucester St., London, WCIN 3AL, England

Library of Congress Control Number: 2024935913

ISBN 978-1-957869-17-9 (paperback)
ISBN 978-1-957869-18-6 (ebook)

Cover design: Lindsey Cleworth
Cover art/illustration: Angelina Nasso
Creative director: Marisol Villanueva Méndez
Interior design: Milenda Nan Ok Lee
Managing Editor: Noelle Armstrong
Production Editor: Allison Felus

Printed in Malaysia

Dedicated to

the Divine Mother,

Her children,

and

the future generations.

Contents

Foreword
Celebrating our Sacred Earth Family

DR. VANDANA SHIVA

Grandmothers' Wisdom: Living Portrayals from the International Council of Thirteen Indigenous Grandmothers contains more than the collective wisdom, creativity, and amazing life stories of thirteen grandmothers—Grandmother Tsering Dolma Gyaltong, Grandmother Clara Shinobu Iura, Grandmother Beatrice Long Visitor Holy Dance, Grandmother Julieta Casimiro, Grandmother Rita Pitka Blumenstein, Grandmother Aama Bombo, Grandmother Margaret Behan, Grandmother Flordemayo, Grandmother Rita Long Visitor Holy Dance, Grandmother Bernadette Rebienot, Grandmother Maria Alice Campos Freire, Grandmother Mona Polacca, and Grandmother Agnes Baker Pilgrim. It is the distillation of wisdom teachings across space and time, across diverse cultures and faiths, across history. Grandmothers are the embodiment of all cultures. Their wisdom is the cumulative wisdom of humanity. It shows the path to our future and the future of all beings, all our relatives.

Grandmothers' Wisdom can help us reclaim the sacred; it can help us reclaim our future in times of collapse and extinction. Through over 500 years of the rule of greed, colonialism, and mastery over nature, biological diversity and cultural diversity have been destroyed. Attempts have been made to erase the sacred in our lives and install new gods of money, market, and technology. Terra Madre, Sacred Mother Earth, has been reduced to Terra Nullius, the empty, dead earth—mere raw material to be extracted from and polluted. Greed and the will to mastery led to the false, arrogant, and anthropocentric assumption that humans are separate from nature and superior to other species who have no intrinsic worth, value, intelligence, or creativity. They are not recognized as sacred, sentient beings but instead reduced to objects to be owned, manipulated for profits, and pushed to extinction.

The colonial process of desacralization colonized nature, women, and diverse cultures. An example of this can be seen through Robert

Boyle, who became the governor of the Society for the Propagation of the Gospel in New England in 1661 and the first president of the Royal Society. Boyle sought to implement Francis Bacon's mechanical philosophy, which defined living earth as dead matter to be manipulated and controlled for exploitation to expand "man's empire" over nature. For him, nature had to be tortured to extract her "secrets." He described the project of domination over nature as "The Masculine Birth of Time" and saw this philosophy as an instrument of power not just over nature but also over the indigenous people who held nature as sacred. He explicitly declared his intention to rid the New England Indians of their ridiculous notions about the workings of nature and attacked their perceptions of nature "as a kind of goddess," arguing that "the veneration, wherewith men are imbued for what they call nature, has been a discouraging impediment to the empire of man over the inferior creatures of God."[1]

I have called the illusion of separation of humans from nature and superiority over other species ecological apartheid ("apartheid" being the word for apartness and separateness/separation in the Afrikaans language). Eco apartheid is the false assumption that humans are separate from nature, are her conquerors, masters, owners. It is a denial of the fact that we are part of nature, not separate from her. This worldview also engenders hierarchies and the illusion of superiority—of humans as superior to other species, men as superior to women, white

people as superior to Black people and people of color, colonizers as superior to those they colonize, and one faith as superior to the diversity of belief systems that have nourished cultural diversity. Separation and superiority create structures of violence against nature, women, and every "other" defined as lesser beings, with the objective of colonization. Inequality and injustice are rooted in the false assumption of separation and superiority.

Grandmothers' Wisdom shows us that in spite of centuries of attempts to build an empire of man over lesser creatures, grandmothers have kept the reverence for all creation alive. Their stories are stories of resilience and a sacred journey that teaches us to live as members of an earth family, with veneration for all our relatives. This work declares that the earth is living, that we are not separate from the earth—we are a strand in the web of life, we are members of one earth family, and all beings are our relatives. There are no strangers, no hierarchies, no superiority and inferiority. Oneness is the path to sustainability, justice, and nonviolence that will bring peace and harmony.

It is not an accident that all the grandmothers whose stories are brought to you in this book are also healers. They are co-creators with healing plants to create harmony, well-being, and health in their communities.

Grandmothers' Wisdom creates the possibility of reclaiming the sacred and, through reverence for all creation, protecting and regenerating the biodiversity of life, abundance of living economies, and cultures of peace, nonviolence, and well-being for all. Through the

1 Brian Easlea, *Science and Sexual Oppression; Patriarchy's Confrontation with Woman and Nature* (London: Weidenfield and Nicholson, 1981), 73.

sacred bond with our earth relatives we can heal the world. We can heal ourselves.

As the ancient sacred hymn of the *Rig Veda* on healing plants reminds us, plants are mothers, plants are creative, plants heal. And grandmothers who carry this ancient knowledge and wisdom are healers on a wounded earth.

HYMN XCVII. Praise of Herbs
(translated by Ralph T. H. Griffith)

1 HERBS that sprang up in time of old, three ages earlier than the Gods—
   Of these, whose hue is brown, will I declare the hundred powers and seven.

2 Ye, Mothers, have a hundred homes, yea, and a thousand are your growths.
   Do ye who have a thousand powers free this my patient from disease.

3 Be glad and joyful in the Plants, both blossoming and bearing fruit,
   Plants that will lead us to success like mares who conquer in the race.

4 Plants, by this name I speak to you, Mothers, to you the Goddesses:
   Steed, cow, and garment may I win, win back thy very self, O man.

5 The Holy Fig tree is your home, your mansion is the Parna tree:
   Winners of cattle shall ye be if ye regain for me this man.

6 He who hath store of Herbs at hand like Kings amid a crowd of men,—
   Physician is that sage's name, fiend-slayer, chaser of disease.

7 Herbs rich in Soma, rich in steeds, in nourishments, in strengthening power,—
   All these have I provided here, that this man may be whole again.

8 The healing virtues of the Plants stream forth like cattle from the stall,—
   Plants that shall win me store of wealth, and save thy vital breath, O man.

9 Reliever is your mother's name, and hence Restorers are ye called.
   Rivers are ye with wings that fly: keep far whatever brings disease.

10 Over all fences have they passed, as steals a thief into the fold.
    The Plants have driven from the frame whatever malady was there.

11 When, bringing back the vanished strength, I hold these herbs within my hand,
    The spirit of disease departs ere he can seize upon the life.

12 He through whose frame, O Plants, ye creep member by member, joint by joint,—
    From him ye drive away disease like some strong arbiter of strife.

13 Fly, Spirit of Disease, begone, with the blue jay and kingfisher.
    Fly with the wind's impetuous speed, vanish together with the storm.

14 Help every one the other, lend assistance each of you to each,
    All of you be accordant, give furtherance to this speech of mine.

Preface

I embrace you as beautiful relatives of the world. I offer you an open hand to show that I greet you in peace.

I come from a culture that has been on this North American continent since time immemorial, surviving and thriving despite many hardships and challenges. Over the ages, simple and fundamental truths have supported our survival that I think are relevant more than ever today for society at large. Principles of humility and making decisions with the consideration of seven generations to come might seem basic and easy to take for granted. Our heartfelt efforts have been focused on the basic call to consciousness: We are all related. This is based on the principles of interconnectedness and humility. It is precisely these principles that need to be integrated into our lives in a deeper way. Everything is my relative. This helps us to see the value in each person and each living thing. We have an everyday existence, with family, tribal community, and our spiritual and earth-based practices with the lands, medicines, language, and ceremonial ways of prayer. The council Grandmothers have commemorated our existence by traveling the world, visiting each of our sister Grandmothers' home country. We celebrate that accomplishment.

By stepping forward between and within cultures and languages, we can overcome boundaries. We can cross borders not only geographically but also psychologically and spiritually. If we were to look at Earth from two hundred miles up in space, we would see that divisions do not exist, and it is very clear that we are one family on Mother Earth. This simple point of view could guide us to act in a way that is life-sustaining, and our worldview would be more open and inclusive. We would listen more and have greater patience in finding solutions.

It has been a long journey that continues in our everyday life. Now is the time of awakening, where we become aware of our fundamental relationship to one another and most important, of our existence in this world.

As we move forward, the Grandmothers Council will celebrate its twentieth anniversary in October 2024. Through prayers, spiritual action, and social action, we have worked tirelessly for peace, respect for nature, conservation, and recovery of ancestral traditions, our traditional medicines, and the preservation of our cultures. In our villages, towns, and cities, we are spiritual activists, medicine women, tribal elders, and advocates for sustaining earth-based ways of life. As individuals, each of us is recognized for our work to preserve our traditions and indigenous culture.

The Grandmothers have been weaving our shared life experiences, cultural lifeways, and wisdom by coming together unified in spirit, heart, mind, and body. Though we walked together in our sisterhood over the years, as life would have it, several have journeyed on into the realm of the spirit world. This reality is not easy. About the lives of my dear, departed Grandmother-sisters, it is a great joy to be able to say, "They were there with me on the great journey of being the International Council of Thirteen Indigenous Grandmothers."

This is a time of deep reflection on the lives of my dear Grandmother-sisters and how the precious memories of them shine love and light, and inspire a deep sense of gratitude for how they influenced my life and those of many others in this day and age. In my time of reflection this morning, tears came and flowed. I was overcome by some sadness, followed by a little moment of being uplifted in my heart.

Many have asked if the Grandmothers Council no longer exists. "When are you going to replace the Grandmothers?" There was a time when all the Grandmothers were present and we addressed the matter of succession. We had a dialogue where each Grandmother had a chance to speak on the matter. The consensus was that there would not be succession. The agreement was that our place at the table of the Grandmothers was like a divine intervention, that it was spirit-driven that we all came together in October 2004 when we established the council and made the commitment to carry out our mission. The foundation of our work was the ceremony and medicine each of us came to the circle with, our own unique lived experience and instruction, which could not be replaced. We then made the commitment to carry on until the last of the Grandmothers leaves this world. Therefore, the remaining Grandmothers continue the mission as we continue to grow through our life cycle. We offer presentations and gatherings, and participate in activities with those who are like-minded in fulfilling our mission. Each Grandmother individually continues to do their work as called upon by our supporters, and in their own businesses and organizations.

Looking forward, we are certain we will see concrete results of our actions and our collective intent to unify and carry forward the message of our elders, teaching respect for the natural laws for all of life.

GRANDMOTHER MONA POLACCA

Introduction

The Earth is our loving grandmother. For all time, Cheyenne storytellers, generation after generation, have repeated this belief with both their minds and their hearts. As they say, The Great One, Everywhere Spirit, created the universe and all life with power so vast it defies human imagination. Entirely with the force of thought, the four powerful spirit beings came into existence to witness creation and to eventually safeguard and shelter all life, especially human beings. Next came the water of life, the fire and light of the sun, the infinite sky air, and compassionate Earth. The Great One, Everywhere Spirit, contemplated creation and thought the Earth to be the most beautiful of all, then declared that the Earth be known as our grandmother.

Grandmother Earth is also, more commonly, referred to as Mother Earth. Indeed, she is first woman, first mother, first teacher, oldest mother, and oldest grandmother. The Thirteen Indigenous Grandmothers whose magnificent lives are encapsulated in the chapters of this book represent Earth's titanic spirit, power, beauty, and love. Individually and collectively, they are rooted in the Earth and carry her wisdom as a perpetual trust. They are committed to sustaining their Earth home and to educating and defending the hearts of all the world's children.

The Grandmothers are border crossers. They have crossed cultural boundaries, language divides, unique spiritual traditions, and continents to visit each other in their respective homelands and to offer collective prayer at their sacred places. Their homelands and inherited knowledge sustain them as the Keeper Women of Earth, who hold a reverence for all creation. They are symbolic of the great love and constant, peaceful devotion of Earth.

These sister grandmothers are the brave-hearted voices of their ancestors, who entrusted them with their strong indigenous ways of being and of seeing. With clarity, they see a world irrationally off balance, rapidly consuming the precious resources of Earth, a one-time gift of The Great One, Everywhere Spirit. They see many people who have lost respect for life and who have abandoned their divinely mandated stewardship responsibilities for the Earth, which the Grandmothers are prepared to defend.

With heavy hearts, the beloved women elders observe the greed of the corporate world, with its blatant disregard for the health of Earth as they drain her life-sustaining blood-water and vital organs, such as fossil fuels. In early 2016 thousands of indigenous protesters, high-profile individuals, Indian organization representatives, and allies converged at Standing Rock to dispute the construction of Energy Transfer Partners' underground Dakota Access Pipeline. They were there to protect the tribe's drinking water source and cultural resources.

The pipeline would pass under the Missouri River and Lake Oahe near the Fort Laramie Treaty lands of the Standing Rock Sioux. The tribe was concerned about a possible crude oil spill, which Senator Bernie Sanders described as the dirtiest oil on the planet. Such a spill would contaminate their water supply, posing grave danger to reservation residents: their mantra is "Water is Life."

Energy Transfer Partners hired TigerSwan, a private security firm, to quash the protesters, and they used military-style counterterrorism tactics and guard dogs. There were 300 injuries and more than 487 arrests. President Barack Obama directed the Army Corps of Engineers to conduct a further environmental impact assessment, but President Donald Trump subsequently reversed this directive. The Dakota Access Pipeline was opened on May 14, 2017.

This was a desecration of sacred ground that could only intensify the heartbreaking grief of the Thirteen Indigenous Grandmothers. To their unimagined horror, they saw their beautiful Earth Mother, Grandmother to all, under relentless attack from culturally materialistic resource extractors. Seventy-five percent of Indian sacred sites are located on federal lands, and the federal government all too often works with pro-development entities. Although the U.S. Congress passed the American Indian Religious Freedom Act in 1978, it has no legal enforcement remedy. Thus, this country's indigenous population

has yet to enjoy First Amendment protection, especially as it relates to their sacred sites.

Sacred sites are critical to the continuity of indigenous ways of life. Like those who walked before them, indigenous people continue to make pilgrimages to sacred sites to pray, make offerings, engage in ceremony, renew and strengthen their spirits, seek guidance for the heart and spirit, revitalize their healing gifts, and maintain their accountability to their ancestors. This concisely describes the spiritual heart of these grandmothers, especially their reverence for creation.

They regularly visit their ceremonial gathering places, altars, temples, or other prayer places, such as sweat lodges, Sun Dance arbors, Native American Church tipis, or churches. They pray in their homes to greet the morning sun and at night to express appreciation for the day. As contemporary prayer women who carry valuable ancestral knowledge, they each maintain an active prayer life.

As articulated in their Mission Statement, the International Council of Thirteen Indigenous Grandmothers are spiritual activists, prayer women oriented toward peacemaking, galvanized by their suffering. India marked a significant event on their earth journey when they had a private meeting with His Holiness the Dalai Lama, a like-hearted spirit, and blended the messages of compassion and peace.

They are troubled by the state of the world, global warming, and the defilement of the four basic elements of life—earth, air, fire, and water—brought about by human activity. Indigenous life has always been about the children, and they see the obligation to nurture and educate them. Through them they seek to sustain the strength of indigenous ways of knowing and their profound teachings, which are desperately needed in the world today.

Thirteen grandmothers answered the call for spiritual activism. They brought their knowledge and expertise with them as spiritual keepers, visionaries, spirit travelers, healers, sweat lodge leaders, Sun Dancers, and water women in the Native American Church. They combined their strong individual prayer lives into a colossal collective prayer, which has to be mighty to restore oneness and a just and peaceful world. Though their lives are big, they are humble about the places they occupy on the sacred circle of our one Earth. They work for the good of humanity, especially its health, physically and spiritually. They honor indigenous wisdom, especially in the original sacred languages in which it was initially expressed.

Some may wonder about the number of sister grandmothers, which corresponds to the thirteen cycles of the moon in a year. The moon, "night sun," second only to the light of the sun, is another powerful grandmother. She lives in the distant night sky and revolves around the Earth, controlling the ocean tides and sacred menstrual cycles of all the Earth's daughters. Thus, the number of council Grandmothers is culturally congruent with indigenous worldviews.

The grandmothers' lives are perfect studies for all the generations, male and female, and for the universal community of the world that is disturbed by the disoriented state of contemporary life. This book would have been a perfect textbook in my Native American Studies classes, were I not retired from Montana State University. It should be embraced by academicians and those concerned with today and all our tomorrows, especially the quality of the life that our children will live.

The Thirteen Indigenous Grandmothers walk in the footsteps of all indigenous grandmothers who have ever lived within the sacred embrace of our first grandmother. These grandmothers carry their combined wisdom and reverence for all life. I thank them and I honor them from my heart. They have embraced the teachings of our one Grandmother Earth and are her wisdom keepers. They just do what grandmothers do.

HENRIETTA MANN, PH.D.
Tsetsehestaestse (Cheyenne)
Hoostah-oo-nah'e
The Woman Who Comes to Offer Prayer/Prayer Woman
Professor Emerita, Montana State University, Bozeman

Editors' Note

The voices of the Thirteen Grandmothers are as diverse as their homelands: the bounty of the South American Amazon rainforest; the fertility of the Central American highlands; the magic of the Sierra Madre of Oaxaca; the wide expanse of the Alaskan tundra; the immensity of the Grand Canyon; the majesty of the old-growth forests; the vastness of the plains and deserts of North America; the sacredness of the Black Hills of South Dakota; the ancient shrines of the northwest coast of Japan; the contemplative Himalayan mountains of Tibet and Nepal; and the ancestral richness of the Central African forests. Indigenous, earth-based cultures, languages, traditions, and spiritual practices are an expression of the very earth from which the people originate.

For nearly twenty years we have worked and traveled with the Grandmothers Council, accompanying them in their public gatherings around the world, witnessing them touch the lives of so many through their prayers and teachings. Their mission inspires us. The spirit that moves them to share their message with the world has catalyzed the *Grandmothers Wisdom* project.

In 2010 we began production by revisiting each of their homelands to document their personal lives. This intimate process spanned a period of over five years, involving audio interviews, photography, video recordings, and artistic renderings.

In interviewing, transcribing, translating, and editing, it is as if we have been sitting at the feet of our elders, listening to and honoring their sovereign voices in order to preserve their legacies. Many of the Grandmothers still speak their indigenous languages in their families, villages, and ceremonies, yet they have had to incorporate colonial languages (English, French, Spanish, Portuguese) in their broader lives. We faced the challenges not only of translating their mother tongue or the colonial languages into English but also of preserving the cultural nuances so easily lost between an oral transmission and the written word.

Every aspect of this documentation has been approved by the Grandmothers and their family members. This has often involved re-translating their words back from English to their mother tongue to assure their authenticity.

We have devoted ourselves to honoring the Grandmothers' lives, connecting with their struggles to preserve and revitalize their cultures. In this current era and its widespread climate of disconnection, we believe all people can benefit from the ageless wisdom of earth-based ways.

May this book be a legacy for generations to come.

MARISOL VILLANUEVA MÉNDEZ
ANN RENÉE ROSENCRANZ
Content Editors, *Grandmothers' Wisdom: Living Portrayals from the International Council of Thirteen Indigenous Grandmothers*

GRANDMOTHERS' WISDOM

Living Portrayals from the
International Council of Thirteen Indigenous Grandmothers

om târe tuttâre ture svâhâ

ONE

GRANDMOTHER
TSERING DOLMA GYALTONG

both have since passed away, leaving their only son, Thupten Thando, who lives and works in the Tibetan School in Palampur, near Dharamsala.

My parents took a great interest in educating their children. My ability to read and write, my ability to recite prayers and read scriptures is all because of my grand-father's and my parents' initiative and wisdom.

When I was six years old my parents admitted me to the Shol Tatong School, where I received a traditional high school education from a renowned and great teacher. That was fairly unusual at that time, because most of the girls who were sent to school were essentially learning trades more than reading and writing. They would learn knitting and sewing and those kinds of things. The school that I went to had one hundred students with only seven to ten girls. I was one of those few. At the age of fourteen I graduated, passing the final examination with good marks. I was privileged to offer tea to all the other students and teachers as a symbol of graduating.

The Chinese alleged that there was no opportunity for girls to study and also that there were no schools for the general public (only for nobles), which was absolute nonsense and false. In fact, there were schools in every district throughout the country. Young people, not only the sons and daughters of noble families but also the children of businessmen or ordinary people, had equal opportunity of education without distinction by family status. Students who were good at their studies in the monasteries could become monk officials irrespective of their family backgrounds, by studying at the Tse Laptra schools and graduating with meritorious results. It's also true that many families didn't send their kids to school because they were more concerned with survival.

Tibetan schoolgirls' cultural presentation at the Tibetan Children's Village in Dharamsala, India, 2006

While I was in school my father had an affair with my mother's friend, leading to my parents' separation. When I was fifteen years old my father returned to his hometown, Porong. My mother came back home to Lhasa. Before my father's departure from Lhasa, we young children were living with our parents alternately. It was troublesome for us to go back and forth between homes. However, both my grandparents were alive and residing in Lhasa, so we were lucky enough to stay with them most of the time.

I clearly remember one time when I went with my mother to meet my father, who was sitting with his newly married wife. My mother was morally so good mannered that she showed courtesy to our foster mother by respectfully calling her *Nyingla* (a Tibetan way of referring to a noble wife) without any sign of jealousy or bad manners. We children were amazed to see the unchanged behavior of our mother.

The husband of my father's new wife had passed away years before. Through their new marriage, three sons and two daughters were born. We still maintained a close relationship with our half-brothers and sisters.

My family was not part of the nobility, but they were well respected. My father was a government official. My grandfather worked as a treasurer in the treasury department of the Tibetan government. Beyond his salary, the department provided other needs, like bales of *tsampa* (roasted barley flour), butter, meat, cheese, and even fuel. He used to give valuable advice and suggestions even to His Excellency, the Prime Minister Kungoe Lukhangwa. As a child I delivered messages between those two great people. This showed how close they were in their relationship and how they trusted each other. Even across these distinctions in society, I had good friendships with the prime minister's children.

So my parents' changed situation did not affect the studies of us youngsters. My grandmother Tashi Tsomo was from eastern Tibet, from Kham. Our elders greatly influenced the improvement and continuation of our education. We owe a lot to them.

Persecution, Torture, and Imprisonment

My younger brother Jampa Soepa was admitted to Sera Monastery. He excelled in his studies and was finally promoted to *chandzö*,[4] manager of the monastery. After the Chinese occupation, Jampa helped my children and me escape from Tibet and stayed in India. After the uprising against Chinese rule in Lhasa in 1959, Jampa thought maybe he'd go back to Tibet and they wouldn't harm a monk. But he was arrested as a reactionary. They arranged for him to be part of a public gathering, a mass beating. Fortunately, he was secretly smuggled away from the beating in a bag containing comestible items like meat, butter, and tsampa. It's a true story.

Still, he was recaptured and imprisoned in labor camps for twenty-three long years, where he experienced unbearable tortures and suffering. Due to starvation, forced labor, and other maltreatments for a number of

---

4. A senior manager/treasurer of an aristocratic or monastic estate, or the senior manager/treasurer of an aristocratic family or a monastic unit. Generally *chandzö* handled both internal and external issues and were higher in power and status than *nyerpa* (stewards), who only handled the storerooms.

years in prison, he lost his mental capacity and memory. At last, however, he managed to escape into India secretly in 1985 and rejoined his old Sera Monastery in southern India under the name of former chandzö. He is now eighty-four years old, and his health is not too bad.

My brother Lobsang also escaped into India. At that time all Tibetans were hoping to get a chance of returning to their homeland very soon, and the spirit of patriotism was very high. The Committee for Tibetan Social Welfare sent Lobsang into Tibet through the Nepalese border to gather intelligence information. Unfortunately, however, the Chinese captured and imprisoned him for twenty-five years. Taking advantage of a slight relaxation of Chinese policy in Tibet, he managed to go to India in 1981. Soon after his arrival, he had to be admitted to the hospital and stayed for months. But owing to his starvation during the imprisonment and hardships in the labor camps, and especially the tortures he suffered during interrogation, his health deteriorated. I hurriedly went to India from Canada to meet my ailing brother and tried to give him the best treatments and perform the necessary rituals for his recovery, but it was all in vain. Soon afterward, Lobsang passed away. During the funeral, the Department of Security sent some monks from Nechung Monastery to say prayers for him and extended all possible help for continued prayers for his departed soul.

Another older half-brother of mine named Jola Dradul was a well-known *nyerpa*,[5] the general manager of the Porong region. The Chinese imprisoned many prominent public figures around the country, so he was captured and sent for life imprisonment, first in the Kongpo district and then in a prison near the Chinese border, in Kansu Province. He was subject to starvation, persecution, and forced labor even for minor mistakes. Hunger made him eat left out pig slop and even dried human waste. He never returned home, so I never saw him again. It was said that 80 percent of the prisoners died in the prisons due to hunger, hardships, and suffering. Very few had the chance of returning home.

It was strange—both my brothers, Jampa Soepa and Jola Dradul, were in the same prison but in different groups. They never saw each other because the Chinese did not allow the groups to gather. This I learned from Jampa Soepa after he came to India.

Jola Dradul's younger brother Chime, also my half-brother, was imprisoned by the Chinese in Gurtsa, Lhasa. He died in prison after facing a lot of hardships and ill treatment.

Jola Dradul's younger sister, my older half-sister, Phurbu Bhuti, was sent as a bride to Porong Khangsar Karpo's family. The others, including my niece Kalsang Youdon and her family, are leading happy and comfortable lives in Nepal and America, like other fellow Tibetans in exile.

Under the Chinese oppression, Tibetans, irrespective of high or low status, male or female, rich or poor, were subjected to continued persecution and torture with an equal yardstick, sooner or later. There are endless tales about the oppression, but I only write about the people related to my family. This might serve as an example of all the suffering and hardship we endured under Chinese rule. These accounts are without exaggeration and all of them are true.

---

5. A steward or manager. In some monasteries, the *nyerpa* was in charge of storerooms under the authority of a higher manager called a *chandzö*.

Under the Chinese oppression, Tibetans, irrespective of high or low status, male or female, rich or poor, were subjected to continued persecution and torture with an equal yardstick, sooner or later. There are endless tales about the oppression, but I only write about the people related to my family. This might serve as an example of all the suffering and hardship we endured under Chinese rule. These accounts are without exaggeration and all of them are true.

Marriage

When I was nineteen years old, I met Tsering Gyaltong, and eventually we got married. Fifty-seven years have passed since our wedding. Gyaltong had to discontinue his studies at Sermey Monastery in Lhasa due to financial problems. After he left the monastic world, he pursued his interest in business, which involved traveling between Tibet and neighboring countries buying and selling goods. He moved into my house after the marriage. We had three children while living in Lhasa, Yangchen Dolkar (daughter), Gelek Norbu (son), and Yangchen Lhamo (daughter).

During that time (early 1950s), Lhasa was still very peaceful and our people enjoyed freedom. People were free to carry out their own businesses for their livelihood without restrictions. Construction projects could be seen everywhere, signs of development and prosperity.

Chinese Invasion, Tibetan Resistance

Then Gyaltong's older brother, Nangpa, and others arrived from northeastern Tibet telling us about the Chinese invasion and reforms. Tibetans in that region were in unsure and unsafe conditions and suffering hardships under Chinese control. When Nangpa saw that people in central Tibet were keeping servants, wearing precious ornaments, and leading lavish lifestyles, he reluctantly expressed his concern. "Tibet will not remain free as before," he said. "These activities will lead to unnecessary difficulties in the future." But people did not believe

him; they ignored his comments. However, soon afterward, his words proved to be true.

Soon thereafter, Chinese aggression reached from across the border. They proclaimed, "We have come to liberate Tibet peacefully. After successfully making the Tibetan society prosperous, we will return to China." When the Chinese first came into Lhasa, they didn't come with guns blazing. Typically what they would do was build roads, hospitals, and schools. They would dole out money. In the early '50s they didn't invade, they came in as investors, just like they're doing right now in Nepal.

In reality, since 1949 they had already forcefully captured Chamdo, in eastern Tibet. Now they gradually marched toward central Tibet, making Lhasa an unsafe place to live. They also rendered powerless the Tibetan government. Resentment against China grew rapidly and in 1952, a new people's movement came into being under the leadership of Chagzo Dhamcho Sonam and others from Sera Monastery. Soon the Chinese arrested prominent leaders of the movement and it became ineffective. In turn, His Holiness's personal attendant, Senior Chamberlain Phala Thupten Woden, started an underground resistance organization to continue the people's movement.

My husband served as one of the members of the newly established organization and worked sincerely to serve the people. All members took the oath of secrecy by signing a paper with a seal, *Theltse Lagkhor*. The main responsibility of that organization was to fight for Tibet's status: safety of Tibetans in general and particularly in Lhasa. The organization also held the principal responsibility to petition for the return of His Holiness the Dalai Lama to Tibet. His Holiness had left for Bei-

Tsering Dolma in Kalimpong, India, circa 1959

jing a year before, in 1954. Tibetans feared that he might be forced to remain and serve the Chinese interests. A committee consisting of Alo Chozed Tsering Dorjee, Amdo Gyaltong Tsering, and other representatives from monasteries surrounding Lhasa left for China with a special petition. Fortunately, His Holiness had already begun his return journey, and they met him and his entourage along the route. The Tibetan people were relieved to find the Dalai Lama returning home without any health problems or hindrances.

Having taken the oath of secrecy by swearing in the name of Tibet's two protectors, Palden Lhamo[6] (deity) and the Nechung Oracle, all members of the secret resistance discussed new proposals for the good of the community, to keep the Tibetan government informed and to receive necessary guidance. In order to avoid leaks of secrets, to improve efficiency, to have better coordination, and to improve the mass communication network, the committee arranged a program of donating alms to the poor and homeless in Lhasa on auspicious days, the 8th and 15th of every month. This would be seen externally, on the surface, as one thing, while internally they would work to offer a golden throne[7] to His Holiness the Dalai Lama from all the people of Cholkasum: the three provinces of Tibet, Amdo, Kham, and U-Tsang. They also organized public meetings, creating awareness among the masses about Tibet's status by pasting posters on the town walls and distributing leaflets among the people. While carrying out this work, my husband, the late Gyaltong,

6. Palden Lhamo means "Glorious Goddess" and can feature a wide range of wrathful female protectors and dakinis.

7. Ceremonial offerings for the longevity of His Holiness.

went often as a messenger to the Dalai Lama's palace and Thromshigkang to meet Phala Dronyer Chemo, His Holiness's chamberlain. This was very risky, but he rendered service at the cost of his life at that critical time.

My husband, Gyaltong, was not alone. I also helped wholeheartedly to deliver secret letters and get responses from here and there. I was very scared, and very young, probably about twenty-four or twenty-five years old. I was nervous, but courageous enough to do what I had to do. It was very intimidating to see all of these Chinese watching me.

Gradually, the Chinese attitude toward the Tibetans had gone from bad to worse. Hence, it was deemed necessary to appeal to the United Nations and the government of India. And over time, secret memorandums/petitions and important documents were prepared, including signed and sealed oath papers. The time had come to deliver them to India. But no eminent volunteer was forthcoming for the work. So my husband, Gyaltong, volunteered for it, leaving for India in 1957 with the important documents. He carried a gun for protection. Duplicate documents were sent to India through a Nepali businessman. When Gyaltong reached Shigatse he was about to be caught, so he killed one or two Chinese who were chasing him and continued on. Finally he reached Kalimpong, India, and delivered the documents to the Committee for Tibetan Social Welfare.

Gyaltong's return to Tibet was delayed, as he was asked to continue work for the committee. Many times he was close to being captured. A few of the people he worked with to get the documents had already been caught, but he managed to escape. So our family had to live separately for some time. In order to work for the committee actively, he made efforts to reunite the family in India. Although the members received very little recompense for their work, Gyaltong chose to work voluntarily and did not accept any wages.

Exile

The situation in Lhasa was becoming critical and more tense with every passing day. In the absence of Gyaltong, I had to look after three young children. The Chinese came to our house quite often for investigation. They kept a spy at our gate, disguised as a sweet seller, to keep surveillance of our activities. In this situation, it was not only difficult but also risky to live far from my husband. So I was compelled to go into exile in India in 1958. At that time, the fighting had not yet begun. But the Chinese were guarding the borders and other checkpoints without consulting the Tibetan government. So there was no easy passage.

Under normal circumstances, it would take about a month to cross the border. China took over Tibet in 1951, so all of Tibet was now sealed off. We had to escape across the hills and mountains and cross wherever possible. I had to leave my oldest child, my daughter Yangchen Dolkar, temporarily with Gyaltong's brother Nangpa. We had to do it that way so they would think that we planned to return, saying, "Oh, my daughter's here," so they didn't suspect the whole family was leaving.

The strategy was to say that we were going on a pilgrimage toward the southern Tibetan area, not to India. Then in order not to raise any suspicion, Yanchen was left behind. She was older, so she stayed. We left all of our animals and household items.

That was one of the saddest moments of my life, when I had to leave my oldest daughter behind. Yanchen was about eleven. She was going to a Chinese school. She was not told where I was going. Yanchen would come home from school asking, "Where is Mom? Will she be coming back soon?" She was looked after by my brother-in-law and escaped later on, when the Chinese invaded from the northeast. A lot of Tibetans escaped at that time with tales of atrocities that no one believed.

When we escaped we hid during the days and traveled secretly at night. My mother traveled on a pony. My two youngest children were in front of my mother. My brother Jampa was walking the pony with my infant son Gelek on his back. Because the pony moved slowly and was bent, both my mother and my children would often fall off. But

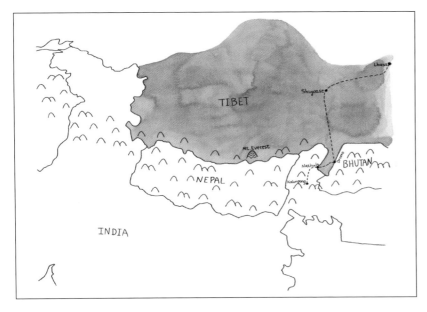

Escape route of Tsering Dolma Gyaltong

since it was dark, you couldn't see it. It was so pitch black. But you'd hear this noise like a shout and I would yell at my brother, saying, "Oh, my son probably lost his eye in that fall," and panic.

All I could hear were the screams when we were going down the steep mountainsides. And it was very steep. I knew my mother was fine because she could speak, but I was so concerned about my son because the child couldn't say, "I'm blind." Anyway, after that incident I decided not to put him on the pony anymore and carried him on my back all the way into India.

We traveled via Shigatse and Dromo, where we were almost caught by the Chinese. But by the grace of the *Triple Gem*[8] and other deities, after traveling almost a month we crossed the Nathu La pass and finally reached Kalimpong without much harm.

After nine months we were able to bring Yangchen, and thus our family was reunited. To this day, I feel good about myself because I traveled that entire journey with my mother. I was able to take care of my mother, and she passed away in my care. I would have felt badly if she had been left behind and passed away without me.

Money will come and go, but that experience of escaping with my mother and taking care of her, bringing her on that long journey with two little kids and with the help of my brother, the monk, I will always treasure.

8. Buddhists take refuge in the Three Jewels or Triple Gem (also known as the "Three Refuges"). The Three Jewels are: the Buddha, the fully enlightened one; the Dharma, the teachings expounded by the Buddha; and the Sangha, the monastic order of Buddhists who practice the Dharma.

"Grandmothers Wisdom, Triple Gem." Gouache on paper by Angelina Nasso, 2019

From left to right, Yangchen Dolkar Lhamo (daughter), Tsering Dolma, Chimi Namgyal (son), Gelek Norbu (son), and Yangchen Lhamo Dolkar (daughter). Calcutta, India, 1966

When you go into exile you leave all of your material things behind, you're not taking them with you. What's really important is love and compassion, helping others; those are the important things. Genuine empathy and compassion for others who are disadvantaged and suffering can help you overcome your own difficulties.

We left for India a year before the actual Chinese military takeover of Tibet on March 10, 1959. At that time Tibetans surrounded the Dalai Lama's palace to protect him. The Chinese killed so many thousands of innocent Tibetans surrounding the palace, thinking he was in there. In the meantime His Holiness had already just escaped in disguise. The Tibetan Women's Association has its roots at that time when on March 12, thousands of women rose up to protest the Chinese occupation.

We lived in Kalimpong, India, for some years. Meanwhile, my late husband received a letter from His Holiness the Dalai Lama graciously asking him to come to Dharamsala to work for the Tibetan government-in-exile. At first he refused, saying he could not work for the exile government because he had no education except the knowledge of reading *Uchen* script. He sought advice and guidance from several great leaders, who encouraged him to render service. I also strongly urged him to report for duty at Dharamsala immediately. Finally in September 1964 he reached Dharamsala and took charge as Deputy Minister of Home Affairs for two years; then he was asked to start and head the Department of Finance, where he served until 1972, working tirelessly per the wishes of His Holiness.

The late Gyaltong was still continuing his wholehearted and dedicated service to the government, and because he was reluctant to accept the monthly wage, I took care of the family expenses. I sold some of the gold items and used some of the money that I had brought from Tibet. Then I started a small restaurant and later shifted to a business of selling sweaters for our living. After arriving in Dharamsala I gave birth to our fourth child, our second son, named Chimi Namgyal.

The administration had been facing acute financial problems. Gyaltong had the habit of giving his salary to his subordinates and helpers as pocket money to encourage them. So he had nothing to bring home. Since he was one of the high-ranking and responsible officials in the administration, I tried to help him procure things he needed like good clothes, shoes, etc. I tried my best to extend every possible help to him for the success of his work as entrusted to him by his superiors. I never challenged his word or showed him disrespect.

Immigration to Canada

In the early '70s we decided to immigrate to Canada. In 1972 Gyaltong pleaded for the acceptance of his resignation from his post, stating that he had difficulties providing education for his children. His Holiness very kindly accepted the resignation but asked that he continue to work until his departure for Canada.

Without bothering the administration and bringing more problems to them, I worked to provide all the documents for our immigration to Canada. I managed to meet all costs, including fees for the immigration forms. In the initial stages, I worked alone without my husband knowing. Later, when legal papers needed to be signed and we needed letters from the local police office, I let my husband know.

Finally, our family, consisting of five members, including three of my children, left for Canada. Three years later we were able to sponsor over my daughter Yangchen, son-in-law Yeshi, and their three children to Canada. Soon after arriving, we sent our children to schools to get the best education per our aspiration. Once again, after coming to a far-off and foreign land, I committed myself to work hard to meet the challenge of a new life, mentally and physically, and to move forward. At first I began working as a caretaker at an apartment building and a community hall. I started at a low level and gained the confidence of the employers, gradually reaching to a higher position.

My last job was at a large-scale hospital where I looked after aged and infirm people and people with mental problems. In the beginning, when I saw those people who were critically ill or with deteriorating health causing death, I was frightened and discouraged, and even wept a number of times. I wondered whether I would be in a position to continue the work or not. Slowly I got used to the job and did not get scared, even seeing people die. Instead I was able to console them. I recited whatever mantras I knew in the ears of dying people, thereby helping everyone. I shared my techniques of serving diligently with the new trainees.

With the motive of helping others, I served the old and infirm people with pity, realizing that it was wrong to think of them as unhygienic and avoid touching them. I used to give biscuits to the hungry people even though mealtime had not yet come. I also used to take special care of those people who were mentally unsound with compassion and kindness. Since they were also human beings, they recognized the warm-heartedness that I showed to them and at numerous occasions they left notes of appreciation of my service to their family members before dying.

To sum up, I was serving the old people and patients with the utmost care, thinking that it was a good opportunity to accumulate merit and to put into practice the valuable advice of spirituality and moral ethics that I had learned from my kind teachers and parents when I was young in my holy country. I shared my experiences with the new nurse trainees, urging them to help people at their time of need. They were able to get job placements easily by winning the confidence of their employers. In this way, I was able not only to earn a good living for myself but also to accumulate merit.

Finally, when I retired from service, people were crying and saying, "We'll miss you a lot." Moreover, at the time of my retirement, thirty to forty people assembled, including the employers and my colleagues, to give a grand farewell party in my honor. During the gathering they offered a large cake to all invitees. I received gifts and souvenirs and a certificate detailing my performance and tenure. I was very proud and honored to receive all these things. Especially in a distant foreign land, which had raised high the name of my country, fellow Tibetans, and the Tibetan women. I was glad that I did not let down the image of all.

Tibetan Women's Association

In 1984 I went to India for a pilgrimage with my husband, Gyaltong. Soon thereafter, His Holiness the Dalai Lama told a General Body Conference of the Tibetan Youth Congress that there used to be a Tibetan Women's Association (TWA) in the past, but it had disappeared like a rainbow. In light of His Holiness's comments, many of my admirers and well wishers approached me and urged me to take the initiative to reorganize the women's association. Although I was lacking education and experience, I made a sincere effort toward the revival of the Tibetan Women's Association by calling volunteers to join the movement. I also approached prominent leaders and eminent educated women to gain their support for the task. In an effort to raise working capital for the movement, I started a fund-raising campaign by donating a small sum myself as a start.

Everyone extended their fullest cooperation and as a result, we were able to restart the association in Dharamsala with branches at various Tibetan settlements in India and Nepal. I worked as a volunteer for the Tibetan Women's Association in Dharamsala for twelve years in various capacities: as the general secretary, the vice president, and the president.

During my tenure with the TWA, branches were established in India and Switzerland. Then, in the wake of the resettlement of a thousand Tibetans in the United States, in 2000 we started a branch in New York and in 2004 we opened a branch in Toronto.

I didn't expect my involvement with the TWA to be for so long. I didn't have any grand plans. But I definitely felt a need to resurrect that organization. Particularly to educate women and the younger generations.

The mother's hand is the first step of teaching, and then comes the teaching in school. Even from His Holiness, the main key speech is that the mother is the most important person in a child's life. The mother is the first teacher in the child's life because they need to teach the child love and compassion. They teach them the real values of being a human being.

His Holiness says if we want global peace, it's in the hands of the human beings. And who develops the human beings? The mother

60

1959-2019

BREAKING THE SHACKLES

YEARS OF TIBETAN WOMEN'S STRUGGLE

ADVOCACY FOR HOME ACTION IN EXILE

TIBETAN WOMEN'S ASSOCIATION

nurtures the child's mind, how he thinks and believes and the values in his life. So it's the parents' role first and foremost to teach those values.

Reunion

In 1983 His Holiness gave a very auspicious teaching for world peace called the Kalachakra[9] in a place called Bodh Gaya in India. I was in charge of the Tibetan Women's Association at that time. We had undertaken the responsibility for all of the food and the sanitation aspect of the gathering.

At that time, after the Nixon and Mao Zedong diplomacy, there was a brief relaxation in Chinese rule over Tibet. Tens of thousands of Tibetans came from Tibet to the teaching. Because of this, I prayed vigorously all of the time: *If my brother is indeed in this crowd, and was able to come, then please let us meet.*

Unbeknownst to me, my brother was one of them. But neither one of us knew.

By the early '80s my brother Jampa had been released from jail in Tibet. Somehow through his contacts he found out that I was living somewhere abroad. So he thought, *I'm going to take this teaching from the Dalai Lama and afterward I'm going to look for my sister.* That was his plan.

---

9. One of the most sacred and rare of all Buddhist teachings, often referred to as the Wheel of Time. Essentially it encompasses the universal concept of the fundamental interdependence of life and nature. Its tradition is passed down from master to master; attending His Holiness the Dalai Lama's bestowing of the Kalachakra teachings and initiation is considered very auspicious.

One day during the teachings, a man came up fairly close to me. He prostrated three times, as all do toward the Dalai Lama, and then he sat down.

I was a fairly sociable person, so I looked at his face and said, "Are you from Tibet?"

He said, "Yes."

I probed him further, "Which part of Tibet?"

He told me, and I saw some sort of a resemblance in his face.

I said, "Are you from Sera Monastery? Are you a chancellor?"

And he said, "Yes."

"Is your name Jampa?"

He answered, "Yes."

I recognized him in a crowd of a quarter of a million people, there, in that spot in front of the restrooms. Once I knew who he was, I asked him, "Do you know who I am?" And there we were, brother and sister meeting again after thirty to forty years.

I was ecstatic!

We embraced each other and I asked, "When did you come?"

He said, "I came last night and my intention was to take this teaching and once the teaching was over, to come looking for you."

Fourth World Women's Conference in Beijing

During my tenure with the Tibetan Women's Association, I attended the United Nations Fourth World Conference on Women in Beijing, China, in 1995. I went to protest the Chinese mistreatment of Tibetans.

(left) Tsering Dolma with her grandson Jingten Nyandak at His Holiness the 14th Dalai Lama, Tenzin Gyatso's teaching in New York City, 1991

Tsering Dolma's younger brother Jampa Sopa at Sera Monastery in Bylakuppe, Karnataka, India, 1999

The mother's hand is the first step of teaching, and then comes the teaching in school. Even from His Holiness, the main key speech is that the mother is the most important person in a child's life. The mother is the first teacher in the child's life because they need to teach the child love and compassion. They teach them the real values of being a human being.

Although it was not possible to attend the conference in the name of the Tibetan Women's Association, I made arrangements to come as a citizen of Canada.

A lot of people were scared and thought that I would be in danger. But I was fearless. I only thought about the good things that could happen from that visit and how I could help ease some of the suffering and the plight of my people. Before I left for Beijing I told my husband, "I just want to make clear that I don't have any debts to anybody." I was at peace to go to Beijing. Others were thinking they would never see me again and were worried about me. They thought that I would not come back alive, or not come back at all. But I didn't worry about that.

There was an incident the day before the conference when we tried to hold a panel to discuss Tibetan issues. Our efforts were foiled by the Chinese when they infiltrated the entire tent with stooges so that we could not hold the forum. So that evening we held a meeting because we had lost the opportunity to express ourselves. We decided that the next day we should protest.

An idea came among the elders that the following day we would do a silent protest. Each of the participants at the women's conference had been given a flowered handkerchief by the Chinese in order to stave off the dust and also to wave. So we used that handkerchief the next day to gag our mouths and made a silent protest at the site. It started raining, but we did not wear our raincoats so that our traditional Tibetan dress, the apron, would be seen.

The next day I attended the inaugural session of the conference wearing my traditional Tibetan regalia, and it drew immense media attention. They held press conferences, generating awareness for the Tibetan cause. As a result, I was about to be arrested secretly, but through the support extended by the participants from foreign nations, I escaped being captured.

When I returned from Beijing, then I had an emotional moment. I realized what myself and others were able to accomplish. Now when I reflect on it, I realize it was a big thing for me to go there. I can recall moments when they were trying to actually capture me. I was escorted out from an embassy there.

After returning to Dharamsala I had the opportunity to apprise His Holiness about the proceedings. I also informed the leaders of the Central Tibetan Administration and the general public.

Tsering Dolma Gyaltong at the United Nations Fourth World Conference on Women in Beijing, China, 1995

(opposite page) Tsering Dolma (third from right) in silent protest at the United Nations Fourth World Conference on Women in Beijing, China, 1995

བཀའ་ཤག KASHAG

September 7, 1995

Mrs. Tsering Dolma Gyaltong
Tibetan Women's Association
Canada

Dear Mrs. Tsering Dolma Gyaltong,

We would like to express our heartiest congratulations and appreciation of your participation in the Beijing Conference on Women despite all the odds against you. It is most unfortunate that more Tibetan women could not participate in the Conference as a result of being denied visas and access to the Conference.

You have shown to the Chinese and to the world at large the undying spirit of freedom and determination and it will serve as a historical reminder to all, that Tibetan women have played a very important role in the freedom struggle and continue to do so. Your participation in the Conference and especially your peaceful demonstration has attracted massive media interest and support for the Tibetan cause.

We are proud of you and of what you have accomplished. You have set an admirable example for all Tibetans and especially Tibetan women.

With best wishes,

Yours sincerely

Kalon Sonam Topgyal
Chairman of the Kashag
Cabinet of H.H. the Dalai Lama

CENTRAL TIBETAN ADMINISTRATION OF HIS HOLINESS THE DALAI LAMA
Gangchen Kyishong, Dharamsala - 176215, H.P., India Tel. (01892)2713, 2218 Fax: (91) 1892, 2357

Spiritual Practices

I must have lived a fairly meritorious previous life. We understand that if you live a positive life, you can be reborn in a favorable realm. It's not something that you can prove, yet a correlation can be made. Just about everyone wants to get a blessing from His Holiness, and for me it came so easily when I came back from Beijing. And he gave it to me, he gave it himself. It just happens that way, you don't plan it.

The main deity I worship is *Naro Khachoma* (manifestation of Vajra-yogini). The propitiation of Her allows me to be personal, comfortable, and close to the path. I've always felt Her presence, all my life. There are so many blessings and things I receive through Her in good and bad times.

Today the power of the female is very pronounced. For years there was no gender aspect of the manifestation of Tara, and now Tara as a female manifestation of the deity is being recognized. It is a path to enlightenment. It just depends on your perception.

Tara is called upon in times of danger. For example, when you are being robbed. If in your wisdom and honesty you recite the Tara mantra, even in the act of being robbed, it has power. The same thing when you are feeling sick. I recite the Tara several times, and with those recitations you can get better.

I've been doing this practice since my teens, roughly at the age of sixteen. Later in life I had to take a major break from the spiritual practice because of all my social work.

I recall an incident in South Dakota when I was asked to visit a young man who was bedridden. They didn't know what had happened, he had been so jovial. So I poured water into his mouth and recited the Tara mantra: *oṃ tāre tuttāre ture svāhā.* Through that recitation he actually stood up.

It's not that I have power, but when I pray, I pray with the right motivation. Motivation is the key. If you have the right motivation, then a lot of positive things can happen that are not explained.

When I was in India it took me almost four months to do 500,000 recitations of the Tara mantra. You do the recitation in a meditative, grateful state.

Our daily offerings are in increments of seven. I do twenty-one. You offer flowers, lamps (lights). We also offer the first food that we have in the morning; then you offer purification and incense. The offerings come in the combination of the wisdom bell and the drum and water, which is life sustaining. We also use hand gestures, *mudras.*

The higher powers above play a big part in our prayers. And the realization that what we have is special already. Being grateful. I don't place a lot of thought on material things. I always tell other people, especially my kids, not to like the material stuff.

There's a lot of happiness in what we currently have. You can look around and there's so much happiness to pull out from what you see.

The essence of the Buddha's teaching gives us the strength to challenge the Chinese and to survive within the Chinese takeover. Our strength lies in our belief. That is our strength. We have no money left, but what we have left is internal. Because of our religious belief, the Chinese cannot control us fully. We've maintained

Tsering Dolma preparing her daily offerings

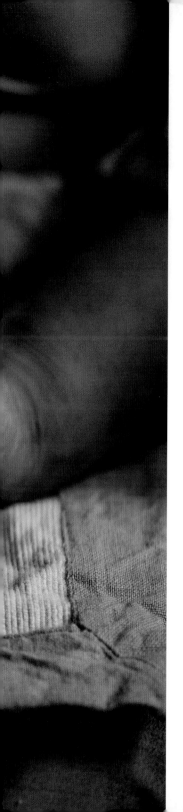

oṃ tāre tuttāre ture svāhā

It's not that I have power,
but when I pray, I pray with the
right motivation. Motivation
is the key. If you have the right
motivation, then a lot of positive
things can happen that are
not explained.

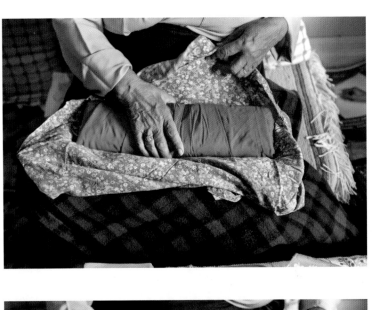

Tsering Dolma reading the Diamond Sutra scripture that she commissioned for her husband, Amdo Gyaltong Tsering

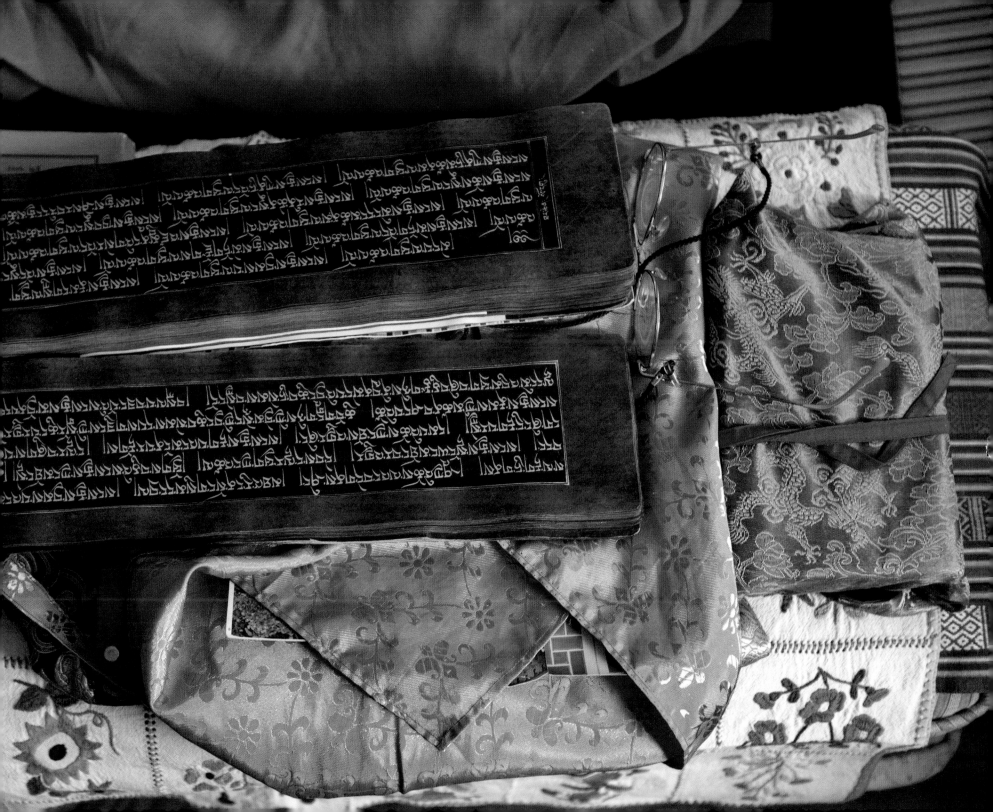

an inner strength. You can't force it and you can't take it away. It's not an object.

In Tibet today, if you go to the Tibetans' homes they no longer have altars now. They'll have maybe pictures of Mao, but hidden behind the façade of the pictures, some actually have altars behind his likeness, or religious relics that they keep out of sight. That's the strength of our spirituality; it's very strong in Tibet.

They destroyed all of our scriptures with the destruction of the monasteries. There were tons of pictures destroyed. But today what has been destroyed is pretty much reproduced. People have actually smuggled things out and hidden them away.

One of the profound messages from His Holiness is that even though China is now enjoying all of the benefits of their power, their lack of compassion will be a major source of harm for the Chinese themselves. We see that now with the natural disasters happening.

The Earth is always cautioning. Like if you hit a dog with a wooden stick, two things could happen: the dog will run away or howl. But if you treat the dog with compassion and gentleness, the dog will come and be your friend. It is the same thing with the Earth. A lack of respect for the environment will cause devastation.

The Chinese invasion of Tibet has definitely been bad, but because of the invasion, Tibetan Buddhism and its teachings have spread to the West. That's one of the biggest benefits of the loss of our country.

Divination

When my husband was doing business in Tibet he would say, "What do you think?" He would ask me to do the divinations. So I have a scripture, a text that I study. On very important occasions I resort to the use of this divination. It's not publicly known, because I have reservations as well, because with every foretelling certain bad things can be foretold. Still, I am fairly confident that a lot of predictions have been proven true.

There was one lady here who asked me to do a divination. She was planning to open a business and she wanted to see how it would succeed. She said to me, "You've got to do this; I'm not going to tell anybody, but you have to do this." In the end I gave in and did the divination. I told her that it was not a favorable divination. In her divination the financing for a store was not attainable. I advised against it, and she followed through and she said, "I'm glad that I did."

I also have the ability to read Tibetan astrology, which is a combined skill with the foretelling. Tibetan astrology and the astrological chart are very complicated. It's the alignment of the stars and the planets, whether it's earth, wind, or fire, the elements.

There's always that disclaimer, though; it's a serious disclaimer. People who seek my advice on that are rare because they know it's very powerful. But I can look up which day is good for you. You don't want to do certain things on certain days. Put off important stuff until the day that is auspicious for you, based on your astrological chart. If you take those divinations into consideration, you can mitigate a lot of unfavorable circumstances.

The Dalai Lama consults the Nechung Oracle, the ancient oracle. A prominent man like him, a globally known person with so much intellect is resorting to the soothsayer for matters of state. He says you take that into consideration and then you formulate your judgment based on all of the factors put together.

Grandmothers Council

The International Council of Thirteen Indigenous Grandmothers came into being in 2004 in an effort to restore the cultural heritage of their respective countries for younger generations, and to safeguard Mother Earth and human rights. I was invited to join the council and I accepted, as the aims and objectives of the council were similar to mine. The first meeting was held on October 17, 2004, attended by thirteen grandmothers from different countries.

It was decided that the next gatherings were to be held alternately in the countries where the Grandmothers were living. So the fourth meeting was my turn. Since my country was under Chinese occupation, I decided to hold the meeting in Dharamsala, the seat of the Tibetan government in exile and His Holiness the Dalai Lama. A year in advance, I sent a letter dated May 31, 2005, to the Private Office of His Holiness the Dalai Lama with a request to arrange an audience with His Holiness for the Grandmothers sometime in October 2006, at his convenience. The request was graciously accepted and the fourth conference was held in Dharamsala from October 14 to 22, 2006. A total of 157 participants from around the world, including

His Holiness the 14th Dalai Lama and Grandmother Tsering Dolma Gyaltong at a private audience held at the Tibetan Children's Village in Dharamsala, India, 2006

His Holiness the 14th Dalai Lama and the International Council of Thirteen Indigenous Grandmothers at a private audience held at the Tibetan Children's Village in Dharamsala, India, 2006

the Grandmothers, congregated in Dharamsala. During the day the Grandmothers met in private council to discuss the agenda, while in the mornings and evenings they were invited to visit the Tibetan educational and cultural centers around Dharamsala. They visited the Tibetan Children's Village, Tibetan Institute of Performing Arts, Tibetan government offices, Nechung Monastery, the Tibetan Medical Centre, the Tibetan Library, the Norbulingka Institute, and the Dolma Ling Nunnery.

The inaugural function was held in our traditional way by lighting the butter lamps for purification, singing the Tibetan national anthem, and serving Tibetan tea and sweetened rice to all guests and participants for good auspices. The festival went very well, serving the purpose.

His Holiness the Dalai Lama attended the founding anniversary celebration of the Tibetan Children's Village. There he graced the Grandmothers and staff with a private audience. This was a memorable day for all. During the audience, the Grandmothers Council donated US$50,000 to His Holiness as an offering for peace and to lessen suffering in the world. These funds were distributed for Tibetan Children's Village scholarships, Gu-Chu-Sum (association for ex-prisoners), Jampaling (home for the elderly), and the Tibetan Nuns Project of the Tibetan Women's Association.

When the Grandmothers get together, we don't think enough of the greater needs of the council in our mission. We get too micro in terms of individual Grandmothers. So if we really want to think big and lift the Grandmothers movement, we really need to think for the council as a whole.

It's time that we think less of our self-interest and we put the greater good first. And then everyone will benefit.

I, I, I . . . too much *I.* Too much self-interest, too much talk about the I instead of the us. Other people should always come first.

I worry about the sustainability of the Grandmothers, the continuing viability and the strength of the council. How can we properly advise or provide counsel or guidance for others? The Grandmothers can never get where we want to be if we don't all have that same frame of mind. How do you focus your mind on what is right? If your mind is for the greater good, you're going to apply yourself and use it for the greater good.

Husband's Passing

My husband Gyaltong's illness was a surprise. When he passed away peacefully at home at the age of 95 on May 7, 2008, things really fell into place, as he had lived a very fruitful

Grandmother Tsering Dolma's handwritten note to self, after the grandmothers' first meeting:

International Grandmothers' day/event. Indigenous peoples from nine different countries gathered and participated in the event to select thirteen indigenous grandmothers to form a council.

From the ensuing discussions between the elected members, we reached a common desire and hope to pass on to the next generations of our respective places, the preservation of religion, culture, ethics and good values through prayers. We also hope for the revival of the same.

One of our biggest concern in today's modern world is the growing fear of wars and more so of the dangers posed from nuclear activities, the consequences of which would result in no peace and ultimately negatively impact the well-being of all human beings and as well sentient beings in this world.

Therefore, grandmothers of this world express deep concern and encourage our next generation to get good education, so that our future generations will benefit from it and hopefully become valuable and better citizens of this world.

It's time that we think less of our self-interest and we put the greater good first. And then everyone will benefit.

life. He was very lucky because we were able to do a whole lot of the ceremonies that are usually done or should be done when someone passes away in much grandeur.

On the evening of his passing, the entire family and all the children were present. The coroners allowed us to keep his body in the house until we did our prayers instead of taking his body right away. So on that evening we invited a Tibetan to do the last rites. When someone passes away a Tibetan scripture has to be read, it's called the *Monlam Namgyal*.[10] The following day or two days later, the actual funeral was held at a Tibetan temple.

Then we perform a ceremony that lasts forty-nine days, called the *Bardo Thödol*. During the time when we do all the prayers, the soul is in a transitional state. I called India, to a lot of the heads of the monasteries I knew, and asked them to perform numerous prayers. During the bardo stage, every week I performed special recitations and again had the monasteries in India do the same. These prayers have meritorious effects on the person's rebirth.

Then he was cremated. The ashes were divided up. Some were sent through some traveling monks who were returning to India. So I actu-

ally sent some to be disposed of in the rivers there. I had enough ash to take with me as well.

My husband accumulated merit. If he lived a compassionate and altruistic life, then his rebirth would be a favorable one. Prayers would assist him to get into a favorable realm. There's a saying, *Benefits from your previous life manifest in the positive side of this life*. For instance, good health or wealth. Fortunately all of the positive things that we have in this life are dependent upon a good past life.

During my long lifetime, starting from the age of twenty-six when there was political upheaval in my country, my family and I have served our country with the fullest efforts in both temporal and political fields and all spheres or forms (externally, internally, and hidden or secretly). In retrospect, I do not have to repent for any shortcomings from my side.

I look back and see that my life has been full of many different elements, from family to national Tibetan issues. Moving from country to country. Now I sit here, hoping for a moment of peace. But I continue to be concerned about the troubles that may be lurking out there and I ask myself, *What else can I do?*

---

10. Also known as the Eight Prayers or the Eight Precepts.

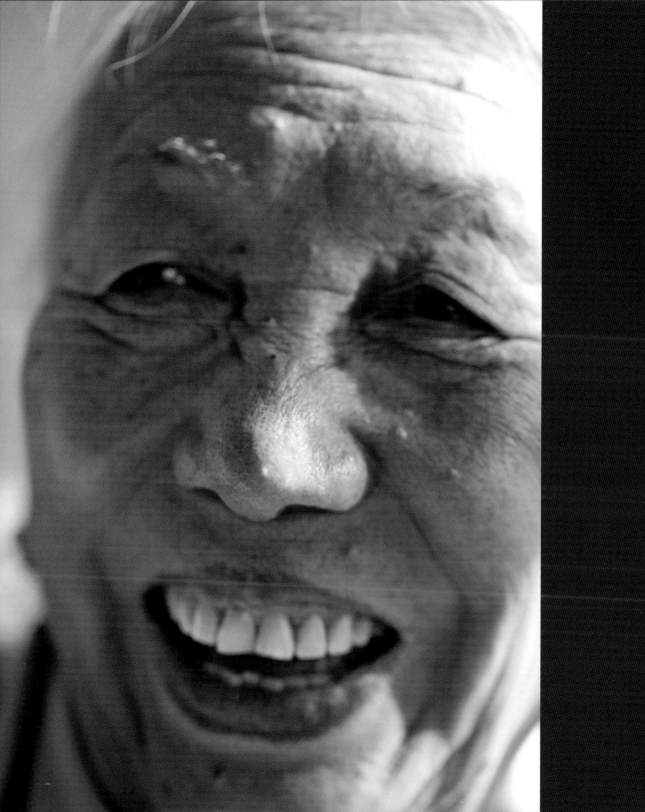

Our mother, Tsering Dolma, better known as "Grandmother Tsering," was born in Lhasa, the capital city of Tibet, in 1930, the year of the Iron Horse. She led a very impactful and purposeful life, but always believed she could have done so much more if only her English language skill was better. In 2018, at the age of eighty-nine, she passed away peacefully in Toronto surrounded by all her children and loved ones. She leaves behind four adult children, six grandchildren, and seven great-grandchildren.

Grandmother Tsering was a remarkable Tibetan leader. Her legacy is a story of unwavering commitment to the Tibetan cause, human rights, and her culture. Her journey began in a free and thriving Tibet, where she received a formal education, setting the stage for her future as a trailblazer.

In 1958, just before China forcefully attacked and annexed Tibet, she made the painful decision to leave her beloved country and escaped to India. She and her family settled in Dharamsala, in the northern part of India, until they immigrated to Canada in 1972.

She was strong willed—believed that love, compassion, and genuine empathy for others, especially those who are disadvantaged and suffering, can help you overcome your own difficulties. Her commitment and dedication extended beyond her family. She was a strong advocate of the empowerment of Tibetan women and was one of the key founding members of the Tibetan Women's Association (TWA) in India. In 1984, she returned to India and volunteered her services for several years; she led TWA Central to help accomplish many important goals and initiatives and was instrumental in initiating TWA branches around the world. She would be proud to know that, as of today, the organization has expanded to fifty-eight branches worldwide, all continuing the good work.

However, her efforts and determination did not stop there. In 1995, she and eight other Tibetan women delegates from the United States, Canada, Norway, the United Kingdom, and Australia attended the Fourth World Women's Conference held in Beijing, China. With their mouths bound in white cloth and hands held together, they made headlines with an unprecedented, daring move: openly conducting a silent protest against China's ongoing human rights violations in Tibet, in particular, the treatment of Tibetan women.

In 2004, she was invited to join the International Council of Thirteen Indigenous Grandmothers. She was passionate about and felt drawn to the organization's important mission in preserving indigenous culture, embracing elders' wisdom, and reverence for the environment for the next seven generations. In 2006, she successfully hosted a visit and conference in Dharamsala, India, with the Thirteen Indigenous Grandmothers and managed to secure a private audience with His Holiness the Dalai Lama, where they held a joint prayer for world peace. In private talks with our mother, we learned that was the highlight and one of her most proud moments.

Our mother's difficult journey from Tibet, her selfless nature, her sacrifices, her unwavering love and determination to provide a better future for her children, along with her strong desire to serve the Tibetan community, stand as her remarkable legacy. She instilled in us strong family values—to embrace our culture, to not lead a selfish life, to always try to give back and serve our Tibetan community whenever opportunity presents itself.

We hope to carry on her message of love, resilience, compassion, and striving to help the Tibetan cause in honor of the indomitable spirit of Grandmother Tsering.

We conclude by sharing with you one of our mother's favorite daily dedication prayers, written by the great eighth-century Indian Buddhist master Shantideva:

བྱང་ཆུབ་སེམས་མཆོག་རིན་པོ་ཆེ། །
མ་སྐྱེས་པ་རྣམས་སྐྱེ་གྱུར་ཅིག །
སྐྱེས་པ་ཉམས་པ་མེད་པ་དང་། །

གོང་ནས་གོང་དུ་འཕེལ་བར་ཤོག །

May the Supreme Jewel "Bodhicitta"
That has not arisen, arise and grow;
And may that which has arisen, not
diminish
But increase more and more.

With our love and deep affection,
Daughter: Yangchen Lhamo (Mimi) Nyandak
Daughter: Yangchen Dolkar Loden
Son: Gelek Norbu Gyaltong
Son: Chimi Namgyal Gyaltong

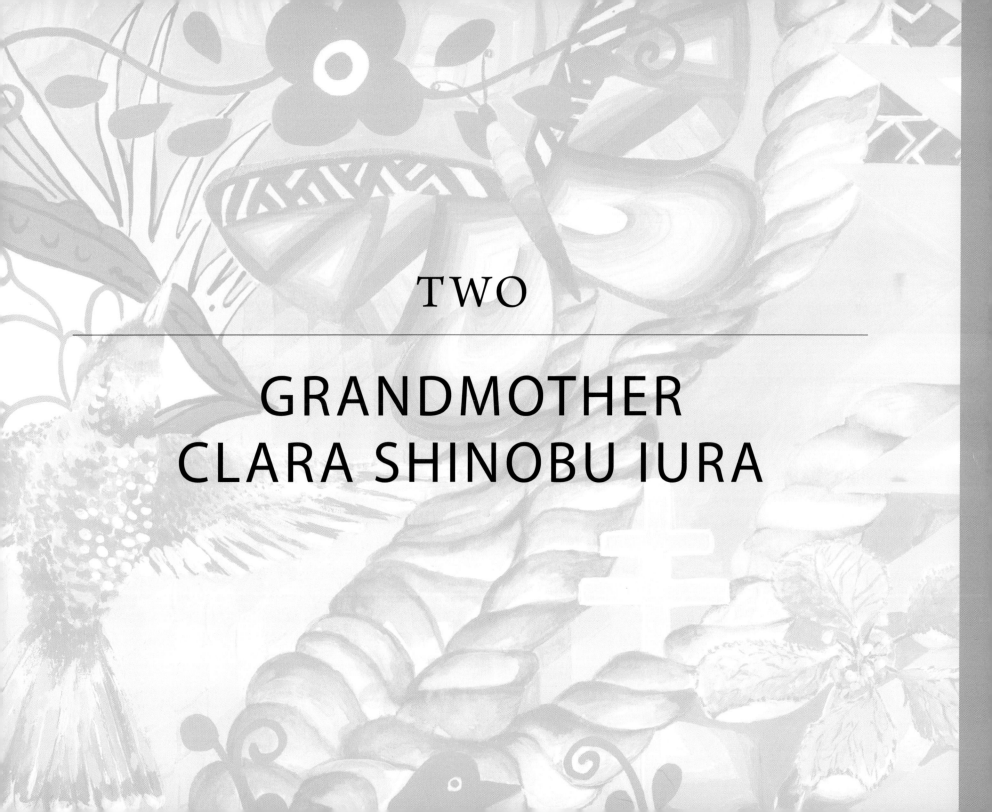

TWO

GRANDMOTHER
CLARA SHINOBU IURA

MY NAME IS CLARA SHINOBU IURA; I was born on the first of September,

1950, in the state of São Paulo, in a city called Mirandópolis.

I am the youngest of nine children. All my siblings had Japanese names. I was the first in my family to have a Portuguese name. When my mother realized she wasn't returning to Japan, she decided to give me the Portuguese name Clara. *Clara*[1] because I had white skin. My siblings had slightly more reddish skin when they were born. I was born with very white skin, so they thought I would begin something new. The meaning of my Japanese name, *Shinobu*, is written with the ideogram of the "heart's sword." They guessed this name would fit me well because, being the youngest, I would live much less time with my parents than the rest of the family and I would need a sword to defend my heart. *Iura* means "the other side of the well." My mother used to say that a well does not have another side. But what it does have is another side to the well's depth. So this is my name, which reveals the meaning of a little of everything I do nowadays in the world: defending hearts, defending the heart of the people so that they can bring out the truth that is inside their heart.

My father was Kiuso Iura and my mother Misao Iwasaki. Both were born in Japan, in the city of Niigata, in the northwest coast of the island of Honshu. Before my parents came to Brazil my mother had a background story. Her husband was supposed to be from another family.

And then, on the wedding day, someone came to tell my grandfather that this person who was going to marry my mother had tuberculosis. The family hadn't told them. My grandfather felt betrayed and decided to break up the wedding on the wedding day.

My mother, in shame, went to become a nun in the family's monastery, a Buddhist temple. My mother's people are descendents and guardians of a Buddhist temple in Niigata, Japan. When my father, who wanted to come to Brazil, heard this story, he thought, *Well, I will see if this young lady who was refused, who didn't marry, wants to marry me, because naturally no one else will want to marry her. And she is probably trying to run away from that story.* So he went to my grandfather's house and asked to marry her. My grandfather spoke to her, and my mother considered it. She realized that she didn't want to be a nun and that she wanted to have children. So she accepted my father's proposal, to live in a country she had never heard of.

My father and mother arrived in Brazil in 1928. The Second World War had not yet taken place, but the First World War had. In that period, a lot of propaganda about Brazil was being made to Japanese youngsters. So many young people didn't agree with the Japanese feudal system. So the Brazilian government offered an invitation to the Japanese people to create a new life in Brazil, with the hope of a new world. Because of so much social injustice in Japan, many decided to come. The Japa-

---

1. A female given name, from a Latin word meaning clear, bright.

nese were invited to work in rice agriculture and on coffee planta-
tions. They were offered houses and everything. And because my
father was an idealist, he thought he could build a new world. He
thought that he could create a new system in Brazil together with
his sons and daughters, and with the people of Brazil.

So my parents hopped into this dream. My father worked in
a Japanese agricultural cooperative. But my father was different
from most of the people. He was born to an affluent family who
owned assets, and he received an inheritance. With this inheritance he came to open up a place in Brazil, and they gave him
a piece of land. Before arriving, he didn't even know where this
land was, close to Mato Grosso. At the time Mato Grosso was like
the Amazon today, a jungle. It had all kinds of animals, jaguars,
snakes, and much more. My mother was a young lady from a noble family. She belonged to nobility as a descendent of the family
of a temple. Both my mother and my father were cultured and
educated people.

I was raised in the countryside of the state of São Paulo, Brazil.
Afterward we went to live in the city of São Paulo. And there my
life in Brazilian society began, so to speak, because until then, in
the countryside we lived in a Japanese community. I didn't know
how to speak Portuguese until we went to live in Registro, a city
near the coast in the state of São Paulo.

Clara's home wall with photos and images of her father and mother, Padrinho
Sebastião, and Mestre Irineu. Céu do Mapiá, State of Amazonas, Brazil, 2011

Takachiho-gawara Shinto shrine
in Kirishima, Japan, 2010

Grandmother Clara at the
entrance of the Takachiho-gawara
in Kirishima, Japan, 2010

My mother and father had a very private life. Both of them made poetry. They were very contemplative toward nature, something that comes from Japanese culture. My mother demonstrated this contemplation to us children as well. They also attached themselves to Japanese groups for their social life. They joined groups who wrote *haikai*.[2] They joined charitable organizations that took care of children and people in need. My mother worked in these charitable organizations, and her children didn't like that very much because she was absent from home a lot of the time. But she didn't mind that. The Japanese people always come together in their own culture, gathering to prepare food, create entertainment groups, have readings, and more.

Once they arrived here in Brazil, the Japanese experienced a huge culture shock. They did not continue with their Buddhist practice. They tried to find ways of preserving themselves and their culture. When they arrived, the food and everything else was very different. So there was a great violation of everything they believed. Actually, I believe that especially after the Second World War, many Japanese became very sad because God wasn't on their side and they lost the war. Many had really surrendered themselves to Japan, and the country was their god, see? They were very concerned with the racial issue, so much so that sons and daughters of the Japanese could not even marry Brazilians most of the time. There were families in which sons and daughters married Brazilians and their parents committed suicide because they felt so ashamed.

From then on, they had to transform themselves, seek a very radical transformation in their daily lives, but at the same time, they began to worship their own race. Also because there was this propaganda in Japan due to the war. The Second World War brought many things, causing an extreme modification in the Japanese way of being.

After losing the war—this is my analysis, right?—they lost a lot of their trust in God, because all those things they were doing were for the sake of God, the Great Emperor. The emperor was their god. So when the war was lost the credibility of this Great Emperor was lost, the existence of this great god. And they started not to believe so much in spirituality anymore. So much so that nowadays in Japan we see many abandoned temples and a very small number of faithful inside houses of worship.

And so here in Brazil, the Japanese, like my father and mother, decided to become Christians. They became Christians in the early 1960s to enter Brazilian society. Then they began to have more faith in Christ, to believe more in the teachings of Christ. This fulfilled their need to become religious in this connection with God, because the connection with the god of Japan, that illusion had gone down the drain from the Second World War onward.

A Healing Gift

My mother, as a daughter of a whole legacy of a house of God, brought the gift of healing with her. She took care of people who had problems of neurosis, depression, laying her hands on them, and people got better. She did not pray, she just touched them with her hands. In Japanese

2. Japanese poem of seventeen syllables, in three lines of five, seven, and five, traditionally evoking images of the natural world.

teate is to lay the hands, to touch with the hands. *Te* means hand. *Ate* means touch. There was no mysticism involved, no connection with God. My mother became well known, and people sought her healing ways. She taught. She was very forward. She learned things. She knew how to make *miso*, knew to make *shoyu* (soy sauce), she knew how to make many preserves. She knew how to cook French, Italian, and German foods. She was full of knowledge about cooking and herbs, and had a passion for nature.

So this woman who was my mother, I didn't understand much. Now that I am older I find myself very similar to her. I believe that this gift comes from her, from my grandmother's family. I don't know the complete history of my ancestors, but my mother used to say that we were descendents of the Ainu people, the native people of Japan, linked with Siberia. My mother used to tell me I was white because my ancestors came from Siberia.

A representation of the Ainu people of Japan at Grandmothers Clara's Grandmothers Gathering opening ceremonies in Kirishima, Japan, 2010

Young Adult

My connection with God, my mediumship, and my spiritual knowledge opened up like a bolt of lightning in the air. From one moment to the next my state of being changed completely, in the same way that it happens with the shamanic people of Siberia. Until twenty-something years in their lives they are common people, lead common lives, study, work as normal people of society. Then suddenly out of the blue, a power comes from the astral plane and the person changes completely. She or he begins to have visions, begins to hear voices. That's what happened to me. In one moment my life transformed.

After my father went bankrupt, I entered the university as a philosophy student. I began to long for more freedom, and at twenty-two years old I left home. But I was always leaving home and returning. I lived in communities with friends, always seeking to live in a communitarian way. Also for a part of my life I lived in the streets. When I was young I also drank a lot and got into drugs.

During that time in college I was discovering a world of other people. I was very connected to black people. I felt very compassionate toward the black people's pain, for the racism they suffered. From the time I was five, six, seven, I was very connected to the poor, always seeking justice. The first time I went to an open street market in São Paulo, I was so outraged to see beggars on the street. When I saw beggars or people who had open sores, I kept crying in front of them and my mother, my sister had to give them money.

I began to take part in left-wing groups: the communists at college, seeking new directions for society, new directions for the minorities, seeking justice for blacks, for women. I worked with Indians, teaching classes to them. I went to Brasília in 1972, 1974, when the homosexual world began coming out. I had admiration for those people as well. Everything that questioned society, I was there together with them. I didn't believe in the system and sought to have a more natural life. I believed that life amid nature was the best that existed. I still had to live in the city, working and studying at college, and I worked in a big telephone company with the first computers that arrived in Brazil.

Until 1977 I lived this whole story of being a rebel, living the nightlife, having several boyfriends, and being very bohemian. I'd work from six in the morning until one or two o'clock, sleep during the day, and at night I went out into the nightlife. And from the nightlife I would go directly to work. That was a period of my life. Then I decided I didn't want to work for the system anymore. I left Telesp, entered a phase of major depression, began to drink a lot. I used to fall down in the streets. I was living in abandoned houses, carried my clothes in a straw bag.

Then there came a Saturday of Hallelujah.[3] In Brazil, on the night of Saturday of Hallelujah there's a carnival. So my friends and I were out on the street, sitting on the curb at four in the morning; I was drunk, my skirt torn. Then a very tall black man appeared. He came directly to me, pulled me up by the blouse, and said, "Have some shame on yourself! Look at yourself, see who you are!" Then I said, "I'll slap you if you don't go away now!" Then several people said, "No, no," shouting around this man and me, and the man held my arm and pulled me up, saying, "You've got to get out of here! Go to your home! Look who you are! See who you are!" He shook me hard. I felt so ashamed I took a cab home.

After that I spent a week in depression, thinking that life wasn't worth living. I saw my father's life, my mother's, all their sacrifices, struggling for their survival in a rental apartment because we had lost everything. I thought, *What are we living for? I think the thing to do is to die.* So one fine day I decide to make some poisonous food to kill my father, my mother, and myself. I had heard of a "medicine" that someone ate and died, so I thought, *I'm going to put that in our food.* When I

3. Between Good Friday and Easter Sunday.

was about to leave the house to get the "medicine" at the drugstore my mother spoke: "Ah, are you going out, my daughter?" I said, "I am, but don't worry because I will be back to cook our supper. I am going to cook today."

When I got to the drugstore at around 11:00, midday, it was very crowded. I was ashamed to ask for the "medicine," guessing everyone would know why I was going to buy it. I thought, *It's better to walk a little, I'll come afterward and buy the medicine*. At the time, I wasn't even twenty-eight years old. So I went walking and I walked, walked, walked … Then I walked into a street that had a museum. It was called the Lasar Segall Museum, after a great Brazilian Lithuanian artist. I entered this museum, spent some time looking around, and then a woman called me. She said, "Hey! We have an art room here. There's clay, there's paint, there's everything you might want to do." The clay attracted me, so I sat down. It must have been around noon. I had never played with clay. I started playing with it, stirring it around.

Then someone tapped on my back. He said, "Lady, aren't you going to leave?" I said, "Oh, but why?" "Because it is already 8 p.m., we are going to close the museum." Everybody had already left and I was still there. When I came to myself, I had really disappeared during those—I don't know how many hours, eight hours? When I looked, I had made a tree trunk with many beautiful roots, cut in half. I had never done that; to me it was the greatest thing ever, I was very happy. And I said, "Wow, eight o'clock!"

Then I remembered that I had to buy that certain "medicine" and that I was going to cook for us. And then I thought, *My God, I was going to make that food, wasn't I? What now? Ah, but now I don't want to die anymore. Look at that beautiful thing I made!*

I was reborn in that clay! I left very happy and joyful, got home, and my mother opened the door and said, "Clara! I was waiting for you! Didn't you say you were going to cook supper?" And then I felt like crying. I went straight to my room and cried, ashamed of what I had been thinking. And that moment was as if I had been reborn, and I saw that my life could have some hope, that I was able to do something beautiful in life.

Awakening

Some days later, a friend invited me to a meditation led by some folks who had come from India. It went on for two days. In one of the exercises I had an instant regression to when I was three months old, when my sister put me on top of a wardrobe and I fell and hit my head. I started crying and screaming like a three-month-old child. They held me close and cared for me like a baby. When I was coming back to myself, I looked at those people and saw that it was as if there were glitter, something like that, around them. Today I know that was the people's auras. I saw colors: blue, yellow, and green. In some of them I saw a wolf's face, saw some weird things, in others beautiful things, like beautiful colors. And all that was awakening me.

That was with the group of Bhagwan Rajneesh, also known as Osho. Afterward, when I looked at the sky, it seemed that I was seeing the sky for the first time. It gave me such a great love for nature. I looked at the flowers, and it seemed as if I was seeing the flowers for the first time in my life. I looked and everything was new to me. I began to have a new life, as if I had opened a new window in my life.

I kept opening a book called *Meditation: The Art of Ecstasy* by Bhagwan Rajneesh, and there he said, *Believe in the Master that is inside you.* And then a voice said: *Do this thing. Go to such and such a place....* And I kept following that voice. I had no distrust of anything.

That night I went back home. My father was admiring the moon, playing a flute. He played a *shakuhachi* flute, a Japanese bamboo flute. Then we started talking about love. Something I had never talked about with my father, or with my mother. It was a very important moment ... my father and I talking about love. We talked at length about love for mankind, love for nature. It was a new Clara talking there. I marveled at myself and at what I was seeing in me.

From that moment on, I began to hear voices and went on following the voices. A lot of things are said about people who hear voices. Thank God I hadn't heard much about schizophrenia at the time, because maybe if I had I would have thought I was schizophrenic. The instructions from the master that dwelt inside of me and those voices I was hearing were voices that were really guiding me. Everything they said were things that went on to happen. There were moments when I felt afraid, because it was so real. Yet it was all so true.

But there came a moment when even those voices, which were so true, began to hinder my relationships with people. I'd look at a person and say, *Tomorrow you'll get a phone call and you will lose your job.* And it happened! I said everything I saw and didn't even think it was bad!

Then people began to feel a lot of anger toward me, because everything actually happened. So I began to be afraid of it, because it started to harm me and harm people. I began to know when a person was going to die. I was beginning to know too much. And I began to have a power that I didn't want to have. That power started to hinder me, and I wanted to run away from it. I didn't know what to do with all of that. I had no emotional structure, and my ego was not prepared to have so much power. So I asked God to take that power away from me, because it was hindering me. I helped many people, but at the same time, when I exposed the truth, people didn't like hearing it. I also started thinking it was a thing of the devil, because I lost many great friends that way.

I so wanted to get out of that, I wanted to forget all of that, but I couldn't, because it kept accompanying me. That time in my life was very powerful for me. One day I was sharing all of this, as it was unfolding, with a friend and he said to me, "Clara, I'm going to take you to a *pai-de-santo*[4] for him to bless you and pray over you." After much hesitation, we ended up at the craziest of places, which had people dressed as pirates and all sorts of characters. There I received my first real spiritual cleansing. Today I understand that the healing I received was a work of transport mediumship,[5] as they removed many of those "things" that were in and around me. I saw people do more or less what

---

4. Name given to a male priest, the head of a temple in Afro-Brazilian traditions such as Umbanda.

5. "Transport" in this context refers to a type of channeling work done by mediums in the Umbanda tradition, to free someone from "obsessor spirits" who are clinging to this person and having a negative influence on her/his life.

I had been doing, but it was much more exaggerated. Still, when I left that place, I felt relieved. I was very impressed. It was as if something very heavy that I perhaps had acquired in this life or in a previous life had been removed.

When I was laying hands on people, I thought I was doing the same thing my mother did. However, my mother did not scream or cry, fall on the ground, and say things. I honestly didn't understand what was happening to me. I felt so ashamed I could've died. But it healed people. When I placed my hands on people, I manifested their illness. When the person became aware of what I was manifesting, they healed. I discovered that that very awareness of the moment when you get ill brings the healing. That was the first big lesson, through what was happening with me.

During that time I spent a couple of days seeing many past lives, who I had been and where I had lived. One of the places I had lived was

Clara at a spiritual work in Brazil, circa 1990s

France. I saw an incarnation in which I had been very much in love with a French lord, living in a castle. In the visions I had, it was as if I were seeing a mental screen, and on the screen I watched as if it were a projected film. It was very magical. I saw that I had a husband, but I fell in love with this lord. I could not bear the passion I had for him and committed suicide. Some great tragedy, right? That past life had a great influence on this lifetime. Since I was little, I always wanted to speak French. I read French and studied it when I studied philosophy. I was certain that I had known this spirit, who came back as an *Exú Veludo*[6] in this incarnation. This story, this knowledge, is something that came about in the middle of my spiritual development. I really never had read much about *Umbanda*[7] or about mediumship because I had always studied Spinoza, Kant, Nietzsche, Descartes, and

6. A spirit in the Umbanda tradition belonging to the "Line of the Crossroads" between life and death.
7. A syncretic Afro-Brazilian religion that blends African traditions with Catholicism, spiritism, and indigenous beliefs.

the like. I really never believed in God or in religion and thought all of that was a construction of the mind. But I saw myself ensnared by a whole network of paranormal occurrences that left me very curious to get to know another possibility of existence, apart from this dimension.

Macrobiotics

I started to wash dishes at a macrobiotic restaurant so I could eat, because I had no money or place to live. The restaurant belonged to a Japanese man. I continued having visions. I was seeing Saint George the Warrior, seeing beings of the most diverse kinds. One day, some beings came and said, *Go to a place, look for Zanatta.* I said, "Zanatta? Zapata? Zapata, the Mexican revolutionary?" I had already heard of a Zanatta but couldn't remember where. In my search to find him, I met a friend who said, "Clara, I'm neighbors with a man called Flávio Zanatta.[8] He brought macrobiotics to Rio de Janeiro."

When I arrived at Zanatta's house, he said to his friend, "Didn't I tell you I was expecting someone? This person has arrived." I said, "Well, sir, how come you were expecting me?" He said, "This morning I went to do Tai Chi Chuan and I heard a voice telling me that a woman of oriental origin would come looking for me and that I had to help her." I told him I had a vision as well that I had to find him, and that I was looking for a place to live. He said, "You will come live here, because

you need to return to your origins. I am a specialist in macrobiotics, I do shiatsu, I do acupuncture, and I will teach you about these things." So I went to live at Flávio Zanatta's house and I began to have a super-balanced macrobiotic diet.

Extraterrestrial Beings

During my stay at Zanatta's I began to receive very clear transmissions, including a central vision that has marked my life to this day. One day, while in a deep meditation, I saw three beings with clothes that looked like Franciscan monks' robes, except that the color was metallic indigo blue. Three extraterrestrial beings. I could not see their faces, only their hoods. It looked like they were two meters (over six and a half feet) tall. The visions were projected on a floating television screen. A tube connected the screen to my throat. I screamed, calling my friend, but my voice wouldn't come out. Still today I have a mark from this tube in my throat.

After a little while, inside of me, a voice, not my voice, a metallic voice started to speak: *Toin, tain. . . . We are here.* They were saying that they were here to bring a warning to the population of Earth, that the people needed to begin to have consciousness of all the destruction that was being done on Earth and toward nature. That at the rate that nature was being destroyed, there would come a time when nature would retaliate against the human race in a severe way. It was necessary for the people on Earth to wake themselves up for the times that were coming. It was necessary for people to begin to care about their nu-

8. Flávio Santin Zanatta is credited as the introducer of macrobiotics in Brazil. He was a direct disciple of George Ohsawa, the founder of macrobiotics.

trition, to begin to care about eating less industrialized, more healthy food—to seek more natural foods and to be careful with genetic modifications. They said Earth's population would be decimated by wars, by the interventions of beings that only wanted power, the technological power installed here in this planet. And that we had to be to careful even when talking about this, for we could suffer many attacks. But it was necessary to start talking about this to the population of Earth, and they were part of a group with the mission to rescue planet Earth. That was in 1978, when nothing was being said about this yet, when no ecological movement had started.

They also talked about the totality of the universe, and about the cosmic universe . . . words I'd never used in my life. I didn't even know what all of this meant properly. And they spoke of God. To me this was all a great idiocy I was inventing, because it wasn't possible from my own words that I, a philosophy student, could be speaking about totality in the universe, speaking of God, of cosmic beings and such. So then they told me to take care, from that moment on not to eat anything industrialized and to have healthier nutrition with macrobiotics, because it was they who had taken me to Flávio Zanatta, and from then on, I should take this message to the population of Earth.

After that, I was left with a scar on my throat that today has formed itself into a little cyst, a little ball. But it's powerful. It is the mark I have from the power of those extraterrestrial beings. At the time I did not talk to everyone about this experience, because I knew I wasn't insane.

After this experience I didn't sleep well anymore. It was at this time that I discovered that I was a descendent of the Siberian people, that my shamanism came from there, that what occurred with me had also occurred with the Siberian shamans. I didn't call myself a shaman, but I was that kind of a person with mediumship and sensitivity.

To sum it up, a lot of things happened. At that time the spirits talked to me about people on Earth who were already studying the possibility of a very strong disaster in nature, and that these people were already planting manioc because there would come a time when we wouldn't even be able to eat many plants from outside the soil. And I was told that I would meet these people above Serra das Araras.

Serra das Araras is a place below Visconde de Mauá. It was there I found the Daime, the Santo Daime.[9] They were already concerned with planting yams, manioc, and potatoes, and there was a prophecy from Padrinho[10] Sebastião that there would come a very difficult time on Earth, and it was necessary for us to prepare ourselves physically and spiritually for that time. They were living in the middle of the forest, people from the city who had created a community in Visconde de Mauá.

I kept that message with me, of how they said there would come a time in my life of rescuing people's consciousness toward God, toward the totality of the universe, toward the preservation of the forces of nature, and of nature itself. That I would walk with a group of people

---

9. A syncretic religion founded in the 1930s in the Brazilian Amazonian state of Acre by Raimundo Irineu Serra, known as Mestre Irineu. Santo Daime incorporates elements of several religious or spiritual traditions including Catholicism, spiritism, African animism, and indigenous South American shamanism.

10. Literally "Godfather"; refers to the name for the male spiritual leaders in the Santo Daime tradition.

throughout planet Earth, taking the sacred knowledge of all forces of nature. I discovered what they had told me was true when I was invited to take part in the International Council of Thirteen Grandmothers. Even though it took some time for me to believe that I was part of this council, I was placed there, and with them I traveled around the planet.

After I had all this spiritual passage, I could only surrender myself, couldn't I? Things happened and were so clear, and so evident; there was no doubt those voices I heard were true. Many things I saw have come to happen today—where I am, the places I've lived, where I have traveled, the contacts I have had. To me, the utmost of such contact was with Padrinho Sebastião and with His Holiness the Dalai Lama, who, for me, was the pinnacle of the story.

His Holiness

When I was in California in May 2005, I channeled that I would be beside His Holiness. I was in a spiritual work, and I felt a little sick and had to go outside. A whirlwind came, and I clearly saw Yogananda's master, Sri Yukteswar, telling me that from that moment on I was to stop eating red meat, because I would be at the side of His Holiness, so I should purify myself. And that's what I did. From May on, around Mother's Day, until I went to Dharamsala with the Grandmothers Council in October 2006, my daughter Tai Lin and I stopped eating red meat. It was there I was chosen among the Grandmothers, in a drawing, to be at the side of His Holiness. When I was there close to His Holiness the Dalai Lama, at the Tibetan Grandmother's gathering, I channeled that I had to do my gathering in Japan.

Grandmothers Council wearing traditional Japanese kimono at Grandmother Clara's
Grandmothers Gathering in Kirishima, Japan, 2010

Daibutsuden (the Great Buddha Hall) at Tōdai-ji in Nara, Japan, 2010

Clara with her daughter Tai Lin and her sister Eiko in front of the Daibutsuden (the Great Buddha Hall) at Tōdai-ji in Nara, Japan, 2010

I felt I was receiving the message from Buddha to do my gathering in Japan. We did the gathering in 2010, and it took four years for us to organize. Afterward I went to see the largest Buddha in the world, in the Great Buddha Hall of Nara, visited by five thousand people daily. I said, "I don't like seeing Buddha just for tourism." When we arrived at the door of the temple, I started to cry. I went into a corner and asked Buddha to give me a sign that he had received my work, this work I had done in Japan with the grannies.

A week later, the Japanese producer who helped us organize the Grandmothers' gathering let me know she had received an invitation for me to go to a meeting of His Holiness the Dalai Lama with all the ministers of the Tibetan community in Japan. When we arrived at the great temple, the same temple we had visited the previous week, His Holiness entered the main hall, prayed, left the hall, and went down the staircases where thousands of people awaited him. Suddenly he came in my direction. The only people he spoke to in the hall were me and my friend, who had invited me. He came to greet me, ask me how I was . . . and gave me the flu . . . because he was suffering from a very bad flu.

That was the great present I got, that I really could not deny. Buddha answered me in such a beautiful and wonderful way. So today I see it like this: my life is made of these voices I hear. I have not been deceived by the voices. I have followed them because I surrendered myself to God to be one of His channels, to be able to bring to Earth the divine consciousness, the consciousness of the spiritual truth, the consciousness of God, for all of us who live on this planet.

There exists wisdom and knowledge way beyond what vain philosophy can teach us. That is a part of my life. I am like this. I even feel sometimes like a puppet of God, but I give thanks for Him to have chosen me, for me to be able to be this person, and I know I have to improve a lot to be able to say that I'm a channel of His, because I also have my flaws, my negative parts. I know I'm here on Earth to evolve, to be able to indoctrinate myself, so I can be closer and closer to God's truth.

All of us have a way of having this contact, of giving testimony of the divine truth. All of my sister grannies also had these experiences in some other way. They're here to give testimony of the reality and the truth of the Great Spirit. We're all witnesses of this truth, and we're here to be able to pass this possibility on to all humanity. As long as you truly surrender yourself to God without thinking of receiving anything, you are surrendered, you are open, you are ready to search for and receive this wisdom, this knowledge that comes through the spirit.

Padrinho Sebastião and the Santo Daime

When my mother was seventy-four years old she finally fulfilled her big wish: the government was going to give a present to the immigrants, a return trip to Japan. And she was preparing herself to go to Japan. We lived at the time with a sister of mine, at my brother-in-law's house, and my mother, like every Japanese woman, always worried that she was disturbing her hosts. One day I arrived from the street. My mother was working a lot, tired, she'd made a special dish, and I argued with her, saying, "You don't need to work so much! Rest a little, why work so much?" We argued. Just after we argued, I went to lie down, and after a little while my father came and said, "My daughter, your mother is feeling sick." They took her to the hospital and she'd had a heart attack. Then two or three days later she died. I felt very guilty, very sick. I entered a state of severe depression. I felt my mother had died because of this quarrel with me. I spent a year of my life in the, so to speak, *mea culpa, mea culpa, mea maxima culpa.*[11] I stayed buried inside that story.

11. Part of the Penitential Act at the beginning of the Mass of the Roman Catholic Church, meaning, "Through my fault, through my fault, through my most grievous fault."

I know I'm here on Earth to evolve, to be able to indoctrinate myself, so I can be closer and closer to God's truth. All of us have a way of having this contact, of giving testimony of the divine truth. All of my sister grannies also had these experiences in some other way. They're here to give testimony of the reality and the truth of the Great Spirit. We're all witnesses of this truth, and we're here to be able to pass this possibility on to all humanity. As long as you truly surrender yourself to God without thinking of receiving anything, you are surrendered, you are open, you are ready to search for and receive this wisdom, this knowledge that comes through the spirit.

After one whole year of suffering, I had a dream that I had to go away, leave São Paulo. In the dream, a car came to pick me up at my house, a black car from the 1940s. A woman friend was fetching me to go to Rio de Janeiro, because a very big flood was about to happen. The sky was dark, very dark. And when we arrived there, by the sea in Rio de Janeiro, on the beach, there was a very big ship that looked like Noah's ark. And there was a bearded man with a bare chest, in trousers, saying, *Get in, get in!* And he said to me, *You almost didn't make it, huh? Get in soon, get in!*

At that time my daughter Tai Lin was one year and a half old. The path opened for me to go to Rio de Janeiro, where my daughter's adoptive father lived. When we arrived, he was in the Santo Daime doctrine.

I had no interest in the Santo Daime doctrine. People wore uniforms, some weird clothes. I found it ridiculous, felt that there was no sense in taking a beverage to be able to contact God. I didn't believe in it. One day they took me to get to know the church. We got there and I was scared when I saw those women with the clothes of a *normalista*,[12] a white blouse and a pleated skirt. They said, "Get in the queue, get in the queue! Take the children!" When I arrived where the man was giving out the beverage, he opened the bottle and I heard a thunder . . . the voice of thunder, *BAAAAA!*

I was so stunned that when I looked, my daughter had already drunk the beverage they had given her. I felt so outraged. How come my daughter was going to take a beverage I hadn't even taken myself? She was a child! I didn't know what to do anymore, I wanted to hit everyone in there. I got very angry.

Padrinho Sebastião Mota de Melo traveling by boat on the Purus River in the Brazilian Amazon, 1987

12. Young women who went to a *escola normal* (normal school), where they graduated to teach at elementary schools. They wore a uniform of white blouses and navy blue pleated skirts.

My daughter asked me to put her somewhere where there was earth. We took her to lie down on the earth under the house, which was on stilts. She remained there for around five to ten minutes, lying down with her arms open, and then got up and said, "Enough, that's okay." And she got up and was fine. And I, extremely scared, extremely outraged, went away.

Then some time passed. There was going to be a ceremony again at this church. The leader of this church, called Padrinho Sebastião, had come there. And I said, "I don't want to stay in this house, because those *daimistas*[13] will start to appear. I'll run away from this house." And then two friends came by and we decided we'd go to Visconde de Mauá. Then a friend said, "You're going to Tânia's house, she lives inside the Santo Daime community. You won't be able to run away anymore. You can go there and take this Daime."

I was so outraged but saw I had nowhere to run to, so I took the Daime. The moment I drank the Daime I had the certainty that this was the place the ETs had spoken to me about, it was these people. I didn't know anything yet about them, but at that moment I had the certainty that God was there too, present. And that this beverage opened my eyes for me to enter into contact with a greater connection with the Divine, and there was no harm in it. And that was when I accepted the beverage and surrendered myself to it.

This first experience with the Santo Daime led to a new stage of my spiritual life. That happened following the death of my mother, after I had spent one year in reclusion. I am grateful to this day for having the

Santo Daime in my life. It has been more than thirty years that I have been part of this holy doctrine.

All the people I met from Céu do Mapiá[14] were saying to me, "Ah, you belong to Padrinho Sebastião! Ah, you're going to Mapiá!" And I replied, "Never will I live in the Amazon! I don't want to know about mosquitoes!" And then I met a man named Padrinho Manoel Corrente, who laughingly said, "You? When Sebastião Mota meets you, he will take you to Mapiá. You don't belong here."

My father wanted to experience the Santo Daime. He asked, "Oh, that beverage leads to sacred knowledge and reveals its secrets? I want to experience it." So I took him to a Daime session. He took Daime and was very touched by it. The next day, he said to me, "My daughter, take me to the administrator of this community." So we went to Padrinho Alex Polari de Alverga. My father said, "Thank you very much for receiving my daughter and my granddaughter in your community." I was outraged because he was speaking for me and he was simply handing me over to the community. So Mr. Alex Polari, the chief, the president of this community, said to my father, "Look, it's not me who's going to receive your daughter. You are handing over your daughter to this person." And he took my father to the altar, where there was a picture of Padrinho Sebastião.

I still was extremely outraged at my father for handing me over. I had even decided to leave the doctrine, see? Three months passed. One

---

13. A practitioner of the Santo Daime religion.

14. Céu do Mapiá (Portuguese for "Heaven of Mapiá") is a village founded in 1983 by Sebastião Mota de Melo. It is located within the Inauini-Pauini National Reserve in the western Brazilian Amazon.

fine day, a woman friend of mine from Visconde de Mauá phoned me and said, "Clara, come to Rio de Janeiro, because Padrinho Sebastião is here! Come meet him, you must meet him! He's a saint, Clara! He's a saint on Earth whom you have to meet." And I said, "I'm all set already, I've already discovered that this doctrine is not my story. I'm oriental, I have nothing to do with Christ." My daughter, who at that time was two years old, suddenly started screaming, "I want to go to Rio de Janeiro! I want to go to Rio de Janeiro!" My father said, "Go then, my daughter. I will pay for the ticket for you to go to Rio de Janeiro."

And so we went to *Céu do Mar*,[15] where they were celebrating Padrinho Paulo Roberto's birthday. Once we got there and I took the Daime, when I saw those people again, I saw that they were so dear to my heart. But I was still certain that I wanted to get out of the Daime.

That same night I met Padrinho Sebastião and he said to me, "Ah, you came to heal me!" I said, "Not me, I didn't come to heal anyone. You, sir, have so many healers, men and women healers . . . I haven't come to heal anyone." And he said, "No way, it's you who's going to heal me." He had something in his lungs at the time. The moment he said that I said, "Oh, only if I can first cleanse myself." He said, "What do you need to cleanse yourself?" I said, "I need to go in the waterfall, I need to go in the sea, I need to put my feet on the earth." He replied, "So do that and come back."

I gave him a massage, but as he was very ill with heart problems, I did a normal shiatsu massage. He said, "I think this is not your massage."

I said, "Well then, can I be me? Because I might fall, I might scream, I might cry, several things will happen when I do my massage. Can I do it?" He said, "Of course, do it!" And then I asked him for three candles: "One candle is to be lit for your guides, my guides, our guides, and for Jesus. The second one is for the *povo da rua*,[16] and the third one is for the *povo das almas* (the souls)." And this how Padrinho Sebastião got to know my work and me. Then he invited me to live in Céu do Mapiá, where I've been living for over thirty years. I'm very grateful to be here, in the Amazon rain forest, and for having had the courage to cross the forest to get to this place, such an incredible place.

When I first arrived in Mapiá, I couldn't take so much Daime because I was already so sensitive. Padrinho said to me, "You're the one who's going to direct the work (ritual) now." So I said, "Let's do an 'Om.'" So we did the Om greeting three times, and after that I spoke about bioenergetics. Saying that energy passed through our body, and that if we blocked our body out of fear, for any reason whatever in any corner of our body, we could create an energetic block, and from that energetic block there might occur an illness. It was important for us to liberate energy from the body, and there were exercises. And I started to do exercises. I did a hand exercise; I did an exercise to loosen the shoulders. And then I said, "Okay, and now we're going to loosen the waist, we're going to wiggle our hips, place our hands on the waist and wiggle our hips." For me, who came from the city, it was a very normal

15. Santo Daime church in Rio de Janeiro.

16. Literally "people of the streets," meaning entities who are *exus* (male) and *pomba-giras* (female), messengers and mediators between humans and spirits.

thing, but imagine those men. Imagine a place of rustic forest men who have never done such a thing! And so I commanded them, and Padrinho Sebastião looked at those burly men and said, "You have to place the hands on the waist! You have to do what this woman is saying!" Poor guys! I had no idea who those men were, who those people were. And I had no idea those people knew nothing about such things.

That was how Padrinho introduced me to Céu do Mapiá. And I remained around eight months doing that kind of work, being criticized by those who didn't like it, being frowned upon. I was also thinking I was in a high position, thinking I knew something. After something like fifteen days, I started to see that there was something I didn't know. A month passed, and I knew even less. And then, when three months had passed, I saw that I knew nothing, and that those people who were all yokels, all odd, they were the ones who knew. They had such an incredible wisdom, and I had no idea. And today I respect a lot the people who lived there, who learned with life, with suffering, with the hard day-to-day life in the forest, planting their own food, building their own houses, waking up with the sun and praying and singing, and having joy in their hearts.

I have lived in Céu do Mapiá for over thirty years already, I'm very happy to be there. Padrinho Alfredo[17] says, "Clara came to help and she always thinks she doesn't know how to do anything, but she's here to help us." To tell the truth, I am the one being helped. I learned to respect life, to respect each human being that exists, because one's appearance is nothing. There is much more wisdom in our day-to-day than in books. That's what the Céu do Mapiá community teaches us. Céu do Mapiá offers us a foundation, to live and not only to survive. It is to live, to plant our food, to wash our clothes, to have daily contact with nature, to be together, to be able to live in a communitarian way, to be able to help one another. I will remain there, if God allows me. We never know what tomorrow will bring. We are in connection with the wealth the forest brings to us in our daily life, in our

17. Alfredo Gregório de Melo (Padrinho Alfredo) is one of the sons of Padrinho Sebastião and Madrinha Rita. He took over the spiritual leadership of CEFLURIS in 1990.

Madrinha Rita Gregório de Melo at her home in Céu do Mapiá, in the Brazilian Amazon, 2013

Padrinho Sebastião leading a healing work at the *Casa da Estrela* (Star House) in Céu do Mapiá, in the Brazilian Amazon, circa 1985

coexistence with nature. We have very little contact with all those billboard advertisements, with all that movement that's out there in the world. But we have contact with life, essentially with the life that's in there. To learn to really live in the forest is the most incredible thing in the world . . . for me, at this moment.

One of the greatest experiences was my contact with Madrinha[18] Rita and Padrinho Sebastião, who are, so to speak, my masters. Madrinha Rita is my great master, my great godmother, my dear one. Padrinho Sebastião left me assigned with a series of things, mainly connected with spirituality in Céu do Mapiá, connected with healing. I always wanted to run away from any responsibility, and he kept giving me more and more, wanting me to go and help people who were ill, so I went to help people who were ill, but then these people, they remained ill, and he wanted me to keep on helping. Oh my God! One day he reprimanded me, he said, "Have you no charity? You must have charity, you must help people!" Padrinho Sebastião was a man like this, of much love. In short, Padrinho believed in me.

After some time living in Céu do Mapiá, Padrinho Sebastião opened up a house, called *Casa da Estrela* (Star House), which is a place where we do the smaller works and mediumistic works too. One day he called me and said, "My daughter, I want you to go to the Casa da Estrela, call your women companions who know how to heal, do massage, how to read stories, cast the I Ching . . . you all go there and help the sick." On Wednesdays we opened the space for everyone who was sick. We worked all day and night and we went straight into the *trabalho de cura* (healing work). Padrinho said to join all the sacred knowledge of the planet to help each son and daughter of

18. Literally "Godmother"; refers to the name for the female spiritual leaders in the Santo Daime tradition.

the Earth. All knowledge was valid, all spiritual traditions could join inside that place to bring some comfort to the people who were ill and soothe humanity. In this way our doctrine is eclectic, as it embraces all knowledge and all sacred lines.

After some time Padrinho made his passage. It was very painful, one of the most incredible things that I have lived through. We held a work for him. Padrinho Alfredo, his son, called us together when Padrinho was already about to receive the extreme unction. Padrinho Sebastião called me, (Grandmother) Maria Alice, and Cristina Santos. And the three of us went to do the transport of the spirits who were harassing Padrinho Sebastião and could be bringing him to death. I had a very strong passage, because while a person caught one spirit, I caught ten, because I was already doing this work even before the Daime.

I had a vision that was unforgettable, in which I went to a place called the Valley of Clamors, a place where human souls remain suffering for eternity. It's as if the clock stops in time. . . . And you begin to say a phrase and that phrase remains for eternity. You cannot get out of that phrase. And I ended up in that place, and after that place I saw myself traveling with Padrinho Sebastião, flying with him. I had never dreamed that I was flying, but on that day I was flying with him. And he said, *My daughter, I'm going to take you to my new dwelling.* I said, *Your new dwelling?* He said, *It's done, we have arrived.* It was a crystal castle. And inside this crystal castle he said, *Now you go back to Céu do Mapiá. You will see me there. But I won't be there. But I will be. But I won't be . . .*

After that, Padrinho went to Rio de Janeiro. He was taken in a helicopter and never returned. Three months later, he made his passage. In the early hours of the 20th of January, the day of São Sebastião (Saint Sebastian), Sebastião Mota de Melo, Padrinho Sebastião made his passage. For me it was very strong, because he was everything to me. He was my father.

Sickness and Healing Works

After Padrinho's passage, I began to have problems in my ovaries. I went to a healing work, and it was revealed to me that I had cancer in the ovaries. No one could say if it was true or not, but a Daime vision showed this to me. I started to take a little Daime every day in the morning. One day I had a metastatic crisis, an excruciating pain in my ovaries. They held an emergency healing work for me in which I received a spiritual operation from the doctors of the astral plane. I felt them really rummaging around in my ovaries. When the operation was over, a doctor, who looked more like an angel than a doctor, came to me. He called himself Doctor Jorge de Albuquerque. Although I didn't know it, he did exist. Jorge de Albuquerque is the son of Mário de Albuquerque, a surgeon. In the work he said I was cured. He told me to go to my house, lie on my bed, and the next day spend the whole day lying down. And so I did. At one point when I got up to pee, a ball of blood fell out of my vagina, the tumor. It came out, perfectly round, into my hands.

During this time when I was operated on (spiritually) in the ovaries, they also did an investigation in my head and discovered that I had a slight alteration in the right ventricle in my brain. And so they (the

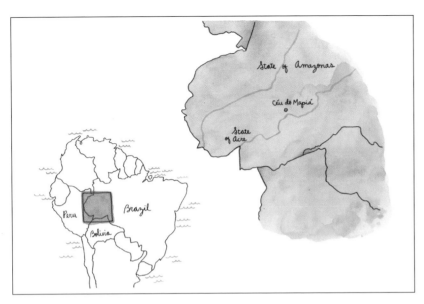

Céu do Mapiá is located in the headwaters of Igarapé (river) Mapiá, 19 miles from the Purus River. The village is located within the National Reserve of Inauini-Pauini, one of the most preserved areas of the western Brazilian Amazon.

Aerial view of Céu do Mapiá

spirits) were asking me to go to a doctor to do a more detailed exam of my head and do the exam of the ovaries.

I went to the doctor in Brasília. It had been three years since I had left to live in Céu do Mapiá. We live a very simple life, truly deep in the heart of the Amazon rain forest. It used to take us three days by canoe and car to get out of the jungle, depending on the season. When we arrived in the city, my six-year-old daughter didn't even remember paved streets anymore.

When the doctor examined me, she believed I still had a tumor. She thought they would need to operate and remove my ovaries. So she told

me to do an iconography, a more detailed exam. When the exam was over, the doctor asked me, "Where did you have an operation? Who operated on you? What hospital was that?" I said, "It was God's hospital." She said, "No, I'm not kidding. Which hospital operated on you? Because I'll tell you one thing, they removed even the tumor's root. That's something that usually doesn't happen. It's impossible to remove the tumor's root. And a very perfect operation was done on your tumor, very perfect indeed. You don't have cancer anymore." She was so impressed.

Then I went to the neurologist. I told him about my astral operation on my head. I described how I saw the astral doctors open up a part of

Amazon rain forest caiman. Igarapé (river) Mapiá, Brazilian Amazon, 2011

"Ponte Padrinho Nel" (Padrinho Nel's Bridge). Céu do Mapiá, Brazilian Amazon

my head, put in a kind of tube, remove some water, and insert something like a valve and a little plate with two screws. That's what I saw in the Daime vision.

The doctor ordered a brain tomography. After the exam he said, "You know that those of us from a public hospital cannot let just anyone do an exam, right? This vision you had is an operation we do for people who have hydrocephalus. And you do have an alteration in that right ventricle, in that place. You have a slight alteration, but for the brain any alteration is an alteration. So you have to be careful. Now you'll have to do exams every year, because I can't tell you if that opera-

tion they did on you really happened and you're cured, or if that thing might grow. If it grows, it's dangerous and a procedure has to be done that is this kind of operation." I spent much time deciding whether I would do the operation or not. Then I decided to ask for help. *Look, Padrinho Sebastião, I'll do the following: if I can sing* Nova Jerusalém[19] *from start to finish, I'll return to Mapiá. And may it all be as God wills.* I managed to sing *Nova Jerusalém.* And I returned to Mapiá.

Then, one month after Padrinho Corrente's death, in 1996, I re-

19. *Nova Jerusalém* (New Jerusalem) is a hymnal received by Padrinho Sebastião.

Clara before her altar in the forest

ceived another operation from the astral doctors. They came with a saw and *Vrrooommm*. They said, *Look, if you continue to smoke cigarettes, you'll lose the benefits of the whole operation. You can't smoke anymore.* And so I quit. After that, I began to do the magnetic resonance every year, and it said that I was well, that I was already healed. After some time I didn't need to return to do the exam anymore. It's been years since I last did this exam. And so I received my physical cure.

Then I went into a whole healing process. In the Santo Daime healing doesn't happen from one moment to the next. It takes a very long period to reach an awareness of your illness. It took more than six months to really receive my healing. There are many things inside us that lead us to our defeat, so to speak, that create much illness inside us, which are our feelings, our anger, our suffering, our internal unresolved issues. After a long period, I realized I had difficulty forgiving myself. I discovered that I still had huge feelings of culpability about my mother's death. Because of my mother's death it was like I had a prison guard, pointing his finger at me, saying I wasn't worth anything. I spent twenty-two years of my life with this suffering. This jailer inside of me was a great teacher. He prevented me from becoming grand, allowed me to keep my humility, to see that I was really nothing. This being kept me from feeling powerful, despite all the power God gave me.

There are many **things inside** us that **lead us** to our **defeat**, so to speak, that **create much illness** inside us, which are our **feelings**, our **anger**, our **suffering**, our **internal unresolved issues**.

The cancer was dismantled after I learned to ask for forgiveness in a really profound way. It's the great sword that we have, the sword of forgiveness. It liberates us from our guilt, and from the ways we blame other people for things that happen to us. This passage of mine with cancer was a passage of great gratitude for my understanding today. Every suffering we go through is always to bring us greater understanding and comprehension, for our evolution.

Santa Casa de Cura

After my healing, in 1998, a Japanese woman was interned in my house in Mapiá for several months because she was very ill. She stayed with her son. We did many healing works for her, and then she returned home to Japan. One fine day, she had a dream in which *Mestre Irineu*[20] told her that she had to give me some money to start a clinic in Céu do Mapiá, because there was no health center in the village. In the dream, she went to a bank and asked for a loan. The dream was so real that she actually went to the bank to ask for a loan, as she had no money. When Padrinho Alfredo went to Japan that year, she gave him the money. So in this way we built the *Santa Casa de Cura* (Holy House of Healing).

The house's original name is *Santa Casa de Cura Padrinho Manoel Corrente*. Maria Alice, Isabel Barsé, and I wanted to honor Padrinho Corrente because he was the women's Padrinho, he gave us protection. The Corrente family always has this connection with charity. His daughters are very charitable. The Santa Casa has been around for over nineteen years now.

When the Santa Casa was ready, I became ill with fever. I was alone, crying. What was I going to do with that monster of a house? How was I going to do it? And then it came to me that everything was prepared. That I was going to have everything, that I wouldn't worry about a thing, that the people would all show up, that everything was right, and I didn't need to worry about anything.

The Santa Casa lives and survives. I also work and go around the world and work for it, to bring a little money

20. Raimundo Irineu Serra, also known as Mestre (Master) Irineu, was the founder of the Santo Daime religion.

Clara at the Santa Casa de Cura in Céu do Mapiá, Brazilian Amazon, 2011

Isabel Barsé preparing remedies at the Santa Casa de Cura, 2013

Six o'clock in the morning ritual setup at the Santa Casa de Cura, 2011

Grandmothers Clara and Maria Alice, and the Corrente sisters at an Umbanda ceremony in the Santa Casa de Cura, Céu do Mapiá, Brazilian Amazon, 2013

to it. It has maintained itself, it maintains itself, as if by a miracle. It has a life of its own. There are many people who receive cures from the Santa Casa. It seems as if the Santa Casa even travels to people's houses.

We also receive a sort of pension. So everyone there has a little money nowadays. But it has become easier for people to find a doctor outside Mapiá. In the old days, the seeking for natural medicine, for the Santo Daime medicine, was much greater than nowadays. Now people prefer to take pills. That's something that Padrinho used to ask, that people not keep on taking pills. There are still people in Mapiá who rely on the Daime and seek their healing through the spirit and within our holy doctrine.

We say healing in the Daime is a little expensive, because it takes a longer time. It's not immediate, comes with self-consciousness, with self-knowledge to be able to receive the cure.

We're trying to keep up with the times that have changed, with people's mentality, and see how we can move forward. Our Santa Casa has become more for people who come from abroad or from other places, who come to seek the Santo Daime to heal.

We are experiencing what I believe is a very big transformation, a very big transformation out in the world, as much as in our healing house in Céu do Mapiá. There was a moment when I thought that the Santa Casa had to close down, but Mestre Irineu and Padrinho Sebastião have been coming to me and I have followed the messages from these masters of mine, my spiritual guides.

Mestre Irineu

I'll share a little about my contact with Mestre Irineu that's been going on from 2007 until now, as it is a very profound contact that led me to start a spiritual work at six o'clock in the morning, which is the Rosary we do at Santa Casa for mediumistic study, for our healing, that I received from Mestre Irineu.

In 2007 a problem I was already having since Dharamsala got worse, a very big pain in the arm. This pain was so strong I could not move. And then, as I was unwell, I decided to go to the doctor and seek some spiritual assistance too. I went to Rio Branco and the doctor found I had a herniated disc, a bone spur, and arthrosis in the seventh cervical vertebra. And that was making me paralyzed and unable to sleep. The doctor said I might need an operation. I continued to try other things and take analgesics, and I felt a bit better.

When I returned home to Céu do Mapiá, the pain started to worsen. So we decided not to do the operation and instead went to pray at the Santa Casa. I decided with Isabel, my companion who works with me at Santa Casa, that I'd remain interned, as a patient. Until then I was the director of Santa Casa. This was the first time I entered there as a patient. At the time my daughter was also ill, so the two of us went in. When I entered the Santa Casa I gave thanks to Padrinho Sebastião, to all the *pretos velhos*,[21] to the *caboclos*,[22] and to Manoel Corrente for my health and for the Santa Casa. Then I heard the voice of Mestre Irineu saying, *Do you remember me? I am that same one who spoke to you at Bujari*—which is a place near Alto Santo,[23] where Padrinho Luiz Mendes church is. At that time I had a very big pain all over my body, I asked Mestre Irineu for help, and he answered me.

And so Mestre said, *I am that same one who spoke to you at Bujari*. Then he said, *And you, lady, you give thanks to so many people. Won't you give me thanks?* Then he said, *Who is the provider of the Santa Casa? Who is the person that gave you the Santa Casa?* I said, *It was you, sir*. He said, *Yes indeed, and you did not thank me*. I said, *I did not indeed, I forgot*. He said, *Yes, you're always forgetting me*. And then he spoke like this: *That's the way it is, you forgot and do not know my* hinário[24] *properly, with so many* caboclos *you keep on channeling*. So I said, *It's true*. And then he spoke like this, *And you're always searching for procedures to heal the sick who come to the Santa Casa. Well then, now I'll give you a procedure*. I said, *Which one is that?* He said, *The procedure is for you to pray the Rosary at six o'clock in the morning*. I said, *Oh, what horror!* Because I didn't like praying the Rosary much. *So this will be the first procedure for your cure. With this, you will get to know what prayer is and how to illuminate all the suffering beings who*

---

21. *Pretos velhos* (old black men) are spirits of those who died enslaved. They are wise, peaceful, and kind spirits that know all about suffering, compassion, forgiveness, and hope.

22. Entities related to the spirit of the indigenous people of the forest.

23. Literally "Tall Saint"; refers to (1) the original church founded by Mestre Irineu; (2) the district of Rio Branco where it stands; (3) the line followed by other Santo Daime churches that stick strictly to the original liturgy set by Mestre Irineu.

24 Literally "hymnal"; refers to (1) a hymnal of sacred channeled hymns received by members of the Santo Daime that are sung at every Santo Daime work; (2) the works that represent the apex celebration of the official Santo Daime calendar, where the sacred beverage is ingested, and the hymns are sung and danced to.

are with you, through prayer. You will also get to know the sufferers who are with you, know your mediumship. Then he said many other things that I must keep private.

So I started waking up at six o'clock and doing the Rosary every morning. One day I started praying, and I started to feel a very big indisposition and went to vomit. And I vomited and a voice spoke like this: *It would be good for you to visit a woman colleague of yours.* I said, *Why? I'm not on such good terms with her.* I kept finding justifications because I didn't want to go talk to the woman. So I went there. It was great, it was very good to have visited this companion, because I was really having problems with her and wasn't able to forgive her. I learned—once again—that I needed to learn to forgive. I needed to see what that pride was. So I entered a study of myself, of forgiveness.

The pain got so bad that I got to the point of using a (cervical) collar. A friend and I continued praying every day. One day an immense force descended upon me, and I began to raise the table where we prayed. It seemed as if I was going to knock that table down with just one finger, so strong was I. My friend approached to give me Daime and said I looked as if I was going to rip everyone to shreds. The strength of the being in me was the strength of the guilt in me, the strength of nonforgiveness. And then that being in me wanted to kill everyone. I started to scream and cry. When I saw myself, I had the vision of myself getting out of a prison. I was even wearing blue and I was getting out of the prison. It was that being who accompanied me, who was escaping out of me.

For twenty-two years I had suffered. And then I experienced a washing of my soul, a forgiveness that I gave to myself. I experienced a very incredible catharsis. And when I got out of that place, there was a woman who had done much harm to me. She passed by the Santa Casa beaming a beautiful, wonderful smile that made me so happy. I said, "Look, I want to tell you something: I forgive you for everything you did to me. I'll just apologize for still not being able to trust you. But I forgive you, let's be friends. But to trust you is going to be difficult for me for a while. Still, one day I'll trust you again." That was an act of so much love and so much truth in me that I set myself free by forgiving. We have so many things to work on inside ourselves to be able to forgive.

I thanked Mestre Irineu a lot for being able to live this moment. And my cure came. I stopped aching, everything got better. After twenty-two years.

My daughter had always had to take care of me during those twenty-two years. She fell into depression because that being had disappeared. She no longer needed to take care of me and she didn't know what else to do. She had never lived for herself; she always had to be an adult. She was always giving me strength. And then I had to relearn to live, and my daughter also had to relearn. So we set ourselves free from this process. This is a story of truth that I lived. I believe many people might be living the same thing without even being aware of it. Beings come to disturb us and diminish us, beings who take our value from us but who also bring us some knowledge.

So I always say that no matter how much suffering comes to us, we should give thanks. Only God knows why we're going through that, and that which we're going through is for our growth, it's for our evolution. I'm sure of it. As painful as it might be, God is allowing it to happen to us for our indoctrination, for our growth, and for our understanding of life. I'm very grateful for these difficult moments I've gone through. It's those difficult moments that give clarity to our lives, give comprehension, bring mercy, and bring compassion to us. I'm very grateful for all the passages I am passing through, and have been passing through, as each moment that happens in our lives is very important so we can overcome and conquer obstacles that have been keeping us from *being*... mainly from *being*... because we are here to *be*. We want to have, but it's not to have, it's to *be*. And that was a great teaching I received.

Santa Maria

During one of my prayers at six o'clock in the morning I had a vision of Saint Anthony of Padua. At the time I didn't even know who he was or what he meant. I learned he was a monk from an esoteric line of profound knowledge. Saint Anthony took me to a room to receive some instructions about the sacred plant *Cannabis sativa*, which Padrinho Sebastião named *Santa Maria*.[25] He considered it a feminine plant that works on our hearts. In the vision I was taken to talk with four gentlemen in black suits. They asked me to take this sacred plant to the Grandmothers Council and make a declaration about it, consecrate it, asking the grannies to place this sacred plant in our basket of talismans. The basket already held the Santo Daime, mushrooms, iboga, and peyote.

25. Literally "Holy Mary."

(top) Clara at her studio in Céu do Mapiá, Brazilian Amazon, 2013 (bottom) Clara's home in Céu do Mapiá, Brazilian Amazon, 2013

The gentlemen also said, *You shall go to Italy to meet the pope*. I said, *Oh, and now this! What could I possibly do there with the pope?* He said, *You will take this energy, this intention to Rome*. So I said, *But I don't even know if I'm going to Italy! No one's talking about going to Italy*. Then some time passed, and the news came that there were preparations being made for the Grandmothers to go to Italy, to support Grandmother Beatrice's desire to rescind the papal bulls.[26]

When we went to the Vatican I made a special prayer, since the pope (Benedict XVI) ended up not receiving us. I prayed internally, because I wasn't prepared to reveal this in public. I asked Jesus to be able to receive this sacred plant so that one day we could reveal it, and perhaps the Church could support its use to help young people.

When I returned from Italy, another instruction came that it was necessary for me to meet with an important politician in Brazil to ask for governmental support. I kept thinking of many politicians, but I couldn't imagine who it could be. Then a week later, Maria Alice let me know that Gilberto Gil, the Brazilian Minister of Culture, would receive us to talk about the Grandmothers Council.

Gilberto Gil agreed with me: "I'll give you advisory support for you to talk about *Cannabis sativa* so that you have this freedom to talk about it in the United States." In 2009 I brought this proposal, a decree, to the Grandmothers' gathering in Oregon, where the medicinal use of *Cannabis sativa* was already liberated. And there I could speak. Many people stood up and gave testimonies about the plant's healing powers, saying that it was really important to liberate it.

Seven years passed, and in the beginning of 2016 we learned that we were going to New York for a gathering to close the cycle of the Grandmothers Council pilgrimage. Padrinho Sebastião told me to bring Santa Maria to New York and ask the council to accept Santa Maria in their basket as a sacred healing plant. At that council, we did the Santo Daime Santa Maria hymnal, a spiritual work calling the force of Santa Maria, of our dear mother. And we prayed. And I felt that Santa Maria touched the hearts of many of the grannies and those in attendance. I believe we will be able to receive this approval one day. There's no way to deny the healing power that this plant is revealing to humanity.

All these stories I'm sharing are examples to say that there exists a greater force that reigns over us. There really exists a divine force, like voices we hear, which propels us to go ahead with instructions that come to us from the astral plane.

---

26. In 1452, Pope Nicolas V issued the bull Romanus Pontifex, declaring war against all non-Christians throughout the world, to "capture, vanquish, and subdue the Saracens, pagans and other enemies of Christ," to "put them into perpetual slavery," and to "take all their possessions and property."

THREE

GRANDMOTHER BEATRICE LONG VISITOR HOLY DANCE

MY NAME IS BEATRICE LONG VISITOR HOLY DANCE. That is my maiden name. My married name is Weasel Bear. I was born on May 12, 1927, and raised in Slim Buttes, South Dakota, and I've lived here all my life. Eighty-five years of it here. I was born across the river, the White River.

My father, Rex, delivered me. My father's name was Rex Long Visitor Holy Dance Senior. His Indian name was *Tashunka Wakita*. His Indian name means looking horse.

My mother's maiden name was Antonia Sierra. And her Indian Lakota name was *Ta Canku Skala*. Her Indian name means her road of life is pure.

My mother was from here, Oglala. Her dad, my grandpa, was from Mexico. My grandpa's name was Cevrano Sierra and he married my grandmother, Mary Runs Between, who was Oglala Lakota.

I had nine siblings. All together there should be nine of us, but some of them died when they were babies, and they're all gone now, except for my sister and me. There were four of us who grew up together: my sister Rita, my brother Rex Jr., my brother Stanley, and me, Beatrice.

One of our grandmothers, the Long Visitor Holy Dance grandma, she had two houses. One big log cabin and a little log cabin. She lived in that big log cabin in the summertime and in the little one in the wintertime, to save wood.

My grandmother's name, Mary Runs Between, means somebody who "runs between the lines." She was named like that because she did that during the Wounded Knee Massacre. She escaped and she was

pregnant with my dad. She got out of there, and when she came back she gave birth to him on January 15th.

My first husband's name was Ernest Afraid of Bear Senior. We had four children together, Fontanelle Pancho, Antonia Loretta, Michael, and Anita.

My second husband was John Tex Weasel Bear. We had two children, Madonna Faith and Aloysius John. I was also with an Arapaho man named Herman Caldwell and I had two children from him, Virginia Lorraine and Norman Caldwell. They both passed.

I had another child, Roger Bruce. I had to give him up for adoption because I had no place to take him. I had no job, nothing. I went to welfare and asked them for a place for him to go, so they took him.

That's why I kept my maiden name. When I joined the Grandmothers Council I was thinking about my son who was somewhere in this world, so I used my maiden name because when they took him from me, I was using my maiden name. So I put my name Holy Dance out there. That's how his wife found me. She read about me through the Grandmothers Council. She saw the name Holy Dance, and she told my son: "I think I found your mother."

First she emailed the Grandmothers Council organizer's office, who called me saying, "Grandma, I've got news for you." I said, "What?" She said, "You know, there's a family member looking for you, your son Roger. Do you want them to contact you or not?" I said, "I want them to contact me!" So she said, "All right." I said, "Yes, send the information to Loretta, she knows about computers."

Loretta received the letter on the computer saying that Roger was looking for his mother. The lady who sent the email was his wife. Loretta wrote back saying that I was still here, and that they could contact me at Loretta's email. Then we talked on the phone in 2011.

So they came to visit. They had a room at the hotel and they told us to go over there. So we went over there and I sat in that lobby waiting and waiting. Pretty soon he came down and there he was. I said, "Roger!" And I started crying. He came running, and we just hugged and cried.

When they took him from me at the hospital, when he was just newborn, I talked to him, I prayed with him, and I told him, *I don't want to give you up, but I don't have no place to go with you.* So I said, *I'm going to let you go for a little while.* But I said, *As soon as I can, I'll get you back.*

I have been praying for him all of these years.

He was fifty-one when he came back. May 3rd is his birthday. So he came back. The next time he visited, his daughter, my granddaughter, came with him. Her name is Angelica. She's so beautiful.

Left to right: Moses Delmar Blindman, Carmelita Long Visitor Holy Dance, Anita Afraid of Bear (daughter), Rex Long Visitor Holy Dance Senior (father), Antonia Loretta Afraid of Bear (daughter), Yvonne Long Visitor Holy Dance, and Fontanelle Pancho Afraid of Bear (son)

All together I have many grandchildren. I have about thirty grandchildren and I lost four, sixty great-grandchildren and I lost three, and eight great-great-grandchildren. I didn't even see some of my great-grandchildren yet.

Childhood

My own childhood in Slim Buttes was good.

I was six years old when I was taken to boarding school. I received the Holy Communion on March 19th of that year at the Holy Rosary Mission, now the Red Cloud Indian School. I learned how to pray like that and sing; I could even sing in Latin.

They didn't accept the Lakota ways, I suppose. But I didn't really pay attention to it then. I used to sing

Holy Rosary Mission—Red Cloud Indian School—Immaculate Conception Sodality, 1945. From front to back: first row, second from left, Beatrice Long Visitor Holy Dance. Pine Ridge Reservation, South Dakota, United States

Lakota when I was there. It was when I was older, though, because I was about fourteen, fifteen years old when I sang in my native tongue in boarding school.

Dad was a *pow wow*[1] singer. I learned to sing Lakota from him. A pow wow is a gathering of tribes where they put on the best regalia they have and they perform. They'd enjoy themselves, dancing. My dad and his mother, they were singers. They'd sing all kinds of songs. They'd sing pow wow, Kettle Dance songs, Sundance songs, Rabbit Dance songs; any kind of songs. They'd also sing songs where the men and women dance together and other songs where everybody dances.

Nowadays the pow wows we go to are with Lakotas and other Indian nations. Years ago, when I was growing

1. A Native American social gathering involving feasting, singing, and dancing

up, they never gathered like that. But nowadays they have those national pow wows. Every summer they gather, all nations gather.

Prayer Ways

My spiritual life began at home. I used to stay with my grandma. My dad built his house here, and right next door was my grandma's house. I used to go sleep at my grandma's house all the time. When she got up in the morning, she and Grandpa would go outside and I'd go with them. She'd stand out there and reach toward the sun and pray.

Both of them, they did that every morning. So I'd stand out there and pray with them in Lakota. That's where I learned how to pray. It was something that we'd do every morning.

When we entered womanhood, they put us into a tent by ourselves and they kept us there for all the time that we had our period. My mother would give us needlework, like sewing quilt tops or beading or anything like that. She'd give it to us and she'd tell us to cut these up or sew them up, and we'd sit in there and sew.

I learned to pray and do everything from my mother and grandmother. I followed suit, whatever way they presented themselves. My mom said, "You don't do this and you don't do that. You don't go to these ceremonies, you stay away from them when you're on your period." So I'd do that.

Holy Rosary Mission—Red Cloud Indian School—Student actors, religious sister, and adults by tipi, circa 1940–1950. Back (standing) row: second from left, Beatrice Long Visitor Holy Dance. Pine Ridge Reservation, South Dakota, United States

The women never did sweat lodges with the men in those days. The men would be by themselves. They had their own ceremonies.

One day my younger (spiritual) brother, my aunt's son, Bernard Red Cloud, had an accident. He parked his truck and was going to go in the house. Then he heard something and he looked back. His truck started rolling backward, so he ran to it and tried to get in. He was trying to stop it and he fell. He fell out and that truck ran over him. Just missed his head. Isaac Yellow Bull just happened to peek out of the house and saw him fall off the truck. Right away Isaac ran out, but before he got there, the truck ran over Bernard.

I was working at that time. I was coming down the street and Isaac was waving at me, so I stopped. My sister-in-law said,

Beatrice walking behind her newly wed grandson and wife, Kakwira Cook and Sarah Elkashef, at the Afraid of Bear/American Horse Dance Sundance grounds. South Dakota, United States, 2012

"You have to come. Your brother got hurt." I said, "What happened?" She said, "His truck ran over him, he fell out of it. They're taking him to Rapid City right away."

I just went in and told my coordinator, "I've got to go." "Go!" she said. So I called home and told Aloysius to get some stuff ready to make a ceremony right away. I said, "Uncle Bernard got injured and they flew him to Rapid City." Right away we got a puppy. I called Loretta; she got a hold of Roger Byrd. He was living out toward Gordon. He said, "I'll start the sweat lodge." So we brought the dog for sacrifice and took the pots and everything with us. And we made prayer ties and everything right away and we went over there. We went way out to the river by Gordon, to the sweat lodge.

His wife prepared the dog for sacrifice. They put red paint on it clear up to his tail, red paint facing the west, and then they choked it with a rope, on each side, they pulled on it until it died. Then they put it on the fire and singed it all up. Burned all the hair off it and cleaned it and washed it and cut it open. She started cutting the pieces. She got it all ready and started cooking it, and by that time they were heating the sweat rocks. As soon as they got done we all went to sweat, and they took that pot of soup into the sweat lodge, right next to the water. We sat in the lodge and prayed for my brother. Roger prayed and he told us that Bernard was going to be all right. So when they were singing, you could just smell that dog soup, and it was getting sprinkled all over us by the spirits in the lodge. It was really good.

Roger prayed, and after a while we ate some of the meat. He told us to take the head part to the hospital. So that's what we did, we took it over there. We made some *womiye,* tobacco ties, with little offerings to help my brother get well. His lungs collapsed two or three times until he got well.

I'm telling you this because if someone is on their deathbed because of an accident or illness, that's what we do, we make a commitment to pray. Maybe we'll say, *I want him or her to get well, so I'm going to do a vision quest and make that offering there.* We make prayers for them.

Or maybe you decide to pray because you've had dreams. Someone may not have problems or an emergency, but they might go on a vision quest. The spirits come to them and tell them, *We want you to do this. Sacrifice yourself like this, and do this and that.* And they have to do it. Some of these dreams, I don't know what they're about, but people make commitments to vision quest. That's their business, I don't question it.

The Sacred Peace Pipe

My dad, my brothers, my grandmas, and my grandpas were all pipe keepers, they all had pipes. The pipe is learned from one generation to the next. So if you want to use a pipe, you make your own pipe and you use it.

The pipes are made mostly by the men. In those days the women hardly handled the pipe. My grandmother had the pipe because she was past the age of having her period. So she could carry that pipe.

Nowadays everybody wants to Sundance and be a pipe holder, and everybody wants to know what's going on. Which is good for the generations to come, because they need to keep passing that on. And they need to learn about it while they're young. Grandma and them were so sacred with it; they keep it inside their house, that big log house. They kept it in there and then they didn't let anyone in there unless there was going to be a ceremony. Then they'd go in.

I became a pipe holder after I didn't have my period anymore.

I started Sundancing way back with the Black Crows out there by Wanblee. I started Sundancing there. I didn't become a pipe keeper, but when I was going to Sundance, I had to have a pipe. So that's where I started using the pipe.

The pipe was given to my son Aloysius by a very traditional family. They had a pipe from their grandparents. When their brother died, they passed it on to Aloysius when he was still a little boy to keep for when he was older, because he was singing and doing those things and their brother was no longer there. Aloysius asked me to take care of it, so I took care of it for him. Then when I started Sundancing I used it. It's a real old black pipe. It still has quillwork and the sage they had put in it. I still keep it like that, I don't change it. The black pipe comes from the center of the earth, and from there it eventually turns into the red. So that's why the black pipe is hardly ever used. It's old.

The center of the earth is the black pipe, and from there it goes up. Like the colors, everything starts with the black. The black people are the first. The black pipe represents the black people and the dark races.

The pipe of peace is our Lakota peace pipe, the one given to them by the White Buffalo Calf Woman, who is a spirit. It's not a human being who brought the pipe; it's a spirit. White people think they can make white buffalos by mixing the herds, but there will never be a white buffalo. It's a spirit that brought the pipe. No person can make one like that, only God.

Sundance

The day before Sundance begins we have what is known as Tree Day. The tree is life, right here. It grows just like us. And that's why the tree that stands in the center of the Sundance arbor is known as the *Tree of Life*.

So on Tree Day, a tree will die when they cut it and bring it to the Sundance area. We give thanks to the Creator for that tree so we can go around it and put our humble prayer ties on it. We pray and decorate it because it gave its life for us. So in honor of its life, we put our

humble prayer ties and tobacco, whatever we can offer to Creator in exchange for us destroying the tree that Creator grew.

The Sundance tree is always a large tree. The Tree of Life is always a cottonwood tree. The center of all trees, the cottonwood. We prefer cottonwood to burn in the sacred fireplaces because that wood can be burned in a tipi and it won't pop and sprinkle all kinds of ashes on you, live ashes, live coals. There are other trees here, but they're not as good as the cottonwood.

I make the spiritual food[2] so that it can be put down in there as an offering, under the Tree of Life. I make spiritual food just like we do with our loved ones who have passed on. When we put our loved ones away, we make a little bag, put that food in there with water as an offering, and we pray. We ask that person's spirit to take that food and give thanks to the Creator for his or her life and for the food that is provided from the Creator to us. We ask the spirit of the one who's leaving to take that food and give it back to *Wakan Tanka*, *Tunkashila*, the Great Spirit. We give thanks to Creator for their lives and the people's lives here on earth, and for the ones who have gone beyond.

According to what I've heard ever since I was growing up, the buffalo, *Tatanka*, is our breed. That's where we come from. We came out of the Black Hills with the buffalo. We were nourished by the buffalo all of our lives. They provided us with shelter, clothes, and food. They took care of us.

In the Sundance grounds we have the buffalo skulls. We're not worshiping them, but we're giving thanks,

"I make the spiritual food so that it can be put down in there as an offering, under the Tree of Life."

2. Spiritual food is an offering of corn, meat (often buffalo), and fruit (chokecherries).

(opposite) The *Tree of Life*

because if it weren't for the buffalo we wouldn't have survived. We wouldn't be here today; we would have starved to death. They gave up their lives to feed us. So that's why we're not worshiping the buffalo, we're giving thanks to the buffalo because we would have starved to death without them.

I'd go to Sundance and sing there, but I never thought I'd Sundance because it's too sacred. I never bothered to go and get involved because it's too sacred. For many years I just sang and sometimes I'd look on, but I didn't try to get in there.

I had a son named Norman Caldwell. He was part Arapaho. His dad was Arapaho. And as a little boy I just raised him up like a single parent. One day my dad went fishing and came back and brought a catfish. And Norman was standing there. He was just a little tot, standing there looking at it, when my dad brought it in. And Dad threw it down on the table and it scared him. It scared him, and he got sick from it. So we took him to the medicine man and he doctored him up and said that he just got scared of that fish. But he said, "He's going to get well." And then he said, "The spirits are choosing him to be a medicine man." They wanted him to have the Indian name *Wambli Hupahu,* which means eagle wings.

Wings of an Eagle, that's what they named him. After that he got well, and every time we'd go to the ceremonies, the spirits, they'd tell him, *You're going to be a medicine man, you're gonna take care of Sundances, you're going to Sundance.* They told him that, but it didn't happen. He was in Pocatello, Idaho, and somehow he died over there. He passed away over there in Pocatello and didn't become the person that they told him to be, that they wanted him to be. He was supposed to be a Sundancer. He was supposed to sponsor Sundance and all of that.

So, some years after he died, about four years or something like that, I sat down with my family and I talked to them. I said, "You know, Norman was supposed to be a Sundancer. He was supposed to take care of the pipe, he was going to be a pipe carrier, and he was going to

be a medicine man. He was going to help people. But he didn't, he didn't, he died." So I said, "I want to have a Sundance. I want to start having a Sundance and keep having the ceremonies on his behalf."

We all agreed. My daughter Loretta and her husband Tom, we all agreed we'd have a Sundance right here on the home grounds. So that's what we did. Right below where my sister Rita's house is, that area down there. That's where we had the Sundance. We had it for four years. There was no name for it. It was just a Sundance that I sponsored or we sponsored together. We all got together because of Norman's death.

That's how we started Sundancing, and after the fourth year Rita's son, Delmar, started to be the Sundance leader on behalf of Norman. He started doing ceremony, doing sweat lodges, and he fasted on the hill and all of those kinds of things.

That's how Delmar started taking care of the Sundance, for he wanted to remember his younger cousin/brother Norman. So that's what he did, and I went over there and supported him and his Sundance because my son Norman was also supposed to be doing all of these things, but he died.

So after those four years, we never had any more Sundances on our home grounds here.

After my husband Johnny passed away in 1983, we went and talked with a man named Dayton Hyde. Because Dayton had told us before, "I've been asking people to come here, Lakota people, to come and make prayers here. I want them to pray on this land. I want people to

Beatrice and her daughter, Loretta Afraid of Bear Cook, at the American Horse Dance Sundance grounds. South Dakota, United States, 2012

pray here." He said, "This land belongs to the Lakota people and when I'm gone, I want prayers here from the Lakota people, so I'm asking you to do that if you can."

He took us all over his land; he showed us all of the places where he wanted to put prayers. He took us to where the Sundance site is now; he took us across the river to some petroglyphs. So we stopped and prayed at every spot. We all prayed. They had Aloysius put up all of the tobacco ties, wherever they needed to, sometimes way up high, where they couldn't go. So he did all of that. Al made all of the offerings.

So we talked about it and we went ahead. We had sweat lodges up there for four years. We used to come at four o'clock in the morning when that sun was coming up. Four years we'd sweat up there. Then the last year, the fourth year, we decided to have the Sundance.

Ernest and his brother decided that we should have a Sundance there, the way that Dayton Hyde wanted. So they went and asked Dayton and he said, "Yes, go ahead, that's what I want to see."

The American Horse/Afraid of Bear Sundance started in the '90s. We placed our prayers there, and then Ernest and the rest of the men, they went and made a sweat lodge down there by the river.

I Sundanced with my daughter Loretta two years there, and then I went to Nevada where Delmar, my sister Rita's oldest son, was Sundancing. I danced with him over there in the mountains. He danced out there with no shade. Up there in the mountains, the ground had hot stones all over. We danced with our shoes off, and I had blisters all over my feet. Other tribes joined him to go down to the valley to get the sacred tree, and they'd walk with that tree up that mountain. They

carried it up the mountain, and it couldn't touch the ground. There was no shade or nothing for us to sit under on the mountain. My feet were blistering, but I danced with him out there. I supported him.

I went there and supported him. And it was good, I liked it. I'm glad that I could bring my other children into Sundance.

My son Mike (Michael) was also a Sundancer. He was a Sundancer and he also sang. But then he lost his only son, the only boy he had. He got killed in Idaho; they cut his throat, and he bled to death.

After that, my son Mike passed away too. Mike lived here, but he was over in Oregon when he got killed. Somebody beat him and someone saw him on the street. He wasn't dead, but they couldn't save him because they'd bashed his head in. He was around fifty-seven.

He's buried here in the Catholic cemetery, and we had his funeral there. It's a Catholic cemetery, but we got permission from the Catholic Church to do Native American traditional funerals there.

A lot of my relatives Sundanced. Some, not everyone. You know, it's really a sacred thing. Everybody doesn't Sundance unless they have to. It's so sacred that they're afraid to do things like that.

We grew up knowing about Sundance, knowing about the ways of my father's side of the family. My dad would say, "Be careful what you do," and my mom would say, "Don't go there. That's powerful, if you don't know anything 'bout it. Don't go there, because you'll do something wrong." So we'd see it done and everything, but we kept away from it.

The young generation now, they get into it right away, thinking it's okay, but it isn't. There's a lot of things to it, especially if you can't live

If you don't live a righteous life and try to do ceremonial ways, you're going to get hurt.

a righteous life. If you don't live a righteous life and try to do ceremonial ways, you're going to get hurt. I tried to live a righteous life but couldn't. I was already deep into sin before I started using a lot of ways of worship. I know about it, I prayed and I learned about it, I know it's wrong.

Drinking Problems

When you go drinking, you think you can do anything. When you're drunk, you think you can do anything.

I had drinking problems for years. But I stopped on my own, I did it all on my own. I got myself into it, I got myself into trouble, and I got myself out of it.

The only one who helped me was Al's dad, John. I got real sick from drinking and he went and got a medicine man, offered him tobacco, and brought him back and had him talk to me. After that, I went to the hospital, sick. The doctor said, "You're starting to get cirrhosis; you're going to have to stop drinking." The doctor told me, "If you don't stop your drinking you're going to die." He said, "You're going to start hemorrhaging. You're going to hemorrhage this way and then you're going

to hemorrhage this way, and when you hemorrhage this way, you're going to die. So you make your choice." I thought about my kids and then I thought, *What is going to happen to them if I die?*

So then I made a prayer. I wanted to get out of that hospital. I prayed that I could get out that day and start using the sacred medicine that I'd used in 1946 when my mom had cancer. She and I took the medicine together when she was sick. After that I didn't use it. In 1956, I used the medicine again. I used peyote with that Arapaho man I was with. That was the first time that I brought water in.[3] It was all men having a peyote ceremony. It was on Easter Sunday, and I stayed in the house during the ceremony because it was all men in that meeting. I stayed in the house taking the medicine and praying.

Early in the morning our friend came over and said, "I want to ask you something." I said, "What?" "Could you bring in water for us?" he said. I said, "I don't know nothing about it, I know about peyote ceremonies, but I don't know about that. So I don't know what to do." He said, "I'm asking you to bring in water; I'll show you what to do. You

3. During the Native American Church ceremony, in the morning, a woman brings water into the tipi and prays.

know how to pray, don't you?" I said, "Yeah!" He said, "This is Easter Sunday. I want you to bring water and pray for us. It's all men in there," he said. "I'll roll tobacco for you, you'll smoke it four times and give it to the leader. That's their ways. And then you can pray. Pray on this Easter Sunday for us." So I said, "Okay!" And so I did.

His mother was there too, but she was old. I stood outside the tipi with that water, facing toward the east, and thought about my folks; my mom, my dad, I thought about everybody and I started praying. Then they said, "You can come inside the tipi and bring in the water." They showed me where to set it, so I set the water down. Then they gave me the tobacco and said, "Do you want to say anything?" I said "Happy Easter" to all of them and told them it was my first time, but I'd do my best. So they let me light the smoke, and I made the Lord's Prayer. Then I passed it on to them. So that was my first time carrying water, on Easter Sunday. I always carried water on Easter Sunday after that.

I didn't go back to drinking after that. They prayed for me, and I stayed with it right up to this time. I got back up. I keep telling people, young girls and boys who drink, I say, *You should eat that medicine, it's good for you.* I tell them, *Look at where I'm at. You can be like that too; you can stop drinking and be much happier.* I took a position where I could talk to kids about alcoholism.

Native American Church

I started going to Native American Church (NAC) meetings in 1946, when my mom was dying of cancer. My uncle was an old peyote man.

His name was Joe T. Sierra. That was way before some of the people even knew about peyote. He went to Texas. That was back in the 1930s or whenever—he was already using medicine. And he'd go to Texas, make a trip over there and get the medicine (peyote). He'd harvest medicine, stay over there, and he'd be cutting medicine, as much as he could load on his cart. He'd load up and come back. Sometime in the '70s I asked him, I said, "Uncle Joe, what does it cost you to go to Texas? How much money do you spend?" He said, "For gas? It only takes us about thirty-five dollars to get there and back." At that time gas was cheap. I remember when gas was twenty-five cents a gallon.

I said, "How much money do you take?" He said, "Sometimes I take a hundred fifty or two hundred dollars, because sometimes we go shopping and stuff." During that time they never bought peyote. So he'd harvest the peyote himself and bring it back in gunny sacks, they called them. And he'd bring it back and he'd bring some to the Pine Ridge (Reservation) area, give some to the Rosebud area, and give some to the Yankton Sioux. Every spring and every fall he'd go, and he didn't sell it to them, he just gave it to them because it's sacred medicine. So that's what he did.

My relatives' knowledge about the medicine comes from our Mexican relatives. That's how come Uncle Joe knew about it, and he started bringing it back to our people.

I learned about it in 1946. I learned more about it then. I knew what was going on with Uncle Joe and them. But some people would tell us, "That's not good for you, that's a drug." Even then, they would say, "That's a drug, you can't have that, it will make you crazy." People who didn't know about these sacred ways would say stuff like that.

So I never prayed in that way until my mom got sick. My uncle Joe came over here. He told her, "I am going to put up a (tipi) meeting[4] for you. I want you to get well. I'm going to give you some peyote." And she said, "All right." My dad agreed too. So we went to Scottsbluff, Nebraska, where my uncle lived. He put up a tipi and he had a ceremony for my mom.

Uncle Joe uses the *half-moon fireplace*.[5] A half-moon fireplace has a mound that is put inside of a tipi. My uncle never ran meetings, but he was the fire chief.

He made that fireplace moon. They use dirt to make the moon. They just make that moon right inside the tipi, and then they light the fire inside of it. It's really a pretty thing. Uncle Joe explained how the half moon is put there because it represents life. It represents women's cycle of menstruation and having babies, according to the moon. It represents a mother when she's having a baby. When that half moon shows up in the sky, that's when most of the mothers have their babies. So that's why it's placed there on the earth, in the fireplace altar. There's a line on top of that half-moon fireplace. That's the road of life. So your life starts from this side (in the south) and you go all the way to the middle (in the west) and then when you get to that part (in the north), you start going downhill again. If you're lucky, you'll get to the end of the moon. So that's the *road of life*. They put the peyote in the middle. You set it in the middle of the fireplace.

We have a Lakota half-moon fireplace; it was blessed by an Arapaho. My uncle set it down for us, for our home, for me and John. We first

used it when my son Aloysius was one year old. Uncle Joe would poke fire[6] there. A man named Phillip Eagle Bear took care of that birthday meeting for Al when he was one year old. We have a fireplace here, and we've been brought up traditionally.

When I talk about the medicine, I say that medicine is so sacred that there's no reason for anybody to try to stop us using it. But we need to stop the people who abuse it. That's the thing. And it's not our fault that there are some abusers out there. Phillip Eagle Bear told me, he said, "Niece, I'm going to tell you something." I said, "What?" He said, "We named this the Native American Church. Native is us, American is those people coming into our country and they have these churches and nobody bothers them, so we had to use that word, 'church.' We have a Native American Church. That's the name of it. We're not going to say 'peyote ceremony' anymore; we're going to say 'Native American Church.'" So I said, "That's good." "That way," he said, "they can't bother with us. We made it legal, and they can't do nothing to us as long as it's a church." So that's how Phillip Eagle Bear put it. He and Uncle Joe Sierra talked about it. That's how the elders talked about it.

Father Paul Steinmetz was the priest of the Holy Rosary Catholic church. He was a good friend of my dad. He used to come out here and visit with him. That's how he learned about all of these traditional ways, from my dad. Before Father Steinmetz went on a trip to Italy, I sponsored a NAC meeting for him, to take care of him while he was gone. I said, "I'm going to ask you one request after that prayer meeting." I said,

4. Native American Church ceremonies are known as "meetings."
5. Native American Church ceremony altar.

6. Be a Native American Church ceremonial fire chief.

"We need to save our Native American Church. We have to do something. I want you to go to the pope and ask him if he would bless our NAC and explain to him that you have been in the meetings and you know what it's about." "Yes," he said, "I'll put in a request to the pope." So he explained everything and asked the pope to bless the Native American Church.

So Father Steinmetz brought back a paper from the pope, blessing our Native American Church. I wanted to fix my old house into a nice building where we could have prayer meetings in the wintertime when it's cold—have meetings in there, and have Native American Church doings there and make it a church. I wanted to hang that paper from the pope in there next to the fireplace. But somehow it's been lost.

So I got that blessing, but it cost. It didn't cost me money, but it cost me tears. During the time that Father Steinmetz was gone, my son passed away. He passed away, and when I was having his memorial, the father came and brought that paper back to me. So it's sacred, it's holy.

I was happy for it, but I was in tears too. But it happened, so it was good. I knew my son was blessed. So anyway, that is part of the Native American Church. It's an important part of the Native American Church that we have here.

Papal Bulls

Those papers have got a seal on them. They came from the pope; he signed it. Just like I wanted him to do away with the papal bulls.[7] But when I prayed about it, I thought, *Well, if he doesn't want to do away with the papal bulls, he's going to show that the pope who had it done will*

---

7. In 1452, Pope Nicolas V issued the papal bull Romanus Pontifex, declaring war against all non-Christians throughout the world, to "capture, vanquish, and subdue the Saracens, pagans and other enemies of Christ," to "put them into perpetual slavery," and to "take all their possessions and property."

Father Steinmetz, S.J., with pipe pointed upward, 1975. Pine Ridge Reservation, South Dakota, United States

Beatrice at her family's Native American Church ceremonial grounds

Grandmother Beatrice with the Grandmothers Council at Vatican City in 2008

never be forgiven. If he signs it, then he does away with it, it takes away all of the evil things. That evil is there and it's trying to keep those papal bulls, to continue to grow and destroy. I can spot the evil in any place, even in a meeting. You can spot it when people act in certain ways too.

When we went to the Vatican with the Grandmothers, there was a policeman who tried to stop our prayers. He was really raging on. Pretty soon I thought, *Hey, this is the evil spirit here.* I looked him right in the eye and I told him, "Do you have a mother, a grandmother?" And I said, "Do you know anything about praying?" I looked at him right in the eye, he looked at me and I said, "We're praying here, you'll leave us alone." He looked at me and didn't know where to look. I said, "Leave us alone." And then he took off. Before that happened, I was looking at the Blessed Virgin Mother on a statue in a corner. I was standing there praying to Her, and the baby Jesus in Her arms. I was praying to Her, thinking about the Catholic school I grew up in, praying to Her. And just then the guard came up to us and tried to stop us from praying.

I pray to the Blessed Virgin Mother and Jesus. I do that every day, every morning. I say my prayers all day long, talking to the Creator about my needs, about my family's health, and about the rest of the people, their health and sickness. I pray like that. When I get ready to go to bed I pray to the Blessed Mother, I pray to the guardian angels. Then I go to bed, I'm out.

[Beatrice's daughter, Loretta Afraid of Bear Cook, reflects on the continuation of her mother's lifelong prayer and work to rescind the fifteenth-century papal bulls that led to the Doctrine of Discovery—the basis of European claims in the Americas and the rationale for the United States' western expansion:]

The work to undo the papal bulls continues. I'm still working in the trenches with our own Native American scholars. With the very public news today of the heinous sexual abuse imposed on children of the masses by Catholic priests, bishops, cardinals, and nuns throughout the world, Pope Francis appears to be backed up to the wall with nowhere to turn but to make big changes. Perhaps we will see those man-made laws of religion change for the better for all people of the world. We can continue to hope and pray for compassion, unity, and peace.

My mother, Beatrice, said to us in her teachings: "Have courage, for without it we have no justice, without justice we have no freedom, and without freedom we have no peace."

Can I live up to these ideals of my precious mother, Beatrice?

Some days I have no courage left, because it hurts and it's tiring to keep her prayers for a better life for our people moving and focused.

I have to get out and lick my wounds, and when I feel courage again I jump back into the fray.

Beatrice's daughter, Loretta Afraid of Bear Cook, was part of a delegation of indigenous leaders who formally presented Pope Francis with the "Petition to Revoke the Papal Bulls of Discovery" in 2016.

I'm not alone. There are many more of us working together since we started this journey!

So my work continues: perhaps we may see our sacred sites opened, protected, and wholly able to receive us when we go there to release our prayers in the *He' Sapa* (Black Hills).

We may live to see federal Indian laws within the federal government that are based on papal bulls changed in our lifetime. We pray that it can be. Mom's humble fights are now mine to fight. I try to meet the challenges because I'm a grandmother. I want my precious grandsons, Tokala and Omani, to grow up in a far better world than the one I grew up in.

"Have courage,
for without it we have
no justice,
without justice we have
no freedom,
and without freedom
we have no peace."

Grandmothers Council

Loretta was asked to take me over to a grandmothers' conference they were having in New York. She said, "Mom, let's go over there," and I said, "Okay! I wonder why they want me?" She said, "Well, they want grandmas over there!" I said, "Okay, I'll go." But I said, "What about Mama Rita, can't she go with us?" She said, "She can go, do you want to ask her? We can take her along." I said, "Okay." So that's how come she went with us.

Once we got in there we were dressed in jeans because we were traveling. And we got in there and we hadn't even cleaned up since the morning, nothing.

We got in there and, *Oh my gosh!* I looked at Rita and started laughing. "How can we get into something like this?" I looked at her and she started laughing too. We sat there and a few days later we found out that they were going to form a council . . . and we were in it!

I felt like, *Oh my God.* I was thinking, *I'm going to be riding a plane and going here and there to all of these places and everything.* Every time I was going up in a plane I prayed really hard, but after a while I didn't even mind it.

I felt like we were chosen, I felt like we were chosen people to guard the earth and guard the children and guard the people and talk to them so that they can get on track. I don't know how the other grandmas feel. Maybe they're perfect women, but I'm not, not me. I'm the biggest sinner they ever picked. Anyway, I'm where I'm at, and I'm happy about it. And Creator provided me with things like that. He would look after me

like that. I was so naughty and stupid, and Creator still took care of me and watched over me. And in those days, when I was drinking, wherever I'd go, wherever I was at, before I'd go to sleep I'd hold my rosary and start praying until I fell asleep. I'd keep praying even then, because I'd think about my mom all the time. I'd miss her, so I just keep praying even though all of those bad things happened to me.

All that I had to go through, all the beatings I had to take, I still prayed. I didn't want my marriage to fail when I had my first four children. I didn't want it to fail, but it did, and my dad got me away from it because he said, "You're going to be dead sooner or later. I'm getting you out of there; you're not going to stay there anymore. This is enough." I was all black and blue.

Traditional Food and Making Relations

Most of the time I make traditional food for our Native American Church dinners. I'll make dried meat soup and *wásna*. Wásna is the dried meat. Wásna and *wagmíza*, dried corn, and chokecherries. Chokecherry juice, *wojapi*, is also used at ceremonies. It's good, it's pure juice.

Making relations, I told my grandson Kakwira when he got married, "That's a real powerful one." That wedding they had was powerful. In the *joining the pipe* ceremony, they hold a pipe together and pray and they smoke it together. They pray.

I prepared the traditional food for their wedding. I took the chokecherries, the dried meat and corn up to him. I made chokecherries and

Beatrice hanging meat on her outdoors drying rack. Pine Ridge, South Dakota, United States

buffalo. The buffalo could be the male people and the chokecherries could be the female.

So I put those two together and use oil to fix it. I use buffalo kidney oil to fix it. I took it in my hand and I told him, "Okay, grandson." I said, "This food is used to make a relationship. The people use it to adopt each other as brother and sister. But you're getting married. You and my granddaughter are going to live together. You can be related. You can make a relation here. And you're going to keep it that way and you're going to bring children to that relation." So I said, "I made this food for you. I want you to take one of it and put it in her mouth, and you'll always remember to feed her and take care of her. And she will take one and put it in your mouth, and she's going to always remember to take care of you, and your relatives and so on." I said, "You feed each other like that, so now you're making a relation with this woman. You're going to bring forth children." That's what I told them. So they did it.

I also have many adopted children. It happens when they come up to me and say, "Could I call you Mom?"

I learned to prepare meat myself because I'd seen my grandma and my mom doing it, and because my dad used to butcher his cattle and started slicing meat. Whether we knew how to or not, he told us to do it, so we did it.

We had cattle and a big corral. Down there where they were Sundancing on the river was a big corral, so all the men would get together and all the cattlemen would round them up and dehorn them and do all that kind of stuff. We rode the calves.

The government provided us with the buffalo only at Sundance time, to the ones who were having Sundance. Other than that, why would you want a buffalo if you have to pay 800 dollars for it?

I make beef jerky, but not with spices. When I start slicing meat, I just want to keep slicing meat all day. When you prepare meat it is like a continuous loop, a continuous row. You have your fingers under there. I dip them into salt water and then I hang them up and the flies come up. But I cover them with home curtains.

The meat rack is really high. So when the dogs were around, I was okay with it. But now that they're all gone, I need to have a lower rack where I can reach.

To cook a prairie dog, you have to singe it and you wash it clean, scrape it clean, all the black stuff. Then you cut it up and cook it in a pot. You could put a little bit of soda in it, boil it for a little bit, rinse it and then re-boil it. It tastes like dog. They're good to eat.

Work and Community Service

I've had many jobs in my life. I worked in the potato fields. I used to pick 400 bushels a day. They'd pay us ten cents a bushel. It was tough, but we had fun. All of us did it, the whole family.

I even attended college classes at the Oglala Lakota College School of Nursing in Pine Ridge, South Dakota.

I started work in 1975 as a health aide for the Oglala Sioux Tribe Community Health Program. I worked under the leadership of Margie Mills Morgan (Billy Mills's sister—Billy won the 10,000-meter run to receive a gold medal in the 1964 Olympics held in Japan). I retired in 1995 after working for them for twenty years.

After a less than a month of retirement, I started working delivering TB prevention medicine throughout the reservation, and I still do that today. I worked with the state of South Dakota and the Field Health I.H.S. Nursing.

Spiritual Commitments

A medicine man is a man who had the dream to be that. He was appointed by the Great Spirit to do that. That is the only kind of man who can learn how to do medicine, by dreams. The ones who are told to do that by

Beatrice delivering medicine at the Pine Ridge Reservation. South Dakota, United States, 2012

the spirit are the real ones. You can't just be a medicine man. One uncle of mine was a medicine man. His name was John Gallagher.

My dad was mean to a horse one day. He got so mad at this horse, he hit it in the face. He hit that horse in the face, and the same day he started having a bad pain and he couldn't get rid of it. It was so intense that he told my mom to go after his brother John. "Go tell him to come and doctor me up, this pain is killing me," he said. So my mom got on her horse and she went and offered tobacco to him, so he came. It was in the wintertime. He came over and had supper, and after supper my dad cleaned up the dishes and everything. Then he sat down at the table and was talking to Uncle John.

"What happened?" John said.

"I don't know, but I got a pain in here and it just won't go away."

It was wintertime, and John went outside and made a snowball and brought it in. He brought it in and held it against the side of my dad's face. He put that snowball right to the side of his face, and a horsehair came flying out. My uncle said, "See, that's horsehair." He said, "What did you do to that horse? You were mean to him, that's why." So with that snowball he knew it, and it just came out.

I knew this timid person, kind of bashful, the kind who keeps quiet all the time. And he had a dream and he told me about it. *Wakinyan*, the "Thunder Beings," told him to do some things that were impossible for him. They told him to go into a crowd where there was a big gathering, to dress and present himself out there like that. But he said, "I can't do that." He said, "They wanted to give me powers, and I never asked for powers or anything. They want me to do that, but I can't do it."

So I said, "You should see a medicine man who knows about those things to pray for you and intervene for you. They can ask the Thunder Beings to leave you alone."

He said, "I keep dreaming about them and they keep bothering me. I don't know what to do. I'm scared. They told me if I don't do it they're going to kill me, they're going to get rid of me because they want me to become a medicine man and to help people and to do all of these things, but I can't do it." And so he went on like that, and one day in July he was out there. He told me, "When those Thunder Beings are coming from the west, from the great waters, I can hear the rumble. And right in front of me I can see that light."

"I'm scared," he said. So he was working on the tractor, driving the tractor and plowing for a rancher out here. That thunder came real quick, so he headed for the ranch house and parked the tractor. By the time he parked the tractor all those Thunder Beings were on him. He leaned against the shack and he stood there. And that's where they killed him. They went right through his heart. That lightning went through his heart, went through his body, and split open his boots.

I felt bad, we all felt bad. We all knew about it because he told my mom and all of us about the Thunder Beings. I don't know too much about it, but I hear these stories about how they persuade people to do the work, to do healing on this earth, and if you don't do it, why, they kill you. If you refuse to do it, they will kill you.

This one lady, her name was Swift Bird. She had a dream and they told her to take her hair down in front of a gathering they have in Pine Ridge, where they have Sundance. They told her to ride a horse naked around the place. They told her they were going to give her powers to heal and doctor people. But she didn't want to do either. When the Thunder Beings came, she just cried. When she came to that gathering, the Thunder Beings were going to attack her. So she went to these medicine men and asked for prayers.

The Thunder Beings were coming, and she cried and cried. She wore a black dress. I was just a little girl, but I remember she wore a black dress, and she had her hair down like they told her to, and she stood with these medicine men and they had their pipes and they all stood there facing the Thunder Beings and started praying for her. Just started praying for her, and they didn't want to let her go.

She didn't want to do it, but they prayed for her and asked for forgiveness for her and asked the Thunder Beings to release her because she was humble. They prayed like that for her. When you fill that pipe to those Thunder Beings and you pray, they can't come near. They have to depart. They have to go around where you're holding that pipe. So that's what happened. That pipe is powerful, but some people don't take care of it right. So she was all right, they didn't bother her anymore.

I don't ever have dreams like that. I think dreams like that have passed away with all of the old people who have gone. I don't know of anybody ever having dreams like that or talking about it. But there's a lot of medicine men out there, and I don't know how they became medicine men. They don't know the truth of it. They don't know the hardship of it. So they're claiming to be medicine men, they're claiming to be this and that out there, running around. If they ever run up against it, it's a death scene. If they don't do what they're told, they could die. But they don't know that. Nobody told them, so they think that they can be healed.

It's a tough thing, if you're appointed by the Thunder Beings and you don't fulfill their wish before you become a medicine man, they'll kill you. They'll electrocute you.

There are medicine men and there are roadmen. The roadmen, they learn with the peyote. They learn how to conduct themselves. If they're appointed a roadman or if they're asked to run a meeting, they don't have to go through all of the procedures, like the pipe. They learn by experience how to take care of it all. When you become a water woman or a roadman, you are going to take care of those prayers, you are not just going to sit there. Some people show off like a water woman or a roadman and forget about the prayers, but that's not what it is supposed to be. That's powerful to the Native American Church. The peyote's

Germaine Garnier with her daughter Bernadine Garnier at a pipe blessing at the Afraid of Bear/American Horse Dance Sundance grounds. South Dakota, United States, 2012

You have to learn the ways, you have to conduct yourself accordingly, and you have to live it.

Live your prayers.

powerful. It's powerful, and you cannot presume to be a roadman or a water woman when you aren't. You have to be ready for it. You have to learn the ways, you have to conduct yourself accordingly, and you have to live it. Live your prayers.

You can stand there and pray and fan people off and act like a chief. But if you don't live it and you don't take care of your prayers, you could get hurt. Even up to death. People who are roadmen can experience things like that. When it comes right down to it, some of their loved ones die. Are they still going to pray? Like me, I was a water woman and they killed my grandson, and the way of the pipe is that I still have to pray. The pipe ways, they tell our people, if you're going to use this peace pipe, you'd better use it right. Because if you don't, you're going to hurt yourself or hurt somebody.

But are you going to keep praying if one of your children or other loved ones is killed in front of you? Are you still going to pick up that pipe and pray? Or are you going to turn around and have revenge? Which one are you going to do? If your loved one was laid down in front of you, someone did that to them, what would you do? Keep praying or what?

Once you start praying, you cannot stop! You cannot give up. Like I say, you can't give up if anything like that happens.

Everyone has faults, and everybody makes mistakes. So you can't really condemn anybody. It's not up to me to condemn anyone. That's up to the Creator, not me.

BEATRICE LONG VISITOR HOLY DANCE

May 12, 1927–March 18, 2016

Beatrice Long Visitor Holy Dance walks now in the eternal. She was my friend, and in the Oglala tradition of adopting new relatives, my dear mom. I have seen her sometimes, as in a dream, circling around us, walking in a steady dignified balance of moccasins lightly touching on the earth. She is wrapped in a red and black shawl and a long-fringed dress of incandescent beads, showing a bright holy trail of completeness.

Beatrice lived out many roles, for her people and for all peoples. Born and raised at Pine Ridge Reservation in South Dakota, Beatrice was a midwife, public health nurse, traditional herbalist and healer, ceremonial leader, and grandmother of many great-grandchildren. She was a truck driver for reservation families without transportation, delivering medicines, food, and other items needed by her community. A woman of service to her people, Beatrice was a formidable elder who was also headwoman, the wise matriarch of a large Lakota *tiospaye* (extended family). Largely descendants of significant chiefs and headwomen of recent generations, these clans of extended families encompass a world of many relations.

Beatrice Long Visitor Holy Dance had the character and the perception to gather that great tribal inheritance to her heart. She surrounded herself with her people, their needs amid serious destitution and hardscrabble poverty. She also lived in their hopes and dreams. She did this in her constant commitment to prayer. Beatrice was an accomplished matron in the peyote prayer tradition of the Native American Church, and she was also a devout Catholic. She saw no contradiction in any of these ways of prayer. She was a leader among those who sustained the movement within the Catholic Church to support the use of sacred peyote medicine in the ceremonies of the Native American Church. She was a leader in challenging the Catholic Church to rescind their papal bulls that ushered in the Doctrine of Discovery.

Beatrice's mastery of ceremony and the way of meaningful prayer for the people flowed most naturally and robustly through the sacred Sundance (*Wiwáŋyaŋg Wačípi*). Deeply meaningful for her relatives in several *tiospaye*s, her leadership in the annual Sundance was central to her devotions.

Despite war and massacres, dispossession and resettlement on reservations, when all indigenous spirituality was banned and persecuted, the Sundance ceremony regrew and was revitalized in every Lakota generation to the present. The sacred Sundance of the plains is a ceremony of the Oyate ("the people") led by the people's relationship to the Buffalo People and their gift of the sacred pipe, brought to the Oyate by Buffalo Calf Woman. It is a men's ceremony that emerges with the sacred woman, the beautiful woman, and flows from the authority of grandmothers, their certainty of knowledge.

The Sundance Beatrice sponsored by the American Horse and Afraid of Bear *tiospaye*s, with much participation by the Red Cloud and other Lakota families, has its unique narrative. Grandfathers and grandmothers of the previous generation, embraced by Elder Beatrice and guided by Larue Afraid of Bear and Ernest Afraid of Bear, journeyed over four years throughout the Black Hills, holding ceremonies to bring the Sundance of their *tiospaye*s back to its ancient ground. They deemed it important that Lakota people reestablish themselves and their culture in their ancient sacred ceremonial grounds in the Black Hills.

The family elders deliberated together and agreed that friendships and alliances strengthen the *tiospaye*. It led them to state: "There's four colors of man—red, white, black, and yellow. Anyone who wishes to come pray with us can come pray." Beatrice and her family would note the instruction of honored ancestor Chief American Horse, who stated in 1898, "Anyone may dance the Sun Dance if he will do as the Oglalas do."

Although their decision did not lack controversy, Beatrice and other el-

ders deepened their conviction over the years that while their ceremony must remain rooted in the Oglala families and Native leadership, *kolas,* good friends, of other peoples and races should be invited to participate.

Through her expansive group of Oglala families, *tiospaye*s of the Afraid of Bear, American Horse, and Red Cloud lineages of chiefs, Beatrice for over twenty years called her sons and daughters, nephews, nieces, in-laws, and all her other relatives to pray and dance together in the grand ceremony.

She danced too, under the open sky, joining into her eighties the grueling, prayerful sacrifice. For decades, every summer solstice, she led the women into the circle for the four long and powerful days, the rounds of many hours of dancing-praying under a searing, generous *Tunkashila*, the Grandfather Sun Spirit.

Beatrice prayed for many relatives, always, and she also always shared the intention of a main prayer as she entered the ceremonial days. Her main prayer—among the many individual prayers—produced commonality of purpose in all the dancers, drummers, and other active practitioners. You could feel the complete sincerity of this grandmother, a genuine elder of her people and of all who came to know and appreciate her special capacity as prayer woman. She always prayed for all humanity, as it would take "all of us peoples" to make peace in the world, to not allow starvation in the world. "Pray for no more violence," she would say. "No more hunger in our kids, no more poisoning of the world." In the call of the Four Directions, hers was a prayer for all of humanity.

Hatueyael (Jose Barreiro)

FOUR

GRANDMOTHER JULIETA CASIMIRO

I AM JULIA JULIETA CASIMIRO. I was born in the neighborhood of Agua Abundante in the city of Huautla de Jimenez, Oaxaca, on the second of April, 1936.

Soy de la gente de raíz.	I am of the root people.
Soy de la gente águila.	I am of the eagle people.
Soy de la gente venado.	I am of the deer people.
Soy de la gente de Huautla.	I am from the people of Huautla.
Soy mujer mazateca.	I am a Mazatec woman.

No one is born wealthy and wise, that's how the saying goes, no one. All of my family, my parents, María Petra Estrada and Maclovio Casimiro, were very poor.

My mother had nine children. My sister Hermelinda was my mother's first daughter. The second was my brother Porfirio Genaro. I am the third. Born later were: Federico, Julián Pablo, Teodora, Concepción Guadalupe, Angélica Juliana, and Angelina Cutberta.

Three of my sisters died because we did not have any money and there was no doctor to cure them of their illnesses. One died of whooping cough and another died from the measles. My three little sisters died, but not at the same time. They died at three years, two years, and four years old. How it hurt me, how it hurt us all. We would cry all day and all night because our little sisters had died.

My father worked by hired task. If asked to clear twelve large parcels of land, he would work it with a hoe, clearing it in two to three days, and would earn five *pesitos* (twenty-five cents).

That is probably how they were able to send us to primary school, where we learned how to read and write. Later on I left school to begin working, helping my mother. My sister learned from my mother first. She never went to school, she never wanted to. But when they sent me, I went willingly. I liked school.

When I was a ten-year-old child, my mother didn't let me go to school anymore. Even being that little, ten or eleven years old, I washed other people's clothes with my mother and sister. My sister knew more, washed more, and I did very little because I was so young. But I had to help. And it's not like it was in the house. We had to go downhill to wash at the stream, where there was water. At three o'clock we would finish at the river and return home with my father, my mother, myself, my sister, while the younger siblings took care of the house.

The corn had already been washed to be ground on the *metate* (grinding stone) to make *las gorditas* (tortillas) to eat, and the beans had already been boiled and baked by those who had stayed home.

The time came when we were *señoritas* (young ladies). My sister Hermelinda had to do everything, start the fire, grind the corn, and I would help by blowing on the fire. In the morning she would say, "Wake up, help yourselves." Soon I was able to do everything too, grind the corn and make the tortillas.

My mother would say, "You will be in charge in the morning and

(left photo) Julieta with her husband to be, Lucio Isaías Pineda Carrera, circa 1950s

Left to right, front to back: stand-in father of the groom and Don Maclovio Casimiro (Julieta's father), Doña María Petra Estrada (Julieta's mother), Doña Regina Carrera Calvo (Julieta's mother-in-law), Julieta, and Lucio Isaías Pineda Carrera on their wedding day, December 31, 1954. Huautla de Jiménez, Oaxaca, Mexico

your sister will be in charge in the afternoon. In the afternoon you will grind the corn to make the tortillas." And there is no way that one can say no to a mother who is giving orders! My older sister would wake up as well and begin to embroider in the morning, while she took care of me. We would place a little wick in the *candilito*, what we called our oil lamp, so we could see the stitches we were embroidering. This is how I spent the first years of my life.

Of all my siblings, I married first. I met Lucio Isaías Pineda Carrera when I was fifteen years old at my aunt's house, where they had sent me to work as a maid. There were several other men who asked for my hand. They would arrive at two in the morning. This is what people would do when they wanted a wife. But the men themselves were not the ones who would come to the house. They would send someone else, their mother or father, their elders. They would have to knock at the door. And then they would talk, talk, and talk until dawn. My mother and father would have to sit with the person bringing an offering, in order for them to ask for my hand.

That's what happened with Lucio. He was thirty years old and I was fifteen. We were engaged for three years. We were married on the 31st of December in 1954, and we had ten children together: Jorge Adalberto, Lourdes, Jacinto Librado, Jesuita Natalia, María de los Ángeles, Magdalena, David Lucio, Eugenia, Jazmín, and Omar.

Apprenticeship

After around two months of marriage, Doña Regina Carrera Calvo, my mother-in-law, asked me, "Daughter, would you like to accompany us tonight?"

"Where?" I asked.

"There, in the house. I want to teach you about the *ndi shito*, *los honguitos* (the mushrooms).

I agreed. "Well, of course."

There we were with Lucio and Doña Regina's husband, my father-in-law, Professor Librado Pineda Quiroga. The ceremony began with my mother-in-law praying and entrusting herself to the power almighty. The *copalero* (copal) and *cera* (candles) were already lit. My mother-in law used *cera grande*, large candles. After praying we ingested the mushrooms, or what we call the *niños santos* (the holy children). Then she said, "You will try this, daughter, because we do not have money for doctors. Here, we have better medicine." That's how my mother-in-law said it.

She continued praying. I became kind of afraid, of course, because I had never tried *los niños* before. A little while later, around thirty minutes, my journey began with a feeling of lots of *azulitos* (songbirds) swooping down. She gave me a little bunch, "Eat, daughter," and then said, "Are you lit up, my child?" "Not yet." "Well, here is another."

Copalero. Huautla de Jiménez, Oaxaca, Mexico, 2011

It wasn't until a lot later that the honguitos took hold of me—lit me up. That's how it goes! There we were praying and everything, and what had to happen with me and the *niños santos*, happened. My mother-in-law was praying and singing about what she was seeing. Because as a healer and guide, one has to tell what one sees in the other. That is why I tell everyone who comes here, "Tell me where it hurts, what else is happening, so that I can touch you and clear it out, all right? Tell me, child, what is happening to you?"

I remember my first journey, of course. We sat down and all of a sudden the earth came to me. It was something big and wonderful. I could see the earth in her round form, spinning very slowly. Everything I looked at was very beautiful; I saw big palm trees that swayed to and fro and giant bells,

Ndi shito, los honguitos (the mushrooms). Huautla de Jiménez, Oaxaca, Mexico, 2016

like the ones in the Huautla de Jimenez church tower, in Oaxaca. I saw how they swayed and how the bells sounded. They sounded like *Pom, pom, pom*. I was taking in and receiving all that was happening to me.

"What are you seeing?" my mother-in-law asked.

"I am, like, inside the earth."

"Ah yes, I know what it is, we will cleanse you." I don't know what she was doing. She blew smoke from a cigar into the shape of a little globe and gave the globe to me. "Here, take it." And, well, I had to take it because the *curandera* (healer) told me to, right? And we continued to journey on and on and on. She'd work on another person, and another, and on another. And that is how the night continued, until five in the morning.

My mother-in-law, Regina, was very different from other people. The work itself made it so that people held a certain level of respect for her. She carried herself very differently from the people of Huautla. She was tall in stature, with a strong body, very firm and big. Very different from the Mazatec physique. I imagine that her family was made up of tall people. My husband was tall. On my side of the family we are *chaparritos* (short little people).

They loved me because I married their son, my husband. That's how we started together. My husband was wily, he never told me that he knew these things.

My mother-in-law continued to teach me with kindness. She was a great, wise woman. Indeed, all of her family on her maternal side were great shamans and diviners who were wise. My mother-in-law talked about her mother, Señora Cecilia Calvo; her great-aunts, Gregoria Calvo and Natalia Calvo; and her sisters, Aurelia Carrera and Martina Carrera.

The trust she had in me was very important. It was powerful. That kind of trust gives you confidence on any terrain. A big commitment was established between the two of us on the rights and obligations to educate her bloodline, that is to say, her grandchildren. In this way, continuity of the bloodline and continuity of the spiritual work would be assured. This is the commitment that a woman or a man makes, that they can give to humanity.

We made a pact between us as *maestro* (teacher) and student, which bloomed into a very strong commitment of great reciprocity. We created a relationship of student and teacher, my mother-in-law and I, but we also helped each other, since she would teach me and I would help her while learning for the future, for when she would no longer be present.

My mother-in-law taught me a lot. She taught me how to conduct the ceremony of the honguitos. She taught me how to have courage and to know how to fight when it was necessary. She taught me how to handle the crises of patients in trance, ways to control situations that, if not managed properly, can get out of control. This kind of work has to deal with everything that can come up at any moment, during the time that the session lasts. One works with all the energy, all the strength that each person brings with them, along with the way they manage it, and how to guide and direct it. A sacred space and time are created for the ceremony. Song and prayer help create this space so that the patient can feel well. The guide should offer security, trust, kindness, love, and service so that the moment arrives when the patient's spirit finds itself at its highest point—the moment it meets with God.

A ceremony with a solid ritual facilitates the relationship between God and man. It gives proof of God's existence. A good ritual will help, transform, raise, bring about awareness, and lead us to reflect in a deep way on who we are. It is in this moment that the presence of the guide, who is aware of everything that is happening, is very important, prepared to use every single tool available, to make use of their whole self. She/he

A SACRED SPACE AND TIME ARE
CREATED FOR THE CEREMONY.
SONG AND PRAYER HELP CREATE
THIS SPACE SO THAT THE PATIENT
CAN FEEL WELL. THE GUIDE
SHOULD OFFER SECURITY, TRUST,
KINDNESS, LOVE, AND SERVICE
SO THAT THE MOMENT ARRIVES
WHEN THE PATIENT'S SPIRIT FINDS
ITSELF AT ITS HIGHEST POINT—
THE MOMENT IT MEETS WITH GOD.

is a warrior, an intercessor for the patient. The guide surrenders and commits through their work. This is the moment when the healer manifests her or his power, strength, and desire in service to the patient.

When I work, I find myself always using invocation. I do it through songs and prayers to God, Mother Earth, the rivers, the mountains, and of course, to all the angels and saints. I do it in my mother tongue, Mazatec, and in Spanish as well. I also do it with my thoughts, my feelings. This is how I work to do good. I turn myself into a channel for the patients; I am watching everything that is happening to them in order to help them through my own strength and knowledge.

Work with Foreigners

I started my work in earnest with foreigners—Europeans, Americans, people from the city of Mexico and other states of the Mexican republic. My mother-in-law, Doña Regina, never did what I am doing. She never cared for it. She never liked to work with people outside of the region. At that time people were very protective of their traditions. My mother-in-law was very protective of our traditions. She worked more with the townspeople than with the foreigners.

A large number of foreigners arrived at the end of the seventies. In those days no one wanted to work with them. These young people arrived in quantity—"hippies" with their slogans of love and peace, and without much more. They came as they were, hairy and disheveled. It felt bad to witness how they were treated. I would welcome them into my meager home, and later the townspeople would send the authorities. They would say, "Why do you care about these hooligans, dirty people who smoke marijuana and smell bad?" And I would say, "You know what, you know why I care about these people? Because they are the daily bread for my children. This is why I receive them and give them permission."

This is how I started to work hard in the company of my husband, Lucio, in secret, so to speak, because it was not looked well upon to give foreigners los honguitos, los niños santos.

Julieta rendering beeswax from honeycomb. Huautla de Jiménez, Oaxaca, Mexico, 2011

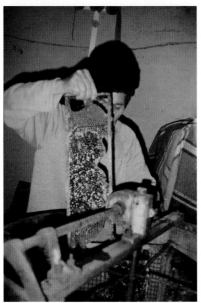

Don Lucio inserting a honeycomb frame into their homemade honey extractor. Huautla de Jiménez, Oaxaca, Mexico, circa 1990s

This is to say that we worked against the wishes of our culture and ran the risk that comes with opening doors to those who do not belong to our culture.

María Sabina was exploited by foreigners. They used her and then left, obtaining the knowledge they wanted without it costing them anything. They went and then left her like that, poor thing. She lived poor her whole life, and died in extreme poverty.

María Sabina was a little younger than my mother-in-law, Regina. Both of them were from the same tradition. María Sabina would come over to leave me medicine, the honguitos. She took up the tradition of the niños santos with her grandparents, which is how it normally happens. I learned from my mother-in-law.

Candles

When it is the feast of each virgin, when her day arrives, much like the day you were born, we celebrate her, and candles are made in quantity. These candles can be made at different times of year if it is urgent for your work. People like to go on pilgrimages here. These candles can be lit in the daytime as well.

My husband, Lucio, preferred to have his own medicine tools because he would charge them with his own energy. *Elementos* are objects that are a necessary complement to your ceremony, they have to be there, right? It's like us with food; if there is no salt you can't eat, or for coffee, if there is no sugar or milk you can't drink it. Just like that, it's a complement. He would make his own candles. Well, light is a complement in order to do this spiritual work. Light is the most important complement for these works.

And for this, we take care of our beekeeping, collecting honey and wax from the bees.

My husband always liked that part of living with nature. He had a very beautiful relationship with nature. With humans it was different, he had to be with them, and by consequence he felt compelled to share because he liked to teach them. But when he returned to his land, he was free because he connected with the birds, with the bees, with the plants. Because when he would be on the land, like me, he would talk to nature, talk to the earth, with a flower, with a bird . . . strong connection of communication; a very magical connection.

[Omar, Julieta's son:]

Although the soul of a person may not be present, the spirit always is. I ask for them and give thanks, because even though they aren't with me in the flesh, they are with me in spirit. So these lights that are created, or these candles through a wick or a thread, are made to light the path for the deceased when they come to visit us in the month of November. And they also light our own path during the rest of the year, in ceremonial works, relationships, jobs, trips to other places, to cure people. So every person who wants one of these special candles has a lot of faith, and may that light illuminate their way. May their faith grow, and may they believe in people and in themselves.

Omar, Julieta's son, pouring melted wax on the wick. Huautla de Jiménez, Oaxaca, Mexico, 2011

Don Lucio making beeswax candles for ceremonies, circa 1980s

Julieta cleansing her daughter Eugenia with *ramos de limpia* before a
Niños Santos ceremony

Julieta blessing her daughter Eugenia with ceremonial beeswax candles

My father taught me this, a long time ago. He taught me the art of candle making. And after his physical death I was graced with the task to work with the wax and candle making. It is an artisanal craft because there are no molds. They are not from a factory.

Originally the candles are from here, in Huautla de Jiménez. There are approximately 55,000 inhabitants. The majority of the population is concentrated in Huautla de Jiménez because it is an important trade center. Here they call it *En'yoma* in Mazatec, which means the place of the twelve eagle warriors or the twelve eagles. In the world of spirits, when a Mazatec man dares to enter in contact with divinity, his flesh is no longer the same, and neither are his thoughts. The evolution of this state is the spirit that trans-

A patient in prayer before the *Niños Santos* ceremony begins

forms into an eagle. Huautla is said to have been founded by twelve warriors who came from a very different place where they taught the art of mysticism in working with the people.

Los Niños Santos

The point of our ritual, as we have learned it, is to make contact, to make prayers so that through our words, our feelings connect with our higher self or God. For many people the word "God" feels very heavy, because they immediately relate it to religion. But when we are talking about our sacred, holy plants, we are talking about the same energy, are we not?

Julieta praying over the *Niños Santos* and cacao for a patient

The point of our ritual, as we have learned it, is to make contact, to make prayers so that through our words, our feelings connect with our higher self or God. For many people the word "God" feels very heavy, because they immediately relate it to religion. But when we are talking about our sacred, holy plants, we are talking about the same energy, are we not?

It is a kind of energy that if you have faith, it can reach a point where a miracle happens. Or one is given the gift of new knowledge. So we have the elements that are commonly used, such as candles, cacao, incense, or copal. But every one of them has its own special meaning. There are many people who might use them in a more simple way. But for us, no, because everything we engage with has a meaning.

We use cacao as another element. The *cacaocito* is like the passport to the spiritual world. It is used to open a portal, a way to enter into the spiritual work with permission.

Copalito (copal) is used for the physical part. It's like when you clean a house, right? When you clean a house you say, "Well, I will use some kind of chemical like bleach, because it will disinfect and take the dirt off of everything." And at the end you will use something extra, some kind of scented freshener so everything will be left very physically cleaned. This is a simple example. But in our case, this is precisely what our copalito takes care of.

In terms of its use in spiritual cleansing, that's where the magic exists, and it's a bit secret. Not everyone should know about it, because there are two ways of using it—for good or bad. So for us, in terms of our ritual of light, we offer the copalito. It's an offering that says, *I give you this perfume. I give you this offering that comes from the earth so that you can guide me, so that I can face difficult things on the path.* You pass them and keep going. So it is like a guide to where I want to go, where I am being taken or toward what I will be given.

Another element that we use are *ramos de limpia* (bundle of plants for cleansing). Each element has a job, its own function. The *hojitas* (leaves) are to get rid of things, to cleanse things here in the physical world so that when you are in the ritual you can transcend that part, so that it's permissible. This is what the hojitas and the cleansing bundles are for. Many of the plants that we use for cleansing are the ones that grow here around Huautla: *ruda* (rue), *salvia* (sage), *hojas de sauco* (elderberry leaves), and others that we know by their Mazatec name such as *Xka' ntjao'o*.

Honey

We are about to start harvesting our honey. This work happens twice a year. It is not a daily task. When it's very cold we save the honey that they are working on for the bees to eat. Even now, when we are extracting the honey we have to leave some for them and other animals to eat. You have to be careful.

You can leave them alone for a while and they will work well unsupervised. However, every fifteen days it is important to go to take a look at them to see if another queen has been born or not. If so, we let the other bees take her away. You have to kill the old queen and find the new one.

The honey has to be taken away so the bees can continue working.

We go to sing and say prayers for the *abejitas* (little bees). We don't only pay attention to them because of what we can harvest, the pure honey and beeswax that we use. It's no small thing what they do. They are deserving of respect. They are nature beings.

And what do these animals do? They dance, jump, sing because they are going to collect pollen to make their honey and beeswax.

The Casita Where I Was Born

We lived in extreme poverty in my mother's house. I was born there. My father's mother, my grandmother María Toribia Martínez, was the midwife. All nine of us were born and raised there. I am the only one who remains. My sisters and brothers have all died. We still preserve that small piece of land and *casita* (little house). All that is left there are some pots and religious figures belonging to my mother.

The house had adobe walls and a dirt floor. We would sleep on the floor. My mother and father did not earn any money at all. We did not have mattresses or beds, which my children now all have. My siblings and I would be put to bed with a blanket on the floor. It makes me laugh nowadays, how we get past those moments in life. That's why now that I am old, nothing is a problem for me. God lifts us up, bit by bit.

Everything we needed was in our patio. We had *guayaba* (guava); coffee; *chayote* (mirliton squash); leaves for tamales; nightshade plant; San Pedro, our sacred plant; tobacco; dragon blood, to get rid of parasites; Mexican pepperleaf to eat when there weren't beans; grapefruit; custard apple; and *yerba de borrego* to use when children were dying from vomiting and diarrhea. We make a kerchief with the yerba de borrego's young leaves and we place them on the child's head.

Julieta at the *casita* where she was born and raised

Gratitude to God always has to be given when we eat the fruits of our Mother Earth.

My mother ended up being alone for a long time. I was seventeen when I married and left my home. My father; my brothers Pablo, Federico, Genaro; and Hermelinda and Teodora still remained, but one by one they began to die. My father died when I had my first child. Because he was always working in the countryside I am not sure what happened to him. I married and I live here now, in my poor home, my place, where my mother-in-law first received me with nothing more than my white dress and flower crown.

We were all very poor. When we didn't even have beans to eat my mother would say, "You can eat this, it won't hurt you, it's natural." She would make us *yerba santa* (Mexican pepperleaf) with tortilla. Do you want to know how much my husband would earn in those days? Just one meager peso for clearing a large piece of land, that's all he would earn. It was hard.

[Eugenia, Julieta's daughter:]

There are people, or beings on this plane of existence that God, our creator, sends to earth with special magic. I believe that my mother is one of those beings, because she would learn and take in from everything that surrounded her. And what she saw around her was never suffering, she did not see suffering despite the shortcomings. It was as if she would transform that reality. She saw how hard her father worked, how much he pushed himself and could not be with his family, that her grandmother most likely had many, many financial shortcomings, difficulties of all kinds. But she was never a weak woman. She was always a fighter, figuring out a way to help her children get ahead, to do everything that was in her power in order to get ahead. In those times, many people worked the land as a sheer obligation in order to survive.

So she saw all this and this is why, I imagine, she is a special being . . . a chosen one, to be given all this magic and the ability to learn to plant, to learn to embroider, to learn to sing, to learn to pray. It's like she came with her pure essence from birth in that poor little house. So many things did not present themselves as difficult for her. It was simply what she was living in that moment, right? That is why she holds everything she does with so much purity and so much love. You see it in how she prays. Everything she does, she does with lots of love.

It isn't a commitment or obligation that she takes on. It is natural for her to do so and it flows from her being.

Magic lives in that casita too. Because that is where she was born, the place where she was conceived with a lot of love. I imagine that she was conceived with so much love to have reached this point of her life with her essence intact, a pure essence that she lives daily. My mother has a big heart and humility to match, with and for everyone. She never gives up on others.

Café and Panela

We make our café at home. I harvest my little trees, gather the beans. It takes work to dry it all on a *petate* (straw mat) in the sun. Once they

Julieta roasting coffee beans on the *comal*

Eugenia getting ready to open the *panela*

dry, we collect and store them. We move the coffee when it's still a fruit; this way I can dry it with all of its natural sugars, so that the coffee tastes good. Once it's dried, we remove the coffee's pulp in order to remove the skin. . . . Now it is the pure coffee bean and it is ready to be roasted on the *comal* (a flat griddle usually made of clay).

This is how we live here. We do not grind our coffee in a machine. We grind it in a hand grinder so the coffee tastes more delicious. A machine grinder would take away from its taste.

Coffee is harvested once a year in March, following its natural cycle. Mother Earth is the one to grow it for us. The work is of my hands, since I am the one who strips my trees.

This is the work of a woman, a peasant woman.

We sweeten our café with *panela* (raw, unrefined cane sugar loaf), which we call here *piloncillo*. It's the pure sugar cane. The sugar is boiled down in the fire until it turns the color of coffee. That's when I remove it and it hardens in the shape of the mold.

[Eugenia, Julieta's daughter:]

We vent the coffee in order to oxygenate it, so that it doesn't harm us when we drink it later. Those were traditions of our grandparents. Nowadays, people don't normally use these methods. Actually, people don't really remember anymore. It's by imitating what one sees that many things are done. We do it because our grandparents taught us how to do certain things in our culture, and we carry out what both our *abuelas* (grandmothers), Regina Carrera Calvo and María Petra Estrada, told us to do. That's how they made their coffee.

Ancestral Knowledge

Traditional medicine—our ancestral natural medicine—has suffered a bit from the problem of commercialization, because of the narrow way people approach the medicine.

In times past, people used to live far from the cities and the roads, and open spaces were unpaved and all that. We didn't have doctors. Our only option was to use the plants to give us results for our healing, sometimes physical and usually spiritual. As humans we are used to locating ourselves physically; we are very earthly, very terrestrial. We are used to relying on our sight, on the material, the physical. So we need to heal the soul first, in order to obtain physical healing.

My mother-in-law brought with her a lineage. Ever since I knew her, even as a youngster, la Señora Regina always brought that knowledge forward. It's an ancestral knowledge that comes from my husband's ancestral line.

[Don Tiburcio, Grandmother Julieta's friend and a Mazatec healer:]

Some people can see (read) melting candle wax, copal, and corn. I learned about this working together with my grandfather.

Julieta grinding coffee beans on a stone *metate*

My grandmother also did healing work. That's how our whole family learned how to heal. We learned to heal people when they are sick, when they don't feel well, when something has happened. We talk to *el Señor* (the Lord) above for a cure.

I learned to see with the niños santos as well, if it were some kind of magic. That's how I learned. Every time I eat the niños santos, after a few hours I reach a point when I connect with el Señor. When I ask him what is he going to do, how he's going to do the cleansing, he says, *Look, talk to me. I am with you.* And he carries on, saying, *Do this, do that.*

The *dueño del cerro* (tutelary spirit of the hill) also speaks here, as if he was present. That's how each of the dueños speaks: the dueño of the hill, of the town, of the earth, of the water, of every river, of the wind, and of every single place. There are people who meet the dueño of the hill. We call the dueño of the hill *Duende*[1] *Aquiles.* That's what we call that beautiful young man. That duende talks to God, and that's why people are cured. We ask them, "What happened to that person?" because we know that the duendes are in contact with God.

All of the elements can speak. When we light a candle, that's when we can see and talk about what we feel and what is going on. It is a gift from God. The copalito also speaks when we are lit. Its smoke travels up and reaches our Lord and cleanses the disease. It's by listening to everything that speaks that one heals.

1 Elflike nature beings recognized by different cultures around the world.

Guadalupe

My *Devocionario Mazateco* (Mazatec devotional prayer book) and the rosary give me strength. We have learned through prayer and connection with the feminine, with Guadalupe. We are all generally *Guadalupanos* (those who revere the Virgin of Guadalupe). Perhaps many people don't think she's that important, but we do. And this is because through femininity, which is connected to Guadalupe *Tonantzin,*[2] we have the strength to accomplish many things. So we connect with the elements, with energies that exist and that are feminine, without competing with the masculine, like Mother Earth and Mother Water. There are many elements, many things that relate with femininity. So Guadalupe gives us that strength.

In the end, we Mexicans, as Guadalupanos, claim her as our spiritual leader. We gain strength because we believe. We believe in her. We believe in this figure, and that is what gives us the guidelines to continue working as we gain many, many privileges along the way.

The Holy Rosary

The rosary that is given to you as a Catholic comes with a small guide. However, I transform the way I do the rosary, in that I also include my Mazatec prayers. Every mystery. Every line. I have my own way of praying. It's very personal. Very particular.

2. The natives recognized Our Lady of Guadalupe as Tonantzin, the Aztec mother goddess.

In times past, people used to live far from the cities and the roads, and open spaces were unpaved and all that. We didn't have doctors. Our only option was to use the plants to give us results for our healing, sometimes physical and usually spiritual. As humans we are used to locating ourselves physically; we are very earthly, very terrestrial. We are used to relying on our sight, on the material, the physical. So we need to heal the soul first, in order to obtain physical healing.

Don Tiburcio reading the corn for a patient

In the past, in Huautla's congregation there were priests who spoke in Mazatec and they would even give the mass in Mazatec. Nowadays they don't. Now the the mass is in Spanish. The priests used to interlace songs in both languages. Now, in some masses there are choirs that will include the Mazatec dialect in the songs. Mazatec is a very interesting language because it has its own unique play on words. We adapt it in our own way to sing Mazatec songs during the mass.

The mysteries of the rosary that we pray for are chosen in the moment and correspond to what I feel in my heart, depending on the connection. Every day corresponds to two mysteries. That's how the rosary that I pray with works. For example, Monday and Thursday are the joyful mysteries. Wednesday, Saturday, and Sunday are the glorious mysteries, and Tuesday and Friday are the sorrowful mysteries. That's how the days are chosen.

The mysteries give thanks for a new day, for what we have, right? They connect us with the energy to give thanks to the earth or to ask for something that one needs in this moment. The rosary is Mary. My devotional prayer book is the rosary dedicated to the Virgin Mary, Saint Mary of Guadalupe.

El Don

Every person has a *don* (gift). The don of the word, the don of feeling. Every time a patient comes to see me, I talk to them. I prepare them before I do my work through ceremony. So that once the patient is ready to transition, in that state, together with my connection with the energies that I work with, we are able to experience a gentle *velada* (evening ceremony).

There are certain aspects and elements that are indispensable to the ceremony, and in order to conserve its essence, they are best not spoken of. It's not that we are being possessive, it's just that they require a lot of respect. When you speak beyond what you are allowed, you can corrupt the magic and the sanctity of the elements and ceremony.

[Eugenia, Julieta's daughter:]

> My mother does not have a closed heart for anyone. The truth is, she is very humble. Perhaps the use of humble words is very strong. She accepts everyone, equally. At times, even as a son or a daughter we get upset because the people who come to the house are dangerous. But my mother will not close the door of her heart to anyone. And her huge heart is very valuable to her work. She will never, never say no to people. She is always open to offer her work to others. To her, we are all children of God.

Embroidery and Designs

When you're poor, you learn at home. When you don't have a place to go when you are young, that's what you have to do. I learned how to embroider with my sister because my mother spent her days outside the house washing other people's clothes. My older sister, Hermelinda Casimiro, taught me how. Later, some men came here to work with the holy children and they began to make drawings of the niños santos to have them embroidered. At that time, no one sold anything like that. I began to make all kinds of clothing, including vests, skirts, bags, shirts, *huipiles* (traditional female garment). People began to come to me wanting to work and help me draw the designs. Huipiles, shirts, and skirts were the first of my creations and boy, how they sold.

And later, well, they started to take my clothes out there, all over. It wasn't so expensive back then. My husband would help me to wash the raw cotton cloth and would help me cut it. He would go to get up to twenty-five to fifty pieces of cloth, each around twenty-five meters long.

Nowadays there is a lot of competition. But we also have our other work that God helps us with as well.

That's how it was, we were poor, but I helped raise us up. Really, I would pray to my personal saint to find the women who would come help me to embroider. And they would show up. They would take the finished pieces to sell for one peso each. It's not like today, where these clothes are sold for at least 100 to 200 pesos, no sir. We were very poor, but thanks to God, he raised me up, and now we have this cherished, humble home.

Our embroidery work began as a way to save a little bit of money. People saw I had able and fine hands to make this type of embroidery. Then people brought clothes in bales to me to embroider in big quantities, not just individual pieces. In those times they would bring clothes like T-shirts and denim. I was one of the few women who could embroider very well. There were others who embroidered, but their work didn't hold up as well. Actually, in this case I was the one who truly brought foreign trade to the town. We call them foreigners

Eugenia and Julieta embroidering at home. Huautla de Jiménez,
Oaxaca, Mexico, 2011

Julieta's daughter Lourdes (Lulú) working on an embroidery at her store in Huautla de Jiménez,
Oaxaca, Mexico, 2011

because they come from outside our town, including even the Distrito Federal
(Mexico City)—our capital. For people in Huautla it was strange to see other
people and understand why they had come. No one would welcome them because they would label them negatively.

So I took the opportunity of the moment and said to myself, *I'm good at this
too. I can do this too.*

And this is how I began to earn a little more capital. At the time there were
still many money shortages, so I saw this as an additional way to subsist. I also

took it as another job to do, apart from the fact that I made very fine-looking embroidery designs and until this day, still do.

[Eugenia, Julieta's daughter:]

I learned how to embroider with my older sister's guidance, Magdalena. I liked to do it. As a child, I remember watching how skilled Magdalena was at embroidering, and at that time we were visited by many foreigners. We lived in a different time period than my mother. Many people would visit us here in our meager home and, well, I could see how one could make some money that way. So that's how I started to see and learn, thanks to the curious nature of a child.

My mother transformed the world of embroidery here in Huautla. She had various designs of mushrooms and flowers in colors that would prompt people to say, "Oh, they look like they are influenced by the psychedelic time period." But if you think about it, it wasn't a fad to her, it was intimately related to her spiritual work in ceremony. Nowadays this type of design is common. However, in those days it was seen as a sin to even talk about the hongui-tos. Our townspeople were very afraid of the plant, especially because foreigners came to investigate and study the mushrooms—why they were hallucinogenic and what they were being used for.

So my mother, inspired by and out of respect for the honguitos, would translate for them and say to people, "Our plant is sacred, not evil." She fought for the *holy children*—worn on clothing like a badge of honor for her. And she wasn't afraid.

She created many designs. An infinity of ideas. She was the one who founded Huautla's commercial trade in embroidered textiles, which helped the town and other people, using our way of life.

The famous cloth, we call a cotton cloth. It is made of pure cotton. People come from other towns and supply us the raw cloth, which isn't originally white but is later treated to make clothes.

In those days, many people would come here, especially young men and women. After finishing their ceremony they would say, "Mamá Julieta, this is what happened on our journey." They would draw what they saw and what affected them most during the work. So they would leave their designs with her. They were very personal, very intimate sharings. My mother would look at them, ponder, and make her own internal connections and later translate the drawings into images on clothing.

Processions

Here in our town, the townspeople select a person who can care, for years at time, for the feast of the Virgin of Guadalupe. In these days a person can ask for the responsibility. However, traditionally, the town would choose an adult. They had to approach the town, present themselves, and say, "I come from the fraternity of the Virgin of Guadalupe because you have chosen me." They begin their job on the day that the Holy Virgin is celebrated. Later they do a *novenario* (a dedicated, nine-day prayer) for the Virgin of Guadalupe.

The Virgin is celebrated on the 12th of December. A *víspera* (eve) takes place on the 11th. A *víspera* is a celebration that includes the "Mañanitas" with other songs, and a whole town procession. So when one awakens on the 12th, the *novena* is complete. The first procession begins nine days before. The image of the Virgin visits each house. It will stay at a different house each night, and every day it travels to the next house that has been given the opportunity to receive the image of Guadalupe.

The people who organize the procession are the ones who sing, speak praises, and make petitions along the whole way, until they reach the next house. As they approach the house they do a prayer. It may be the rosary or what the family has chosen. The prayer is finished and an invitation is made by the household. They invite them to have coffee, bread, or some other kind of food. Then the day of prayer is formally closed. The townspeople and those in charge of the image leave and the owners of the house do their own personal prayers, connecting intimately with the Virgin, depending on their needs.

Every organizer is given a certain period of time to take care of this feast. There is a council here in town in charge of deciding who will take care of these saints and for how long. For example, right now, I have been given the responsibility of the *Señor de las Tres Caídas* (Lord of the Three Falls), which is celebrated here in Huautla. I am in my second round, and next year I will close with my third year.

I was in charge of the procession of the Virgin of Guadalupe for eight years. The town's council saw how much devotion and responsibility I had for the Virgin's visit, so they gave me an extra year. Usually it's seven years. They gave me an extra year because they saw my dedication and that I would take care of every aspect of the Virgin's celebration. They liked that.

Sadly, it was during this time that my husband began to get sick, and I had to give up my position.

The parochial council of Huautla, which is a group of people who works with the church to organize the festivities for the saints, chose me for the biggest festivity. In the case of Jesus, it's about his sacrifice. That's why he is called the Lord of the Three Falls.

Julieta leading the *Señor de las Tres Caídas* procession in 2016

It's when Jesus was imprisoned and lived his process of detention, the way of the cross of our Lord. So one could say that I organize the biggest feast, because it's the most powerful celebration. I was given three years to take care of this image and to carry out its novenario in the springtime. This feast occurs on different dates during Easter week. It is the way of the cross.

Traveling Abroad

My first trip abroad was with my husband, Lucio. We went to Switzerland, to the Institute of Anthropology. From there we traveled to Rome. We went to the Vatican. We were there, in both Italy and Switzerland, for a month, and we traveled everywhere. We even ended up going to France, imagine that. Later we traveled to the United States and we both also returned to Europe.

A German woman who knew me for many years asked me to come and work in the United States with the niños santos. And so I went. And I got to know them. I went back many times, and on one of those occasions I met a doctor and she told my German friend, "We need another grandmother for a council of thirteen grandmothers because it is time to begin this work."

And she told her to call me immediately, because at that point I had just arrived back home from the United States. So my hostess in the United States called me, and I said to her, "Why are you calling me so soon? I just got back. You are frightening me."

She said, "You need to come again immediately because there's work for you."

I said, "What work?"

And she said, "There are going to be thirteen grandmothers."

I said, "I have to ask my children to see if they will let me go or not."

She said, "Don't ask, you just come to do your work."

I accepted the work. And it was difficult, believe me.

Lucio, my husband, died the 31st of March, 2003. That's how I was able to move on faster. We went all over the world, right? Oh, I

Julieta and Lucio on their first trip to Switzerland

felt a deep pain that I would forget my husband. I was still in mourning when I received the invitation to join the council.

Visions, Dreams, and Prophecies

Everything we do through our hard work and the way that we get along with other people nurtures our understanding and knowledge of what is possible in life. When we give rest to our thoughts, the universe opens up, and all of the energy that we have used during the day will present itself in our dreams.

Many people misguidedly seek to see and understand the relationship that exists between man and Mother Earth as two separate entities. These same people have hurt Mother Earth, and now we live in a time of very powerful changes. We need to keep moving forward and teach people the correct path to live in peace and harmony as one.

There is a lot of news about the changes occurring in these times, as much in the mountains as in the pyramids, in all parts of the world. Brothers and sisters, know that this change will occur on the level of human consciousness, spirit, energy, and in all the ways that we choose to work with positive actions while eliminating the negative.

The moment of change is already upon us. We need to help more people in their evolution so that it is easier for them to change and to listen to counsel. May they know that we, the Thirteen Grandmothers, are carrying and spreading the message for a new beginning.

For our brothers and sisters who do not want to change, it will be very difficult for them to accept what is happening in front of their eyes. No one can predict the destiny of millions of people in the world; only the Great Spirit can speak to awaken the ancient consciousness within, which has been long slumbering in the bodies of the people who do not want to wake up to our spiritual reality.

Many of our brothers and sisters take advantage of people who are looking for a message of relief, an answer, a helping hand to lift them from their suffering, due to the love they lack for always being out of the house, and when at home, fighting with their brother, sister, mother, father, and everything in their life.

We can change our tomorrow, which is already sounding loud in the now. We can do it by knocking on the door of each heart, each mind, of each person. Our younger sisters and brothers need to gather close so that they can hear and understand what we are trying to say, including the children as well, so that they can be the leaders of tomorrow.

Let it be known that there is light, and that hope and faith do exist. And above all, know that there is still time to amend what we ourselves, brothers and sisters, have destroyed with violence, death, and wars.

If we want our future generations to live in harmony, we have to teach them respect, courage, and all things that Mother Earth provides.

Remember, the most difficult struggle we all face in the world is with fear—the fear that is inside our hearts, deep inside our mind, in the deepest parts of ourselves.

We must do what is right today. In this moment. Not tomorrow, or next year. No, the time is now.

JULIA JULIETA ESTRADA CASIMIRO

April 2, 1936–July 23, 2018

To speak of Grandmother Julieta's legacy, one needs to mention the various ways she was able to influence the people who knew her and the people she met through her work. To this end, we can say that her inheritance is incorporeal for both her blood and nonblood relatives. To continue, advance, Grandmother Julieta's legacy is a big job to take on. Anyone who claims to be her disciple needs to know that such a claim must be based on a powerful truth because it involves loyalty, charity, empathy, completely giving of oneself, so as not to leave anything behind for themselves.

To give and teach wholeheartedly is to see with your eyes what your fellow man/woman sees through their own. Her blood children who have chosen this path know that the path has rules and that they need to be followed. There is no other option except to do good, always seeking to find the balance in all that happens around us. Balance is what gives meaning to life.

And to say it is a legacy is to act, it is to carry out a healing therapy for the spirit with the purpose to see many happy and satisfied faces afterward. So that those who have participated in these spirited encounters are able to see with different eyes, see another reality.

And there are those who are her spiritual children (nonblood relatives) who will also continue her legacy, with other tools, other forms of healing, other sacred plants. All with the objective to help heal others.

My mom, Grandmother Julieta Estrada Casimiro, was born on April 2, 1936, in a place named in Spanish Agua Abundante, Abundant Water. In Mazatec it's called Nda kjin. She married Don Lucio Isaías Pineda Carrera. All this is important to the cosmovision of the Mesoamerican peoples. All these symbols make up the essence of men/women, which give meaning to their existence. Just like Mamá Julieta was born in a place where there was an abundance of water, this characteristic of the place served her well as she took on the charge given to her and she washed and cleansed. Clothes, but she also helped others to wash themselves, those who needed water to cleanse themselves, refresh themselves.

She used to say, "To find peace, one needs to work and offer it up to the heavens." She helped others learn how to cleanse themselves with water, with clean water. Water that cleanses the spirit, the soul, thoughts, and flesh.

This is a place called Huatla in the Náuatl language and Naxinanda Tejao in Mazatec. A place in the mountains where eagles fly. A place where people still give offerings to Mother Earth, precious offerings of objects, seeds, rare bird feathers, in order to find healing, to find balance.

It is the place of the Mazatec language that inspires travelers. A place with landscapes that delight those who look upon them. A place with traditional dances, like Naxo Loja, "the orange flower"; Naxinanda Tejao, located 1,150 feet above sea level; rich, oh so rich and exuberant, the upper as well as the lower Mazatec region. God gave this place with all its heart, a marvelous habitat for the sacred mushrooms, *los niños santos*, the holy children.

Who would not want to know, experience, all this bounty? What better legacy could God and his maestros, guides, disciples offer us?

Julieta's husband, Lucio Isaías Pineda Carrera, was born in a place called Sobre la Piedra, On Top of the Rock. I highlight that name because from what I understand, it ended up being vital to her story to have a firm footing, to step firmly, safely, with the support of her noble husband. A man, a faithful husband, a loving father, a hard worker, a believer in something higher, what he would call the *ser supremo*, the supreme being.

Lulu, the eldest daughter, also cleans, *limpia*; she continues to clean and arrange the flowers and altar where Grandmother Julieta would conduct her ceremonies. Lulu works there now, much like Grandmother Julieta did. She has also, little by little, taken on the commitments my mother previously held with the community, like how to attend to, give condolences to those who have lost a loved one. Her presence at weddings is important.

Malenita, another of Mother/Grandmother Julieta's daughters, has journeyed deep and works the sacred plant (*los hongitos*, mushrooms; *niños santos*, the holy children) as well. Her knowledge comes through the

Pineda family lineage, along with that of her husband's family. She has added elements from both families in her work, and she has also worked in communion with her children, husband, and husband's grandmothers. It's extraordinary that she speaks Mazatec better than the rest of us, with a fluent vocabulary that allows her to communicate with the people from the neighboring indigenous settlements. She works in her home, Xochitonalco, which belongs to Huautla de Jiménez Municipality. She's a very active woman; she likes to help people who are impeded from accessing the justice system because they do not speak fluent Spanish.

One can see the commitment and responsibility that is needed to continue with the work of precious ceremonies. The rules that can't be broken. What one should say, or not say. And what one says is chosen carefully, and what has value is said with great care.

David, one of Grandmother Julieta's sons, is another great supporter. He also is committed to the philosophy of helping others, within his abilities and limitations. He plays an instrument called *zampañas* (pan flute) beautifully, with which he accompanies his sisters when they are singing. The sound is lovely, it is very pleasant to listen to. Music is an instrument, a tool to achieve a calm state. It can also elevate the spirit. In the past, David has also spent time making candlesticks with pure beeswax from our family's farm.

Eugenia is known to many, for she was the one who traveled with Grandmother Julieta and lived and experienced much with her. She knows how to do many things, and most importantly how her mother, Julieta, did them.

Omar also works with the *niños santos*, the holy children, with *limpias*, cleansings; conducts ceremonies, prays. Omar travels from the mountains to the city to do the work he knows so well. It is an important source of employment, one that provides for the needs of his family.

For all who make the commitment to follow this spiritual path, the work is constant. It calls you, the work will call you; one cannot be without working.

I am Jesuita Natalia Pineda Casimiro,
daughter of Mamá Julieta, Grandmother Julieta.

FIVE

GRANDMOTHER RITA PITKA BLUMENSTEIN

MY BIRTH NAME, THE NAME I WAS GIVEN when I was born, is *Pamyuran.* It means the tail end of the old ways. Pamyuran is my Yup'ik name, my great-grandma's name—my mother's grandmother. I have her spirit.

My mother gave me three names. The first one was Pamyuran; *Can'irraq* means to clear the way, and *Tanqiar* is little light.

I got my English name when I was three days old. Rita. Our priest was Belgian, and he named me after Saint Rita, because Saint Rita is the sister of the poor people. My full English name is Rita Martha Pitka Blumenstein. *Pitka* means long. My grandpa, my mother's dad, was Pitka. He was Interior Athabaskan from the Yukon. He came from Eagle, a city in Alaska, and moved down to Stevens Village, which is in the Yukon. He traded tanned caribou hides on the coast of Hooper Bay. He was a trader of sealskins and leathers.

I don't have my father's name because he died a month before I was born, so I go with my mom's maiden name. My father's first name was Josef. He was Aleut and Russian. I never saw my dad. But I heard stories and a little bit of how he was. He was a really good man and very generous. My father was a fisherman, and he saved all of his bonds. That's how I went to school, with his bonds.

My grandfather, my father's father, and his sister stowed away from Leningrad in a fishing boat to Massachusetts. The guy who found them kept feeding them with extra food and they got to Massachusetts. He took them to New York and kept them in his house for a while. Then my great-aunt became a nanny for rich people in New York. My grandpa joined the army and went to the Aleutian Islands, where he married my grandmother.

Agrafina was my paternal grandma. She was from the Aleutian Islands. They made baskets that are really fine down there. My grandma was a famous basket maker. In 1948 my mom sent me there for two years and I learned how to make baskets from her. I was around fifteen years old then.

I was born in a fishing boat. My cousins Nick, George, Dan, and Ben Charles were taking my mom, Nina Pitka, to her parents' village of Tununeq (Tununak) in Qaluyaat (Nelson Island). My mom was going to have me with her parents there, but I was born five days before we got there. So I was born on the Bering Sea outside of Bristol Bay, near Kuskokwin Bay.

I was most well-to-do. I was doing better than the ones who had both fathers and mothers. I had everything. We never went hungry and we never got cold.

My mom had seven kids. We all have one mother. One mother and different fathers. My mother was married three times, and all her husbands died. One drowned, my father died of diphtheria, and the last one died of tuberculosis. I have two sisters and one brother older than me. Myrtle, Francis, and Peter are half Danish. I also have two sisters and one brother younger than me, Alfonse, Sophie, and Mary, who have another father. I'm in the middle, so I'm the fourth.

My mom's spirit emblem was a bird. The first three children born were her first wing, the younger three children were her second wing, and I'm in the middle, I'm in the body.

My mother died in 1976. She tripped and broke her hip, and died on the operating table. That's why I'm scared of operations. I was in Corona, Italy, when it happened.

My father wanted me to have education of some kind, to know how to read and how to understand another language. He said to my mom when she was pregnant, "I'm saving it (his bonds) for that one, boy or girl." My siblings also went to school; some of them graduated. I never graduated from anything.

I grew up on Nelson Island until I was three. Then I went to the Montessori school with the missionaries in Seattle. Back in those days kids went to school at three years old. My mother took me to Bethel and put me on a big plane. She put me on the passenger side with three pillows. The pilot strapped me in and said, "Do you want to be my co-pilot?" My mom said good-bye to me and she said, "You're going to go far, far away and I'm going to be far, far away. When I think of you, you'll be thinking of me, and we'll be close." That's why I never get lonely.

I would come home in April and return to school in October. Every year when I came home my mom told me to follow the white people's

Front to back: Rita's great-grandmother, Pamyuran; grandmother, Rosalie Inuq; and cousin, George Sipary. Village of Tununak, Nelson Island, Alaska

protocols, what they did, what they ate. Not to criticize them. I was in Seattle, in the Montessori school, for seven years.

My grandma and my great-grandma, before I was born, they told my mom, "You're going to have a special lady." That's me.

I had many visions and things from three years old to nine years old. First I saw the lights, three lights. I'd see the lights, and they talked to me in my mind. The first thing the lights said was *Don't be afraid*; they said, *Don't be afraid*. My head tingled when I first saw them. My whole body tingled. I'd see the visions, and people said that I was going to be a special seer. I was going to be traveling the universe with my visions.

I never talked about this back then. When I went home from the Montessori school in April that first year I saw the lights. That spring, in May I saw a vision of a caribou or a reindeer with a big tail and I told my mom he was dancing. I didn't know what it was. Then when I was five the lights told me what was going to happen to our land, what the new government was going to do. Telling me in my head. Then I told my people.

They'd say, "What are you, a devil?" They called me names. My mom told me, "It's not going to be easy; they'll probably try to kill you. But it's your gift. So it's okay."

My mom told me, "Don't answer them, don't fight back." She said not to fight back because if you fight back, your gifts will stop, but if you keep listening, they will grow and in some cases you'll understand, and then you can use it for talking like I do now, for energy. The gifts never stopped.

Left to right: Lucy Post, Clara Aluska, and Rita's mother, Nina Menegak. Village of Tununak, Nelson Island, Alaska

Aerial view of part of the Bering Tundra, Alaska, 2014

I come from several generations of healers. One of my grandmothers was a healer who knew how to take care of the kidneys, the back, and the pelvis. So when I do healing, when it is something that I don't know about, one of my ancestors from the spirit world comes and helps me.

I work with mind, body, and soul. The spirit and the soul are different. The soul, the way I understand it, is God. It has no body, it's free. It's everywhere. Spirits are the guides that come to you, that's spirit. Our people are named after these spirits. Our ancestors who were good hunters, good people, these are the spirits that help our people.

I'm helped by my spirit guides, my mom and my grandmother, my uncle and my aunt.

Education and Assimilation

I never had friends my age. I had friends who were older people. When I went to the Montessori school at three years old the teacher came and talked to my mother about how I needed to learn how to be with the children. She said that I needed to learn how to get along with other people and how they live. My teacher told me I was going to learn to speak English and eat different kinds of foods.

Mr. and Mrs. Moreland, the principals at the school, took me to their big house, a mansion. When Mrs. Moreland opened the door there was a mask, an Eskimo mask. And I said, "I'm not going in there. I'm not going to go in." And she said, "Why?" And I said, "That mask up there is a spirit." When someone's face is covered with that mask, you're

not supposed to know who is behind the mask. I told her, "I don't want to live here. I don't want to be here." So she took the mask down. She put it away in a box. I cried that night, thinking of my mom and wondering what she was doing.

They brought me food that I had never seen. The bread looked so white and ugly. I wanted my mom's bread. I was thinking about those foods that I used to eat. Mrs. Moreland said, "Eat that sandwich." I said *Sandwich, sandwich, sandwich* in my mind. So when I broke up the bread it was sad and I didn't want to eat it. When I learned how to read I looked up "sandwich." It's food between two pieces of bread.

Two weeks later I started school. The food I ate while at school took everything away, taste, smell, everything. I ate it, but I didn't like it. The people with me would say, "Agh!" And I'd just keep quiet. A guy came over and turned my bowl upside down and asked me, "Are you done?" I said, "Yeah, I'm done." He turned my bowl upside down, so I learned that when they finish, they turn their bowls upside down.

The Montessori school had one big room, all the kids in there. They put me with the little ones. They were really noisy. We learned from the older kids. We learned how to do math and everything. All of the white people learning was really difficult for me to understand. I didn't understand it, but I was learning because my mother told me long before, "Everything they do, you do. Whatever they do, don't answer and don't look at them in the eyes when they're talking."

And then the teacher told me, "Look at me when you're talking." I told her, "I can't look at you." "Why?" I said, "I see what you're thinking. I know what you're going to say." And she said, "What are you?" I said,

"I'm Rita." In the Yup'ik way we do not look at people in their eyes. To answer them we need to think about what they are asking, and then answer when the right time comes.

That was my first school. It was a good teaching for this day and age. Learning to follow the other. That's how I jumped way out there in the missionary school and then I jumped way back here, to my people. It taught me to be here, right here.

They criticized my people, you know, like we don't know anything and they know about this or that. When I got older I understood not to criticize other people's protocols because that's what they know, and that's how they learned to be. So I don't blame the missionaries. They taught us how to be healthy, how to live life. Still, they brought bad water, a bad mind, and killing. Our Native way is not to kill. We use and kill only what we need. When we kill an animal, we have to use every bit of it. We even bury all the dead people so they go back to the earth. I have lots of grandkids and great-grandkids who are in the army and are in combat, and they've killed lots of people. The military doesn't take care of their bodies when they die.

Many of the things that the missionaries brought us are good things. We learned from them about taking care of our house and cleaning, the healthy way. The missionaries also taught us about religion, about the Catholic Church. My family was Catholic and Russian Orthodox. I grew up Yup'ik, Catholic, and Russian Orthodox. The Catholic Church is still there now, but the Russian Orthodox priests don't come anymore. There were lots of Russian people there. When I was growing up we had a school, a doctor's office, and a Native store. That's all we had.

That was the big thing in Tununeq. People would come and get things because it was the port for the ships. It was an important village. Villagers would come and trade their baskets, art, and whatever they had with the ship people. That was in the '30s and '40s.

Blessed Mother

When I was seven I learned how to read and write. I wrote poems and I talked to God. And because I was Catholic, I went to church. In the month of May, they'd have rosary for thirty-one days. Father Pascal asked my mom if I could be the flower girl.

He let me light the candles and talk to the Blessed Mother's statue. From the first of May I asked the Blessed Mother, *I want you to ask your son, Jesus, what I shall become when I grow up*. I prayed every day for thirty-one days. I never got an answer. I was getting discouraged, impatient. I thought God didn't hear my prayer. So on the last day I told my mom, "I'm going at 5:30 a.m.," and she said, "Why do you go so early? The rosary starts at 7:00." I said, "Oh, I just want to talk to the Blessed Mother." She said, "Okay." So I went to church. I cleaned up everything and I talked to the Blessed Mother. I was looking at her. *I just want you to ask your son, Jesus, what I shall become when I grow up*. And she blinked her eyes! Maybe if I'd told my mom she would have said: *It's your eyelashes*. But She was standing like that and a tear came down her face. Yeah, a tear came down! When

(overleaf) Village of Tununak port, Nelson Island, Alaska, 2014

Moose antlers and musk ox skull.
Village of Tununak, Nelson Island,
Alaska, 2014

I went there I touched it and it was wet. I extended my hand and it dropped . . . I licked it and I rubbed it on my face and on my head and on my body.

I ran out, I got scared. I had to go home to change because I peed my pants. When I went home I told my mama, "The Blessed Mother answered me!" She got a cotton thing and she wiped my face. She be-lieved me! She wiped my face, and I still have the cotton. After that, I changed my clothes and went back to church.

I asked Her what I would become when I grew up and said that if I failed or succeeded, I'd accept either. I succeed and I fail sometimes, and I accept them because the Blessed Mother told Her Son to talk to God . . . that's powerful.

Nellie Lincoln cleaning fish at the village port. Village of Tununak, Nelson Island, Alaska, 2014

Fish-drying racks. Village of Tununak, Nelson Island, Alaska, 2014

So the answer was, *Use your gift*, my gift, whatever it is.

My mom said, "I believe you. I believe you and I think you are my special daughter."

Oh, Blessed Mother!

Visions of Light

Being gifted is not easy. It's scary.

I'm really careful with my gifts because they're like angels. It's about the future.

My first vision was of three lights. They appeared over the years in odd numbers—three, five, seven, nine. . . . They mark the four quadrants of the universe, the four sacred directions of the universe to unite all into one.

When I was five, I saw a horse and then I saw five lights.

Later on, when I was seven, I was eating at camp and I saw seven lights. They were talking to me about the future and what it was going to be like. I was sitting there with my mouth open and shaking when they were talking. I told my mom, "I saw a polar bear, a musk ox, and this animal, I don't know, it was white." I later found out that it was a white buffalo because the musk ox has a big head and this one had a little head and a hump. And my mom said, "You're just imagining, or seeing things." Mom never saw those seven lights. I wasn't imagining, they were there.

When I was nine we went to fish camp on the Yuukaq River to get ready for the winter season. There were all kinds of fish in there, whitefish and so on. I was eating my lunch, and my mom had a hook in the water. Then I saw these lights. One light there, four lights there, and more there. There were nine lights. Nine planets. All of them were in a circle. This time all of them were talking to me about the future.

I was sitting there, and my mom sat down next to me. And we saw them; my mom saw them for the first time. We were shaking. Hugging each other. Really beautiful, really something. Really scary. Because we knew, both of us felt that power.

They told me and my mom, *Before the world becomes one, before the people become one, before your beliefs become one, people will go crazy. But not until you understand that God is in all breath, in all that breathes, then it will become one. One faith.*

The ancestors told us to heal the world.

When I was nine years old my great-grandmother Pamyuran gave me thirteen stones and thirteen eagle feathers, saying that I would be a part of a council of thirteen grandmothers. Thirteen is the number.

Thirteen Grandmothers. Thirteen planets. Thirteen white tail feathers of the eagle. Thirteen full moons in our year. The world will become one. The world will become one when you learn to believe. One Creator, one perfectly balanced tail feather of the bald eagle.

When you really believe, the world will become one. That happened to me and my mom.

[From journal entry]

HERBS ARE SACRED BEINGS

Finally, after a long hard winter, spring is upon us. And with the coming of spring I can remember the ways of my great-grandmother (Pamyuran), who was a Yup'ik great medicine woman. She would say to us: *The harshness of winter often brings colds, flus, and mental contamination, being cooped up. Spring is a time to re-create the body, mind, and soul. The best medicine to use for this purpose is a spring harvest of stinging nettle.*

Great-grandmother always had a prayer pit in the back of her house. Even at the age of ninety she took pride in chopping her own kindling wood, setting up her spring equinox ritual, and making special prayers for Mother Earth and the plant people, who would soon awaken from the deep sleep under a blanket of winter snow.

The ceremonial prayer pit had exactly thirteen medium-sized round stones. It was constructed upon a model (where the four cardinal points of the universe allegedly converged) and always kept clean of debris. She built her sacred fire upon a wood-stacked altar, always making sure to leave a space for the eastern door, where the first rays of sunlight could be invoked to provide answer to the sacred fire.

As a child I asked: "Why only thirteen stones, Grandmother?"

With a loving smile and contemplative pause, she replied:

"Because there are thirteen tail feathers on a perfectly balanced eagle, thirteen planets in our universe, and exactly thirteen full moons in a year, my dear grandchild. Someday the white people will realize

Before the world becomes one, before the people become one, before your beliefs become one, people will go crazy. But not until you understand that God is in all breath, in all that breathes, then it will become one. **One faith**.

Rita gathering seasonal herbs. Hatcher Pass, Willow, Alaska, 2014

Rita and Marie Meade harvesting valerian root. Hatcher Pass, Willow, Alaska, 2014

this truth and come to learn the meaning of this symbol as a source of power."

Then she would walk toward the eastern door of the circular ceremonial fire pit. Entering clockwise from the east, she walked westward, as Grandfather sun travels. Puffin beak and clam shell leggings rattled as she circled four times in a sacred manner. The family and friends humbly followed.

Golden eagle and falcon feathers, an old tobacco basket, a tube-shaped soapstone pipe, and a set of small flints made up the basics of her regalia. Four small tobacco ties in colors of white, red, yellow, and black were carefully placed with prayers upon the circular rock pit.

Each of us was handed a pinch of wild but cured tobacco; then Great-grandmother lifted her lit pipe to the eastern sunrise and prayed:

O Great Spirit whose life-giving force flows through all things, I call upon you in a humble manner. Accept my pipe and tobacco as an offering. To the four powers of creation, I ask, to the four sacred directions of the universe, I ask, to the four elements of creation, I ask. To the spirits of the fire in the north, to the spirits of the air in the east, to the spirits of the earth in the south, to the spirits of the water in the west.

Four times she blew smoke, four times she cried and sang her prayer song. Then she struck the flints by the eastern door of the fire pit. Sparks ignited the wood shavings, smoke curled up to the Great

Creator, and a sudden gust of wind blew in from the east. In a mystical way, the fire started to blaze and dance. A white cloud drifted in from the north, a red flicker bird flew in from the east, a caribou suddenly walked out of the bushes while chewing a plant in the south, and a raven hollered from an old house to the west.

Upward the smoke danced with a small gust of wind. Toward the center of the sky a shadow appeared. We heard a cry of a golden eagle. With outreached claws, it flew into the swirling smoke, as if trying to capture the ancient prayer. Still screaming, it spiraled upward, then began its descent and continued to circle overhead while Great-grandmother kept praying:

We come together in this sacred circle of life to give special thanks to our Mother Earth and all our relations in nature, seen and unseen. To our ancestors, we ask, to the plant people, we ask, to all of creation, we ask. Now it is time for you to wake up, to be reborn and loan us your medicine. We are sorry we have hurt you, but we need your life in order to survive. Thus, according to ancient custom and law we offer you this tobacco, food, and prayer as payment before harvesting. We thank you for your medicine and power.

All those in the circle made similar prayer offerings in gratitude. Then we walked counterclockwise around the ceremonial fire four times, exiting the same way we came in. We shouted: "All my relations!"

The first herb Great-grandmother gathered in spring was stinging nettle. Perhaps that was her secret to long life.

My mom told me that I was going to be like the dandelion. It doesn't grow in the village, but there's an area where it grows, on a mountain where there are little lakes. Dandelion is a flower, but a flower that people don't like. It's a nuisance. My mom told me that they would try to get rid of me. And I know that.

Dandelion is a medicine for the liver. Sickness in the liver is hidden, and sometimes it's too late. So the dandelion is the one that can reach it before it develops. It can sometimes detect cancer of the liver. The dandelion is about caution.

Like the polar bear liver. If you eat polar bear liver, you get white spots all over. Like the dandelion, it's dangerous, but very powerful medicine.

Elders and Storytelling

When I was young I went to the storytelling every night, and the elders used to talk about the plants and animals, that they have life like we have life. And they taught us how to talk to the animals, how to talk to the seals and the musk oxen, and thank them for clothing us.

And when we take the plants, we talk to them and thank them for our health. And the elders used to tell us they're like people, they have feelings and they'll let you know if they don't want to be picked. Like yarrow root. We call it *anuqetuliar*. That's an emergency medicine. Talk to that plant, because in summertime it will grow when you need it. *Caigglua* is wormwood. Sometimes they'll have purple flowers, sometimes they'll have yellow flowers, and they glow. Some plants glow for the medicine when it's an emergency. I didn't believe that then, but I didn't know what they were talking about at that time. Now I believe. Now I know.

When the elders talk, it's important, because we're losing them now. Elders are, like, sitting in the boat, and if we don't listen, we cut the rope off. They're floating away. Now I can understand what they were talking about. Our young people are floating in another direction, chewing on their nails, and don't know where to go. They don't know what they're doing because they didn't listen.

When the elders talk, it's important, because we're losing them now. Elders are, like, sitting in the boat, and if we don't listen, we cut the rope off. They're floating away. Now I can understand what they were talking about. Our young people are floating in another direction, chewing on their nails, and don't know where to go. They don't know what they're doing because they didn't listen.

Now the elders don't even want to talk to their young people. The ones who really followed the stuff are all gone.

So I am just me.

Myths are examples of our lives. Elders would never say *Don't do it.* They'd never point. Because when they tell someone *Don't do it*, they do it anyway. And when they tell them *Do it*, they don't do it. So we are the opposite of that. If you do it and you don't want to, then you really haven't done it. You know? It's kind of hard to understand. People say that we don't remember anything anymore. But if you name me after my grandmother, my grandmother might really come back.

We're in the computer age right now. You know, sometime before the first Grandmothers gathering, maybe in 2000, I saw a visitor come to the planet and the computers blow up. No computers. I saw that. But then I don't know if it's true. See, the planets in the galaxy, some are blowing up, yeah? It's the cosmos. It's today. It's before we become one.

Four hundred thousand years ago, everything was far away. We knew nothing. Today you push a button and you know everything on the other side of the world. Our ancestors had it already, they had it.

Everyone has attributes. Everything has a name. We all have a spirit, all of us. We all have a soul. We all have gifts, all of us. I'm not the only one. I'm just me. Elders used to say: *Listen to your instincts.* And instinct tells us: *You go ahead and do it, you try it.* That's why I asked the Blessed Mother. That's why I talked to her. I said what I had to say, *whether I would fail or succeed.*

My elders used to say, "Life is not a competition." Life is not a competition. You do better than me and I do better than you, or not. We do the same thing, we do what we know. You know what you're doing. And I know what I'm doing, whether I'm wrong or right.

If you do it and you don't want to, then you really haven't done it.

I work with lots of patients with very difficult physical problems and mental problems. And I say, "You know, you're the only one who can heal what you have." I'm not the healer. I'm just your friend and you know, I don't know what's going on with you. But you know your troubles. Look at them, look at them and do whatever's best for you. That's how I work on my patients because I don't know what they have. When they open up it's just like Jell-O, like Jell-O melting out.

Sickness and Healing

When I was around three or four, my mother was mauled by dogs. She came home from fishing in the fall. The dogs had bitten her, and two of them had rabies. I was on the bed watching my mom moaning, groaning, and my grandpa picked me up and said, "Go work on your mom." My grandfather told me to heal my mom. I went over while my mom was sleeping. I put my hands over her body and felt a shock. That was the energy needed to take out all of those yuckies.

When I'm doing healing I'm nobody. I'm nobody. I do things that come to me, that's all. I don't use somebody's talent. I use what comes to me. My mother and my grandmother told me, "You own nothing, you are you. Whatever comes, use it, that's all. That's all."

Rita and Tununak elder relative sharing family stories.
Village of Tununak, Nelson Island, Alaska

I was in school until I was nine. Then I went back to Nelson Island, I went home. After I came back from Seattle I was very sickly and angry.

Nothing comes to you for no reason. I had polio, a touch of polio, and one side of me was paralyzed. That's why every once in a while I fall down. Then I had diphtheria and I couldn't talk. We were quarantined for two years. I was home, in Tununeq, for two years like I was in prison. My mom and I couldn't go out. I couldn't talk for two years. And now, you can't stop me from talking.

I had scarlet fever and my medicine was wild chamomile, you know, pineapple weed. I'd eat it, I'd drink it and chew on it, and my fever would go down very fast. I had to stay home for all of those sicknesses. My mom took care of me. There were four people who didn't live. Nobody caught it from me.

For two years we couldn't communicate. That's why I didn't have little friends my age.

First Menses

I wasn't supposed to get married. I wasn't supposed to have children, because I was chosen to be a healer. Before my mom gave me permission to get married, I went through the women's ritual. I had my first period when I was nine years old. I was taken to Qilengpak, an old volcano where Raven's daughter had her first menstruation ritual. That's where she sat. They called it a sitting down ritual.

The story about Qilengpak on Nelson Island is that Raven's daughter, when she had her first menses, did this ritual. Raven is the Creator.

She sat in Qilengpak for a period of time, some say from five to seven days. When she deposited her blood in that area, it became ochre, red ochre. We call it *uiteraq* in Yup'ik.

The elders took me up. Only women could go up there. It's forbidden for men. Men can't go up there unless they have permission from women. There were five holes on top of the old volcano, one of them in the middle. During the first menstruation ritual, every time we were going to eat, we'd bring a food offering to those holes, those five holes.

Qilengpak is a sacred site. It's very windy there. You can hear it. When you talk, it just echoes. So when you put the food in there, you listen. I don't know how deep the holes are, but they were pretty big.

All the girls my age did the rituals for their first menses. You were not to eat animals. You could eat bird and fish and seal, but not four-legged animals. And you were not to handle knives, needles, or scissors. And you were not to go to ceremonies or dances. You couldn't go to the men's house and when there were people and the wind came . . . you'd have to walk away. You were not supposed to walk on the windward side of boys . . . boys or men.

In the past, we were taught to let menses go to the earth—no pads or tampons.

Usually your menstruation period starts from the beginning to seven days, but for me the restrictions lasted for fourteen days, every month. My mom talked to the priest and talked to the teachers, saying that I wasn't going to be doing things for fourteen days.

They don't do those rituals anymore. We're at the tail end of the old ways.

WHEN I'M DOING HEALING I'M NOBODY. I'M NOBODY. I DO THINGS THAT COME TO ME, THAT'S ALL. I DON'T USE SOMEBODY'S TALENT. I USE WHAT COMES TO ME. MY MOTHER AND MY GRANDMOTHER TOLD ME, "YOU OWN NOTHING, YOU ARE YOU. WHATEVER COMES, USE IT, THAT'S ALL. THAT'S ALL."

I am Pamyuran, the tail end of the old ways. I saw the end of the old ceremonies and happenings.

There was another ceremony I watched two times, where they prepared for six days. The little boys made torches. All the women and girls stayed outside, chanting. We stayed outside. We didn't go in and bother them. The little ones had no clothes. My brother was one of them making torches out of *tarnaq*, wild celery. They built them for six days. After they finished, they wrapped them and put them into the fire. When the ceremony ended, they used animal bladders as an offering.

The men wore capes with no clothes. They'd run to the ocean and talk to the water and the animals, tell them to come back next year so we would not be hungry or have a shortage of food. And then they'd come back and dance with the fire, and the little boys would light the torches. And then we'd dance around the camp. This was a fall ceremony.

So those things I caught, and to me they were so interesting, it was very powerful. That's the ceremony for asking the big animals, the walruses, the whales, and everything to come back to feed the people.

The Little People

The Qaluyaat mountains are the home of the *Ircenrraat*, the little people. The whole island is the home of the Ircenrraat.

This girl was at one of the ends of the village, I'm not sure which side exactly. But she was playing with friends and they heard a thundering sound and ran home, scared. The next day a man asked her, "What happened? What happened up there?" She said, "We heard a thundering sound and then we ran home." And he said, "What direction was the sound coming from?" She told him where it was coming from and he said, "Oh, that means I'm not going to be here much longer. I'm from Kalukat. The Ircenrraat from there know that one of their members is going to be coming home soon. That's the sound they make, they call it *tuka'arluteng*. The word means to kick." He said, "They are making that sound because they are expecting me. They know that I'm going to come home soon."

The Ircenrraat don't steal. These guys have three doorways into their world. The only way you can go through and go to their realm or their dimension is through the middle hole. And then it's up to them; they can send you home, they can send you back, after they take you into their place.

And the only way they can send you back is through that middle way again, the middle door. If they send you back through the top hole or the top doorway or the bottom doorway, you don't come back. You don't come back to this world, you are lost, you are in the other dimension. That's what these guys are, these guys, the Ircenrraat.

I think the Ircenrraat are coming back. The Ircenrraat are not dangerous. They are attracted to light. They only present themselves to people who have light.

I saw another kind of being, I saw the *Cingssiiget*. These are smaller than the Ircenrraat. They looked different, a little different. My brother and I were checking the black fish traps. When we got up to the little mound, he turned around and said, "Shhhhh." Then he motioned for me to come. I went up there and there were two little guys. They had sleeves and they put fish up their sleeves. We looked at each other, turned around, and they were gone. They weren't there. We were scared. We were really interested in watching them, but when we looked at each other and turned around they were gone. That's the last time I saw them.

The Cingssiiget and the *Egacuayiit* are supernatural beings, the mischievous kind, but they also can help, they're helpful. It's not about good and bad. When I encountered them loading up their sleeves with the black fish, they were being mischievous. They were stealing.

I'm not sure exactly where the Cingssiiget and the Egacuayiit reside. These guys are little and pointy, like gnomes. In the museums, you might run into some masks, shaman masks, that represent their pointy heads.

They say that the orcas, the killer whales, and the wolves can also be these guys. The Ircenrraat can transform. They can also transform into human form.

Cultural Preservation

A long time ago my grandma told me, "There's going to be intermarriages. Even though we're intermarried, we're supposed to keep our culture, our identity, and our heritage alive. Do not forget it, keep it with you. Don't forget your culture. Don't forget your language, and don't forget who you are."

When grandkids, great-grandkids marry, some don't even know their blood anymore. I have all kinds of grandkids and great-grandkids, and they all know who their mama and dad are. That's why I always remember I'm Aleut, Athabascan, and Yup'ik, and a little bit Russian too. So I am me, Rita. It is important to know every little bit of who you are.

We are the last people on my island. We have kept our dances and our traditions because we didn't listen to missionaries who were telling us that we were going to heaven or to hell. We didn't listen, we danced and performed ceremonies.

We believe the world was created by the Creator. It provides us food, it provides us air, it provides us water, fire, and everything else that we need in our lives. Some of us know how to connect with the land. Some of us know how to connect with the water, and some of us know how to do other things. Everyone has a gift.

Everyone has to remember their own grandmothers. We're not fixer uppers.

Basketry

We made baskets with grass, wild grass. We stained them with plants, berries, and charcoal. If you mix ochre with blood and charcoal, it sets. We'd also use the dyes for paint, use them for tattoos, or whatever. I grew up with it. I never learned it. I observed.

The first basket I made was a little one. I traded it at the store and bought sugar, crackers, flour, tea, and coffee. The storekeeper said, "What else do you need?" I said, "Oh, lard." So I also got lard. That was the first time I traded. The guy at the store kept asking me, "What else do you need?" So I brought all of these things into the house, and my mom asked me if I stole them. "No," I said. "You know that little basket I made? That's how much it cost!" So that was my first little one.

I made a basket that got awarded a lot of ribbons. It won a gray ribbon, a blue ribbon, big ones, red ones, yellow ones, different ones from the first Mother's Club. And it went to different places, Kodiak, Ketchikan, and other places. The last place it went was Juneau, and it didn't come back. My mom and I got a letter from the Juneau people that they were going to enter it into the Smithsonian Institution.

On top of the basket it has a crow. Instead of the knob, an ivory carving is the cover handle. My mom

Basket made with wild grass by Rita

Dance fans made with wild grass and caribou hair by Rita

carved it. She had a vision of how to do it. I painted the ivory with charcoal, ochre, and blood until it was black. At the bottom are Raven's feet, and the tracks go in a spiral up to the top. It went to the Smithsonian, where it won more awards. The government sponsored that.

They still have a basket of mine somewhere at the Smithsonian National Museum of the American Indian in Washington, D.C.

Travels

My mom signed the papers for me to travel all over the world, and I did it. My mom and I went to see Eisenhower. Yeah, they all came out, big shots, they all came. I didn't get paid, but I had first-class accommodations.

When I met Eisenhower I gave him yo-yos. Yup'iks are like bouncing people. We bounce from here to there. I went all over the world. Just me and the Smithsonian chauffeur and their guards. I went to Morocco. I went to Greece. I went to Italy. I went to China. I went to Easter Island. Anyway, when I was born, I think I was a millionaire in spirit so I could travel.

It's scary to travel though, but it's also my gift. Lots of people want to be like me, they all wish to have something, and they have it already but don't appreciate it. They don't know it. And they get scared. Lots of people come to me and say, "Oh, this came to me," and I say, "Good. Are you going to use it?"

One time there was a little boy who was being pushed by a negative spirit. So I went to his home. The priest came with me. He had holy water and was saying prayers and reading his Bible. I talked to the spirit and said, *This is not your house. Get out of the house, leave them alone.* I just talked to the spirit, gave it food, swept the house, and opened the windows. The spirit never came back after that. What I tell the people who go through something like that is, "Put a little food in one dish from all of you in the household and give it to the spirits; maybe they're hungry. You know?"

Sometime later, his mother called me and said, "You know, Rita, we put lots of food out there and when I looked outside there were no cars, no animals, nothing, but the food was gone." She said, "I'm scared." I said, "Did you say thank you? Go out there and say: Thank you for leaving us alone."

We may be crazy as Natives, but we talk to the spirits. Some spirits are asking for help and some help us. We ask our Creator too much sometimes and then blame the Creator. Some spirits must have a reason for not answering right away.

For a long time our prayers hadn't been answered much. So I want to learn how to take care of the prayers when they are answered.

Marriage and Children

I got married to Bernard Blumenstein in 1960. Bernie was from Brooklyn, New York. He came up to Alaska in the '50s to make money. He came with a Chinese friend to make money to go to South America and open up a chicken farm in Peru. But he never did.

I had eight children. Just three are alive.

Ayagnera	Chorus
Tarvarnauramken	Let me purify you with
Ellugarnauramken	Cleansing power of *ayuq* (Labrador tea/*Ledum* sp.; both plant and infusion)
Pikaniraniartuten	Let me stroke your body
	So you can be strengthened and be well

Apalluan ciuqlia	First verse
Yugiyamaa	My semblance
Tarvarnauramken	Let me purify you with
Akuluram kat'um	Power of that bay down there
Tarvartainek	
Elluarrluten	So you can do well
Qamigaquniartuten	When you go seal hunting

Apalluan kinguqlia	Second verse
Yugiyamaa	My image
Tarvarnauramken	Let me cleanse you with
Kinguqat-gguq-qaa amkut	Strengthening power of
Tarvartaitnek-qaa	Land over there
Elluarrluten-qaa	So you can do well
Makiraquniartuten-yaa-aa	When you gather plants and berries

Marie Meade wearing her traditional Yup'ik regalia

Lyrics to "Tarvarnauramken (Let Me Purify You)," a traditional Yup'ik song

The first one was mine. She's twelve years younger than me. I was only eleven when I got pregnant. I'm not bashful to talk about my baby. Later in life, we talked to her about what happened. I said, "You are twelve years younger than me because this man did this. You know, they play with you and tickle you and pretty soon . . . that's why I don't wear scarves, because when it's right there on my throat . . . And he put wash cloths in my mouth."

One Sunday, the priest, Father Deschout, said, "We have a little girl here who's going to have a baby." After that, nobody talked about it in the village. People never made fun of me, except for my little friends. My mom, my grandma, my aunts, and other people in the village helped raise her. The teachers I babysat for put her through college. She's a doctor in biology now. I never see her.

I feel that if people can talk about their hidden things, like what they store away and never bring up, if people can bring that to their center, they can heal. The center of the earth is right there in the tailbone, where we hide things. And all of those things are the matrix of the human. The cosmos of the brain has muscles, glands, bones, everything. So we hide them here in our tailbone, and that's why we have problems with everything. It's like a bubble, and then when that bubble bursts there's more little bubbles going into the nerves, glands, head, everywhere in your body.

And that's how we get sick. It goes especially into women, into their wombs. For men it is in the prostate. The elders used to say, "The way we are going to make the world one is by talking about ourselves." So my students are learning about all these things. I tell them, "Let's learn about ourselves first. Talk about the hardest things, the most angry things that you feel. When you learn who you are, you can't become like me. I am me, Rita. You have to become like you."

I was a very angry person and had lots of disappointments in my life, but I didn't fight

Rita playing her drum at her native village of Tununak, Nelson Island, Alaska, 2014

back. I kept it to myself, you know? I had to heal myself, to work on my healing, to become a healer. I had to go through the galaxy. I met all of these meteors, big rocks, coming toward me. To do energy healing, you have to chop all of those blocks. All my anger. Chop it into molecules. And then I was feeling a little better. After the molecules, I chopped those molecules into atoms. Then I chopped those small atoms into dust. That's the way my healing worked.

I'm going to get them, whatever physical things I can work on, like the anger in my body. Because nobody is going to work on them but me. So I do that. They're not going to go away, they're always going to be there. You can still feel them when they become dust. Through the sun's rays, through the light, you can see the dust. My grandma told me about this last stage; she said, "That's when it becomes dust, *makuat.*"

Twenty-four years after I had my first baby I met Bernie. We met in Bethel when I was working as a medical assistant. I had lots of boyfriends before meeting him. We never called it boyfriend then, we just knew.

Back then, marriage was arranged through the parents. But I didn't want to marry any of my boyfriends. Then when I married Bernie, it was really arranged by my mom and Bernie's dad. Because Jewish people are not supposed to marry non-Jews. But Bernie's spirit was stronger than the Eskimo's spirit.

We didn't get married for two years because I had to tell him about me. I told Bernie about my restrictions around my period. For fourteen days, I wasn't going to cook, I wasn't going to handle knives or anything like that. I was going to just be. We had two beds. So I slept on the other side during my period. That's how I went into the universe for fourteen days.

I didn't say yes to Bernie, I said, "I'll think about it. I have to tell you about me." I already had a spiritual education, so I told him everything. I told him I needed to take care of my gift, *whether I failed or succeeded.* He understood; he was a really good man. I traveled a lot, and I never suspected him of going with another woman.

So that's what I told Bernie. And after two years he said, *Yeah.* Then he asked his family if it was okay if he married outside of the Jews, and they gave him permission. My mom gave me permission to be with him. So we went to New York to meet his family. They're mostly doctors and lawyers, educated Jewish scholars.

Bernie told me, "In my culture, my faith, my people, men take care of women." So that's why I never learned how to pay bills. He took care of everything. He never slapped me, he never yelled at me. He'd just be quiet if I was yelling at him. He never yelled back. He was studying Jesus. He felt that he was not Jewish if he didn't believe in Christ.

Bernie died in Anchorage. He had many physical problems. He had three strokes in a row and on the third one, he died. He was a real good person. He never fought back. He had a gold mine, you know? Brought me lots of gold. People tried to kill him, and he never fought back. He was a good man.

I still miss him.

Midwifery

When I was fourteen, the village midwife used to take me with her to help with baby deliveries. We'd go by sled a lot of times, or we'd go in a kayak or boat to different villages. We'd go to summer camps and winter camps to deliver babies. In my time, when I was fourteen, we only had three deaths. I assisted her in many deliveries, and I never panicked.

Then I worked for Dr. Harriet Jackson, who was a doctor for the administrator in a Native hospital in Bethel. She hired me because she knew I helped Margaret Lantis, an anthropologist, when she was on Nelson Island. I was helping Dr. Lantis that summer when Dr. Jackson came and joined us on Nelson Island.

The elders used to say not to touch the bones of dead people, but as an anthropologist Dr. Lantis gathered all of these bones, legs, arms, heads, and put them around the tent. At night she would write in her tent with bright lamps. I told her, "The elders say not to touch the bones. They'll come to you." So later my mind said, *Scratch the tent*. I was lying there and I scratched the tent a little bit. And she stopped writing, but then she'd start again. I did that maybe four times, and pretty soon she turned the lights off and went to bed. The next morning when we were at breakfast she said, "Rita, you know how you told me not to touch the bones of heads, arms, and legs? I think they came last night." I laughed and I said, "I just wanted to be silly and I scratched the tent." I was mischievous like that.

One day Dr. Jackson said, "I'm going to open a private practice and I'm going to hire you." I said, "I don't know a thing, what am I supposed to do with you?" She said, "You can diagnose for me." Later on, when I was living in Palmer, the doctor at the hospital would take me to accidents to comfort the children or the parents.

Sometimes we'd deliver breech babies. Babies have their heads down or their butt above, or their butt is to the side and the head is on the other side. I would feel the heartbeat first and then go up through the head and then go to the butt. Then I would follow it and feel the baby when the head would go into the pelvic end, and I'd push it in place.

The midwives don't put anything inside the mama, anything except hands. Sometimes the cord would be wrapped around the neck. I was still a little girl when Dr. Jackson washed my hands and put duck fat on them. I put my hands inside and I closed my eyes. The cord was really tight. I moved my hands around with my eyes closed and I pulled the cord over the baby's head. When the cord went over the head, the baby slipped out into my lap.

It just slipped out and right away it was crying, and the mama was so happy. It was a little girl. Before we cut the cord, we tied it and put it on the mama and let them hug. That mama was really happy, because she had had four boys and that was a little girl. She thanked me. That lady gave my mom mink skins and told her to make me a parka. I had a mink parka, that was the payment.

Clothing, food, and things like that, that was our payment That's how shamans work. I got food for my family, and I provided for them.

Tribal Doctor

I think I delivered around four hundred babies. I took in Natives for the most part. I worked at a clinic. I lived upstairs and it was beautiful. One time I saved a baby. There was this family, I forget their name now, but their great-grandkids always send me a seventy-five-dollar check, every year, ever since. They'd had four miscarriages. I worked hard to save the

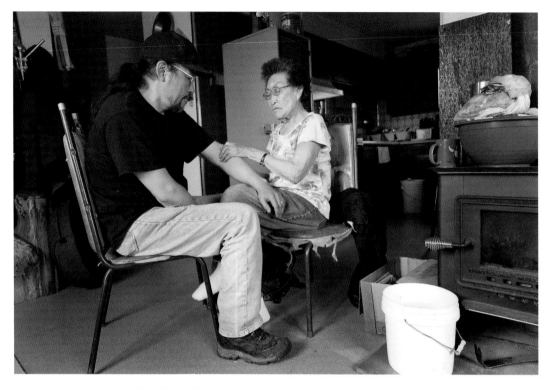

Rita treating a relative at the village of Tununak, Nelson Island, Alaska

last one. I told Dr. Jackson, "Just leave me alone, I'm going to be traveling." So I traveled in my mind to the baby. I cleaned his throat, I spanked him, turned him upside down, tickled him, everything. Three or four times he would turn into a little ball and relax. I was working on him just as if I was in space working on meteors. Then finally, after thirty-six hours he cried, his voice came out. The baby's mom fainted. She started crying. The father fainted too.

When I was done, when I moved, even my eyes hurt. My whole body hurt, everything, even my hair hurt. After I did that they put me on the bed and brought me brandy. I slept for like twenty-four hours.

I put the baby in my goosedown parka. I had him for five months, until he weighed five pounds. I fed him with a medicine dropper every hour. One drop, every hour. Now he's 6′7″ and he's got five children, sixteen grandkids, and great-grandkids.

His great-grandkids still send me seventy-five dollars. He told me, "For your lifetime, we'll send you seventy-five dollars." So every Christmas I go to the post office and there it is.

When I went to Bethel in '55–'56, I was working at EMS (emergency medical services) as a nurse's aide. Dr. Jackson hired me, and all of the registered nurses were jealous. "How come they hired you?" I said, "I don't know!" Once she hired me, we would work with the FBI and the state troopers. I did autopsies when there were accidents. We'd go to emergencies; we'd go all the way up the river sometimes. And we'd deliver emergency babies too.

While I was there, she and her mom took me to Long Island. We went to an underground hospital, like an asylum. There were children and old people. Then they took me to Oregon to the Morningside Hospital, a psychiatric hospital.

We went there and picked up a mentally ill man. They had four troopers who were going to put the restraining jacket on him. So I said, "If you're rough, he's going to be rough back." People would just say, "That's the way that crazy people are." But by handling him gently I took him all the way to Salem, Oregon. Because when you're rough with people like that, they'll get rough with you. Anybody, even normal people.

In 1959 I came to Anchorage and got married. In 1960 I moved up to Nome, and I stayed there for thirteen years. I have five children in the graveyard there. When we would come up I would go fix their graves.

We stayed in Nome, and I worked at the hospital delivering babies. After Nome, we stayed in Palmer for twenty-six years. In Palmer, I worked in the school district and in college. I'd teach basket weaving, sewing, beading, and storytelling.

Then I got a certificate from the UAF (University of Alaska, Fairbanks). It's like a college professor certificate so I can teach college. To me they are just papers. I worked as a professor for many years, and then I worked part time in elementary, high school, and college in Anchorage. I commuted back and forth from Palmer to Anchorage for over two years before we moved permanently to Anchorage.

When we moved to Anchorage I started working at the Southcentral Foundation (SCF). There were some people from Seattle studying me in Anchorage to see what kind of a healer or what kind of a doctor I could be. A group of elder advisors from the SCF got together and chose which healers to study. They studied me for two years. They were telling me what to do, and they told me not to touch anybody.

They told me not to touch anybody for three years, almost four years. They'd come and check on me. I had to write to the head of the program and say to her, "If you want to know what I'm doing, don't send these people to my office. You come and talk to me." And they did. They came and said that they were afraid. They were afraid of political things, of bureaucracy.

I worked with alcohol and drug substance users, women who were pregnant. I noticed that some babies were drunk and some babies smelled like cigarettes or alcohol. These people came from different villages and tried to have healthy babies here in Anchorage. So as soon as they'd get pregnant they'd be put in a program to try to get well. And now we have lots of healthy babies.

In 1995 I got the certificate and registered as a doctor. I was the first certified traditional doctor in the state of Alaska. I was certified in Anchorage, at the Native hospital. After I got certified they were still checking on me.

In the late '90s I started working at the Alaska Native Tribal Health Consortium (ANTHC). I still have an office and work there. Right now I'm working on writing a book and talking about these things, for our Natives to be recognized as healers, as a people, to help the Alaska Native Medical Center (ANMC), so Native healers can work at the ANMC.

We're all known by our people and we are there when they need us. Even from a long distance the ANMC calls and says, "I'm sending

Rita in front of the Bahá'í House of Worship in Wilmette, Illinois, circa 1979–80

my daughter there, can you look at her?" There are a lot of healers, but they're not working because of politics.

The Oneness of Humankind

I became Bahá'í in 1959. I believe in the Bahá'í faith. The Bahá'í teachings say that when the time comes, different teachers will be chosen. Like Krishna. Like Moses. Like Buddha. Like Jesus.

I believe that all religions come from the same one source, God. And if God wants to do something to me, it's up to Him. It's all up to God.

Grandmothers Council

Soon after Bernie died on January 6, 2004, Marie Meade asked me to join the Grandmothers. I told her, "You do it, they invited you," and she said, "No, I am too young." After that, I agreed to go. I didn't know what I was doing. I was doing it because she asked me to do it. I told them, "I'm not involved in politics and I don't know anything about paperwork. I just do what grandmothers do, that's all." Because you know, in the old days everybody helped everybody when they needed something.

So like my grandma used to say: *Maybe we are a little late, but we're here.*

When we heal ourselves, we also heal our ancestors and our children. Healing ourselves, also heals the Earth, Sky and Universe.

- Ancestors occupy the bone marrow; the bones are our parents (structure or pillars); the flesh and skin represent the person in the present moment.

- Past lives? I acknowledged reality of past lives. However, I expressed grief over the fact that many people go back energetically and dwell on the past, thereby diminishing their current vessel and attention energy. I noted that everything we need to learn will be in front of us and that going forward is a quicker path to healing.

PAMYURAN TANQIAR CAN'IRRAQ

July 11, 1933–August 6, 2021

Rita Pamyuran Tanqiar Can'irraq Pitka Blumenstein was born in 1936 in the Bering Sea on a fishing boat en route to Tununak, and she died in 2021 in Anchorage after an extraordinary career as a traditional healer and peacemaker. Gifts of visions and healing hands that were apparent by age five were nurtured by a protective mother and grandmothers. Rita continued to develop and freely share those abilities for the benefit of others throughout her life.

I heard about Rita in the mid-fifties when she worked with her longtime friend Dr. Harriet Jackson in Bethel, not far from her Nelson Island home. She must have been about twenty years old when Jackson introduced her to alternative Western medicine. But I didn't get to know her until much later in Anchorage. By then she was well established as a tribal doctor, medicinal plant specialist, and educator, with many patients, students, wellness colleagues, and health professionals competing for her attention.

My relationship with Rita really started after my son and daughter-in-law Karina Moeller asked her to officiate at their marriage. Karina had met her earlier as a patient and was immediately captivated by her restorative energy. Our families became close after that.

Then in 2004 my writer friend Mary Lockwood asked me to represent Natives of the Northern Regions at Menla, at the first gathering of what would become the International Council of Thirteen Indigenous Grandmothers, with members from all four directions. I felt unqualified, so I recommended Rita instead. Event organizer Ann Rosencranz, of the Center for Sacred Studies, asked me to escort and assist Rita in her role as indigenous Grandmother from the north. Our adventures together—Nepal, India, Brazil, Mexico, Japan, Europe—are documented in two books and a film. It was a deep honor to travel with and support Rita, who I later found out was my close cousin. I have been privileged to participate in the ceremonies and Grandmothers Council meetings, sharing my own gifts of song, dance, and culture.

Throughout her life Rita followed her own path, despite a dominant culture that would dismiss or try to suppress her traditional healing arts. Rita embraced traditional spiritual beliefs and possessed obvious abilities, yet she was very humble and expressed genuine love for everyone. With these qualities she effectively collaborated with the Western medical establishment, opening a path for the next generation of indigenous healers to follow. Her legacy lives on in all the people whom she touched, taught, or shared with throughout the world. Her lifelong work has been crucial in shaping how Western-oriented health-care providers treat and promote wellness for Alaska Native people and indigenous people worldwide. We remember Rita for her compassion, her unconditional love, and all the healings freely given during a lifetime of service to a suffering world. When praised, she would say, "I am Rita. Don't try to be me, be yourself."

According to Yup'ik custom and the wishes of Rita's daughter, Sandra Palmer, I made a trip to the beach at Tununak to ritually burn Rita's wedding fur parka and fur boots, to commemorate her life on earth and celebrate her spiritual journey on to the afterlife.

Marie Meade

SIX

GRANDMOTHER
AAMA BOMBO

WITH OUR *TAMANG* PEOPLE IN NEPAL our birth name is different than the name they call us. They do not use the name we are born into right away. In our culture, the name we are born into is used in situations where there is no other option. My father used to tell me that when I was young I was a very disciplined, good child. He had thirteen children from three different wives, and he used to tell me that out of all his children, I was the most disciplined. This I came to know later in my life. Because I was very good as a young child, the common name given to me by my father was *Gyani* (meaning mage or scholar). The name that I grew up with is Gyani, and in official documents my name is Buddhi Maya Lama. Today, I am mostly known as Aama Bombo. In Tamang *aama* means mother and *bombo* means shaman.

I am Tamang, and Tamang people are all of Tibetan origin. A long time ago our ancestors fled from Tibet and stayed in Besi, a small village nestled in the foothills of the Himalaya. We are *Bhote*.[1] After our ancestors stayed in Besi, we became Tamang. To be more specific, *ta* means horse and *mag* means rider. So our ancestors came to Besi riding horses. We are the oldest tribe of Nepal. If it hadn't been for that migration, we would still be Tibetans.

As Tamang people, we are committed to our cultural preservation. We are saving our language. Small children are taught to write and speak the Tamang language in order to preserve its essence. There are people who do not understand the language as a whole. Many people have lost the knowledge of our indigenous tongue, and speak Nepali. That is why we run programs that initiate the preservation of the Tamang language through music, like Tamang songs, Tamang instruments, etc.

Childhood

I have a lot of childhood memories. Because girls are not educated, our parents used to send our brothers to school, but not my sisters and me. Since we didn't go to school, we would go to the forest to graze the sheep, buffalo, and cows. While the animals were grazing and eating, there were small ponds and big rivers where we would take off our clothes completely and place them on top of a rock. We would swim the whole day and when it would tick five o'clock we would collect the domestic animals and bring them home. I remember those days so much, splashing water and playing with friends in the forest.

---

1. The term *Bhote* means people of Bod (Tibet).

As Tamang people, we are committed to our cultural preservation. We are saving our language.

While we were in the forest, we all would gather and sit down. Ever since I was a kid I used to play-act being a shaman. I used to take a twig of bamboo; in Nepali we call it *patyang*, which we use to play the *dhyāngro* (small, flat drum). I would cut that kind of twig and use it to play the drum. I would mimic my father and others who would dance and jump. We used to watch them do all those movements and then we would go to the forest and play the drums and dance.

We used to climb the trees and take the *charo* (bird) and place them on two stones. Then we would pretend to sit like a deity (goddess) and play the self-made dhyāngro and dance. We would mimic what our fathers used to do by sacrificing the charo and pretending to put it in front of the men. Our people did not do that for the women then. We would cook the birds in the fire,

Grandmother Aama dressed in full regalia playing the *dhyāngro*.
Kathmandu, Nepal, 2012

making an offering to the stone and then dividing them equally among us to eat. I used to do these kinds of things when I was eight or nine years old.

Back in the day, my grandfather was a renowned person in the village. He was the *dware*, like the head of the village. My father came from a family where the male figures had a high status and were well recognized. Men from such a family would look for women from good family backgrounds or women who were beautiful and also from respectable families. They would just snatch them and bring them home.

I have three mothers. My father married only one of his wives and brought two of them home by his own volition. My grandfather and grandmother arranged his first marriage. They had a very grand wedding. My mother was the middle wife. My father brought my mother home because he fell in love with her, yet he did not marry her. Later he found my youngest mother—a really beautiful woman. Hence, he also brought her home. That is how my father had three wives.

We come from a very large family. My mother is also a daughter of a very rich man. My mother's father had a lot of property and money at that time. Out of the three wives, my mother's family was the richest. That is another reason my father brought her home. In a way, my mother was very intelligent and also very strict. She had a very bad temper. From my own mother I have four siblings. The youngest two are twin brothers and there is an elder brother too. I also have a younger sister. Our mother loved us very much.

In our society at that time we were made to work at a very young age. It was mandatory. We were asked to do chores such as cutting grass, collecting fodder, plowing the fields. After we became a little older our parents, especially our mother, used to send us off to work. My mother loved us a lot, she used to give us good food to eat. In the Himalaya we did not have access to lavish food, but whatever was available she used to give us, and from time to time she used to give us good food. After we had grown up, when we started earning on our own, she did not have to do as much for us.

When I was seven years old, the Nepali Congress, the social-democratic political party in Nepal, won. Those party members didn't care if women or girls were someone's wife or daughter. They would just lay their hands on them irrespective of whose wives or daughters they were. My father and other elders were observing the congressmen's behavior and were keeping their wives and daughters safe from them. Within one year of the election, a congressman took my mother forcibly. He told my father, "I am taking your wife with me." At that time if anybody talked back to them, they would shoot that person with a gun. They would threaten to kill them; nobody could tell them anything.

Orange tree at Aama's village in Khopasi, Panauti, Nepal, 2014

After my mother was taken away by force, we felt really sad. I could not make sense of my surroundings. I used to keep calling, "Aama, Aama!" (Mother, Mother!) I did that for so long because I could not sleep without her. I used to be so worried. Every night, when it was time to go to bed I would ask my father where my mother was and would keep calling for her. After waking up in the morning I would start crying, raising questions like, "My mother is not here, where is she?"

Later on my father agreed to let me go with my uncle to see her. Her home was a three-day hike away from our village. My father told my uncle, "She is so worried and stubborn about seeing her mother that she hasn't even eaten a meal, so take her with you to see her." In three days we reached my mother's home. When I finally reached her, my mother started crying. I ran into her arms and started cuddling her. I remembered everything, like what my mother used to make us for food and give us. My uncle was instructed by my father to allow me to stay there for only two days, not longer. But due to my stubbornness I stayed with my mother for four, five days. Then my uncle said that my father would scold us and asked me to leave for home.

I returned with my uncle and stayed home. But after five or six months, again I started missing her. I told my father that I would visit my mother and come back. He would not allow me. He did not know how the people at my mother's home would treat a stranger like me. I told him that I would go and come back the next day. He agreed and sent someone along so I would be safe. I was almost ten or eleven years old then.

During that time, every three or four months I used to go to see my mother. She would smother me with all the love she could, crying, "I don't know what curse this is. Because of the Nepali Congress I have to leave my children behind and come here." When I turned thirteen or fourteen years old my father told me that he would not allow me to go see my mother alone because I was an older girl and at that time, girls were not allowed to walk around alone. Therefore, my mother would send me gifts and goodies through other people.

Life as a Young Adult

When I turned fifteen years old my father said, "Since my daughter is fifteen now, we will get her married." Back in those days girls were married off at a very early age. The suitors came to ask for my hand in marriage and my father gave me to one of them. I really didn't want to get married. My family talked with my suitor's family and arranged the marriage. I did not like the guy or his family. Even though I was young, I was very smart for my age. My father forced me to marry at the age of fifteen, but I didn't even stay with my husband for one day. From the day my husband's family returned me to my house, I never went back there again. My father kept scolding me, saying that I should build a family because if I didn't, the family name would get a bad reputation. So he asked me to return to the house where I was married off. I refused, over and over again.

My aunt (my father's elder sister) was living in the Durbar (the royal palace) of Kathmandu. When she came to visit, I told her I wanted to go to Kathmandu with her. She told me that my father would beat me if I left. She also said that because I was a married woman my husband would come looking for me, and they would put my father in jail if I was not at home. My aunt said she was leaving for Kathmandu the next day. So when she left, I had a plan. Early that morning I packed a few of my clothes in a bundle and left it in the forest. Later, I went with my friends into the forest, taking my cows and sheep along. I knew exactly what time my aunt would pass nearby. So at that moment I told my friends that I had forgotten something at home. I asked one of them to look after my animals, promising to return. I knew the path my aunt was traveling, so I ran to meet her. She scolded me, saying that my father would beat her, and asked me to go back home. I was very adamant and kept on following her.

It took seven days to reach Kathmandu. While I was following her

I kept crying, and in this way we reached Kathmandu. My aunt lived in the Narayan-hiti Durbar palace, and I stayed there with her. The people of the palace asked my aunt, "What name should we give to your *bhadaini* (niece)?" My aunt replied in a very respectful dialect, "I don't know, you look into it and decide." I was fifteen then, quite big for my age, hence they called me Nauli. They gave me work washing the silver plates on which offerings were made to the gods, then cleaning the room where they used to do *puja*,[2] keeping it clean and fresh before the rituals. So after I ran away from home they gave me work in the palace.

Aama as a young woman

After six months passed my father came to pick me up. He said that as a father of a married daughter it was his duty to return his daughter to her husband's house. So I returned with him to my village. My husband and all of his family members came to my home, prepared to take me back to their place. I told my father that if he forced me to go back I would jump in the Koshi River and commit suicide. My father got scared. Still he tried to convince me, saying, "Go to his home for only one day and then come back. When you come back I will give you your share of my land and keep you in my house." I refused again, saying I would jump in the Koshi River. He could not convince me, so he told my suitor and his family, "My daughter cannot be convinced. Please marry someone else."

After all that I stayed home almost twelve months and then ran away again to Kathmandu. I thought I could work in the palace like I did before, but they had already replaced me with someone else. So I got together with friends and did some wool crafts. From time to time my aunt would come to see me and would take me to the palace. While I was adjusting in Kathmandu my father sent my elder and younger brother to get me. I told them that I would not return home.

2. *Puja* is a prayer ritual performed as devotional worship to one or more deities, to host and honor a guest, or to spiritually celebrate an event.

Later I cooked for a renowned *subba* (a high-ranking government official) in Basantapur. He used to come to the *Ganesthan*[3] and feed us, and I came to know him more. After three years he tried to convince me to live with him. I refused, thinking my father would kill me if I did. First of all, I had run away from my village and left my husband. If I went ahead and married this other man without their consent, my mother and father might come here and beat me. I did not know where the subba lived. He told me he was not married to anyone. Also he was just five years older than me and knowing his age, I thought that maybe he was still single.

Later on I went with him. I found out that he had another wife in the house. His wife and I got along and lived together. So now I had his four daughters and two sons. From the age of eighteen, I have taken care of these six children and lived like that ever since.

Someone from my village residing in Kathmandu informed my father that his daughter had gotten married. After hearing that, everyone—my father, brothers, uncles, every one of them—arrived in the city. They asked if I had gone with him on my own or been trapped into it. Then they said they were taking me back to the village. My husband said he would not let me go. He said, "You can kill us or do whatever to separate us, but we are not going to separate." Upon hearing those words, my father and family returned home.

My father worried about me a lot. When he found out about the first wife of my husband, he said, "What if my daughter was killed by her husband's other wife?" I think that he passed away because of the tensions he took on for me. Two days before he died he said to my brothers, "If my daughter faces problems, give her this much of the agricultural land." He also told them to give me a pure silver coin. He said that if they did not do this they would be cursed.

The coin is somewhere on the altar, as I offered it to goddess *Laxmi* during a Laxmi puja (offering ritual to the goddess of wealth, fortune, and prosperity.) There are a lot of coins there because we have offered so many coins in Laxmi pujas.

I don't think my father knew I had shamanic gifts. When I was younger, I had a very big mole inside my nose. This mole started growing, and I couldn't breathe. While that was happening, my father read my Nepali *patro* (astrological birth chart). He also decided to bring my chart to a *Brahmin*.[4] He told my father that if they cut the mole on my nose it would put my health at risk. I might fall sick or even die. When my father looked into my chart he saw the same thing. They both said the mole would become small on its own. The Brahmin also told my father that I would become someone renowned later in life. So my father thought that a god or some higher spirit would fall upon me. Later the mole disappeared by itself. It's there, but you can barely see it. When there are little ups and downs in my income, you can make it out as a tiny bump, but now it is no more.

---

3. *Ganeshthan* is one of the four major Ganesh temples dedicated to the deity Ganesha, the remover of obstacles, located in Kathmandu.

4. *Brahmin* represent the highest of the four Hindu *varna* or castes.

Shamanic Practices

Jhākri (shamans) existed even before the time of *Guru Rinpoche* (name of a Buddhist master, Padmasambhava). Before any other way of prayer, jhākri existed in Nepal. The first creation in the world was *Brahma*, *Vishnu*, and *Maheshwar* (the basic forces of creation from which all other forces are derived) and right after them, the jhākris were born. The *lama* (Buddhist monks) came later; before that everything was called jhākri. They were there from the time of the deities' existence.

At the age of seven my father was taken to a *banjhankari* (a forest shaman). My father had a wound made by the fire. Because of this serious burn he was taken into the forest for seven to ten days. I was told that during that time my grandparents cried a lot, wondering if their son had been eaten by a tiger. They searched everywhere, and after seven days the banjhankari brought him back.

When my father was twenty, the gods came upon him. He became a Tamang shaman because of the banjhankari incident. The gods used to come upon him and our *kulpriti* (ancestral spirits) used to come upon him too. Also the goddess *Kali* came upon his body. Some people learn such skills from another shaman, but the gods came upon my father spontaneously. The gods used to come upon him a lot. After he passed away, they entered my body as well.

My father was a man with great knowledge and many skills. He was very educated as well. As a *vaidya* (ayurvedic practitioner) he would apply plant medicine as well as use *jhankari*, shamanic practices of the forest. He was very well respected in our village. People would come to our home at any time of the day or night to pick him up. People would come to him saying, "Brother, my mother is about to die, please come and see her." So he would be away from home a lot. At home, I would see him harvest plants. Then he had to travel great distances to meet patients.

My father would take care of the people who committed suicide and do the final rituals for them. Sometimes he would help people who were harmed by *kachopai*, a form of black magic. Powerful witches would place the leg bone of a dead person somewhere in the ground, inside the victim's house. In that state the person would be vomiting, screaming, and crying and would be in great pain. They would cry and beg for help from my father. Then my father would sit in one place and pray for the victim, holding a rope in his hand. He would find the bone and remove it with a knife. After taking the bone out, he would burn it in the river to bring peace to the unsettled spirit of the dead person.

Initiation

While I was living with my subba husband in Kathmandu, my father sent several letters saying that his asthma was getting worse and that he might even die soon. He asked me to come home. My husband and I decided to leave for the village. But soon I received a letter saying that my father had already passed away.

After my father died I was really sad for several months because I could not see him before his demise. I kept thinking that I should have gone to see him. Also I got scared that my family would punish me. I had left home on my own volition. The culture, religion, and customs

of our own caste were very strict. For instance, we would not marry into a family of lower status. We would not marry outside of our caste. After our parents agreed and gave our hand in marriage, we had to go with the new husband. But I left and got married on my own. Having done so, I felt scared, thinking that my father would scold me or the village people, like my uncles, would think ill of me. I thought my sisters and brothers would scold me. Because I was scared, we kept on delaying our visit to my father and while we did so, he passed away. Even then I didn't return to our village. Nine years went by; my sisters, brothers, and uncles kept visiting me in Kathmandu, but I never went back home.

After nine years I went to a place where a jhākri was playing the dhyāngro. While watching them perform the ritual, I started getting little *kampa* (shivering). I felt scared as I started to think, *Why am I shaking?* Then my husband said, "Let's go to our room." From then on I started shivering and every day I would shiver more and more. I went to so many doctors and jhākri. I went to so many places and tried so many things, but nobody could do anything to help me. I kept shivering. The doctors could not figure out what was wrong with me and the jhākri would say that someone had called on bad spirits and unsettled souls to make me sick. They said someone did black magic on me and that I was going crazy. They even talked about admitting me to the mental asylum. This kept on happening for two or three years. I couldn't work and ate very little.

I became a little better, started to work and grow my appetite again. Then after three months I started shivering badly. I just could not eat. I kept shivering for fourteen whole months. At times I would say, *I am Kali Mata* (goddess Kali). I would eat maybe once in seven days. After shivering for fourteen months, I spent all my money and sold all my jewelry for my medication. But that treatment didn't help me. After all this, they could not find anything wrong with me.

I told my middle brother, *I am Kali Mata, and these are the things that I want you to bring: on*

Aama performing a puja at her village home in Khopasi, Panauti, Nepal, 2014

the top shelf in the house there is my dhyāngro, and a few beaded necklaces of mine have been given away, but some of them are in the house; bring them to me. Then he asked, "What day should we come?" Then Kali said, *Come by anytime you want.*

My brothers and uncles, almost twelve of them, got together in my room. This is when my father, who had conducted all the rituals in the past, came into me. My brother said that none of them believed that our father was coming through me. He said my father would not come through a daughter who was already married. He needed to come within his *kul* (patrilineal ancestral pool). My brother began to ask all sorts of questions to the spirit of my father coming through me. "Tell us what you can say about when you died! Who was there? Who saw you first? Who brought the lama?" Then my father's spirit said, *I will tell everything, but before that, I will enter everyone's body once.*

At that very moment he left me, and each of my twelve brothers and uncles started shivering. My father said that he would not stay in one body for more than ten minutes. Then he came back into my body and started saying, *It is me. On Wednesday at four o'clock I died. Salminti's uncle saw me. He started calling me, Jetha, Jetha! (My son, my son!). I did not respond to him and he was curious why. So at four o'clock when he came up to me to see what was wrong, I was already dead.* He stated all of this information. Then he said, *All of my sons had gone to the market. When they came back, everyone started crying.* Then my father gave the name of the lama who had performed his final rites. He also gave the name of the person who had made his *dhung* (funeral casket).

While the spirit of my father was coming through my body, he spoke about what happened when they were taking him to burn his dead body, there in the rest-

Aama treating a 100-year-old Tibetan woman. Kathmandu, Nepal, 2014

At first, goddess Kali came to my father, and that is why she came to me. She is my principal deity. After Kali came upon me, many other gods started coming upon me.

(overleaf) Boudhanath Stupa in Kathmandu, Nepal, 2014

ing place in the forest. He said, *While my body was being taken to be burned, my head moved in a certain manner and my father gently lifted my head. He was crying, remembering all his children, each and every one of them.*

When the spirit of my father told all of this to the people in the room, everyone was shocked. My brothers and uncles confirmed that it was my father who had come upon his daughter's body. Finally they believed it.

They asked my father, "What should we do now?" Then he said, *I will stay in my daughter's body and for our main ancestral house I will select someone else.* Then he said, *Now, bring all my belongings here. My daughter will stay in gufa⁵ in the* chyan⁶ *for one year and after that, she will come out and worship Lord Shiva. She has to sit in gufa for three consecutive years, and then I will give my daughter all the knowledge of all the mantras and procedures.*

And so in the month of *Bhadra* (August), on a full moon night, I went to the Swayambhunath cemetery. After a year of staying in gufa, I went to pay my respects at Gosayathan, where I worshiped Lord Shiva. After that I spent two more years in gufa and then I gained all the knowledge. Then I thought, *I do not want to suffer so much, I do not want to do jhākri. I will do meditation and other things, but not jhākri.*

I brought a statue of *Lord Buddha* home, did a ritual, and asked the lama to bless it. I would offer water to it every morning and every night.

5. Literally *gufa* means cave. It also refers to shamanic initiatory practices in an enclosed space.
6. Cemetery.

I used to smoke cigarettes. The lama told me that after I placed Buddha on the altar, I should not smoke inside the room. If I wanted to smoke, I needed go to another room. One day I forgot about it. I cooked for my son and he had left for work. Then I sat down to cut wool. I had the urge to smoke a cigarette and I did. Suddenly, I threw the cigarette and the lighter out. That force came into me so abruptly, I thought I was going crazy. After that, even though I smoked in my own room, the cigarette would smell bad to me.

For one and a half years I did not treat any people, I just read scripts and meditated. Some time later, a woman who was critically ill needed help. A lot of doctors visited her, but none of them could identify what was wrong. My father's spirit told me, *Okay, now you go and help that woman. Identify what is wrong. All of the rituals will come naturally to you.* I had never done a ritual of that sort. He said, *If you go and perform the ceremony, that person will be okay tomorrow.* I got scared. On the next day when I heard that person cry, my father said again, *Go help that person.* I felt scared and said that I would not go. This kept on happening for five days.

So one day my father's spirit took me there on his own. I went there and I didn't know anything. Then he (my father) asked for one egg. I took the egg and started reading a mantra and performed a ritual with it. I asked them to keep that egg in the crossroads. They went and left the egg in the crossroads. From then on that patient became better bit by bit. The woman would ask her children to call me to come see her. I was scared, so I didn't go. The following day my father did the same thing. He would say, *GO!* and would lift me up. After he did that to me three times, I found myself in her house again. I performed rituals on her for three days. She had been sick for six months, and within three days she got much better. Then the buzz of this incident spread through the family quarters, and people started showing up at my door. After that incident I started doing treatments.

[While being interviewed Aama starts to moan and chant, and her father comes through and says:]

I will always be with my daughter. She is a very good daughter and she follows whatever I ask her to do. I miss her a lot and I love her very much. I was so sad and I cried so much because I couldn't see her before I died. Everything she is saying is true. I have blessed her body and soul to protect her from any bad energy. I have given her the power to help people. Everything she said is true.

Once I started treating people, they kept pouring in; sometimes in a day I would treat around seventy or eighty people. People who would shiver would also become better; people who had become mentally unstable would also become better. The news started spreading faster and faster. People from *Boudha*[7] would come; people would also come

7. Refers to the Boudhanath Stupa in Kathmandu, Nepal, and surroundings. Boudha is one of the largest stupas in the world.

from very far away. People with various types of suffering came. When a person came who performed *bokshi* (witchcraft), even if they were suffering, I could not tolerate them in front of me. I would not allow them to come near me.

At first, goddess Kali came to my father, and that is why she came to me. She is my principal deity. After Kali came upon me, many other gods started coming upon me. Gods like *Dolakha Bihmsen*, *Manakamana*, and *Gorakh Kali* all talk to me.

We have to ask for permission from the *Dharti Aama* (mother earth), *Suryanarayan* (Hindu sun god Surya), and *Chandrama* (lunar deity). We remember all of them in our prayers in order to gain knowledge.

Reunited with My Mother

After my mother was taken away by another man, she suffered greatly. She used to drink and gamble a lot. I would get messages and news about her. People told me that my mother would go out begging to feed herself. She didn't even have proper clothes. She wore rags and walked around in the place called Ramechhap. I feel bad that she had to suffer so much.

I told my husband that my mother did not leave us purposely, she was taken away forcibly. I told him I had to go and bring my mother home and look after her. When I talked to him he said, "If we give a little of what we eat and wear, it should be enough for her. Go bring her."

(opposite page) Aama painting a rock for a Kali puja. Khopasi, Panauti, Nepal, 2014

(top) Aama at her yearly Kali puja, during the *Diwali* festival. Khopasi, Panauti, Nepal, 2014

(bottom) Aama blessing village kids after the Kali puja. Khopasi, Panauti, Nepal, 2014

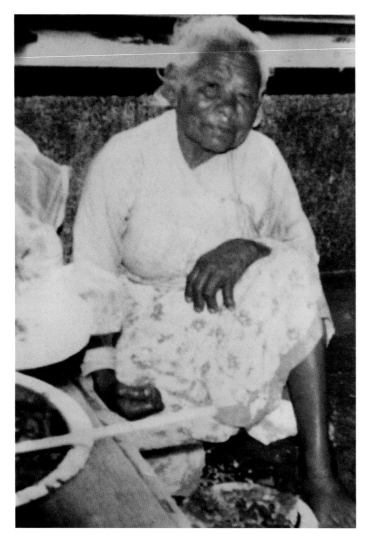

Aama's mother, Ram Maya Tamang, circa 1981–82

I took a bus to Ramechhap and brought shoes, clothes, and everything for her. I brought her here with me and looked after her for twenty-five years. It has been almost twenty years since she passed away. I did her final rituals and sent her off.

Healing Work

Every morning I wake up at 3:30 a.m. and stay in my bed after waking up. While in bed, I recite the Guru Rinpoche mantra 2,000–3,000 times before I actually start my day.

Om Āh Hūm Vajra Guru
Padma Siddhi Hūm

Then I get up and wash my face. I put a little water on my whole body. After getting dressed, I move my legs and meditate for half an hour. After that, it is almost 5:30 in the morning. Then I go down to the puja room. I offer rice grains. My daughter-in-law offers the water. Then I sit down to meditate. Lord Buddha, rinpoches, all of the deities—I meditate about them. After I call all the gurus' and Guru Rinpoche's names, I bow down (prostrate) three times to get their blessings. Then I take incense, rice grains, flowers, and fruits and go to the rooftop. On the rooftop I wash all the gods. I have old stone statues of them there. I wash each one of them, and then I wash the rice grains as well. Then I offer the washed rice grains to them. After that I offer them a flame, flowers, and fruits.

After that I worship the sun. I do a Suryanarayan (sun) puja, then do puja to Chandrama (moon), then I worship all the gods and goddesses. I pray to them and then offer *aarti* (light the oil lamps). It takes almost half an hour to finish that

Oṃ Āḥ Hūṃ Vajra Guru Padma Siddhi Hūṃ

part of my prayer. Afterward, I go to my room and again I sit and recite mantras. Then I drink my tea and have my breakfast.

Then I go downstairs, where people are already waiting for me. After purifying myself, I ask the gods for permission and sit down to heal people. Then spontaneously the gods come inside of me. I ask them, *This person has come to me with this problem, what should I do?* Then the god gives me instructions and procedures to do my work. Some patients are mentally sick. Some patients come to me looking like they are going to die. After I have treated them, some become well on the spot. That is why I have to be clean and pure before I sit down and start my work.

The *mālā*[8] (necklace) I use is a Lord Shiva offering. *Ritha,* the black seed beads, make up the *Rudraksha mālā* that we use to pray, which represents the tears of Lord Shiva.

The *ghanti* (bell's) significance is to let the prayers and sounds reach everywhere. When the gods come, we ring the bell. The louder it rings, the farther the sound will travel, and it will reach out to more gods. That is why we use it.

8. Prayer beads or malas (Sanskrit: *mālā,* garland) are a traditional tool used to count the number of times a mantra is recited, breaths while meditating, prostrations, or the repetitions of a deity's name.

The peacock feather we call *sirbandi,* we wear as a headdress. This is Krishna's. Lord Krishna climbed on the peacock and traveled around, so Krishna's adornment is the peacock feather.

The dhyāngro is Lord Shiva's *bhakti* (devoted disciple). During the *Satyug* (the Era of Truth), in Hinduism we call him Shiva. In Buddhist tradition he is Guru Rinpoche. From the day Guru Rinpoche came to the earth, he created the dhyāngro, the Rudraksha mālā, the bells, and the ritha. All of this Shiva gave to the jhākri. This is the reason we wear them and offer our prayers to the gods and goddesses. When Guru Rinpoche came to earth, all the elements and jhākri were established.

During the chanting period of my rituals, many of Shiva's different aspects come through me. During that period, all of the gods and goddesses come into my head and they flow through me. Shiva sometimes rides Singha, the lion. When Singha enters my body, I start roaring.

Lord Hanuman, the monkey, comes too. Monkeys climb from one tree to another. During the Satyug the monkey was considered one of the gods.

Some jhākri look at rice grains to diagnose illnesses. But I do it by counting my fingers. So whatever has entered the body of my patient flows into my body automatically and it comes to my mouth, and then I

Aama on her home's rooftop doing her morning prayer offerings. Kathmandu, Nepal, 2014

tell them. After I diagnose them, they usually ask me how to treat the issue, but at that moment I don't even know. I have to look at the patient again, call in the gods, and count on my fingers. Then the answers come into me automatically. Then I know everything about their body, their history, their thoughts, and what's in their hearts.

I can also divine the fortunate time for laying the foundation of a new house; lucky dates for a marriage or for when to travel. Other people, like Brahmins, do divinations according to the person's astrological chart, but I look at my fingers. And my predictions are no different from the predictions made by the Brahmins and lamas. There is no caste or religion to my divination; I'm able to see the future of Brahmin, Tamang, or anyone.

I can even know the exact day that someone will die. I can tell if the

patient can't be treated and if they will certainly die. But I don't say this to their relatives because if I say this to them they will panic. So I give them more time. If that person is going to die in two months, I will tell the family that he may live up to six months.

Sometimes I can go for seven days without eating. I do not feel hungry at all; I can just sit like that. Nothing happens to me; I don't feel hungry or thirsty, I don't feel anything. When I'm in a state of devotion I feel my stomach is always full.

In order for me to stay pure, my father's spirit and his spirit helpers ask me not to eat *jutho*, food touched by anyone else. If I share food with someone else, I shiver. In the beginning, even if I spent intimate time with my husband, I would shiver too.

The spirits tell me before I'm to do a healing if there is something

wrong, if there's a reason I should not meet certain people. They inform me if someone is menstruating; they tell me not to touch them. They warn me if someone is a practitioner of black magic and tell me not to look at them. They tell me to send them away.

Of course, I forget sometimes. I forget some of my restrictions and do certain things I am not allowed to do. Then the gods get angry inside of me: they scream, they cry, they pull my hair. If I touch impure things such as pork meat, I go crazy. I pull my own hair. These are the gods who reside in my soul. Sometimes my father's spirit does that too.

Once when I was traveling with the Grandmothers Council, all of us, along with the other Grandmothers, sat down to eat. I mistakenly touched pork meat. I just touched it a little. The gods inside me grabbed and gripped me. They asked me why I was touching the meat.

When the gods came into my body that way, many people got scared and left the dining hall. The gods inside me started pointing fingers at everyone, saying, *Why did they give me food that I should not eat?* My translator and travel companion lit incense sticks and cleansed me with pure water. After that I got better.

When I look at the patients and their conditions, if I know that they will get better with only my treatment, then I treat them myself. When I look at them and know that my treatment would not be enough, I tell them to go to the doctor. Sometimes when the doctors say that a patient will die, it is still not certain. Maybe the gods have written that he may live.

Once I had a critically sick patient from Darjeeling, India. She was the sister of one of the nurses. While she was in India, none of the doctors could identify what was wrong with her. They thought it was TB (tuberculosis) because she lost a lot of weight. They brought her to a hospital in Nepal and kept her there for three months. She lost more weight, and the doctor said that she might die soon. Then the doctor told her a date that she would die on. They asked her family to take her home. So the people of Boudha said, "The doctor has given the date of her death, yet she is still alive. Let's take her to our Aama." Her sister, the nurse, was upset. "Don't talk nonsense like this," she yelled at her family. The people from Boudha came to pick me up and said, "Aama, Aama, can you please come with us to see a patient in the hospital?" I felt a bit uncomfortable because she had been kept in the hospital for so long. *What will the doctors tell me?* I wondered. I went there and saw the patient; she was really thin and fragile, and her mother was sitting

beside her crying. I looked at her carefully; all my gods made me look at her carefully.

When I looked at her I saw that inside her body was a dead soul. Her lifeline was very long, so I told them that she would not die, but a dead soul had entered her body. My gods told her that if I kept treating her with puja offerings she would get better. The nurse told me, "You will not be able to do anything because the doctor has already given her one month to live and asked me to take her home." I went to see her every day for five days. On the fifth day, the patient was able to open her eyes and see. Then she was able to drink water from a spoon. The parents asked me to come for more days. They cried in front of me. On the seventh day, she drank three spoonfuls of lentil soup. Then the patient said, "The spirit inside of me said, 'My friend, I am going, you take care of yourself and sit up.' Then he became a butterfly and came out of my nose."

The parents were shocked, as they did not understand. When I looked at her, I saw that the dead person's soul had left her body. Later on the doctors asked the nurse to introduce them to me. All the doctors were there waiting for me. I felt so shy. The doctors asked me if the patient would get better. At that time I was not able to tell them if she would live or not because I couldn't trust them. I just told them that she might make it but I was not sure.

The next time I visited her she was sitting up and eating a few spoonfuls of rice. The doctors were shocked. I went there to treat the patient for ten to fifteen days. Then she came to my house and I continued to take care of her, doing all the required pujas. She got better. After she got well, a lot of doctors started coming to my house. The doctors started believing me. They would tell me, "Aama, if you do not feel well or anything happens, you do not have to stand in line, it is free for you." *Aama* is what they call me. The patient who they said would die has two children now; one is ten years old and the other is thirteen years old. She is doing really well.

Nowadays, when doctors from different hospitals can't treat someone, they tell the family to bring the patient to me. In the afternoons I usually go to treat people in the T. U. Teaching Hospital, Bir Hospital, Patan Hospital, or the Om Hospital and Research Centre. When the hospital medicine doesn't help them, their staff comes to pick me up. When I do my mantras and rituals on the patients, surprisingly the same medication that didn't work before starts healing them again. Everyone trusts me, and all the doctors also trust me. They trust me a lot.

Many well-known doctors and lamas come to me. Recently, around sixteen nuns from the Gorkha village became mentally ill. A few weeks ago one of them was brought to me. She was grabbing her throat and choking herself. She was so strong that five or six people had to restrain her from hurting herself. After four days of treatment, she became better. She was controlled by a bad spirit. Sometimes even some monks practice black magic. Afterward the remaining fifteen nuns came to me, and they became better.

If the gods in me tell me that I can treat someone, I treat them. But if they tell me that I cannot, then I simply do not treat them.

Sometimes I treat myself when I sense negative energy. When I am traveling, sometimes bad things may come up, but they cannot stay for long in my body, as I have the protection of the *Tetis Koti Devi Devta*[9] (gods and goddesses) in me.

Grandmothers Council

Being part of the Grandmothers Council must have been my destiny. It must have been written on my destiny to walk with the twelve other Grandmothers. This invitation first came to another Grandmother from Bhimsengola in Kathmandu. I think it was not in her destiny to be part of it.

My friend Larry Peters told me that there was a gathering and they were looking for a grandmother from the East. I agreed to go meet with them. That is how I became part of it.

Before I left for Mexico for the Grandmothers Council in 2006, my husband fell ill and was admitted to the B. P. Koirala Memorial Cancer Hospital in Chitwan, Bharatpur. I told all of my sons and daughters that their father would not live and asked them if I should go to such a gathering. I did not want to go because I was scared he would die before I returned. All of my children told me to go. "We will take care of him," they said. "In a few weeks you will return to Nepal."

So I went to Mexico for Grandmother Julieta's Council Gathering. In my dreams, I saw a person in black in my house, people tearing their clothes, and a lot of people from my village gathering in my house. I felt that my husband had passed away. Later on I got the news that he had died. I had been in Mexico for seventeen days and came home as soon as possible.

When the Grandmothers Council came to Nepal in 2012, the jhākri, the Tamang, and many other Himalaya cultures were represented. In honor of the Grandmothers, they danced and sang at the opening procession to Boudha and throughout the gathering's program.

The Council Gathering theme was "Praying for Peace in the Land of the Buddha." I spoke about moving out of the tumultuous *Kali Yuga* into the *Sattvic Age* where only truth will be spoken.

After the age of twenty-five, the gods entered my body. I feel like my destiny was written in my previous life, because gods do not enter everyone's bodies. It must have been written in my previous birth. My father enters my body. He gives me power, because in the beginning, I knew nothing. Ever since I started working, they have been coming and guiding me. It is through them that I have been able to help and heal so many people.

Right now, as I sit here, I am a normal person like you, there is nothing inside of me.

I wish for everyone to have success in life, I wish this from my heart to them. I do not want to destroy or hurt anyone. However it can happen, I wish good things for everyone.

---

9. *Tetis Koti Devi Devta* are the thirty-three gods and goddesses that sustain the world.

Grandmother Aama preparing for her prayer ceremony at Grandmother Julieta's gathering in Huautla de Jiménez, Oaxaca, Mexico, 2006

BUDDHI MAYA LAMA

July 16, 1943–June 7, 2022

Dear Relatives of All Nations,

I am deeply honored to submit these words on behalf of my Nepalese family and in memory of Grandmother Aama Bombo, who passed away on June 7, 2022, at the age of seventy-eight.

I first met Grandmother Aama Bombo in 2009 at the International Council of Thirteen Indigenous Grandmothers Council Gathering in Sedona, Arizona. During the prayer council led by Grandmother Mona Polacca, I witnessed the power of Grandmother Aama Bombo's healing and shamanic abilities. Although we did not speak the same language, we connected telepathically, and I was later asked to accompany her on a journey that would last for thirteen years.

Grandmother Aama Bombo's life was dedicated to healing and helping humanity. Her power and essence were never fully understood, but her endurance and tenacity as a shaman were undeniable. She was a vessel for the gods and goddesses, bringing forth initiations and healings for the benefit of all.

While there are many questions about Aama's lineage and connection to these deities, we can be certain that her lifelong task has been completed with great success. Her healing and *puja* rooms will remain, tended to by her family members in her honor; her daughter-in-law takes care of the village Kali puja and the monastery, as the leader and heart of the family. Aama Bombo continues to have a strong presence and guidance via the teachings left to perform the daily morning and evening puja for all gods and goddesses and to respect the ancestors. Aama would always remind the family to "Never forget to give your respect to the ancestors, who are always at the priority of this life."

As a tribute to Grandmother Aama Bombo's legacy, we have established the Grandmother Aama Bombo Life Legacy Fund to support her ancestral homeland in the mountain foothills north of Kathmandu. The fund will support the monastery, with the ongoing care and feeding of and educational supplies for the orphanage and poor families in the surrounding area, as well as beginning the reconstruction, affected by the 2015 devastating Gorkha earthquake, for the renewal of the Kali temple in her name. We will continue to gather in Nepal to bring peace and joy to this continued prayer in her name.

May Grandmother Aama Bombo rest peacefully, knowing that her life's work of bridging this world to the next will continue to be in people's hearts. We offer our loving gratitude and peace to the gods that you know in name and spirit. Namaste.

Sensei Rev Hanayo of Winnipeg, Manitoba, Canada

SEVEN

GRANDMOTHER MARGARET BEHAN

MY NAME IS *BAA'NEE'AW'TH'SA,* Red Spider Woman. My Arapaho grandmother gave me this name. Red Spider Woman means she will balance the world. My Cheyenne grandmother translated it in Cheyenne to *Ma'eve'ho'Ka'e,* she will be relentless. My English name is Margaret Louise Behan.

I was born on the 4th of July, 1948, at the Clinton Indian Hospital in Clinton, Oklahoma. My mother was Daisy Fletcher Behan. Her people are the keepers of *Ma'hut's,* the sacred arrows. I grew up out in the country in Watonga, Oklahoma, near my grandparents.

At five years old I was taken to St. Patrick's Catholic Indian Boarding School[1] in Anadarko, Oklahoma. When I went to St. Patrick's, it was very cold. I didn't eat all the food on my plate because I didn't know what it was. I wasn't used to it. So they put us in the basement because we didn't eat our food. I hardly ever talked. I did know English, but I don't even remember that part. I remember how they were mean to us. There were a few of us kids who had to stay in the corners of the cold basement. I remember a nun coming over with a pan of toast. I was so hungry, I was picking up the crumbs, eating the crumbs of the bread. And I thought she was so nice to come and feed us the toast. I was told it was leftovers, but it was good because we were hungry.

I remember a nun died and they made us go to the mass. All of us had to march into the church. And that was the first time I ever saw a dead person. It was a dead nun.

1. St. Patrick's Mission and Boarding School.

I remember my older sisters were told: don't be asking questions. We'd be in trouble if we asked questions. There was this big statue in the basement where we were punished. It was a statue of Mary holding Jesus. He had blood coming through the holes on his hands. It was very scary because the statues were bigger than us. I had to work standing on a box. I always carried that box with me. I would be in the laundry room folding towels and I would get hit on my hands if I didn't fold them right. My hands would sting. I spent a lot of time trying to fix the towels the way that the nuns wanted them to be. And so I always remember being hungry and my hands stinging.

We were all Cheyenne. The older ones would tell us, "Do not speak Cheyenne." We would cry. I'd cry for my mother or my father, calling out for them in Cheyenne. My sister came over and she said, "Don't be saying those words, because they're going to punish you again." I had to learn right away not to say those words in Indian. That's the first thing I learned.

We didn't go home for Christmas; we went home for the summer. But in the summer we had to work. We picked cotton and we'd watch other kids, babysit. We even helped with the cooking. I remember I had to peel potatoes a lot.

I remember one time my grandmother made gravy with tomatoes and sugar. After that we always wanted sweet tomato gravy. I remember eating cucumbers out of her garden. My brothers and I liked taking a horse and wagon. We'd pick wild plums. Then we would find turtles, land turtles. My grandfather said, "When you pick them up, put them far away from you because they pee, you know?" We'd put a whole bunch in the gunnysack and go home and she'd build a fire and put all the turtles on the grill. And then Grandpa would break them open and finish cooking them. Then we'd eat the eggs and the legs. I haven't tasted it in a long time, since I was a child. And the plums too. We had plum pudding, plum jelly, and dried plums for the winter.

My grandma would make dried meat out of beef or deer. I learned how to do that with her. I'd sit beside her and slice the meat and dry the meat. I had my own pole or clothesline where I would put my meat to dry.

I only remember the happy times growing up with my parents and my siblings in summertime. Then we would have to get ready to go back to school.

It was very sad. My dad would tell my brothers and sisters, "It's only for a little while, it's just going to be one more year." I used to wonder, *When will it be my turn for him to tell me it's just going to be one more year?*

My parents worked hard picking apples, cutting broomcorn, and picking cotton in the migrant jobs. They made a good amount of money. They'd come to visit us and bring us some fruit. Then they'd take us shopping when we needed something or just to feed us, to share food with us. They came very seldom, but we were happy to see them. A lot of times other relatives would come, like my mom's

Margaret Behan, Classmates Return from Minnesota Trip

Margaret Behan, Watonga, her classmates in the Advanced Foods Class and their teacher of Chilocco Indian School, have just returned from a week in Minneapolis at the American Home Economics Association Convention. Their trip was one of their prizes for taking top honors in a Yeast Menu Planning Contest.

Competing against hundreds of home economics classes from junior and senior high schools in every state and the District of Columbia, the girls and teacher turned in an entry that consisted of a one-week's menu plan for a family of four with recipes for all dishes. The menu plan was nutritionally well balanced, practical and was presented in an original leather binder made by one of the boys in the Chilocco shop class. A great deal of time was spent checking costs and values in the local Dillon's supermarket — and many additional hours were spent testing the recipes in class.

Highlight of the project was a powwow feast where the girls served friends special foods — including the Indian specialty, squaw bread.

Now back to their normal summer activities, the class still has to choose a major appliance for their classroom—another prize for winning the contest.

Their teacher, wins still another big trip. She and a companion have an expense paid trip to Europe. They left July 14 and will spend a day in New York and then will go on to England, the Netherlands, Germany, Switzerland, Italy, Spain and Portugal.

Margaret wears her ceremonial Cheyenne costume to the Standard Brands booth. With her is her teacher, Mrs. Jessie Jordan of Oklahoma City, circa 1970s

Margaret as a young woman

brother. I was at St. Patrick's through elementary and then at Concho U.S. Government Indian Boarding School in Concho, Oklahoma, through middle school. From there I went to a school where I graduated, far away near Arkansas City, Kansas.

Sacred Ceremonial Ways

In the summertime when I was twelve, the Kit Fox Society came to my mother and father and told them I had been appointed to be one of the sacred girls of the Sun Dance of this clan. So I remember going through that ceremony.

They talked to us like we were sisters, sisters to this clan. We were sisters to everybody who was special. It seemed like they were saying that we were to be special, sacred girls and that they couldn't start the Sun Dance without us. It had something to do with the sacred objects.

I was the youngest one. I was kind of curious why the others were older. But my understanding is that they had to include a family that was very devoted to the ceremonies and kept the practices. So I was chosen because of the ways and belief systems of my mother's side and my father's side. I guess they were holy people. My father was Northern Cheyenne, Northern Arapaho. And my mother was Southern Cheyenne.

They prayed daily, but the prayer is also in the service. My father composed songs for the Sun Dance ceremony. People would come to him: "We need a song made for a special occasion." Usually it was a ceremony. He would just make it right there.

My mother was a great person. People came to her. I guess she was a leader. She was in politics. I remember people used to come to her and tell her they were running for office, and she would go around and register the Indians and she would educate them about who to vote for and why they were voting. She was really strong.

Native American Church

The Native American Church (NAC) was given that name when it was legalized as a Native American religion in 1918. My understanding is that the Native American Church was created for the Indians, for all Native Americans who were put on reservations. It seems like that ceremony was what helped them to transition to reservation life.

There are many ceremonies combined in the NAC ceremony. There are parts from the sweat lodge, parts from the Ghost Dance, from the Gourd Dance, from the Eagle Dance. There are parts from the Corn Dance, the harvest, the Animal Dance. All these ceremonies they had, they brought to this one place.

The leader of the Native American Church ceremony is called a *roadman*. The old people used to look for folks who cared about ceremonies. The elders would say, "We see you're very interested in this ceremony, so we want you to be the leader or caretaker of it." In the ceremony there is a crescent moon altar made out of sand, dirt. Along the top of the moon altar they mark a line, a *road*. That road means a lot of things. It means *God*. It means *the road of life*; it means *showing the way*. So if somebody in the ceremony, in the circle, feels like they're lost, like they don't belong or like they're not doing the right things in life, then if the person looks at the road they can see where they are. Kind of like a gauge. The roadman takes care of that road for the people.

"Who made this?" I would ask my father. I would ask my grandfather and my uncles, different ones. I would say, "Who made this ceremony?" And my grandpa, he said, "Go look in the mirror." He said, "The women made the ceremony." And I would ask my father, "How did this woman make this ceremony?" Because I wanted to see if he knew, you know? He said, "The woman made this ceremony.

8 CHICAGO SUN-TIMES, Tues., Nov. 24, 1970

Notake the Press made

Pow-wow princess

Margaret Behan, a Cheyenne Indian from ~~South Dakota~~, flashes a winner's smile after she was named Indian Princess of the 17th Annual American Indian Pow-wow, to be held at the Chicago Av. Armory Nov. 26-29. The 22-year-old North Sider was selected over seven other contestants in pageant Monday night at the American Indian Center, 1630 W. Wilson. (Sun-Times Photo by Larry Nocerino)

She's the one who put this together. She saw all of these things. And everything belonged to her."

My mother and her father were part of the Native American Church. They were preserving the old stories of the NAC. They didn't really talk like the way I'm talking. They'd talk about some things as beings. Like the thing was a person.

Years ago my mother went to this elder woman and asked about a fireplace altar (a NAC ceremonial way). It wasn't being used anymore. So my mother asked this old lady for the altar. And the old lady was so happy. She said, "I was praying for this to happen because this way was not being used anymore." She said, "I know you will take good care of it and it will flourish, it will keep going." My mother said she was a sacred old lady. Her son and husband healed a lot of people with that fireplace.

Then my mother's uncle wanted to use it. He was in the marines. He was so proud to be in the military. He said, "I'm going to put an anchor in the altar." So he made an anchor with the earth, because to the Cheyenne the earth is a grandmother, the great mother. Everything is from her. So my mother's uncle changed this fireplace that my mother had asked for. When he was in the marines, he said, his job was to carry the anchor. It was very heavy. The anchor was put in the water to hold the ship stable. So that's why he wanted to make a shape of an anchor, because it stays in one place—it doesn't move, being in the water and not moving.

I remember my other uncle said, "No, you can't do this, it's from the white man's world." There was an argument and a discrepancy about changing the altar. The Cheyenne were going through great changes in their culture, and my mother was one of the ones pushing the edge of the culture. Both her uncle and then her nephew said they wanted to use the anchor altar too. The Native American troops were returning home, bringing their experi-

Tipi at Margaret's home in Lame Deer, Montana, United States, 2014

ence in the U.S. government military training, in the wars. They were bringing it back to the ceremony. My grandpa liked it. "Our warriors are coming back home, they are veterans. They know something, they earned their life, and so they can put it in the altar, they can change their altars around because every roadman has their own altar."

This white couple came to my grandpa and told him, "Our baby boy is sick. Our friends told us to come here to the Indians because you've got some kind of magic." So Grandpa said, "We've never doctored white people yet. I have to ask." He asked his brothers, who said, "We have to doctor him because he's from the Creator." So they put up the tipi, brought this baby into the ceremony, and doctored him. The baby got well and the parents always reminded him, "You were very ill and those Cheyenne Indians are the ones who cured you."

At that time our Indian people had to go underground with the ceremonies, they had to hide at night. All ceremonies were illegal. So this white boy grew up to be a lawyer and then a senator for Oklahoma, Carl Cunningham. He came to my grandpa and he said, "I can help you to protect and legalize this ceremony." My grandpa said, "This would keep us out of jail, you know?" Carl Cunningham helped draft the papers. He said, "We have to call it a church." So it became the Native American Church.

And see, that's where the men came in. Although the women made the ceremony, they needed men for the government legalization. The government sent people to investigate what was going on in this ceremony. So that was when they put the men in there to disguise, or legitimize, what was going on.

In the very beginning, I was told there was no roadman, because everything was equal. But when they made the charter, the legal church, they had to put a leader. So that's how they now have a roadman. That way, if the government looked at it they would know that they had men leaders. They adopted the model of the priest, you know.

We use the peyote medicine in our ceremonies. The medicine grows only around Mirando City, Rio Grande City, in the southern part of Texas and then on into Mexico. There are many stories about our medicine. There was a man named Quanah Parker, his mother was a white lady, his father was Comanche. He had one blue eye and one brown eye. He was a half-breed. Once he was very sick, dying. A Mexican lady, a *curandera*,[2] doctored him with the peyote and he came back to life. Then he took that peyote back to Oklahoma and the people started using it. They were just using it one to one. And then it got put in the Native American Church ceremony, because the NAC was a healing place where they prayed. That's how peyote got to be considered a sacrament. They had to write it into the ceremony, legalized as a sacrament. Quanah Parker was a very, very great doctor. I heard stories about how he brought lots of people back to life through the peyote.

It has another story to it. Around where it grows down in Texas there's the same thorn they say that Jesus had around his head. They don't know how it got there, but it protects the peyote. And they call the peyote *the little people*. That's another whole story. Different people have stories about the peyote as *little people*.

2. A traditional healer.

There's another story about the peyote. A mother lost her son, and she was walking in the hills or the prairie. She told her people to go ahead and move camp. She was staying behind to find her son, and while she was walking she saw this humble cactus. The spirit of the cactus said: *Eat, eat me. Eat this plant, it's a medicine, and you will find your son.* So she ate the medicine and she began wandering by herself. And the wind, the way the wind would blow, she began singing these songs. She sang these wind songs, and through the wind, through her songs and her journey with the medicine, her determined prayers, she found her people's camp. And there she found her son with her people in camp. So she gave the medicine to her people. She showed them how to have the ceremony. The elements—the earth, the wind, the fire, the water—were very important in this ceremony. And the medicine. And that's how the Cheyenne tell the story. That a mother brought this ceremony. So there are many stories around it that the women were the ones who made this ceremony.

I heard my grandmother and grandfather say, *Peyote doesn't belong to anybody. It has its own life, it has its own way.* Some peyote are called *chiefs.* You know all of this language is disguised for the white people, the government. Because our ways were underground. A *chief peyote* has thirteen markings on it. They are rare to find.

I must have been about thirty-five, and one of my uncles, Rutherford, got a stick out of that fire and started making thirteen markings, or rays, in the coals. He said, "Look, Margaret, you know you've seen this before." And I looked at it and I said, "Yeah." He said, "Even the chief peyote up there has thirteen markings." I said, "Yeah." He said, "And

you, you're one of the lights." I didn't want to believe it. I thought it was really nothing the way he said it, the way he told me, until I was invited to the Thirteen Grandmothers Council. And still, even now I don't tell that story because I don't feel comfortable. I'm shaking. How could I even claim this? That they said those thirteen markings on that chief were going to be the Thirteen Grandmothers, and that one of them was going to be me.

NAC Teachings

Each part of the Native American Church ceremony has meaning. Like the water drum. That drum, it means the heartbeat. It's got everything in there. There are seven rocks that tie the drum, and that is the Pleiades. Then her skin, the mother hide, the mother animal gives of herself for her children. Then the water is in her womb. She has also the balance of that shell from the ocean, the charcoal from the fire in the water. The rope to tie her also represents the umbilical cord.

The drumstick comes from a tree, the *Tree of Life*. I've seen people doctor with it. They can touch where you're hurting, where your pain is, where you're ailing. They just touch the tip of that drumstick and that drumstick pulls that sickness out. You know, whoever's drumming is in tune with the way the world is on its axis. It's moving around. All of that motion, it's all for healing in the ceremony. People go there and get well.

There's a fire in the middle of the tipi, a whole other central being. Two women gave me the fire and told me to use it to help people. They said the fire called me, that was their interpretation. I use it like a

"Grandmothers Wisdom, Mother Tipi." Gouache on paper by Angelina Nasso, 2019

fortune-teller. The one old lady gave me that and then the other old lady, she gave me the coals. The fire's talking to me, it's the one instructing me. I get the coals and I put it in front of me. It's higher than me, higher than a holy person, very holy. Another part of that is when a person comes to me and they're scared and they want protection. I get a hot red coal from the fire and put it in water and I have them drink it. That's the protection. So that's what the old ladies gave me.

Then there's the wood, which has a whole other story. The wood comes from the Tree of Life. And the Tree of Life has its own way of doctoring us. We need these trees, and the trees are there, they're the sacrifice. They sacrifice their life. The fire man, when he goes to get wood, has to get his own wood. So he knows what every notch is and he knows how he knocked the tree down. This fire man, everything that he does with wood is about a prayer of life. It is about the medicine wheel, the movement of that medicine wheel. He's got to keep the ceremony moving along.

There's also a cedar man in the ceremony, usually an older person who has lived his life. He's the one who carries the cedar. The cedar incense is forgiveness. The story is that—it didn't say it was a man or a woman—but that a person came to the Creator and said, *I love people so much I want to do something for them.* So the Creator said, *Go and stand on the mountain or the hill.* And the Creator told them, *You will never change color, you will always stay green, year round. When human beings smell the incense, they will know that they're forgiven and they're comforted. It will be that way.*

Margaret's ceremonial gourd rattle

The sound of the gourd rattle is to touch the heart, the spirit. Calling the spirit.

The sound of the gourd rattle is to touch the heart, the spirit. Calling the spirit. They say the rocks in the gourd came from a volcano. All the parts make electricity, they spark. The gourd shell can be very delicate. To prepare the rattle, the shell has to be cooked and cured in a certain way. And when you're going through the process of curing that shell, it can break. So it's kind of delicate. They also say when you use it to sing it will reveal what kind of person you are. If you're angry, it's going to crack. If it's too thin, it's not going to sound right. You know, there's a certain way to get that sound. It's not just a sound. It's hard for me to explain that.

And then there's the horsehair. The first animal that was sent to help the Cheyenne was the horse. We became horse people. So they put it on their rattles and then they had other animal hairs. There's something like the white one they call ermine, and I think they had some bear and porcupine.

Then there's the staff. I was told the staff represents the lightning. Lightning to light our world and also lightning to doctor—just real quick. Also the staff is the snake. The snake changes life. Transitions, it changes life. The staff too is decorated with horsehair and also an eagle feather, sometimes an eagle plume. It's an instrument used to doctor with because the eagles, the claws can kill you and can heal you that quickly too. The staff is life and death. Then alongside the staff they put the little rolled-up sage. And that sage is to clean our spirit, so our spirit can go ahead. The sage clears a way, clears us off so we can go where we need to go. And when the sage is used to doctor people, they have to put it right up to their nose, rub it, smell it. It cleans our spirits.

Then the feathers, and the different birds. The most important one I know is the flicker. It doctors really fast. Like a bee, it stings you. It's a real fast doctor. The next one is the swift hawk, which is preferred because it's really precise. It's direct and knows where to go. And then there's the eagle. The eagle is the one that is

Golden eagle (*Aquila chrysaetos*)

always watching over us. He's the protector. It protects us. Angel, big angel. They call the red-tailed hawk for newness. New things, like when you don't know something and you want an answer, you call the red-tailed hawk. Another caring or doctoring bird, the magpie, is the one that takes care of death. It's not bad, but it's the one that cleans up death. You know? Then the plumes are more special. They're more special and they're more spiritual, they're more angel-like. If you see a plume, it's like an angel. Pure. It's more perfect. It's more ultimate.

Water is so essential to us, and the water bird showed us where it was. The water and the morning star go together, they're symbols of the Native American Church. For the Cheyenne, we call ourselves the *Morning Star* people, the beginning of the new day, the beginning of time. There are ceremonies with the water birds, the ceremony with the morning star.

In the morning of the ceremony the mother comes in and prays with the water. And with the mother's love she will sanctify all the prayers that have been said, and it will be all true when she sits there. My grandma used to say, "I will lock all the prayers and send them out. It's already that way." She would touch the ground. "Your prayers are already there. It's already happened. So be it, it's already that way." Once she said it, she didn't really go on and on.

My father told me, he said when you bring in the water in the morning, the mother is giving birth to the dawn. When you're bringing in the water, when the woman sits there in that seat, it's holy, it's very holy. Her

Water is so essential to us, and the water bird showed us where it was. The water and the morning star go together, they're symbols of the Native American Church. For the Cheyenne, we call ourselves the Morning Star people, the beginning of the new day, the beginning of time.

presence, when she sits there, everything has already taken place, like God. God granted everything. So when she sits there the star crowns her. Both Arapaho and Cheyenne people, we are Morning Star people. And the Morning Star is the mother of us all.

Then in the final part of the ceremony the sacred food is brought into the tipi. The corn is the mother, the meat is the father, and the berries are the children, represents children. That sacred food represents family.

My grandpa would say, "Before you enter the tipi, drop yourself outside and come in as spirit. Leave your baggage outside and you can pick it up in the morning. If you need it."

My mother fell off a horse and broke her hip. The doctors said they would have to break her bone and reset it. My grandfather said, "No, we're not going to do that. We're going to put up a tipi for you." So she got doctored with the peyote. So she walked out of the tipi. She had a limp, but she walked out. And it is through this healing that I was born.

My mother was very devoted to the Native American Church because of her own healing. And I came through that healing. So I came to be passionate about the church too. I became curious about it. "Where did you get this? Where did you get that? Why did you do this? Why did you do that?" My grandparents loved it. And my uncle, he said, "This one is going to bring the old into the new world."

That's why I'm not afraid now to speak to you about the eagle, the eagle whistle, and these sacred things. This whistle is used at the crack between the old and the new: *Okay, we're finished with this night and we're in the morning now.*

Healing Path

I got married and I had a big wedding in 1970. I married a man who I wanted—educated, handsome, all of that. And then one day we went shopping and I asked for a pair of panty hose that were ninety-nine cents, and he didn't answer until we got in the car. We got in the car and I got a slap in the face. "How dare you ask for something we don't have money for?" he said. From then on I was a battered wife. I remember little incidents like that. I couldn't look out the window. Whoever I was looking at, he'd say, "You want him?" and he'd backhand me.

I remembered parts of growing up where I was always startled, scared. Always on guard because I'd get beaten. I remembered when I was in the mission school, first being hit and how it made me feel. It made me feel like nothing. Like I was nothing. Then here I was getting battered by my love, my husband, and feeling that *nothing* again, remembering that feeling of *nothing*. And so I lived like this for sixteen years. Alcoholism was taking its toll, and I began drinking with my husband. And then I began finding myself not wanting to remember, not remembering a beating.

And I'd flash back and forth between my childhood and my married life, wondering and asking myself, *What did I do to deserve this? Why am I being beaten up?* I had to have done something wrong.

So this went on for sixteen years. When my oldest daughter was turning fifteen, the school reported that she was always fighting the kids or the teachers. My youngest daughter was in Head Start. She was not talking, she wouldn't talk. They came to get me and said she wouldn't speak, and they were sending her to a speech therapist. And then my son, I noticed my son questioned everything. Questioning why we didn't have bread in the house and why his father said that there was no bread. So I saw the behavior of my kids and then of myself.

I was beginning to be very angry and I was hiding a lot of stuff. My kids were reacting to all of this. Sometimes my husband would sit on his knees and he would cry. He would say he was sorry, and I was so willing to forgive. And then within an hour or whatever it was, he would start beating me again. And I thought, *What happened with saying "I'm sorry?"* And he'd do it again. It was the same thing as when I was in the government boarding school. I remember I cut across the lawn and walked on the grass, and the nun saw me and said, "You're not to walk on the grass, you'll be punished."

And so I started drinking with my husband, because he was the one who was the boss. He was the authority, you know? So I became a drinker with him, and I was feeling like I was okay, you know? I was on the same level. I was able to be with the alcohol, to be happy, to pretend I was happy.

I could be the other person, being slapped, being hit, being beaten up. And then the worst would happen when I was drunk and I finally would be able to talk to him about it: "Why did you beat me up? Why did you hit me?" I felt brave enough to talk to him in this way when I was drunk. Then he would beat me even worse. Our children would be screaming and trying to get help, and they would tell people what we were doing: "They were drinking and my father beat my mother up

because my mother was asking him why he beat her up." Or "She was cussing him out for beating her up, so he beat her up again." This was ongoing and very difficult.

Then finally he took me to a breaking point. He'd have this look on his face, and when I would see this behavior I wouldn't want the children to see him beat me up. I thought I was saving my children. So I got in the truck and we drove off. My husband drove me out to this place, stopped the truck, got me out, and started beating me up. I remember images of a rag doll, him throwing me around and kicking me. I played like I was dead. Then he got in the truck and he ran over me. As he ran over me I thought, *Why am I allowing someone else to hurt me, someone else to kill me? Why am I doing this?* This is what I thought when I was rolling back and forth under the truck tires. And then the worst thing was, *I bought that truck.* And so right then, something snapped inside; I began looking at myself.

I had just gotten an inheritance from my father and bought the truck. I bought the truck and I'm allowing him to run over me with my truck. Why didn't I just go and get a gun and kill myself? But the question was: *Why didn't I like myself?*

Then there were people who came to help. I saw a light. It was an old man and an old lady. They came with a flashlight and they helped me. They took me to their house, and in my mind I thought they were grandparents because they were old people.

I thought, *Jesus, they're angels! They came to help me.* I was in a daze. They called an ambulance, called the police. It was way out in a rural area, and these were Spanish people. I thought I was dreaming, you know? Like these were my grandparents saving me, like they saved me from the boarding school.

I called my sister-friend Carolyn. She was one whom I trusted, and she came right away. The ambulance came and took me to the ER. They had to wire my jaw because of the extreme beating. I remember one doctor saying, "I don't know how she's lived." I could have drowned in my own blood. I remember another doctor saying they were going to call a plastic surgeon. Here I was, overhearing these doctors talking, helping me. They were helping me and so I felt like I had to live. I had children to live for.

I remember I was worried because I had to go to the (tribal) council, to the officials of the village, and tell them I was leaving and taking my kids. So I got my car and my kids and I left. The Catholic marriage was really what I believe kept me there all that time. Even through all the beating and the betrayal. He was going with other women too. My story was the classic story of a woman being betrayed by her husband. So I felt I had to stay hidden. And I had the pattern with my family. Over the years I would go to my family when I was getting beaten up. Finally my uncle said, "Don't come back here beat up. I'm tired of it." My sister said the same thing.

So this time I had no place to go, so Carolyn was the one I called. I had to stay in hiding for a year. I filed for my divorce, and I was scared of him. I was so afraid even for my children. My children were always crying for their father, "I want my daddy." I almost gave in to them, but I knew that this time I couldn't. I knew I had to do something.

I was with this group of women who really supported me. I began going to this battered women's shelter to volunteer, to cook or to clean. Just to volunteer, to understand what this battered women's shelter was about and to help in some way, and at the same time to look at myself and learn about myself. I was a battered woman. So from there I learned a lot about women being beaten. I saw women who were in the same place that I was and maybe even worse.

Very, very shocking, but I learned all of this in that battered women's shelter. I must have been there about two years and then I told my story, how I got out. You know, we had a Catholic marriage. My husband was very educated; he held a high position in the tribe. And for others to know that he beat me up, it was really in that time an unbelievable story. So from there I still continued to drink. I believed I had the right or that it was my reward, that I could drink.

I went through the divorce and I met my second husband and had a rebound marriage. My second husband was so kind and so gentle, so different than the first husband. I was a full-blown alcoholic by then. I felt secure with him. He took care of me while I was drinking. He was really not a drinker; he balanced out my first husband. I felt so much kindness from him and my in-laws. Everything was so amazingly beautiful. We got married by a justice of the peace. We got a house, they gave us a house, and we were all set up, everything was just good, and we were together for eleven years. I was married some good thirty years of my adult life. I was also doing my pottery then. I became known as a potter. I received the top award in the art show at Indian Market in three categories. And I was drunk. Something was happening to me. I started thinking, just like with the first husband, that I didn't like myself. *Why didn't I just kill myself?*

With my second husband, we were just drinking and partying. My artwork balanced it out. I would make my artwork and then reward myself with drinking. I decided to leave my second husband because one day I realized I didn't love him. But it was really nothing about that; I knew that I had to get sober. I knew I couldn't live like that. I was tired of living like that. I was coming to that part where it was the same thing over and over: wake up with a hangover with no control over it, and start drinking again. I was neglecting my artwork and my children. And my daughter had her first baby and I was thinking, *I don't want my grandchildren to see me drunk.*

Finally I told my husband, "We need to go to treatment." He said, "Okay." He was always pleasing me; whatever I wanted to do, he was willing to go along with me. We went to treatment together, and he stayed only three or four days. He said, "I have to go home to check the house and pay the bills." So I stayed. I think he was surprised that I stayed. He knew that I was serious and wanted to get sober.

My husband would come and visit me, but he was a pot smoker. The people in the treatment center saw how my husband would come in high. Even the people in treatment with me, they said they could see. It really got my interest when this one man said, "Margaret, we talk among ourselves and we see you, we see you with your husband and he's high. And there you are, you're sober, and it hurts us. We watch you how you deal with him, and you don't even call him on it. We see what's happening with you, you're beginning to understand something."

So when I was getting ready to leave treatment they asked me, "Are you going back to your husband or are you going to leave him? Because we know that you're not going to stay sober if your husband is using marijuana." So I had a plan. I was rehearsing my plan. I went down to get my overnight bag, my important papers, and my driver license. Our bank book, my valuables. I put them in the suitcase and I came out. I saw my husband lying on the couch watching TV with the remote. He asked me what we were having for supper, if we were going to his mom's or to eat out, or was I going to cook or did I want him to cook.

I remember him saying that and I walked out the door. I had to choose which car I was taking, because we had like four cars outside. I chose the Cadillac and I drove off. I was crying on the street: *What are you doing, Margaret? What are you doing?* Even my girlfriends said, "You have it made, your husband doesn't beat you, he cares for you." But I said, "I don't love him," and they said, "But you can learn to love him, you can make yourself love him." I said, "I've been trying. I did my best, but I couldn't do it."

My grandmother was really powerful in our lives. I've thought about her so many times, how she loved her children, how she loved me, how she could give this love that was so amazing, this love that was so incredible. It was completely unconditional. She was a big motivation for me wanting to be sober; even after she died, her essence was still very present. It was my uncle's influence that was pivotal for my sobriety; he stopped drinking after his mother died. And so I began to think these thoughts when my grandchild was coming. It was such an important moment for me in my life to become a grandmother. I wanted to make it beautiful—something so terrible, I wanted to turn it around and make it beautiful.

Margaret kneading and preparing clay to make a figurine

Margaret holding two of her story-teller dolls in front of a tipi

My grandmother's love was so beautiful, and it stuck with me. I wanted to be like her. My mother's was the same way. And I see my mother in my daughters, I see my grandmother in my daughters, I see myself in my daughters, and now my granddaughters. I have three granddaughters and one great-granddaughter. So I started working on myself because one of my sponsors told me that you have to remember you're the world and you're so powerful that you can change yourself. I had to really work on myself and ask why I was drinking alcohol, and when I went there (to treatment) I had to tell my life story and even about the beating. About being first beaten when I was five years old and that it wasn't my own parents and my grandparents, it was somebody else.

I wanted to understand why I drank. And so I kept asking questions, to my psychiatrist, my counselors, my sponsors in AA, women who were in recovery who sobered up. I asked many questions and I began figuring out things for my own self. I had to really look at myself, I had to like myself. I had to remember that my grandparents and my parents loved me and loved themselves.

And I had to remember that I had children and I loved them, and this grandchild that was coming. Then I had many, many women, all shapes and sizes, all coming to me and helping me. One gave me an apartment on my own so I could be by myself. Another one bought my car and traded it in, so my husband wouldn't find me. Then another one would have prayer meetings for me, prayer sessions for me. I began seeing this change. Even my Tibetan teacher came. I had met her before, when I was with my second husband. She said, "When you

Storyteller dolls handcrafted by Margaret

sober up, I'll be there to help you. Call me." I didn't believe her, but I called her and she was there.

I began learning a whole other life, like I had died. I had a living death. I looked back at the many times that I was out of my body and out of myself and I came back and said: *I had a living death again.* My heart was broken, my heart was cracked wide open, and I had to put it back together myself. Nobody could do it for me. I knew that. I had to come to that understanding.

And then I remember making it through. I was sober, and the director of the treatment center offered me a scholarship to go to school to be a counselor. I said no, I was an artist, I couldn't go. I had my own business. Then I thought about it and I thought, *Nobody offers you something like this.*

It's a miracle to sober up, especially as a Native woman. I went back to my daughter's. Her husband shot himself, committed suicide. I had two grandsons who were not going to have a father. I said to myself, *How am I going to tell them? I need to get equipped.* My grandfather would say, "Study the enemy." We used to study the enemy in Cheyenne history. So I went back to the director and told her I wanted to learn about addiction, I wanted to be a counselor. She said, "What happened?"

Margaret making a storyteller doll

I said, "My son-in-law committed suicide. I have two grandsons; they need to know what happened in the correct way, in the best-educated way." I usually had a husband to help me, a man to help me. This time I was by myself. I said, *I'm going to have to do this by myself.*

I went back to the University of New Mexico, in the psychology department. I learned lots of things on the way. Afterward I went to find a job. I remember one employer said, "What is your metaphor for alcoholism in Native country?" I said, "Wildfire." "Wildfire?" I said, "Yeah. I, as a counselor, have to be like a fireman and steady the fire, to steady the environment and the terrain. To make the blocks on the fire, you have to steady the fire where it's going to jump and it jumps." He was really impressed.

By then I had cleaned up two storages of marriage material and had gone to my husbands and asked them for forgiveness. My children were on their own, and I was alone and I said, *My God, that's something. Now I have to go home.* So I came to Montana to connect with my father's side. I moved to the Northern Cheyenne reservation in Lame Deer, Montana, in 2003.

Grandmothers Council

In October 2004 I was invited to become part of the Council of Thirteen Grandmothers. Our mission statement is about world peace, healing Mother Earth and her inhabitants. We were to travel to each Grandmother's home to hold a Council Gathering. So we began in New Mexico with Grandma Flordemayo and finished at Grandma Bernadette's gathering in Libreville, Africa, in July 2015.

My gathering was in 2017. The 11th Council Gathering, July 26–29, 2017. The theme was "Gratitude Brings Freedom." To commemorate my ancestors bringing us back home to Montana, we organized The Ride Home, a historic ride in remembrance of the Cheyenne exodus of 1878. This 1,391-mile journey by horseback commemorated the Cheyenne Breakout, when three hundred of the Northern Cheyenne escaped. My understanding of the story is that it was a Northern woman who led them back, and then they split in the Black Hills

Margaret in full regalia in front of tipi. Lame Deer, Montana, United States, 2014 and Dull Knife went to the Red Cloud reservation, the Red Cloud Agency, and Little Wolf came here to the Tongue River.

The historic horse ride was scheduled for the weeks before the Council Gathering, to be completed in Lame Deer during the council. I joined the riders along the route for prayers and healing ceremonies at these sites of sacrifice: Black Kettle on the Washita; Turkey Springs; Sand Creek Massacre; Punished Woman Creek; Fort Robinson; Noahvose; and Little Big Horn.

The Council Gathering was to be at my house in Lame Deer. But there were eight forest fires going on at the time, so they moved us. The tribal council was concerned that there were no escape routes, so they suggested we move to the *pow wow*[3] grounds in Lame Deer. It was such a big ordeal. It was very amazing. For the first time we had animals coming to the council. The Ride Home completed its journey at the pow wow grounds during the third day of the council. The wolves were there for the first time too.

The highlight of this gathering, I believe, was about historical multigenerational trauma. Alisha Armstrong Custer, a descendent of General George Armstrong Custer, was there. It was amazing. She apologized to the Cheyenne people for her ancestor's actions, what Custer did at the Battle of the Greasy Grass (Battle of Little Bighorn), five generations ago, including the Arapaho and the Sioux.

You know, I was somebody before this council and I still continue to do my work of healing, of dealing with my family, my tribe, and the Cheyenne Elders' Council. I continue to take invitations that are appropriate for me. That's where I'm at. I believe it's all divine intervention, and I really feel it. I feel good about it. The Thirteen Grandmothers Council is a reflection of the conditions of the way we live. The Grandmothers Council is not exempt from that. There is a lot to be learned in council service all over the world. This one council says it's indigenous. There's a lot that is not conforming to the bureaucratic ways. It's a very amazing time.

I'm doing my best to answer this call. So I'm continuing this work.

To be able to talk like this is what I understand, and what I know as a great-grandmother. Many women worked

---

3. A Native American ceremony involving feasting, singing, and dancing.

so hard for us Grandmothers over the years and spent a lot of money volunteering. All the dysfunction shows up, you know. It still comes with it.

Now where I'm at with my life, I've traveled the globe. I see the synchronicity of all religions and I see the different ceremonies, and they're all beautiful to me. I raised my daughters traditionally from their father's side. I raised them in the Cheyenne/Arapaho tradition. We said prayers for each other to *Mahoe*.[4] I came to that understanding after seeing all the ways of prayer in all the countries along my journey.

Maintaining a Healthy Life

As Native Americans, commodity food has been in our lives. My tribe has a food bank, and many of us go there when we don't have any food. I went there a couple of years ago when I didn't have any food and I saw some of the same foods that I grew up with. There was the white flour, yellow corn meal, and powdered eggs. There were canned foods—beef and pork, chicken, canned milk, and powdered milk. There was so much that reminded me of when I was growing up.

I remember we used to mark our softball field with the powdered milk and the cats and dogs used to come and lick it up. We'd get angry with them. Of course we made fried bread with

4. Cheyenne name for the Creator (God).

My grandmother was really powerful in our lives. I've thought about her so many times, how she loved her children, how she loved me, how she could give this love that was so amazing, this love that was so incredible. It was completely unconditional.

the flour, you know? And so there were many ways we filled our stomachs with this commodity food.

The store had apples and oranges in a bag and a bag of potatoes, so they had some fresh vegetables. I really like the beans. I keep asking them, "Give me the beans," so they'll bring them. They have one store here and they do pretty good at getting vegetables in, but sometimes nobody touches them. Nobody even wants them—like the squash and the berries, the raspberries and blueberries. Maybe they don't care about them because we didn't really grow up with those kinds of berries. But bananas, oh, when they bring in the bananas, they're all gone. So we eat a lot of bananas.

Now at my age, I'm finding my digestive system isn't handling that kind of food. My stomach gets bloated when I eat flour or wheat and sugar. I know I'm also unconsciously eating fast foods. It's an emotional eating, constantly just putting it in my mouth. Then my belly is the one that has to really pay for it. And then eating late at night and not getting enough walking around, not moving around makes it even worse.

I do my best to go swimming at 5:30 in the morning. But I have to drive 21 miles one way. I did invite other people to go with me swimming. I like swimming because my bones, my joints, aren't really hurting so much. But other than that, chopping wood around here, carrying wood, and making a sweat lodge, that's my activity.

Everybody's complaining about their joints. Especially at my age. People are complaining about their knees, talking about having knee surgery, hip surgery. It worries me. My own body, I can feel my knees, they're in good shape. I feel like they're in good shape because of my diet. The more that I eat vegetables and turmeric and things that I didn't know were good for my body, the better I feel. I didn't even know I liked these foods. Before, I didn't have time to pay attention to these things. But I'm very fortunate that my joints, my knees especially, are good. I'm very thankful.

There could be some sort of program here to reintroduce the idea of sustainable gardens and growing your own foods. They have gardens around here, but I don't have time, or I don't make time. But can I go and eat fruit? No. Because it's not accessible, it's not right here at hand. Eating fruit here is a luxury. Especially organic food. We have to drive two hours. I believe if good food were accessible and taught and practiced here, then people would be aware and get it. It's a slow thought process, but they would feel the effects.

I've been having smoothies for the past month and I feel good. I even lost a few pounds without having to work at it. But the feeling is really important. It's not impossible to feel this health. But to understand it, to ask for it is like survival, you know? Here on the reservation we just eat what we can, we eat what we've got. We eat sometimes because we don't know when we're going to eat this kind of good food again. It's a hand-to-mouth situation. How to stop the sensation of feeling the food in my mouth but not recognizing that my body has to digest it.

Margaret practicing her horseback riding skills for The Ride Home at Davalon Healing Center in Richmond, Ontario, Canada, in 2012

Ten of the International Council of Thirteen Indigenous Grandmothers at Deer Medicine Rocks, near Lame Deer, Montana, United States, 2012

Nourishment, what is nourishment, feeling nourished? Feeling like you've really had good food. Now in this past month of eating these foods, I know a little bit about it. I had to put thinking and feeling together. I can feel the crunch of the salad and know that it's going to my stomach and that it's okay. I don't have to think of potato chips or something heavy like that. Fast foods, actually those foods that don't have any kind of nutrition in them, are kind of boring.

I think that I just have to take time and make it nice, like in Japan. When I saw the food there, they made it so pretty. A little radish, you know, they made it so pretty, like a flower. And then there were apples and pears. The fruit. The leaves, you know, lemon, wheat, lemongrass, and everything was just so pretty. I didn't even want to eat it, I just wanted to look at it, but we ate it and it felt good.

The things that I saw as a Cheyenne/Arapaho woman, as a spiritual being, traveling the globe! It was so amazing to me to know that I didn't have to chase or want or wish. Now I know what my grandmother, what my grandparents were saying, you know? It was like somehow they already knew. We have it all already, and we share the synchronicity of this understanding with other cultures and other parts of the globe. The synchronicity is really amazing, how the belief systems are alike. People talking about oneness. It takes the whole to make it complete; it takes the little pieces to make this whole being.

EIGHT

GRANDMOTHER FLORDEMAYO

MY NAME IS FLORDEMAYO. I was born and raised in Nicaragua, Central America. My mother had fifteen children, five daughters and ten sons. I was the youngest.

When I was age four, in the middle of the night my mom's voice woke me: "*Hija, despiertece.*" Wake up, daughter!

I immediately opened my eyes. I saw my mom's shadow above me and I answered, "Sí, Mamá."

She said: "Ya viene la cigüeña," the stork is coming. "La vecina va a dar a luz," the neighbor is giving birth.

I jumped up on the bed and my mom said, "We need to hurry, we have to be faster than the stork."

We left the house holding hands and ran through the neighborhood in the dark, guided by the light of the moon. I played with our shadows, making us smaller and bigger.

When we arrived at the neighbors', my mom walked me to the kitchen, where I was served hot cocoa, and she went to deliver the baby.

The person in the kitchen started chatting with me and before long my mom came in with a newborn baby wrapped in a cloth. All you could see was its little face. She handed me the baby and said, "Tell the neighbors what you see around the baby."

This is my first memory of explaining what I saw out of the physical body.

This was my beginning. And that's how I started, journeying with my mom as her apprentice.

Childhood and Migration

Central America is ruled by males. Females have very little opportunity, if any, to be educated, to have a better life, to voice their opinions. My mother was concerned about the life that her five daughters would have if we stayed there. After my father passed away in the '40s, my mother made the conscious decision to begin moving us to the United States.

My mother understood that this is the cultural way in Central America. It's known by many names, but the most common is *machismo*. The women basically have no opinion on who they're going to marry or on how many children they're to have. My mom wanted to give her daughters an opportunity that she didn't have.

Around the 1930s and '40s the United States sent a lot of military to Central America to what is known as the Banana Wars. A marine fell in love with one of my great-aunts. Because my grandmother passed away at childbirth, this great-aunt raised my mom and her sisters. So my auntie was married and living in the United States by 1945.

It was through the help of this auntie that our family started relocating to the United States between 1945 and 1965. We settled in New York City. My siblings stayed back to go to school, but the older ones got working papers or applied for green cards and became factory workers.

My mom went back and forth, bringing the kids into the United States. So over time our family migrated, left our home and everything we had.

My mom gave me the name Flordemayo Rosa María. Flordemayo is the Spanish name for the national flower of Nicaragua, the *sacuanjoche*. I was born in May, when this flower blooms. My mom used the flordemayo as medicine.

When I came to the United States they looked at all of my names and pulled out what was simple for them. When I became an American citizen at the age of seventeen they changed my name to Rose Marie.

In the early '90s, on the airplane moving to New Mexico, I saw my mom in a waking dream. I saw her reflection in the window of the plane. She said, *Hija, from this moment on, I want you to use the name that I've given to you. You are Flordemayo.*

Growing Up

We were not practicing Catholics. I understood from my mom that that was because we did not have money to support the church.

One day when I was six or seven, our very mischievous cousin came to the house and asked my mom if my sister and I could go on an errand with her. My mom gave me *the look*. She always counted on me to do the right thing, just as she could always count on my cousin to do the wrong thing. As soon as we got out the door, my cousin screamed, "You're not going to believe this, but we're going to church!"

"What are we going to church for?" I asked.

She said, "Hey *babosa* (silly girl in Spanish), we're going to the church to get some money. I have a plan." She stuck her tongue out. On her tongue she had a piece of gum. "And here's the other part of the plan." In her dress pocket she had a pocket knife. "I'm going to stick this gum on my pocket knife and pull the money out. And you're going to help me."

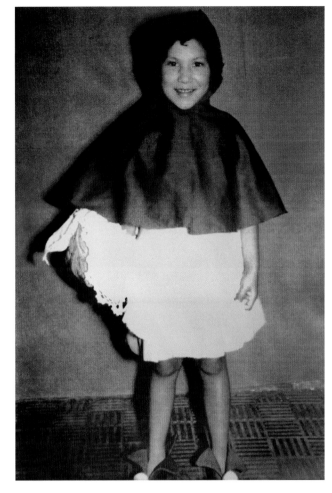

Flordemayo when she was five or six years old. Nicaragua, circa 1954–1955

My sister said, "How much money are we going to get?"

My cousin said, "Whatever we get, we're going to be rich. Not only that, but if you're good I'm going to buy us some gum."

It was the first time I'd ever heard the word "gum," and I said to my sister, "Do you think it's okay for me to have gum?" My sister said, "Yes, if we're rich we can have anything we want."

My job was to be the watch person at the front of the church. I was supposed to make a coughing sound, clearing my throat if I saw the priest or anybody coming. A lot of the elderly people in our community were very nosey, they were always watching all of us getting into trouble. So a lot of times before we'd even get home, my mom would already know.

As soon as my cousin and my sister left me at the door, I broke into hysterical crying. I had snot coming out of my nose, practically touching the floor like melting candles. I was spitting out of my mouth, crying so loud.

Before I knew it, my sister and my cousin came up, shouting, "Hurry up, we've got to get out of here!" I started running and by the time I caught up with them, my sister started shaking my hand. "You're such a baby. Why is it that every time you're told to do something you have to break down crying?"

My cousin said, "Let me wipe the tears off of your face, we are going to be eating *papitas fritas* (french fries)."

I said, "We can have papitas fritas?"

She said, "Yes."

I said, "Besides the gum?" Because I wanted to get everything that I'd bargained for, you know?

And she said, "We are rich, we have fifty-five cents."

Then we went to the store. My cousin said, "We want some papitas." The woman looked us up and down and said to me, "What's the matter, girl?"

I said, "We've come to buy some papitas."

She said, "There's something else going on here!"

I said, "Nothing. I'm just crying because we didn't get some papitas." My sister looked at me, nodding her head. She was proud of my lying.

The woman said, "Well, I know you girls don't have any money, how are you going to buy papitas?"

My cousin said, "We are rich, we have enough money for three bags of papitas."

And so my cousin put her left hand on her hip and her right hand in her pocket and pulled out the money and slammed it on the table. The woman said, "Good, you have enough for three bags of papitas." She made a little cone out of brown paper, folded the bottom, and filled it with papitas.

It was so yummy! I had grease up to my elbows. Then we went to the local mercantile where they had little boxes of Chiclets gum. My cousin said, "You need to eat both of them right away, don't swallow it, just chew on it all day long."

We went back home. My sister had warned me that if Mom saw me with the chewing gum she was going to wonder where we got it. But she didn't notice. I did a really good job hiding it inside my cheeks. That night I went to bed and somehow I lost my gum.

Every morning my mom would comb my tangled curly hair. That morning she found the gum way down in the back of my hair. "Girl, what is this?"

I said, "I don't know."

She said, "I'm sure you *do* know what it is."

I thought about it for a long time. "I think it's gum."

She said, "Yeah, it's gum. Where did you get it?"

I said, "Oh, our cousin bought it for me yesterday."

"Well, now we're going to have to cut the gum right out of your hair. The procession is coming pretty soon, we better have your hair done." It was the day of *la Purísima*.[1]

I was standing outside our door; my mom was holding my hand. People were playing drums, making all kinds of noise, and these two little girls were being carried down the street with a saint. They were dressed like little angels, with little wings and sweet little golden halos.

I started screaming and crying. My mom squeezed my hand. "What is your problem?"

I said, "Mama, I want to be one of those girls."

"We can't."

I said, "Why not?"

---

1. The Immaculate Conception.

"Because we don't have any money."

I stepped back from my mom, put my hand on my hip. "What do you mean we don't have any money? We have money! The church gave us money, we're rich. Why can't I be one of those girls? I want to be an angel; I want to be carried around in a procession!"

My mom put the gum, the money, and the church together and she figured it all out. She turned to my sister. "Do you know anything about what your little sister is saying?"

"No, I have no idea."

My mom grabbed each of our hands and marched us down to my cousin's house, and I thought, *Oh my god, I'm going to get it today.*

So that's how I found out that we didn't have any money to support the church.

My mom said her prayers in whatever way. It was like a personal dialogue. It wasn't associated with the rosary or anything like that. But she had a lot of faith. She always kept a very simple altar with candles and incense burning.

Cumiche

I had a bunch of nicknames. My mom would call me *Cumiche*, the runt. One of my sisters called me *Pipa*, which means baby in baby talk, or *Pipita*, which means little baby. When she was mad at me she would call me *Pipona*, which means big fat baby. Some of my brothers called me *Mica*, which is like a nature spirit, because I was always talking to

Flordemayo when she was around fourteen months old. "I remember my father took that photo. He used to call me *cachetona* (plump-cheeked). I was already potty trained." Nicaragua, circa 1951

everything that was out there. I was the family runt, because I was the baby. I was allowed to do things that none of the other children would do, like walk across the dining room table.

I didn't go to school because public school was very expensive. You had to pay to go to school, for your uniform and supplies. Still, we were always very busy. We took good care of the wild animals in our house who would eventually turn into a meal. I didn't really understand that until I got older. They would disappear from one moment to the other. My mom would use everything she could from the animals. She'd use the fat and make creams and things like that. She took care of feeding the wildlife every day.

We had all kinds of little pet animals. I had a baby sloth and a baby deer. We had iguanas in all different sizes and shapes. We had wild birds. There were a few parakeets that hung around the kitchen door. When they'd hear the church bells in the evening, they would start reciting the rosary together, cackling.

We had a garden. My mom also kept an herb garden. That was one of her passions. I had my own little garden too. When I got old enough, around five years old, every morning I would harvest my greens, carrots, and put them all in my little basket. I would ask my neighbors if they were making soup that day and if they would like to buy some of my veggies. I was very respectful and chatty and I loved receiving payment for my work. So every day I would make fifteen to twenty cents selling my veggies. I'd come home and contribute that to the family.

I was a regular tree climber, and I loved it. I'd climb up and get avocados, mangos, limes, lemons, and any other kind of fruit. I would fill up my basket and go to the neighbors and say, "Are you making juice or lemonade? Would you like to buy some lemons?" They probably had lemons in their yard because in Central America everybody's got all kinds of things. But I think just the gesture of my coming made them buy them from me. I was probably even picking their own lemons, because I would sneak into the neighbors' yards and if they were ripe, they were mine.

We had a lot of fresh fruit and vegetables growing up. Everything we had was fresh. Everything that we ate and drank, including the coffee. I come from a land of coffee. My mom breast-fed me until the time I was four. From when I was a baby she would give me coffee-tea, a very diluted coffee. So I've been drinking coffee all my life. Mom made it special, she would grind it in the grinding stones with cinnamon and nutmeg. Then she would boil fresh milk and put the coffee in. It was really yummy.

Our house had a little kitchen with a dirt floor. The adobe cooking stove had two burners, actually little holes. One hole was bigger, for a big pot, and the other was for a smaller pot. It was a wood-fire stove, very simple.

Our sleeping room was divided by a curtain for privacy, but the other rooms were big. There was a living room and then, of course, the kitchen. We did everyday things on the patio outside. We'd go in the living room for sewing or drawing. We loved to draw as a family, all of us were artists. We'd say, "Let's see who can draw the best parrot!" Once my older brother bought me a set of colored pencils, four or five colors. He would keep the pencil scraps and rub the pieces with his fingers so nothing would get wasted.

My family also did a lot of sewing. All of our clothes were made right in the house. We learned to do a lot of handiwork, crochet and even embroidery on the sheets. Once in a while we would get orphan animals to take care of, if somebody in the neighborhood killed their mom by accident while hunting. My sister and I got the most adorable baby twin howler monkeys. My third oldest sister got into making clothing for the baby monkeys. So we became instant moms. We were too poor to have dolls or toys, but we did have animals. We'd dress them up in very nicely made clothing. When my sisters got older, they worked in the garment district.

Illness and the Gift of Sight

When I had baby animals, if they could be on the bed with me, they would lie down with me. To make a very long story short, one of the howler monkeys was a tuberculosis (TB) carrier and I ended up with TB. I must have been six or seven. So I had a very delicate childhood after that.

My mom tried really hard to heal me. She took me to a lot of different healers, but I ended up in a sanatorium for tuberculosis patients. After that I'd sit on the roof of the house and watch the kids play outside because I couldn't play with them. Being sick was very difficult. I had high fevers and no appetite. The fevers allowed me to do a lot of journeying, a lot of out-of-body work. But my visions and my dreams had started five years earlier when I was around two years old.

In Central America when someone dies, they do the wake in the house and bury them right away because we don't have any refrigeration. When my father died, we, the children, got to witness the body in the house and walk with the casket in a procession to the family burial plot.

After my father was buried, I remember telling my mom and my sister that he was not buried, that he was still in the room. I'd see him standing in the bedroom when we went to sleep at night. Like he was watching over us. My mom would say to me, "Does it scare you?" I would say, "Yes, sometimes."

I didn't particularly like to see him because it was not like an angelic kind of light. I knew the difference between the light of an angel-like being and my father's. My father's light was very dim. Even at that very young age, I was able to see things in different light form. When I saw a nature being that had wings or the *duendes*, which are the little people who take care of the plants, I would go into this ecstatic experience and start talking to them, *What can we do for you?*

All my brothers and sisters, everybody in the family was a seer. Every morning my mom would say to us, "What did you dream?" The whole family went into a dialogue that lasted all morning. Everybody would talk about their dreams and my mom would do the dream interpretation. Some of us learned about it and others didn't. It depended on what kind of interest you had.

I always had an interest in watching nature beings, like the duendes and the little *micas*. The micas are the nature spirits. They're like fully grown people, but about two feet tall. There are different little societies that live in different dimensions, and depending on the person, you can see through these veils of dimensions. They're good beings. They're not mischievous.

The duendes are good too. They are mostly involved in taking care of the land, like forests. They are guardians of the plants, but they're very close to the humans. Duendes travel in groups and they come in different sizes. They're androgynous little beings and they take care of the forest and the plants.

My mom told me, "When babies are born, the duendes are there at birth." The duendes receive the baby and hold it. The baby starts a relationship with the duende, it's a personal little buddy, like your guardian. When you see your duende, you know that you have this closeness with nature.

Duendes develop a relationship with you until you die. There are older folks in Mexico and Central and South America who say, *Oh, I'm getting ready to die, because my duende has come to get me.* The duendes come just before you die and they take you into the spirit world.

When I was a kid I became fascinated with the duendes and wouldn't stop asking my mom about them. One night, my mom woke me up: "Come and see where the duendes have been." She took me into the kitchen, to look at the wood stove ashes. My mom was 4'11" and she lifted me and said, "Do you see those marks? Those are little duende feet." There were marks of little tiny bare feet with very wide fanned-out toes. She said to me, "From now on, if you ever see these little feet in the dirt or the mud you'll know that they've come." I went into a place of total exhilaration.

When I first came to the forty acres in New Mexico, there was an invisible tiny circular door next to the refrigerator that the duendes would go in and out of. They gather together outside around a little fire. Once in a while, I'll see my mom's spirit come and bring wood for

them. One of these days I'm going to paint a little pink round door in the corner of the house so that everybody knows that the little people come in and out of there. So that we don't disturb them. When I have people stay here I tell them, "Be careful leaving your shoes outside because the little people love to play around." I say this because some shoes have gone missing.

Emilio, a colleague of mine, a master farmer from Bolivia, has a farm in New Mexico. Every year he puts over 7,000 medicinal herbs in the ground. He starts them in the greenhouse in February and just before the summer comes, he transplants them out in the field. Once I stood in front of the big cottonwood tree on the way down to the fields and I said to the tree, "I'm asking for permission to enter this sacred place. Do I have your blessings to come in?" I stood in front of the cottonwood tree and the little duendes came out from the back of the tree, thirty or forty of them. I became overwhelmed. They gathered all around me. They were all naked, little androgynous beings circling around me, and I started crying.

One of the little duendes said to me in this sweet duende voice, almost like a child, *Flordemayo, where have you been? We've been waiting for you.* When I heard that, I cried, *Oh, I'm so sorry, I'll never do this again. I'll make an altar for you. I'm always going to take care of you, no matter how old I get.* They were touching me and hugging me and said, *It's okay, we're so happy to see you.*

How do you collect thirty, forty duendes in your lifetime? I've been doing a lot of work. When I told Emilio, we started crying together. We erected a shrine for the duendes right there. We brought little toys,

children's food, things that they would love. We keep fresh flowers for them. All over the world I build little altars for the duendes, it doesn't matter where I go.

Somehow through the love and unconditional devotion I have for these little beings, I can see them. The gift of seeing has always been with me. I think being sick with tuberculosis, having high fevers made me more sensitive. I lived like that for a long period of time, in a state of delirium. That sickness changed my life. It gave me that extra sense of knowing and gave me a lot of patience with people who are sick.

I was kept in the dark all through my childhood, as a kid and a teenager. I could have died. People didn't survive that, not in Central America at that time. My TB got really full blown before I was taken to the sanatorium to be cured. That's where children with tuberculosis were taken. It was the most awful place. I remember every detail of it. It smelled. All of the kids were crying all of the time, day and night. I remember getting a lot of injections, going through a lot of x-rays. But whatever they gave me to heal, worked. I went back home and I survived. I could barely walk. That is one of the reasons my brothers and sisters carried me everywhere, because they didn't want me to overdo it.

It wasn't until I was in my twenties, already with a child, that I went to a lung specialist who said, "Did you know that you have more scarring on one lung than the other?" I said, "No, I didn't know." I now see a lung specialist once a year. You're kind of branded for the rest of your life once you get TB. My lungs are very sensitive. I have trouble breathing, and sometimes I have to wear a mask if it's very dusty or smoky.

The sickness kept me home with my mother, and I really learned a lot with her. She said I spoke very early and was a very clear communicator. I would be very focused and if I wasn't satisfied with the answer, I would continue to ask more questions.

I was always doing everything she did. My generation did everything from scratch. My mother would prepare *cremadas*, which are creams, massage oils. She would teach me as she was doing it. But when she was dissecting animals to get their fat, she didn't go into details. She knew how squeamish I was because I loved my animals too much. We were poor, and that's the way that life was. When she was grinding the corn she'd say, "This is the way you take the kernels, and you place them in the center and you hold them in that direction." I learned to do all of these things like that, it became second nature.

Mom was very fastidious, very clean. She would get up at 4:00 in the morning and take a cold shower and do laundry and by 6:00 she had already ground coffee and got everything going. We never had white sugar. We'd buy a chunk of raw brown sugar, wrapped in banana skin. Everything was very basic and simple. We'd have fresh tortillas with a little bit of beans and a little bit of *queso*, cheese. My mom made the cheese in the house. After it was cured, you'd wrap it in banana skin and put it away in a little basket. She made everything.

Visionary Dreams

One morning, I was sharing my dream in our family dream conversations. I dreamed I was older, in a place where I was speaking a different language. I ran and I fell and it was frozen. I didn't know what snow was, but I knew what ice was because my cousin had a refrigerator.

That same day, my mom was washing clothes and said, "Mija (colloquial Spanish for 'my daughter'), come here. Do you remember your dream? We're going to a country where they speak a different language.

They have a different kind of weather; it gets very cold and there will be snow. We're going to go together, you and I."

Moving away from Nicaragua was very strange and devastating. I went from living a tropical life, being outside every day, surrounded by animals, watching birds, butterflies, bees, and all kinds of little critters, to a life surrounded by concrete and tall buildings. The only trees there were at the cemetery, right next to our building. The rest of it was concrete. It was very difficult and very shocking.

Everything was a new experience: going into the elevator, walking down the metal stairs, getting out of the building. There were metal and glass doors with a key. I had no idea what a key was. I learned how to speak English by listening. And so I speak the way that I do from listening. It was all very traumatic.

Everything changed very drastically and dramatically. We didn't have refrigeration in Nicaragua. I never got used to drinking cold things out of the refrigerator. We didn't have soda or packaged juices in Nicaragua, we'd have fresh drinks. My mom had to cook on a gas stove; we had an indoor toilet, no outhouse. We had a laundry room in the building, learned how to use a washer and dryer. In Nicaragua we used to bathe in cold water because that was all we had. And here you bathe in warm water. Even now, as an old lady, I use cold water to bathe.

Mother's Illness

I had a vision that my mother was walking without stepping on the floor. I told her about it. Another time I had a vision where she had no physical body, just a light body. I was around seventeen and the only one living with her. She was beginning to feel sick. Once my mother was diagnosed with breast cancer in November, she predicted that she would not live longer than six months. She passed in April. She had a mastectomy, but she was never good after that.

I was the one who took care of her. Her body got so frail that she got a hairline crack on her hip bones just by me putting her on the potty. Our lives changed from a mother and daughter relationship to a caretaker and a mom. I was responsible for taking care of her at night. One of my sisters would come during the day to cook all of her meals and bathe her. She would stay home with us until Mom went to bed.

We took care of her until she needed to be catheterized and they admitted her to the hospital. She didn't live much longer after that. I was with her when she took her last breath. She didn't speak English, so she was never left alone, either in the house or in the hospital. The nurses didn't bathe her or anything like that. We took care of her.

I had already been going out with Marshall for about a year. Mom felt confident that he was my man. She absolutely loved Marshall, and he loved my mom. He'd come over every day and she would feed him some of her yummy Nicaraguan food.

Love and Marriage

A month after my mom died, Marshall and I got married. I went from being a young daughter, as my mom would say, a child, to becoming a wife.

I started a new journey with my husband, who is very much a Western man. He is *americano*, born in the U.S.A. When he was seventeen he went to the university for art, and later became an art teacher. He has two degrees, one as an art teacher and a master's degree as a social worker.

We started a new life in a tiny studio apartment in New York City. Marshall shared my passion for pets and wild animals. So we got a teeny-weeny Yorkshire Terrier. We also had a fish tank with tropical fish and a couple of tropical birds.

I became pregnant that year and gave birth to our first child. As a young mom, I remember embracing my daughter with so much love and caring, as I was going through a period of loneliness and missing my mom. We were a very creative family, always doing some kind of art. When Marshall graduated, we moved to a farming community in the Adirondacks. I had a second child there. The children were five, six years apart. It was beautiful, but the cold weather was very severe for me. We had nine months of winter, two months of mud, and one month of actual summer. I kept a garden and always cut and carried wood to heat our house. I had to get used to this kind of winter life.

The Heart of the Center

While we were in the Adirondacks in the early 1970s there was a little yellow school bus traveling across the country, carrying a group of prominent indigenous elders from North, South, and Central America. The inspiration for this pilgrimage began in what is known as the *Heart*

You always have this yearning about where you come from and who you really are.

of the Maya. They were bringing awareness through the Americas, following the guidance of the Mayan prophecies, inviting people to come together through the gathering of the condor and the eagle.

Don Adrián Inés Chávez, a very respected Guatemalan Quiche Mayan elder and linguist, asked me to translate for him. One elder spoke of the coming period of the '80s, known as the *Harmonic Convergence.* He said that the planets were going to align, and humanity would become more aware of the presence of the divine. Many people were being awakened or reawakened around the world. So I was present when these words were delivered to the public, and they stayed in my heart throughout my life.

At that time, I was a young woman, a young mom, still walking around in a state of loneliness and longing, having lost my mom. She had been my one and only teacher I could talk to about my visions and messages. I felt a sense of incredible spiritual loneliness. So in finding these elders and especially in finding that one Mayan elder, I started feeling that I wanted to know more about my people. I felt like I had a hole in my heart. I would go into daily prayer and ask the Creator to bring me a teacher, a traditional priest from my culture who prayed in his native language.

I had taken the path as a wife and a mom, but I knew that there would be a day when I would be able to go out and be with this elder. I held myself in a place of contentment with my everyday life, with the children, taking care of my husband, taking care of the garden and my animals. I learned to make baskets, beading, and all kinds of things. It became a way of not only learning something different but also bringing in additional income.

When I came to the United States, I did not know how to read or write. I had no sense of direction as far as where exactly Nicaragua was in relation to New York. It wasn't until I became older that I started believing I actually could travel back home and meet other indigenous and nonindigenous people of prayer.

So in my twenties, I just barely knew about my own culture. You always have this yearning about where you come from and who you really are. I had this admiration and love for these elders, and a desire to know more about my ancestors, about my mom's and my father's peoples, who originated in Guatemala.

My roots are Guatemaltecas. As I understand it, my people were among many who migrated out of the country in the late 1800s from the old capital of Guatemala, Antigua, because it was destroyed by several natural disasters. Everybody in Central America has a large percentage of native blood, and we also have a percentage of Spanish blood. Our Spanish blood usually shows in someone who has lighter skin and lighter eyes. I found out that my mother's father came from the Canary Islands in Spain.

I was able to journey to the Canary Islands to connect with the teachings of my Spanish side, of my grandfather's people. It was a very beautiful journey for me. I also returned to Guatemala to find the teachings of my ancestors. So I have been on this quest to find out where exactly my family and my people come from.

Vision of New Mexico

While living in the Adirondacks, I had a vision of four eagles lifting me and bringing me across the United States into New Mexico. An invisible voice said, *You need to live here.* I woke up from the vision and told Marshall, "My Creator is asking me to go to New Mexico." He said, "New Mexico? I can't move to New Mexico, I haven't retired!"

So I started packing the house. Marshall would go to work and I'd pack the house like we were moving. One day he came home and said, "My university is calling for social workers from out of state. So how would you like to go on vacation to New Mexico?"

We rented a car and Marshall went to different interviews all over New Mexico. And sure enough, he got a job. He said, "Would you like to move to New Mexico? They want me here in fifteen days."

Photo by Russell Richards, courtesy of Flordemayo's family archive

I said, "We're already packed, all we have to do is drive the moving truck." Sure enough, we were in New Mexico before he was to start his new job.

Meeting My Teacher, Don Alejandro

One day a friend told me that a Mayan high priest elder, Don Alejandro Cirilo Perez Oxlaj, was going to be in New Mexico and that he was looking for someone to translate for him. When I met him I was overcome. I started crying and said, "Beloved elder, I've been waiting for you for quite some time."

He said, "Beloved daughter, what month were you born? What date? What year?" He started thinking about the day on which I was born, based on the Mayan calendar. This cosmic birth chart is based on Mayan tradition and lore. He said, "You have all of the aspects of becoming a priestess, but you need to get going because your chart shows that you should have started seven years ago."

When I showed Don Alejandro a photograph of Don Adrián, for whom I had translated in the Adirondacks, Don Alejandro told me that he was a high priest of the Mayan Nation. He was the one who had initiated Don Alejandro to start walking through South America to meet with indigenous people. That brought my relationship with Don Alejandro to a whole different place. Don Alejandro's teacher was my teacher too. And now Don Alejandro was my teacher.

From the moment that my mom passed, I had a void in my heart. Since then, I'd been looking for a teacher. I said to him, "This hole in my heart, the emptiness of not having a physical person to speak to about my dreams and visions is beginning to close."

In the Mayan tradition, if you agree to study with a teacher, you are together until either you die or the teacher dies, and it doesn't stop there, because it continues even after death. We take our teachers very seriously. We don't separate ourselves from our teachers. We

Don Alejandro Cirilo Perez Oxlaj and Flordemayo in ceremony

might have our differences, and even go through a period where maybe we are not seeing things in the same way. We might even go through a period where we don't see each other, because we are in the process of praying about it all.

Don Alejandro had come from Guatemala to the United States to meet with the Hopi and the Pueblo elders. He had come to invite them to the Heart of the Maya for a gathering of the condor and the eagle. He invited me to travel with him to visit the Hopi and Pueblo elders. I went home, dropped off my groceries, packed some clothes, and got in a van with Patricio Dominguez and a couple of Mayan priests, including Don Alejandro.

We went to Nambé Pueblo and from there we drove to the Hopi. After we had driven all night long, suddenly Don Alejandro said, "Stop!" We stopped the van and rolled down the window. Two people leaned in: "Do you have the Mayan high priest inside?" And we said, "Yes, he's here." They invited us into their home and Don Alejandro shared the prophecy of the gathering of the condor and the eagle with these Hopi people. He encouraged the elders to come to this first gathering in Guatemala.

The invitations were done in this way, going place to place inviting people. Don Alejandro had an intuitive way of knowing where to go. This was the early '90s when Don Alejandro and the Mayan Nation had the first gathering of the condor and the eagle. They brought together 150 indigenous elders from as far south as Patagonia and as far north as Canada. Don Alejandro invited me to come to Guatemala for these ten days of prayers and pilgrimage to sacred sites.

The elders there decided to bring the prophecies and teachings to Colombia, South America. A community in Putumayo, in Colombia's Amazon region, hosted this gathering. It was in an area that was known as the land of the condor.

Then Don Alejandro gave me and a couple of other folks who lived in North America the mandate to bring people together in North America, as a continuation of the gathering of the condor and the eagle. The prophecy said we needed to bring all of the people together before the year 2000.

My colleagues and myself formed a nonprofit organization in New Mexico called the Confederation of Indigenous Elders of the Americas. I held the position of president and vice-president. So in 1999, before the completion of this prophecy, we brought together people from South, Central, and North America. This all began for me in the early '70s. I didn't know I would be involved in the completion of this prophecy in the making.

Growing with My Spiritual Teacher

One beautiful thing that I've learned from knowing Don Alejandro for this long is that teachers are also humans, in the process of learning as teachers. If you meet someone you want to study with, it is human nature to hold them in adoration. It is natural for us to feel that this person is absolutely a divine being, when in reality we are still human beings. There are a lot of expectations put on those human teachers. When I saw the humanness in Don Alejandro, sometimes I was turned off. But

it wasn't his issue, it was mine. Because I had put him on a pedestal.

My mom taught me that as women we need to be respected and honored. She had surrendered so much of herself and her family and her people in Nicaragua so that we could have a better chance. She sacrificed her way of life for us younger women to have a better life. To have choice. Not to become someone's property. These were the teachings from my mom. Don Alejandro and I had a lot of conversations around these things.

In all the years of international travel with Don Alejandro before 1999, I got to know him and I understood that he was very much human, very much a male, and very much a Central American man. I would not agree with him sometimes. But we have been able to resolve our differences.

I see Don Alejandro now being in a place of unconditional love, unconditional with all of his teachings. So in my lifetime I have been able to witness the man becoming very enlightened.

It is a great honor to meet with him in these days that he is a leader and an elder, and dialogue with him on different levels. He told me that he's very honored to know that the Grandmothers Council has come together to bring our messages around the world.

Crossroads

My husband has always been very supportive and open. From the moment that we met as teenagers, we knew that we were meant to be together. We have been together for over fifty years now.

Flordemayo and her husband, Marshall, in front of one of their Airstreams. Estancia, New Mexico, 2014

He does a lot of reading on spirituality and things of this nature. So his support has been from the beginning. He introduced me to some yoga masters. Just before my mom died, he gave me the *Autobiography of a Yogi* because he thought it would be an important book for me to read. It was. That was the first book I read cover to cover.

Marshall would read and hear about visions and dreams, but he'll tell you that he's never had a dream and that he's never had a vision. So when I met Don Alejandro, Marshall was afraid that if I went home to Central America, I might not come back. I would never do that.

But one night he had a vision. He saw me walking down this road and he kept calling me until I eventually looked back. Then the road split into two roads and I split into two. After I reached the crossroads, I continued to walk the two paths, side by side.

My husband is an enormous man. He's about two hundred and fifty pounds, six foot four, a moose of a man, okay? This big man woke up and he was crying, inconsolable. "I've had a dream. I don't know how to talk about it. It was so painful." I said to him, "Come into my arms and let me rock you."

We were sitting on this king-size bed. I'm five foot, and I've got this six-foot-four moose on my lap and I'm rocking him like a baby and wiping down his tears. He was just sobbing, and I said to him, "Marshall, that's a beautiful dream.

"The dream is confirming to you—not to me, but to you—that from the moment we met I've had two paths that I need to walk, and that is the unconditional path of a mother and wife, and the unconditional path of my spiritual work." I said, "I understand my position and my commitment as a mother and as a wife to you. When I made that commitment, I made the commitment *until death do us part.* I also made a commitment to the Creator when I was a child that I would always do the work of the invisible beings. The invisible beings are showing this to you, so that you can be okay with this."

I reassured him that if I went back to Central America I was only going for a few days. That's a commitment that I've made to him. I don't go away for more than ten to fifteen days at a time anywhere, and then I come home.

Marshall supports me 100 percent with my journeys in the four directions. We walk in life together like this so that I can do what I need to do in the way that spirit has me doing it.

I have the sweetest married life with my beloved husband.

Children, Grandchildren, and Dogs

Our grandchildren were raised traveling in Airstreams. I think we've owned about ten different ones. Our favorite traveling Airstream is named Stella. So when you see a 1971 Airstream that says *Stella* on it, you know that is us.

Today, other than having two children and three grandchildren, Marshall and I also have two dogs, Farfel Wonder Dog and Judy. Judy is my cosmic child, because after being with us for about a month she got in bed with me and she took her little paws and opened up the dream veil. She came into my dream, and I said to her, *Little one, I didn't know that you could come into the human dreams. You are welcome into my dreams and into my visions.*

I absolutely adore her. She went from a miserable existence of living with seventy-four dogs in a single-wide trailer to being treated very special.

Flordemayo and her dog, Judy. Estancia, New Mexico, 2014

A Sacred Site: Temples for Humanity

In January 2011, an invisible voice woke me up. *Flordemayo, I want you to bring the people to New Mexico.* I became fully awake and said to the voice, *Oh my gosh, like here, in this little house? You know my house is so tiny. Where am I going to put the people?* I kept arguing with the invisible voice. The voice came back and repeated the same, now in a very stern tone.

It was my usual time of prayer, between two and four o'clock in the morning. I prayed, *Beloved Creator, I know you are giving me these messages, but I need more clarity about this. What is that I'm supposed to be doing?* I spent five months in diligent prayer, 24/7 . . . prayer, prayer, prayer. *Who am I going to bring to New Mexico? Where? How am I going to do this?*

Then one morning I got a phone call from the neighbors. They were leaving the forty acres of land that belonged to our daughter, Heather, and her husband.

So we started to clean and clear out the property. I remember feeling the stillness and the beauty of the land. One day I went into spontaneous prayer: *Beloved Creator, is this where you want me to bring the people?* Out of nowhere I felt this little gust of wind from the right side of the hogan. And the little gust of wind gave me a soft blow in the face, like a kiss.

I thought, *Beloved Creator, I know that this is your confirmation. You are listening to me. This is where you want me to bring the people. I'm going to stay on this land to prepare for a vision so that we can continue to talk.*

It was close to full moon in May. My little dog Judy and I sat all night long. I didn't receive a vision. So early in the morning I went home. That evening I went into a vision. I saw our daughter Heather and me walking together up to the center of the forty acres. Then she and I divided into four people, moving in the four directions of the land. We went into prayer, squatting and blessing the land with our menstrual blood, until we covered the whole forty acres.

I woke up at the crack of dawn, my usual hour, and I started feeling one with the Creator, in a state of grace. I decided that at dawn I would call my older sister, the one who carries the knowledge of my mom's dream and vision interpretation.

We have the Seed Temple and the temples to the elements for the future generations, to remind people that we are of the sacred earth, sacred fire, sacred wind, sacred water. These temples are here as a constant reminder that even though we're humans, we are not different or separate from anything that grows on the earth.

My sister said right away, "The vision is telling you to figure out a way to become the guardian of that land. You and your daughter have already blessed it with your menstrual blood. That land has to stay in the family."

When my husband woke up, I started crying. "Spirit is telling me that I need to buy that land. How am I going to do that?" Later that day Marshall started calling banks. But they would not lend us the money.

I was taking care of my elderly mother-in-law while I had become the devoted caretaker of the land. She really loved being there. One day she said to us, "What are you kids going to do with that forty acres?"

Marshall said, "Mom, we've been trying to get the land, but I think we're just going to have to surrender."

My mother-in-law said, "Marshall, I'm going to leave you an inheritance. Why don't you just take the money now and buy the land?" And that was pretty much it! She walked into the bank and bought the property outright.

My mother-in-law had an incredibly wonderful time working on the land. She was able to see the construction of the different temples. She was able to enjoy the land for about two years before she passed on.

When we first came to the land, the only building here was an octagonal, straw bale adobe hogan. There was nothing inside until I got a painting of the Golden Child by Minouche Graglia. The baby came from one of my visions. I was shown to call this hogan the Temple of the Golden Child. This is where I do my teachings.

After that, I started receiving more messages. I received a vision from the Beloved Mother. She showed me myself, sitting in a rocking chair inside the Seed Temple. It looked like my mom's old rocking chair. I had seeds all around me, and I started making little bundles. And then she said, *You are to make bundles for the future gen-*

erations, for the little children who are being born. Remind the parents that the seeds are also children, and when their children receive the seeds they will become responsible for them, to grow and to protect them.

So that brought on the vision of the Seed Temple and the seed keepers.

I started putting the word out that we were looking for seeds. I delivered the message of the seed bundles at one of the Grandmothers Council's gatherings. The Grandmothers started helping me put the word out. Grandmother Dianna Henry, known as the Corn Elder, brought some seeds over because she could relate to the seed bundles, children, and the future generations. Then Susan Lipshutz, the founder of Everyday Medicine Woman, connected me with a colleague of hers, Nance Klehm, who brought some of her seeds over too. So Nancy became another seed keeper. Dianna also recommended Greg Schoen, our third seed keeper.

Straw bale adobe hogan at the forty acres. Estancia, New Mexico, 2014

When these three seed keepers get together and teach, it's over 100 years of farming knowledge, seed saving, and soil conservation. Everything's being categorized and cataloged, and we've put word out to the people in the four directions about seeds.

I go into the Seed Temple quite a bit and I do a lot of prayer. I also bring some of my ancient skulls so they can receive coded information, genetic information from the living seeds. These skulls are holding that information for the future generations.

When the Grandmothers were here for the Seed Conference in September 2013, we only had the Seed Temple. Don Alejandro and the Grandmothers came out to the land to pray and to have something to eat.

Some college kids were taking care of the fire in an iron pot that belonged to my grandmother. In this way, we initiated the site for the Temple of the Fire. This is how the different temples were built.

I also had a vision of Grandma Mona in front of a big grandmother rock, a vessel that holds the temple of the water. I saw Grandma Mona blessing herself with the water.

One day I went to Albuquerque to purchase a stove and refrigerator for the hogan kitchen. I heard this voice singing, *Hallelujah!* I followed it to an outdoor rock store where I found the huge grandmother rock from my vision! She was singing.

So I didn't come home with a stove and refrigerator. Just then I received a phone call from Ann Rosencranz from the Center for Sacred Studies: "Grandmother Flordemayo, I just got a phone call from an anonymous donor who said that the star beings told her to give you some money." I jumped up in the air. "Ann, can you call her and ask if I can buy a rock?" Ann said, "Well, the star beings told her that you need money for something. . . . So I'm sure that a rock is okay."

When the man came with the five-ton grandmother rock, I said, "Put the rock about forty feet directly in front of the door of the hogan, where I can see it." The beautiful grandmother rock looked like she had fallen from the heavens.

Entrance altar at the Seed Temple at the forty acres. Estancia, New Mexico, 2014

I let everyone know that the Water Temple grandmother rock came from the star beings. And that she's a singing rock.

When we initiated the ceremony with the grandmother rock it was a very auspicious day of the Mayan calendar, 12 kahn. The kahn is the day of the celestial serpents. We placed the grandmother rock in the middle of twenty-two feet of circular stone with petals around it, a flower design, to bring blessings and prayers to the sacred water.

I looked up to the sky and right above the rainbow rock I saw an enormous image of a grandmother. I said, *Grandmother, you're standing above us. This grandmother rock is alive, singing. She's at the center of the Water Temple. Come down from your heavenly place and meet us here at this rock.* And before I knew it, the grandmother rock looked at me and I felt her vibration.

She started moving in a circular motion, the way of the Milky Way, spiraling and coming down. Her energy was so high! There was a cosmic sound in my ear, like when you see something inside of something else. It sounded like it locked, like it was whole again. This grandmother came down and descended into the rock.

We all started crying and praying. I keep her fed with the circulation of the sacred water. She is known to some people as the Water Wheel, and to myself she is the Temple of the Sacred Waters.

I was born seeing energy in cosmic rainbow colors. In Spanish it's called *el don*, which means a gift that you were born with. I see these different forms of light and through the vibration of the light, I can hear it. When I close my eyes and turn toward the fire or the water, I receive a transmission and I dialogue with the different elements.

I believe this is something that everyone has in their heart.

My visions are dedicated to everyone, to all the brothers and sisters of the four directions.

For me, seeing was nurtured as a child. It was expected of me to dream, to vision, and to see. And it was expected of me to dialogue about it, to learn how to interpret it, no matter how frightening.

One day while all these temples were being finished, I received another mandate from the invisible beings: *Bring the iron ore right to the center of the forty acres.* This huge piece of iron ore had already been in my house for about fifteen years.

A few days after, I had a vision. I was looking at the land with spirit eyes and could see the energy underground. A light from each of the four corners of the forty acres touched the center of the iron ore, and it created an underground pyramid, a four-cornered pyramid.

Four huge holy golden beings, twenty to thirty feet tall, stood on each corner of the land. They had their arms embracing, touching their hearts. I placed four monolithic rocks on each corner of the land.

The holy Creator was not done. In the third vision, I was standing in the middle of the forty acres looking at many people coming through the gate: men, women, children, and bitty babies. The holy voice said to me, *From this moment on, this place is known as a place of transformation.*

When I heard the word "transformation," the women turned into men and the men turned into women. We became androgynous beings, balanced in both male and female qualities. We were all bound together. Children, toddlers, teenagers, young adults, middle-aged, elderly people, all united as one, being transformed.

We have the Seed Temple and the temples to the elements for the future generations, to remind people that we are of the sacred earth, sacred fire, sacred wind, sacred water. These temples are here as a constant reminder that even though we're humans, we are not different or separate from anything that grows on the earth.

I don't think too much about how the future will unfold here because I have this incredible respect for how the holy ones and the invisible beings are guiding me.

Ancient Crystal Skulls

Crystal skulls are part of my cosmic chart. In the sacred teachings from Don Alejandro, the Mayan lore and traditions of the crystal skulls say that the Mayan people created fifty-two skulls. These connect to the sacred calendar, to the four cycles of a human life, those cycles of thirteen years, going from birth to becoming an elder. As we go through these different cycles of life, we have these different lords that guide us through the thirteen-year periods.

There are ancient skulls in different cultures around the world, but the Mayans say that the fifty-two skulls from Central America have moved around the globe at different times. They were physically hand-carried, transported by boat through the water, or transported from one dimension to the other.

About eighteen years ago, I had a waking vision about the skulls. I felt the presence of an elder, a spirit being, coming in through the front door. This elder was someone from a long time ago. He was a very small person, barefoot with a little breechcloth covering his groin. I heard his bare footsteps walking on the tile floor. He came into the bedroom and sat on the bed, and I felt the weight of his body make an indentation on the mattress.

Before I knew it, he lay down on the bed, right next to my left side. He took my left hand and cupped it within his. I found myself going out of my body, traveling with this elder throughout the world. We visited different skulls made out of different materials. I remember entering through the eyes of the skull. We went to high-rise apartments where they were doing prayers with the skulls. We went into caves where there were ancient ceremonies being done. We went down through the forests and jungles around the world where these skulls are right now being kept. I dove into the ocean where some of these skulls might be. I experienced people doing ceremony and prayer from the beginning of time. I would be inside the skull, witnessing everything through the eyes of the skulls. The journey with this elder was my initiation into becoming one with the ancient skulls from around the world.

Soon after that, I saw a notice about a viewing of the Mitchell-Hedges skull. Marshall and I went to see Ms. Mitchell-Hedges, stay for her lectures, and have dinner together. That was my first physical experience with an ancient skull. After that, I met JoAnn Parks from Texas and Max, her ancient skull. I also met with Nick Nocerino and his ancient skull, Sha Na Ra.

This was the beginning of my journey. I started bringing Don Alejandro from Guatemala when these skulls were being made public.

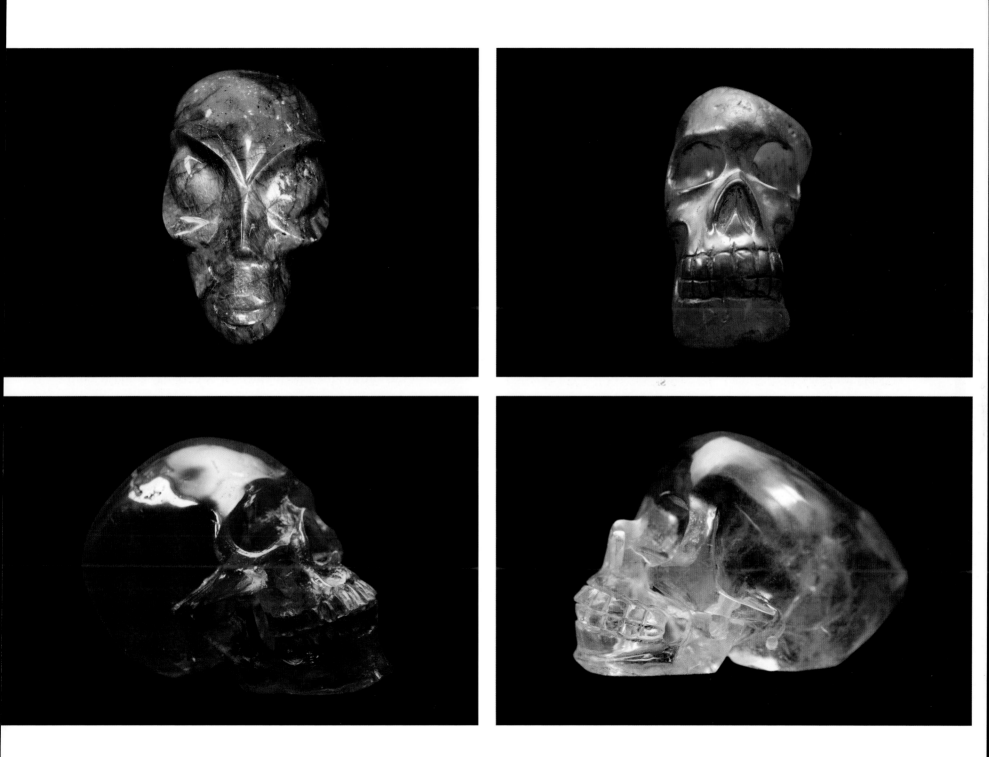

A few times we did ceremonies with the ancient skulls. As I've traveled up and down the globe, I have seen skulls made of many different materials, indigenous to Central America: crystal, jade, obsidian, volcanic stone, jasper, ocean jasper, mountain coral.

The invisible beings have said, *It's through these tangible things that we are able to communicate with you.* In other words, humanity feels more comfortable having a dialogue with something they can see than having a dialogue with an invisible voice.

Mayan people have an obligation to get close to the skulls and to work with them because it is the way that the holy ones speak to us. From the beginning, the skulls were old. They came from the blaze, from the star beings. The four lords of the four directions descended into the earth as shafts of light. These shafts of light became solidified, crystalline beings.

We receive our knowledge through these crystal beings. When they left, they said to the Mayan people, *We have left you with wise counsel. It is time for you to use these teachings and to become the humans that you are to become.*

I personally take care of more than thirteen skulls. They have become part of me and I am part of them. I have a skull that was gifted to the Grandmothers Council that's called the Grandmother's Skull. I have my own other personal skulls that I've traveled with throughout the world.

On my second trip to Nepal in 2011, when Grandma Aama had her gathering, I kept having visions of a couple of crystal skulls. They kept talking to me every day until I found them. I went to a store and said, "I know that there are some skulls here that I am to purchase." And I was able to purchase two Himalayan crystal skulls.

They are very special, rare skulls. Himalayan crystal is one of the first crystals. If you bang them together, they spark just like flint.

The structure of the crystal is made out of triangular shapes. The structure of our light body is also composed of these triangular shapes. It's the only geometric form that has the capacity to amplify and magnify. When we humans come together with these crystal beings, we are able to amplify and magnify each other's light.

I love the skulls. I'm very dedicated and devoted to them. They don't like to be out in the open, like objects for people to see. I keep them enclosed, away from the daylight in a handmade box with Mayan carvings.

One of the lords in the Mayan calendar twenty-day count is Lord Keme, represented by a human skull, responsible for taking us from daytime into nighttime. Lord Keme is the lord of transformation.

Every one of us goes through this transformation on a daily basis. We go into a place of dreaming at night, very active evenings. Then we carry the dream into the daytime, and it is through the daytime that we manifest the dream.

The Sacred Bundle of the Mayan Princess

As a Mayan priestess, you receive your sacred bundle, *la vara sagrada,* after doing your sacred walk. Your teacher will have very specific sacred sites that you need to visit over a period of time. You will have to climb mountains, cross rivers, and go into special caves designed for your sacred walk. You have to plant prayers, do ceremonies, and ask the spirit of the elements—the wind, the water, the earth, the fire—to bless you on this sacred walk.

When you make that commitment, then you have to be available. If the teacher calls you and says, "We're going to do this particular walk on Saturday," it doesn't matter where you are around the world, you have to meet him and do the walk. I had many of those phone calls, where I had little time to get ready and get to a particular site.

The sacred bundle contains what you have seen and picked up on your sacred walk: sacred seeds. When you have gathered enough, you are instructed on doing oracles. These seeds have your prayers, your intentions, the strength and energy from the places you've gone to. You have placed them on Mother Earth. You have washed them with the running waters, you have blessed them with the sacred fire and the smoke. You've done all of that, and so this becomes the bundle.

The bundle is wrapped in a little bag or in a little scarf, tied up by the four corners. No one can give you a bundle without you doing this walk. If the teacher agrees on what you have in your sacred bundle, then you are allowed to graduate.

As a priestess, the other item in your bundle is the Mayan cross, the "square cross." It represents the four directions and the way the Mayans read your cosmic chart. At the center of the cross you have your heart; at the top of the cross, your day of conception; at the bottom of the cross, your adult life; on the right, your maternal aspects; and on the left, your paternal aspects.

We are the people of the center, from the Pleiades. We're the star people. We are born knowing. We must know the positive and the negative aspects of ourselves. These teachings support you throughout your life so that you can become a better human.

Basically, it's a journey between yourself and the invisible beings. The Mayans say that a teacher comes for confirmation, for dialogue so that we as humans don't feel so lonely. So it's a companionship of spiritual dialogue. That is the purpose of the teacher.

Through devotion to the invisible beings, openness, and patience, we receive information. Once you receive these mandates, you have to bring them into a physical manifestation. Without manifesting, you're not ready for another part of the vision.

When Don Alejandro was here at the forty acres he said, "Flordemayo, the ultimate way of the priestess is to build his or her temples." This is an acknowledgment of following your visions and dreams and manifesting them.

Mom was always very clear about words. She would say, "Things are either good or indifferent, but don't ever use the word 'bad,' nothing's bad, only indifferent. You just have to learn to deal with it."

Mom would say, "You can't be asking for help every two minutes, you have to learn to do things for yourself." And learning to survive on the Earth is one thing. Learning to survive with your spiritual self is another thing. It's not going to go away, you can't bury it, you can't put a lid on it.

Through **devotion** to the invisible beings, **openness**, and **patience**, we **receive information**. Once you receive these **mandates**, you have to bring them into a physical **manifestation**.

Grandmothers Council

In late 2003 I received a call from the Center for Sacred Studies inviting me to go to a women's gathering in upstate New York. I told them that I needed to pray and consult with the invisible grandmothers. I also didn't know if I could attend because I had already made plans to go with some friends to India and Nepal in August.

In the summer of 2004 I was in Nambé Pueblo, New Mexico, at Grandma Connie Mirabel's house. She had invited me there to support the Peace and Justice runners coming through.

One morning at dawn I had a profound vision. I watched the ceiling of Grandma's house disappear and was taken to the heavens, out to the stars. I stood there, out in the open, and saw four grandmothers in the heavens with white flowing hair, moving in the cosmic wind. Their arms extended out and they were touching each other's hands, just at the fingertips. They formed a circle, each positioned in one of the four directions.

My hands were extended, my feet were tippy-toed, my granny gown was moving softly in that cosmic wind. The first grandmother called me from the east. Her hands were extended and so were mine. She was gliding in the air. Our foreheads touched in a huge transmission. According to the Mayan teachings, we moved from the east to the west. The grandmother of the west called me, then the grandmother of the north and the grandmother of the south. I received transmissions from the four grandmothers.

Before I knew it, I was back in bed. I was still looking at the stars, looking at the grandmothers beginning to fade. Dawn was coming.

When I woke up, Grandma Connie was in the kitchen. I was all glassy-eyed, half out and half in my physical body. I said, "Grandma Connie, I am right now in a state of grace. I don't think that I can bring hot drinks to the runners." She said, "You take care of yourself first." I sat in her living room chair for hours, praying and meditating, feeling the presence of the four grandmothers.

Soon after that, I accepted the invitation to come to the women's gathering in the fall.

While in Kathmandu in August, we stayed at the base of Mount Everest in a monastery hotel. The large windows faced Mount Everest and the natural wonder of the clouds moving in front of the mountain. A Sherpa[2] elder took me on gentle walks at the base of Mount Everest. One day he took me to a monastery where there were guards surrounding a glass box. I looked at it and almost fell. I started crying in prayer. I was looking at a real, flesh-and-bone yeti skull. It had tissue stuck on the cranium and a tuft of hair. I thought to myself, *I love skulls so much, and my beloved Creator brings me here to see this yeti skull!*

A few days later, I saw the grandmother from the east standing at the base of Mount Everest. I recognized her cosmic voice: *Child, I have a gift for you.* I extended my hands and the grandmother placed a triangular kind of flag with sacred writing in them.

I kept praying, *Grandmother, what exactly is this writing? What does*

---

2. A Himalayan people living on the borders of Nepal and Tibet, renowned for their skill in mountaineering.

You have the knowledge, you have the power, and you have the protection.

it say? Finally it came time for us to leave, waiting for the helicopter. In the moment that the helicopter came to pick us up I said, *Grandmother, where are you? I can't see you. You've given me this gift and I still don't know what it is.*

Just as I raised my foot, I heard a sound like a thunder and lightning storm coming from the heavens. But there was nothing there. Then the grandmother's voice came through the rumble: *You have the knowledge, you have the power, and you have the protection.*

The thunderstorms started rumbling again, even though the sky was clear. There was no wind, no clouds, no rain. I said, *Thank you, grandmother! I've received your message. Thank you for coming to me in this sacred place and for giving this to me.* And I prayed on it for the whole time traveling back to New York.

So it was with this message that I walked into the Grandmothers Council.

When I spoke to the public I mentioned my vision. I said that when the holy ones speak to me, they're not speaking to me as a person, they're speaking to me as a collective. This message was for everybody. We as humans have the knowledge, we're born with the knowledge. These are the words from the spirit grandmother: *You have the knowledge, you have the power, and you have the protection.*

In other words, we all have ancestors and they are always here helping us out.

Having the power means that as humans, we are constantly being empowered. These are the same as some of the original teachings I heard from Don Alejandro. My mother also was always reinforcing to us that we are powerful humans. So I came into the Grandmothers Council and delivered those words:

You have the knowledge, you have the power, and you have the protection.
And they belong to the Human Nation.

Flordemayo at the forty acres. Estancia, New Mexico, 2014

NINE

GRANDMOTHER
RITA LONG VISITOR
HOLY DANCE

I AM OGLALA LAKOTA. My Lakota birth name is *Tipi Ska Win*. It means white tipi, not a house but a tipi. I received that name when I was born; my dad had an aunt whose name was Tipi Ska Win and so he named me after her.

My English name is Rita Long Visitor Holy Dance. I was born on the reservation in a place called Loafer Camp, which is about six miles west of the Pine Ridge Agency. That's where I was born. I grew up in Slim Buttes, where my dad and my grandfather grew up. The land I live on belonged to my grandfather, whose name was James Long Visitor Holy Dance. I never met him. I think he died in the '20s.

My mother's name was Antonia Sierra. She was born in Blanca, Colorado. Her dad was from Mexico and her mother was Lakota.

My father was Oglala Lakota; his name was Rex Long Visitor Holy Dance. My dad was only married once, to my mother, and my mother was married twice. Her first husband died after she had three kids. My parents met at the railroad roundhouse in Chadron, Nebraska. Then she married my dad. He had cattle and she had chickens. They were together for about twenty-five years.

My mother had nine kids, three with her first husband and six from my dad. I had two older brothers from my dad and mother, but they both died when they were babies. So I'm the sixth. Then there's my sister, Beatrice, our brother Rex, and our youngest brother, Stanley.

I went to the Holy Rosary Mission, now the Red Cloud Indian School. Back then on our reservation there was the mission boarding school and the government boarding school, so there were two different schools that the children on the reservation went to. I went to the mission school. That experience is tattooed in my mind, all the things that happened at the mission school. I was exposed to the harsh disciplinary teaching approach the Catholics used on us there. Yes, I am a Catholic Indian boarding school survivor! It was hard on the Lakota students, but also hard on the Lakota parents. If the parents didn't take their children to school, the parents would be arrested by the Indian police. The Lakota people back then had no control over the taking of their children. When I was first taken to the mission school I was still a small child, I didn't know anything. I had not yet been introduced to our traditional Lakota ways concerning prayer. But once I was taken to the mission school it didn't matter how young I was, I was introduced to prayer, the Catholic way, a strict disciplinary way that was foreign to our Lakota ways. Back then the Lakota parents had no control over what religion was taught to their children. It was hard back then, really hard.

The mission school was in English, not Lakota. We grew up speaking Lakota, only we had to learn English at school.

My mom spoke Lakota and English, and she also spoke her language, which was Spanish. So she knew three languages. They were tough on us speaking the Lakota language, but we all did. We were not allowed to speak Lakota at the school. But I spoke Lakota. We were boarders. We stayed there day in and day out for nine months of the year. I was with my sister, Beatrice. We stayed in a dormitory like in the army. There was one stove in that big building where we had our beds. In the wintertime it froze. A couple years after my sister, Beatrice, was brought to school, we were both taken to the IHS hospital to have our tonsils removed, and the mission school didn't even inform our parents.

The mission school taught us the usual things. Everything. But mostly prayers, Catholic prayers. My mom was Catholic, of course. The mission was twenty miles away from home. We had vacations for ninety days.

Coming home was freedom. We played all over the hills and trees and in the river. We were kids. My dad had horses, so after I turned maybe fifteen, we used to ride around bareback all over the place. In summertime we picked berries, plums, and cherries. And then some evenings Dad would take us fishing. He had a homemade fishing pole, all except for the hook; he bought those. We'd catch catfish. That's why I love fresh fish. So we'd go fishing down there.

We'd catch all these different fish. We'd have catfish, bullheads, and we'd have carp and minnows. They're really good. The bullheads have got big heads and it looks like thorns peeking out, so when you catch them they'll stick you, it hurts.

That was summertime vacation. My mom would have us do our chores. We'd clean up, sweep, fix our beds, and clean up again. After we'd sweep and do the dishes, my mom would say, "You can go down and swim at lunchtime." When she said that, we would go down below and swim. We'd walk way over there and pick berries on the way back. We were never hungry in the summertime. Sometimes we'd have our fishing poles down there, so we'd sit there and sometimes we'd catch those minnows.

We'd take their little guts out and pretty soon we'd heat our skillet. We had some shortening, they called it

From left: Antonia Sierra (Rita's mother), Severiano Sierra (Rita's grandfather), two unknown Sierra family members, and Mary Sierra (Rita's grandmother)

I WENT TO THE MISSION SCHOOL. THAT EXPERIENCE IS TATTOOED IN MY MIND, ALL THE THINGS THAT HAPPENED AT THE MISSION SCHOOL. I WAS EXPOSED TO THE HARSH DISCIPLINARY TEACHING APPROACH THE CATHOLICS USED ON US THERE. YES, I AM A CATHOLIC INDIAN BOARDING SCHOOL SURVIVOR!

Holy Rosary Mission—Red Cloud Indian School—elementary school girls, 1939. From front to back: 2nd row, fifth from left: Rita's sister, Beatrice Long Visitor Holy Dance. 3rd row, third from left: Rita Long Visitor Holy Dance. Pine Ridge Reservation, South Dakota, United States

lard. We'd cook fresh fish there and we didn't even go home. We had our matches to light the stove, and we used to hide the fish down there. If my mom was doing something and she didn't want us to be there, we'd have all the good time we wanted. That's what we'd do.

When I was on vacation I didn't pray. I did enough at school. I did nine months of prayers; I'd let that rest.

Being the Oldest

In 1942 my mom got sick. At first I didn't know she was sick. She didn't tell me, she didn't tell none of us. Back then, they didn't discuss their sicknesses with their children. They didn't say, *Oh, I've got a headache!* Nowadays, every little thing is a big deal, somebody stays home because his or her head hurts or stuff like that. But back then, they tended to take care of themselves. But it got to a point where she must have been not doing well at all, or she probably complained to my dad, which I didn't know.

I'd already bought clothes for school. I bought a suitcase and brand-new clothes, because I was going to go into the ninth grade. I was looking forward to school that fall because I wanted to learn shorthand and other skills to become a secretary. Then the day we were going to go back, my dad said in a nice way, "Daughter, I know you're hoping to go back to school, but I'm going to have to let you know that your mom isn't doing very good. So I'm going to have to keep you home to help." And I said, "Why?" He said, "She's not doing well." And he didn't tell me more. So I said, "When am I going to go back to school?" He said, "Maybe you'll go back to school in January." He felt so bad.

He took me to the mother superior's office and said my mom was not good. "So I'm going to keep Rita home. But she'll be back in January." I think I was either fifteen or sixteen. I thought, *Oh my god, I'm going to be behind in my work and in my studies.* But again, I didn't complain. I never sassed my dad or my mom or the teachers. I never complained about anything. When I'm going to do something, I just go and do it.

So I didn't go into ninth grade. I didn't ask my mom what was wrong with her, or why I didn't go back to school. I never did ask her. I just kept quiet. Little did I know I wasn't ever going to go back to school.

Mom just kept getting worse. She couldn't stoop down to pick up anything heavy, so I knew that there was something wrong, *but what*

was it? I just kept quiet and I helped her. My dad used to bring me water from the river. At that time the river water was good. He had two barrels that he'd bring water in. So one of them I cooked with and one of them I washed with. And then he made a thing for collecting the rainwater. We'd drink that.

My mom was getting worse and worse. My dad took her to the hospital. They had to examine her, and my dad said they were going to find out what was wrong with her. She stayed for a procedure.

I think it was around Thanksgiving, because I had to clean the house. I opened a letter and read it and found out that she had cancer. I'd heard of cancer at school. So I just put the letter back down and kept on cleaning. Then as the months passed by, things got kind of rough for me. My mom's health was not improving. Somewhere about that time my dad went to a meeting and he came back and said they elected him to be a representative for the tribe. There are many districts here in the Pine Ridge Reservation. Every district has a representative, and my dad was the one from Slim Buttes, a Sioux Lakota representative for the Pine Ridge Reservation. There are five other reservations.

He said he had to go to a meeting once a month. And it was just me, my mom, and my dad. So I'd clean her up, feed her, give her lunch, and put water by her bed, and then I had to go outside where the horses were in the corral. And I had to saddle a horse and get our cattle across

Young girls riding horses at the Pine Ridge Reservation in South Dakota, United States

the river. So in the dead of winter, I'd take care of the cattle. Feed them and make sure they were on our side of the fence, way up on the hill. I had to ride all the way there and make sure the gate was closed or else the cattle would wander off.

One day as I was cleaning up and putting things in order, I came into the bedroom. My mom was looking out the window with binoculars and she said, "Daughter, I think those cattle are over the gate, I see them on the other side of the fence. You'd better hurry up and go get them before they get into the cedar breaks over there." I hurried up and got dressed. I had to wear my brother's chaps. You know, the kind that cowboys wear. My brother wasn't a big guy. I had to put some extra socks on and put his boots on, and my mom made sure I put those chaps on and oh my god, I got on the horse. I knew the cattle were coming from the north and already they had broken out and were going to where the cedar break was. It was windy. I had a heck of a time driving them against the wind. They can't go against the wind. I had a heck of a time trying to bring them in. I got them into the pens on this side and drove them toward the water.

In the summertime, I had to take care of my mom. But when my dad came back from the school with Beatrice, I was glad, because Beatrice would help her too. She was there for my mom and my two brothers were there for my mom too. But I had to do much more work. Because I'm the oldest one.

It's really hard to be the oldest child of the family. It's hard to be the oldest because everything falls on you. Everything is Rita. That went on for years of me helping my parents during my mom's illness.

Horses and Wagon

Back in those days of the 1940s a part of our lives revolved around horses; they were our means of transportation. One day in the summertime my dad had to brand cattle. So he said, "Well, daughter, I think you have to make a trip to town." And I said, "What town?" He said, "You have to go to White Clay, Nebraska. You're going to go in a wagon." White Clay was about twenty-two miles away. I said, "Okay." Our wagon was like those ones you see in the movies, a horse and wagon. I asked him, "Can I ask my girlfriend if she can go with me?" He said, "Yes, but you've got to leave early from here. When that sun comes up."

The next morning my dad said, "I've got the wagon ready." My friend Fern was up and so we had whatever to eat and we jumped in the wagon and took off. Dad had put a lot of hay in the back of the wagon. He gave me a grocery list and said, "Bring all of this back." He wrote a note to give to the grocery clerk. So I stuffed that in the pocket of my jeans. So we took off and my dad said, "Let the horses trot." He said, "Let them walk and let them trot. You'll get in by noon." We didn't have watches, we just had the sun.

We made it in good time, around noon. We took the horses and put them in the back so they could eat. Then we shopped. I got all the things that my dad wrote down. Then we hitched the horses back up. We jumped on the wagon and came back over the hills. In the distance, the sun was already going down.

My girlfriend said, "You know what? From here to that turn way over there, there's a bad spirit around here." I said, "You have to mention that?!" It was dark and there was no moon. It was getting darker, so we just kept on. My dad had said, "If you're on horseback or driving the wagon at night, the only thing you have to watch is their ears. Watch the ears of the horses." So that's what I did. If that horse's ears go back, get pinned back, that horse is seeing something scary!

I just watched those ears and let the horses lead, because they knew the way to go. But I watched those ears. My girlfriend kept talking about spirits. And it was at night. And I told her, I said, "You know what? We still have to pass a place where I know there are spirits. We still have to go by the graveyard!" Years before I had heard about it. I dreaded it. She said, "Oh my god! I guess we'll have to sing louder!" So we passed that haunted place. There was no other way but to come through there, so we did.

I watched them ears and they were going good. The horses weren't running, they were trotting good. And I gave them a little tap on the behind and we came right below the cemetery. We came through it and passed it and Fern said, "Oh, am I glad we passed that!" We came back to the house. My dad was waiting, standing outside.

Afterward my friend stayed for a couple of days and we sang and sang. I could ride a horse like nobody's business. I practically grew up riding horses. It's fun riding horses, but it was hard work too. I used to have quite a few horses, but it cost me too much money to take care of them. I might have had about twenty head. They were wild, all over. I also had a team of horses, and an extra one. When we were kids our dad's mare had a filly. I named her Peggy. We tamed her with sugar. After that she got to know us. Whenever we were going to the corral, she was always standing there, waiting for us.

My first horse, her name was Baby Ruth. My oldest brother, Pete, and I went to a bingo game in our community. We didn't know what the prizes were going to be. They told my brother that he had to be the caller. So he was over there, getting everything ready. Then this man comes in and he says, there's going to be two prizes, a horse and a billy goat, for this bingo game. . . . And that's how I got her, my first horse! To this day I still love horses, they are so beautiful.

My Mother's Wishes and Passing

My mom died in August 1946 at around 8:00 a.m. She died at home; we were all there with her. We knew her time was close the night before. A vigil of our neighbor ladies from the community formed and came over to sit with our mom. Back then, the ladies in our community were very close. They all worked together at the canning kitchen. My dad and my mom were also very close, so it was a hard time. We had a hard time after my mom passed away.

One day in the springtime, I was cleaning her up. I'd usually give her a sponge bath twice a day, wash her hair with scented soap. I would rub her down and put talcum powder on her, massage her back and legs, and then help her lie down. After I'd get through bathing her, I'd massage her legs so she wouldn't get stiff. Sometimes she would say, "Daughter, I want to stand up."

So I would pick her up and let her stand up. When she got like that, I knew she was really sick. I knew that one day in springtime. After

I cleaned her up she said, "I want to sit up." So I put the pillows up around her and she said, "Bring that trunk over here." So I brought her the trunk and she said, "Open it." So I opened it. She said, "Take all of these clothes out." So I took them all out and put them on the bed. She had brand-new dresses that she had never worn, coats, jackets, sweaters, scarves. Women wore stockings back then, nylons. She had all of that. We had bought her nice things like that, thinking that maybe she'd get well. So I laid those clothes out and she picked out one dress and skirt and some underclothes and put them aside. She told me to give this and that away to certain women. So I said, "All right."

She said, "Daughter, I'm going to die."

I said, "Mom, don't say that."

She said, "I don't have very long to live." And I looked at her and went up to her. She said, "I don't have very long to live, so I want to get you prepared." I started to cry. She just nodded at me and said, "Don't cry, stop your crying. I want you to stop crying. You're the oldest and you have to take care of your sister, your two brothers, and Papa."[1]

She said, "Those four, you've got to take care of them. You've always been strong. I'm not going to be around. I don't want you to be crying. You keep crying and you're going to make your two little brothers and your sister cry too." And she said, "I can't handle that." So I stopped crying.

She just told me like that, she said, "You've got to be strong, promise me." So I told her, "I won't cry." Looking back at that moment, I

1. Dad in Spanish.

never realized it, but I became a parent to my three younger siblings, three teenagers, and at the same time I too was still a teenager.

In the Lakota tradition, when someone passes on, they give away everything. There was one thing that she gave me from all her clothes, a mink coat. It was a real mink coat that we all chipped in and bought her, and she didn't even wear it once. She said, "You helped me, all of those years. You didn't go to school, you helped me. So I want you to have this mink coat." So I took it. She said, "Hang it up and put it away."

I remembered what she told me. After she passed on and we had her funeral, we came back. A lot of people came and started to help cook and all that. So that was good.

But deep inside I was so empty, I felt so empty. But then I had my two brothers, my sister, and my dad. . . . I wanted to cry, but I had made a promise to my mom that I wouldn't cry. I wanted to cry, but I just held it back.

My dad said, "Okay, you give away everything. Take down everything and give everything away." And he said, "I want all the people to come in and help themselves to all of the clothes and whatever they want." He had them come in and help themselves to whatever they wanted. So they took all the dishes, pots, pans, spoons—everything.

Everything was gone.

We didn't have nothing, everything was gone. I think we just had a few blankets. Not quilts, but blankets, and jackets and coats.

I think in the third week of August we went to White Clay and my dad bought all of this new stuff, a big tent and dishes. I don't know how much money he spent on it. But he bought whatever we needed. He said, "Days and months will go by, we'll catch up. But Mom is never going to come back." He said, "She's not going to come back no more, but someday we're going to go over to where she went."

When we returned from White Clay and came over the hill, we could see the house. My dad started crying. He cried all the way back. He cried because we were coming back home and my mom wasn't there. We all cried with him.

We came back and built a fire. We had bought kitchen utensils so we could cook. The dogs were barking. He said, "Somebody's coming on horseback." It was my uncle coming over. That made me feel good. He stayed with us for two months, and every day he would talk to us. Every day. He would talk to us about life and death. He would talk to us in the evenings. He would sing and he would preach to us. He was the one who really helped out, because our dad couldn't. Our dad was so lonesome. My uncle was a distant relative, but everybody's related here. We called him uncle. After that, I felt much better that somebody cared.

Marriage and Children

In 1944, prior to my mom's passing during World War II, I met a young Lakota soldier who was home on furlough, he was on leave with other servicemen. My mother's sister, Aunt Elaria, said, "You'd better go to the Rabbit Dance. Dance with the soldier boys. There is a war, and you don't know if you're going to see them again." She said, "Have respect and ask them to dance."

That's when I met this guy. I went up to him and said, "Would you like to dance with me?" He asked me, "What is your name?" I told him, "Rita." He said, "My name is Moses." And I thought, *Holy Moses!* I thought about the Bible story and thought, *Holy Moses!* But I didn't say that. I said, "I'm pleased to meet you." I danced with him and he said, "Can we dance again?" I said, "Sure, anytime." So we got acquainted with the guys. We went outside and talked to them, and that's how I met Moses Blindman, my future husband.

I remember working at a restaurant as a dishwasher at that time. Fern and I, we worked there. This was during World War II. The soldiers were really bad. Just because they were defending our country, they thought they could treat women as they wanted to treat them. *Oh boy, defending your country, you know?* But we made sure, I made sure, that nobody was brought back to the kitchen. "These women are working in here, soldiers are not allowed in here!" That's what I told them.

Moses went into the service. He got wounded, but he used to write to me every day. He was in New Guinea when he got hit. He was in a convalescent hospital. He didn't know when he was going to be discharged. When he came back, he came over to see me. We just visited around and then he left.

My mother passed away in 1946, and Moses and I got married in 1947. My sister Beatrice and I, we had a double wedding. We married at the same time. At the same church. Beatrice with Ernest and me with Moses. Our father sponsored a wedding feast and dance. A few months later, my dad said that when a girl gets married she goes to where her husband goes. So I had to move away. I was married to him for, gee, close to twenty years.

We didn't have any children for four years. Finally in December 1950 I knew I was going to have a baby, my first child, I was going to become a mother. I was so happy! Several weeks later I told my father. He was so happy he came over and gave me a big hug, saying, "I'm so happy for you, daughter." Because I didn't have any children at the beginning of my marriage, this brought harsh criticism from my in-laws, but all that was now in the past. As new parents, Moses and I were blessed with a son, Moses Delmar, and eventually seven kids, all boys, including twins, and one daughter. And from my second marriage I had another boy. It's so funny how people are, at first they said things to me because I didn't have any kids, then when I had the twins, Stuart and Stanley, they said, "That's enough!" You really can't please anybody! To this day I have a dream catcher that Delmar, my oldest child, made. I have it hanging up in my room. I pray with it. When I pray with it, I pray for all my children.

When we pray we have to be truthful to ourselves. We have to have a conscience. If there is something in there that we're not bringing out or if we're praying with hate in our mind, you know that prayer is not good. We have to clean our closets before we pray. My son would say to me, "Mom, you don't have to go that far." I said, "I have to go that far if I'm going to be talking to the people."

I was blessed with children, but I wasn't blessed with a happy, solid marriage. My husband was never home, but I continued to go forward. I endured hardships as a single parent. There were times I had to walk one-and-a-half miles over and back carrying water buckets by hand to my house for my kids. My greatest support was my father. In the early 1960s he bought me a car, a 1940 Mercury. I used to do my own mechanics.

In 1965 I got pregnant with Twila. While I was pregnant with Twila, my Uncle Joe Sierra, my mom's younger brother, said, "There's going to be some work in Grand Junction, Colorado. If you want to, you can go over there and pick apples. Right now they're picking cherries and pears."

So my husband and I and our children went to Colorado. We picked apples. Although I was pregnant, I climbed up trees and picked apples. Then after apple season was over, we had money. Moses and I worked, and my oldest sons too.

My Uncle Joe got this job for us. Moses was also drawing a pension because he was wounded in action. The boys were working too, so they could buy their own clothes. They would pay us for the apple harvest season. We made good money then, and we could eat all the apples we wanted. That's why I don't eat apples now.

My Father's Passing and My Awakening

About two weeks after coming back from apple-picking season, we went back to Oglala and settled into our house. One evening a car came. I didn't know who it was. I heard a car and then Moses came running in and said, "I'll be back, I have to go." I said, "Okay." So he left. After I got through cooking, we all sat down to eat. I kept looking at the time, and Moses didn't come back. It was after eight in the evening, coming toward nine. Then a car came up to where we lived. The boys said, "Mom, I think Dad's coming."

> *When we pray we have to be truthful to ourselves.*
> *We have to have a conscience. If there is something in*
> *there that we're not bringing out or if we're praying with*
> *hate in our mind, you know that prayer is not good.*
> *We have to clean our closets before we pray.*

And here Moses came in. I didn't say nothing. I just looked at him. Then the priest walked in behind him and I thought, *What is going on?*

Father Steinmetz came in and he just looked at me. He looked at me and I looked at him. Moses was standing over there with the kids, and Father Steinmetz started walking real slowly toward me. He came right in front of me and he said, "Rita, there is a time that we all have to go." That's what he said. And so I said, "What? What's going on? What happened?" And I looked at Moses, "What happened? What's wrong?" I kept saying that. I couldn't hear nothing. Father was telling me something, but I couldn't make out what he was saying. "You have to get a hold of yourself, Rita."

He said, "Your father just passed away." And I started to cry. After Father Steinmetz left I just cried and cried and cried. Pretty soon my whole body was shaking. And I was pregnant. I couldn't hold my legs or anything. I was shaking and shaking. When I stopped crying, I told Moses, "Sit on my legs, sit on my legs." So he went and lay me down, and he sat on my legs. I was in shock. He should have taken me to the hospital, but he didn't. I was in shock.

And so I just cried and cried and cried. He took water and he poured it on my head. He lifted me up and started walking with me. But I was just shaking all over. I couldn't believe it. I had just been talking to my dad a few hours back at his home. He and my brother Rex Jr. were going to go to town. As they were leaving I called to him from the window, "Dad, Dad." He said, "What?" I said, "Remember the brakes are not good." He said, "Oh, don't worry about it, you worry about

Father Steinmetz, S.J., praying with pipe, 1975. Pine Ridge Reservation, South Dakota, United States

everything." And so they left, and that was the last time I spoke to my dad. A few hours later they were in an accident.

The next day, Moses said, "We're going to go to Slim Buttes." He said, "Get yourself together." The boys all started crying, "Grandpa, Grandpa."

The fourth day was going to be the funeral. We went to the Catholic church; everybody was at the church. Our relatives on my dad's side, they were there. I went into the church, and my boys and Moses followed me in. I went in and I saw the casket. I went by and I saw something on top of it. You know, they always had flowers, but this one had a peace pipe on there. And it was already loaded. I went and knelt down and prayed with my dad, and I promised myself what I'd promised my mom, that I wasn't going to cry. I had to be strong, that's what she told me. That peace pipe lying there gave me strength for some reason. After the mass we went up to the cemetery.

There were these medicine men, Uncle John Iron Rope, Uncle Austin Backward Sr., George Plenty Wolf, and Pete Catches up there with Father Steinmetz. They all went and blessed the grave in the Lakota way.

The priest took the sage and the medicine man was standing over there. When he got through, they smoked that pipe.

And that changed my mind. I couldn't even cry. The way my dad was buried with that pipe and the way they cedared him off, I couldn't cry. My life was changed right there. I couldn't cry.

Before my dad died, I was Catholic. I went to church, received communion, everything that goes with being Catholic. Then, the day of my dad's funeral I saw what happened at the church and at the cemetery. My eyes opened up to a new life for me.

I thought to myself, *I am an Indian. I am Lakota, and so were my grandparents.* Since I had been in school, I had tried never to miss mass. I used to want to go to church all of the time. After my dad passed away, buried in the Lakota way, I started thinking about how the Lakota pray. I'm a Lakota woman and a Lakota grandmother of my grandchildren, and I didn't know how to pray Lakota.

After my dad's funeral, I think it was twelve or fourteen days later, I started having pains like I was going to give birth, but I didn't. It bothered me. One day I got real sick. I thought the baby was coming. I went to the hospital and Twila was born, my only daughter.

Working for a Living and My Children

And then came winter and spring. During that time my husband was never home, he was always gone. So I'd go out and chop wood and get water. I had to make sure that the boys went to school. Every day from Monday through Friday the bus would come.

And then in June, my brother came over and he said, "I think they're going to be hauling bales in Hemingford, Nebraska. I was wondering if Moses would want to go." I said, "He's not here now; when he gets back I'll let you know." Moses and I weren't getting along because he was drinking and he was always gone, always gone. Moses had a drinking problem that was years long; although he went to the VA[2] for treatment for his drinking, he would always re-

lapse. So anyway, when he came back I told him and he said, "Yeah, we'll go."

So we went to Nebraska. I was hauling bales with my oldest son, who was of age. But bales are pretty big and heavy. We'd work for I don't know how many days and then get paid. One payday my brother and Moses left with our son. My brother came back, but my son and his dad didn't. When my son finally got back, I asked him, "Where's your dad?" He pointed to a trailer and said, "He's over there." "What's he doing over there?" He said, "Mom, Dad's drinking."

In all the years that I was married to Moses, he hit me a lot of times. But I never hit him back. When he'd get drunk, he'd asked me about this guy and that guy, be jealous of old boyfriends. And he used to hit me.

So this time I went over to that trailer where he was, and I was mad. I knocked on the door; someone said, "Come in." I went in and there he was, sitting right there. Then he says, "What are you doing here?" So I said, "What are you doing here?" Then he tried to get mouthy with me. So I let him have it. I knocked him down on the floor and started hitting him all over. I didn't even give him a chance to stand up.

I said, "I'm leaving you."

I turned around and I left. I went back to the camp and said, "We're going home." My brother said, "You can't do that." I said, "Hey, I can do whatever I want. I'm taking my family back home."

2. United States Department of Veterans Affairs.

Back then when I was a young housewife and mother, there were no safe houses for us abused women and our children to go to. We had to endure what was happening to us. Now it is better for the women, they have somewhere to go where they can get help.

So I went ahead and took that tent down and loaded up the car. I cried all the way back, I cried for the future. I thought of all the moments that he and I were to share as a couple, seeing our grandchildren, everything ruined because of his drinking.

We came back to Slim Buttes, my brother and I, and I told him, "I'm going to divorce Moses. I've been abused too many years. I'm tired of it."

And he said, "What are you going to do with all of these kids?"

I said, "Never mind what I'm going to do with all of these kids, they're my kids and I'm not going to let them go." So I went into Pine Ridge and I reported Moses.

Some relatives told me there was housing in Pine Ridge. So I found a place, and my children and I moved from reservation country life to village life, an important moment in my life with my children. The year was 1966. I had to pay rent, water bills, and electricity bills. I hired my Uncle Alfred Yellow Horse to haul us to Pine Ridge. On the first day I went straight to the courthouse and paid for my divorce. No *ifs* or *buts* about it, I paid for my divorce. That was that, and that felt good.

Moses was a World War II veteran. Since he had been wounded in action, he got a check every month. But his drinking got the best of him; he never did anything with the boys. I had to take care of all of that. While my dad was alive, he helped me too. He knew how I was treated, so he would give me money.

I never applied for welfare for my children. I knew I could handle it. We were happy. My children were happy. Their dad wasn't going to come back and raise hell with me and I didn't have to worry about him coming around drunk anymore. After I left Moses in Nebraska I didn't know too much more about him. I think a couple years after I divorced him we heard he was in the Bay Area in California, where his late older brother's children had settled.

Back then when I was a young housewife and mother, there were no safe houses for us abused women and our children to go to. We had to endure what was happening to us. Now it is better for the women, they have somewhere to go where they can get help.

Less than a year after losing my father, I was in a new beginning as a new divorcee and as a single mother living with my children in the Pine Ridge village. I thought even more about the future and how I was going to survive with my children. I didn't have much formal education in my life, so I had to go to work for a living with my kids.

Around that time of moving to Pine Ridge, my brother-in-law Ernest brought his children over to my place. As usual, I was glad to see my nephews and nieces. Eventually Ernest and I got together, mostly as a partnership to make a better life for our children.

My brother Rex, who worked as a farm/ranch hand, told me that there were jobs in Idaho. So we all moved to southeast Idaho. I worked on a tractor, pulling out the spuds. A lot of us would stand on top of the tractor and when the potatoes went through, you'd stand there and take out all the rocks and the big chunks of dirt and weeds and everything.

That first trip to Idaho was in 1967. I had all of my kids and my sister's kids with me. Some of them would help with the others. We even took a puppy, a little cutie; her name was Sweet Pea.

A couple years later I had my youngest child, another son, Travis; he was born in Pine Ridge but grew up in southeast Idaho. I think I

Nathaniel Blindman at the Pine Ridge Reservation. South Dakota,
United States

was forty-four when he was born. My kids stayed with me there in Idaho, and whether they grew up on the reservation or in mainstream America, they all grew up with a work ethic. Delmar, my oldest, was in high school, and so was Duane, but they quit on the wayside to work and help support the family. My second oldest son, Duane, got married; when he was young he was introduced to and began to follow the ways of the Native American Church. Nathan went to college and Patrick went into the Marine Corps. The rest were still kids. Nathan's my first four-year degree college graduate. I had to put up money for that, but that's good. He was the first in my family to go to college.

When my son Patrick told me, "I want to join the marines," I said, "No. Your dad told me never to let any one of you to go and join the forces."

"Why?" he said.

"Because your dad was wounded in action. He was wounded twice. He said that that is no place for you boys to go. That's a white man's war. It's no Indian war, we don't belong there." That's what he told me and that's what I told my son. I said, "You're still going to school."

He said, "Well, the sergeant already made plans for me to hurry up and finish."

I said, "Well, then you're going to graduate this year." In 1980 after he finished his high school education plans, he enlisted and went into the Marine Corps.

In 1975 when the spud harvest was over I got a job at the hospital as a cleaning lady. So I took care of the rooms and everything. My husband, Ernest, had a government job. I was still working at the hospital, but due to the cleaning fluids, my hands got all white. One day Ernest came back from work and he worried about my hands and the cleaning fluid that I was using. He said, "I want you to quit working there. I'll bring an application back from where I work."

This was a government job, and I was accepted. I had to report to work on December 26. But I had to train this girl who was going to take my place as a cleaning lady. The last day of my work at the hospital was Christmas Day, and then the next morning I had to report to this new job. I didn't have any Christmas. Of course, I had a great big Christmas tree for the kids, but I couldn't be there for Christmas because I had to go to work that day. Naturally I was a bit nervous, my first day on a new job.

That was really a good job. I had to wear a badge to get in. It was the military. The pay was really good, and it had vacation time. After I got used to everything, I changed my vacation days and saved them for summertime. Holidays I'd get double pay. And so all of those holidays were mine. Ernest and I rode the bus to work every day, forty miles away. We were both working, so we moved to a bigger house. Everything was going good and then all of a sudden, he started to drink. And that was the beginning of the end of our marriage. But I continued to work, put in ten years, then I retired.

Sacred Ways and My Oldest Child

Somewhere around 1977/78 my son Delmar said, "Mom, I keep having these dreams; I've got to let you know part of it." So he told me part of it. I told him to write his dreams down. I said, "You keep a good written record on a piece of paper from the first dream to the last dream. So you can read the whole thing as you dreamt it." I said, "There's a message in there for you. Not for me, but for you. And you will know what it is. You don't need to tell me."

One day he said, "Mom, I have to go back to South Dakota. I have to see a medicine man." He must have been about twenty-something years old. I took some time off from work and took him to see a medicine man on the Pine Ridge Reservation. They didn't tell me what the dream was. All they told me was that they had to take care of Delmar.

"We'll take care of him. Don't worry about it." So Delmar stayed for a while, and after four days he went back. He had a vision quest. That was his first vision quest. After that, they told him that every time he had a dream he had to have a vision quest. So that started. These dreams that he had were sacred dreams. In the dreams, he was chosen. He was chosen for a lot of different things to help the people.

I thought about it, *Oh my god, how many years after I got married and had children? How many years later my oldest son has to be chosen for the sacred ways?* After that, every year he Sundanced. And every year he vision quested. He Sundanced until a year before he died.

And so he became a medicine man. The medicine man told him, "There are going to be people who won't like you, but don't pay attention to them. Just keep going and be nice to people."

Delmar was the first in my family to enter the Sundance circle. He led the way for the rest of his siblings into our traditional Lakota spiritual ways. Many years ago when the Lakota people were first put on reservations, they were forbidden to do the Sundance and to practice traditional Lakota spiritual ways.

I was always Catholic, this is what was introduced to me as a child before I knew or was told about our traditional Lakota ways. But after my dad died, that pipe on his casket showed me that I'm Indian, that

I'm a Lakota woman. So I didn't go to the Catholic church anymore. I started going to the Sundance. I prayed and I sang.

I Sundanced for many years. After Delmar turned into a medicine man, I told my son I was going to be Sundancing and he said, "Mom, you don't need to dance, but you could dance four years, one day each year, and it will be four years."

After my son Delmar passed away, I went to Sundance when my sister, Beatrice, had her Grandmothers' gathering in Hot Springs. I went to the tree and talked to it, and I told myself, I'm going to dance. So I danced like my son said, only one day for the next four years. No more. Every year I danced just one day, and that is a prayer. I don't have to go there and dance every single day. To Sundance, you have to see a medicine man. It's strict, very strict.

I started praying with the pipe then. Because my son, the one who passed away, made me that pipe. That's the one I still pray with. He made that pipe for me in 1988, when we had that first Sundance in Slim Buttes.

I sing with my sons in the sweat lodge. It's really good to learn those songs, sitting there and meditating. A lot of good thoughts will come to you. As we sing, we are praying. I picture a lot of things when I'm singing. I close my eyes. I sing with devotion. They're prayer songs.

Detail of Sundance *Tree of Life* wrapped in prayer ties. South Dakota, United States

Rita's sweat lodge grounds.
Pine Ridge Reservation, South Dakota,
United States

I don't care what kind of prayer ceremony you're at, if you're in a white man's church, in the synagogue, or wherever. When you go in there, you pray about whatever is bothering you. Or maybe somebody is having a hard time, you pray for them.

I always say, "I want each and every one of you to close your eyes and meditate and pray about whatever it is that's bothering you." They don't have to listen to me. They have to listen to themselves and pray. What about you? What about how you feel? Your family, your relatives, your friends?

I always say, "I want each and every one of you to close your eyes and meditate and pray about whatever it is that's bothering you." They don't have to listen to me. They have to listen to themselves and pray. What about you? What about how you feel? Your family, your relatives, your friends?

When your prayers are granted, you give *wopila*, thank you. *Wopila* means thank you. Wopila belongs to everybody. You know, we might give someone a cup of coffee or some money and say, "Wopila, thank you, wopila."

Every day is a wopila. Morning sun comes up, goes down, wopila. Morning sun comes up. *Thank you, thank you, Grandfather for shining on us again. Thank you, Grandfather. Everything is thank you, wopila.*

You give with your own feelings. You thank everybody for what they have done for you. And if you want to give something away, that's entirely up to you. A person doesn't have to give everything away to say "wopila."

Tunkashila and My Return to the Reservation

When I was a little girl, our sweat lodge was way back over there in the land. I didn't know what a lodge was because I was a kid. I wanted to know about it, but my grandmother taught us not to go near the lodge. So we stayed away. We couldn't hear what they were saying. Then they'd come out. And even after they came back to the house, we didn't go to that lodge because we were told not to. That was a sacred place.

One time we were playing in the backyard and I saw this skull. I went to it and looked at it. The skull was sitting against the wall of the house. I asked my grandma, "What's that?" She said, "Just don't go near it, don't touch it. It's a skull." I looked at it and it had horns. So we never played back there anymore. We played elsewhere. Even as I was growing up, I never did go back there.

It was a very big mystery that was always in the back of my mind until I went to the Sundance and saw Sundancers. Some of the Sundancers pray with that skull. It's a buffalo skull. But I'm still wondering, I'm still wondering. Nobody ever explained it to me.

All Lakota know that White Buffalo Calf Woman, who came as a white buffalo and turned into a maiden, was a spirit buffalo. The *čhaŋnúŋpa*[3] that she brought, that was real. She gave it to the Lakota with instructions on how to use it, and then she disappeared.

Tatanka Ska is the white buffalo, but we don't say that. When we pray and we say *Tunkashila*,[4] we don't say "white buffalo." We pray to Tunkashila, Grandfather, Great Spirit. I don't know about the rest of them, but when I close my eyes at night and pray, I see an old man sitting there with gray hair and a long beard. It's an old man that I see. I see that man with my own eyes.

God, the God that made this world, the skies, the stars, the air, we don't see him. We never see this Great Spirit. That is not a person, that we call God. He controls everything, that's what we believe. I don't know what the other people believe, but we pray to him, like the white man prays to God's son, Jesus Christ.

When I was in Idaho I was in the process of buying a house. But I left it because I wanted to come back home. I was raised here; my mom and dad are buried here. At that time my son Del was still alive.

3. The Lakota name for the sacred ceremonial pipe.
4. Grandfather, Great Spirit.

Rita circa 1990s

Buffalo skull and deer antlers at sweat lodge mound. South Dakota, United States

After nearly twenty years in southeast Idaho I came back to South Dakota with some of my kids and some grandchildren. But I didn't move back to the reservation right away. My family and I lived in northwest Nebraska for about four years, then we moved up to the Black Hills. Living in the Black Hills was so beautiful. I'll move back there anytime. I wasn't having a hard time off the reservation, but I wanted to move back to my home community. An older-model mobile home was donated to me; it took a few months to do the paperwork, then in 1997 I moved back. Thirty years earlier I had left from there, now I was back. Many memories crossed my mind. I thought of my dad. I also thought of my grandmother and looked at where she used to live. I didn't go over there, but I remembered her advice, "Look forward to the future." Life back on the reservation was difficult: the car broke down after a few months, the blizzards came, and in the summer the heat waves caused the trailer to become an oven. I really had a hard time.

Then in 1998 I had open-heart surgery. After recuperating in Rapid City for one month, I came back to my home on the reservation. With no running water for the indoor facility, I had to walk way over there through the deep snow to use the restroom. Pretty soon somebody bought some skis for me, so I used them and I'd go down to the toilet and on the way back I'd have a hard time.

So I prayed real hard so I would get a house for my children and my grandkids to come to. I'd go outside with my Rottweiler named Mesa and pray, *Tunkashila, I need a house. I want a decent house.* I just prayed and prayed to the four winds.

One time I was outside and Mesa was walking in front of me. All of a sudden she stopped. I said, "What is it?" I looked up and then I saw something. So I stopped and I looked and she stood in front of me. Her ears went up. And I said, "What is it, Mesa, what is it?" I looked and there was something white, and I started walking backward. You wouldn't believe it, it was a grandpa sitting there!

Long hair. Sitting with long hair and a white cape. He's sitting there looking at me, and I just froze. I said, *Oh Tunkashila!* I said, *I'm really happy to see you, glad to see you.* And I stood there and I prayed. And Mesa sat down. That dog, she didn't bark, she just sat down right beside me where I was standing. *Thank you,* I said. He said, *I bring you good news.* He said all of that in Lakota. Then I looked and he was gone. And that's God's truth. And I knew, I knew right there that everything was going to go good for me.

That summer I took some food and went back to the sweat lodges; I went and put an offering there. I made offerings where that spirit came. I believe in spirits. I believe in spirits, but you have to believe in yourself, you have to believe in yourself and your prayers.

People come into the United States to help the Indian people. One lady named Brenda Aplan came from England and said, "Oh, you're living in a small house. I'm here to help people, so I'll see what I can do for you." She went back to England, but she kept calling. One day she called and said, "I think I found somebody who will help you get a house."

It was a real pretty trailer, oh my god!

She gave me a photo album with a white man in it. He was the one who bought me the trailer. It was fully paid. I still have his picture. One day she said, "We have enough money so you can buy yourself whatever you want." And that's when we bought the furniture, all brand new. She said, "I want you to buy a refrigerator and fill it up with food." So all

along, ever since I left my husband and I went to Idaho, nobody helped me. I was not ever on welfare. And these people from England came and helped me.

I lived there four or five years. I was living there when I got a notice from Pine Ridge saying that my application was approved and that I was getting a house, a brand-new house. How many Indian people have been denied help by this office!? I felt grateful, but I also felt bad for all those who didn't get approved.

The Lakota Language

When we first came back to Pine Ridge to apply for housing there was a Lakota girl behind the desk. I told her in Lakota that I was there to apply for housing. She didn't know a word of Lakota. She looked at me, a Lakota woman, a Lakota girl, and she said, "I'm sorry, I do not understand what you're saying."

So that's how things are. When my kids came back from school I always told them, "Hey, you guys had better speak your Lakota language, because one of these days when we go back to South Dakota, everybody's going to be speaking Lakota and they're going to make fun of you if you are speaking English and don't speak Lakota." I was wrong.

But even my grandkids speak Lakota today. They know.

Lakota was my first language. Even though when I went to the Holy Rosary Mission school I got punished for speaking my language, I still spoke it. It was only us girls playing, we'd speak in Lakota. But I don't write it and I can't read it.

These days, you go to Pine Ridge, you go to a store, the gas station, and you hear all the people speaking English! Now as I'm speaking to the people, I push the Lakota language, I push it every time. There's a man, Leonard Little Finger, who is starting a Lakota language school now. He wanted Beatrice and me to go there and be delegates for speaking our Lakota language.

It's not only us Lakota people who don't speak our language, lots of tribes in this United States don't speak their language; they all speak English. And I say, "Christopher Columbus came to conquer America and he's still winning." And some people say, "Why would you say that?" And I say, "Check these Indian kids out. They're all speaking English, not the Lakota language, so he's still winning."

He Sapa—The Black Hills

The Native Americans who live here all go to the Black Hills to worship.

There's the Cheyenne, there's the Arapaho, and there's Standing Rock, where Sitting Bull's people are. It's like a holy land. Some people who go to the Black Hills, they go to Harney Peak (Black Elk Peak). Because that's where Black Elk went.

They go up there to pray, but they all have their land; it's a lot of land. This is my land right here, Slim Buttes. The Lakota go up there in the summertime. That's when our people go up there. "This is my land," they say, and so they sleep there. But the government, the white man has something to say about that, and there are places where it says DO NOT ENTER.

A lot of people have tried to save the Black Hills. That's been going on for ages and ages. All of us Lakota people, all we have to do is protect our land. My grandmother told me when you go to the Black Hills, take some of the water from there and bless yourself with it. My in-laws from Oglala used to go up to the Black Hills and bring water back from there to drink for healing.

Grandmothers Council

In 2004, seven years after I had come back to the reservation, one day Beatrice came over and said that her daughter Loretta told her that there was going to be a meeting for grandmothers. She wanted her mom to go. Beatrice said, "I don't want to go alone," and asked if I could go with her. I said, "Well, I have to think about it." She went home. I thought, *Well, it's been many years that I came through a lot of hard times. But I stuck with my children, and they're all grown up now.*

Beatrice came over: "Did you make up your mind?" I said, "Yeah." Then she says, "I think that meeting is not going to be around here. Why don't you make us some dresses?" So I pictured a grandma right away and I said, "I could do that."

I didn't know where I was going. Nathan took me to Chadron, where Loretta used to live, and Aloysius, my sister Beatrice's son, got up on the back of the pickup and started loading things. It was just Loretta, Aloysius, Beatrice, and me—the four of us. And we drove off in her truck.

On the second day driving, Aloysius said, "Mom,[5] you see that tower?" I said, "Yeah." He said, "That's Chicago," and I said, "Wow,

Chicago, Illinois?" You know, I never did go noplace. The farthest I ever went was Idaho.

I don't like the eastern countryside because it's just covered with trees. I grew up in these wide open spaces where you could see the hills way far away. On the fourth day of traveling we got to New York State. I saw a sign for "Woodstock" and what did I remember then? The hippies!

So we got to the place, and there I saw all of these little colored flags (Tibetan prayer flags) on a light cotton rope hanging there. I looked at them and I said, "Gee, they hang their dishtowels." I said, "Look at the dishtowels they've got hanging out there." Me and my big mouth!

We went into the big building and Loretta said, "I think we have to take our shoes off here." I saw all the shoes there and I said, "Gee, do we have to?" Beatrice said, "Do we have to?" And Loretta said, "Yeah, we have to take our shoes off." So we took our shoes off and Beatrice said, "You'd better put these together. Somebody might take them."

So we went in. I wasn't scared or anything, but I wanted to know what was going on. Loretta opened the door and I peeked over and saw Grandma Margaret, and she had her regalia on. And I said, "Oh my god!"

Beatrice said, "What?"

I said, "They're all dressed up. They've got regalia on." I said, "They'll look at us like we were country girls."

Beatrice said, "Oh dear!"

So we went in and sat down. Someone said something and I went deaf all of a sudden. I couldn't hear. They introduced themselves and I introduced myself. Mona sat right between us that time.

So that's how I met the Grandmothers.

The most important thing I talk about is education and language, and abuse and alcoholism, because that runs in everybody's family. You can't tell me that any family is innocent.

Each Grandmother, they have a past. We each have a past. And so when we pray, are we praying with devotion? Or are we just praying to be heard?

It's just a big world with all kinds of trouble going on. And there's some of us, not only the Grandmothers, but all over the world, some of us could jump in there and try to help solve what's going on.

5. It is customary to call an aunt "Mother" in Native American cultures.

TEN

GRANDMOTHER BERNADETTE REBIENOT

I AM BERNADETTE REBIENOT, OWANSANGO, born January 1, 1934, in

Libreville, Gabon, in the Estuaire province. I am a teacher by career, currently retired. I belong to the Omyènè[1] indigenous community of Libreville. The Omyènè are composed of Mpongwe, Enenga, Galwa, Orungu, Adyumba, and the Nkomi. I belong to the Mpongwe ethnic group, which is my patrilineal lineage.

My mother was part of the Lumbu community. She was married legitimately to my father. In our culture, we follow the patriarchal line, so I grew up in the community of my paternal grandmother. Unfortunately, my mother died when I was just four years old. I did not get a chance to know her.

So I had two surrogate mothers: my paternal grandmother and my aunt. Because I wasn't part of my maternal line, I do not speak my maternal language, the Lumbu. In any case, although I did not know the woman who gave me life, I love her immensely, and the lack of her affection has had a major impact on my life. After her death, my father took care of me and later entrusted me to the nuns from a Catholic boarding school. It is through them that I have followed the religious education that is mine today.

In fact, I received three different upbringings: the Mpongwe education from our paternal family line; a French education, since we were in a Francophile school environment; and a religious education, because I spent a large part of my adolescence with the nuns. This variety of

1. Also known as Myènè.

education makes me who I am today and constitutes three strong pillars of reference.

I completed my primary studies when I was fourteen in Libreville, Gabon. At this time we were under a French protectorate, so there was not an opportunity to pursue higher education in Gabon. We would have needed to go to either Brazzaville or Senegal. Because my mother had died, my father's relatives didn't want me to be away from them, so I had to continue my vocational education in Libreville. In this era there weren't a lot of employment possibilities. My choices were to enter health or education, and because I loved children, I chose education. I was eighteen when I started working; we were still under French colonization. It was only when we gained our independence in 1968 that women started working more widely outside their homes, getting involved in various sectors of society.

This profession gave me a lot of satisfaction. As an only child, I fled isolation and solitude. With my students, I had company all my life. These were my sisters, brothers, and at the same time my students. This companionship helped me evolve a lot in life.

I stayed in education for more than thirty-five years. I taught in primary schools in Libreville and in Port-Gentil. I had students from many places who are grown up today and who hold a variety of jobs. Even today there are students who call me "Maîtresse Bernadette," because I was their teacher. Many people in Libreville know me by this nickname.

Origins of My Life as a Priestess of the Ndjèmbè

Already when I was six months old, a doctor from the hospital in Libreville, Dr. Porteau, confirmed that I was blind. They could not heal me. My parents, distraught by the lack of results within modern medicine, decided to return to traditional medicine.

So my grandmother brought me to a traditional medicine healer named Agnourou-goulè Nkoumouè. This woman healed me with plants, and I recovered my vision. This was my very first encounter with traditional medicine. A sign for my future? Even still, throughout my entire childhood, I suffered from violent headaches that no one knew how to relieve.

Following our customs, young women are initiated rather early in life in the women's rites, the *Ndjèmbè*. I was initiated in 1948, when I was just fourteen years old, according to my paternal traditions. My paternal grandmother was the one who asked that I be initiated. I remember the women came to get me, saying to my father, "We're going to take your daughter, and we'll bring her back when we are done." I remember my father was sad; he never wanted to separate from me. But he was obligated to obey the women.

At the end of the first-level initiation, the spirit of my great-great-grandmother manifested through me, saying she had come back to continue the work she was doing while she was alive. The priestess told my father, "We believe your daughter either has a gift or she has a spirit that's bothering her." These women from my family wanted me to wait before advancing further in the initiatory levels of Ndjèmbè so that I might first

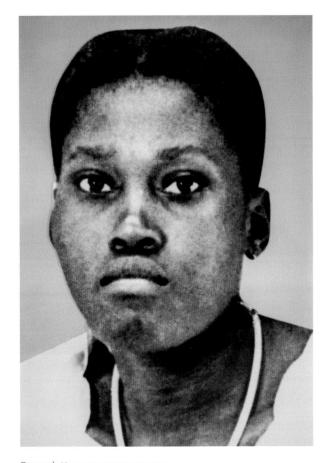

Bernadette as a young woman

Bernadette teaching a seminar in the DRC (formerly Zaire), in 1958. Diploma presentation to participants

Bernadette at a Mpongwé chief funeral, 1986

acquire more spiritual maturity. So I continued my studies with my fellow students.

A few years later, the acute headaches returned and I had difficulty seeing. Both my father and my grandmother had already died. The woman who had healed me as a baby had also died. So they brought me to an elder in Libreville who said, "This child is ill in her eyes because of the ancestors who live within her." It was this man who encouraged me to see if the customs from my maternal line might be able to heal me.

I was twenty-four years old. So in the season of initiations they brought me again to the Ndjèmbè feminine rites to continue my initiations. At this time they confirmed that an ancestor inhabited me and wanted to continue her work through me, the work that she had done while she was alive. This ancestor had been a priestess in the female initiation rites. And so I passed to the level of a master priestess. A young master, because it was necessary for me to be next to the elder priestesses to learn.

In July 2018 I celebrated sixty years of intense spiritual life by orga-

Ndjèmbè young women's rites initiation. Oyenano Village, Libreville, Gabon, 2014

Ndjèmbè young women's rites initiation. Oyenano Village, Libreville, Gabon, 2014

nizing a great Ndjèmbè. I passed the torch to the new generation so that they in turn can initiate the women. I wish them success in this difficult and noble mission.

Origins of My Life as Healer and Initiator of the Sacred Wood, *Iboga*

Several months after my second Ndjèmbè initiation there came a new revelation. I continued to suffer from extreme headaches, to the point that I spent days in a dark room because I could have no contact with light. I kept my head covered with a damp cloth. Every time I was ex-

posed to light I felt an enormous pain in my eyes, which immediately triggered the headaches. I had the impression that my eyes were being pierced. No one knew what to do.

I was already an adult. My relatives who worked in health care decided to send me to the Claude Bernard Hospital in France. I underwent a complete medical profile, which revealed no physical dysfunction. When the doctors explained that they found nothing abnormal, I said, "How is that possible that everything is normal? I'm suffering so much. Doctor, I am very disturbed about my health. My mother died at a very young age. Please tell me the truth if I need to prepare my children before dying." The doctor said, "Do you want me to invent a sickness? If you want, you can return to your country now."

With tears in my eyes, I returned to Gabon to my children and my work. Still no one could help me with the acute pain in my head, my eyes, and my nose. I was so disillusioned that the Western hospital had found nothing. I returned home. I had to crawl to go to the bathroom, because if I stood, I would fall. I could not walk. In all my life, I had never felt such pain.

And so my relatives brought me to an old man named Pambo, who revealed by clairvoyance that I was inhabited by a spirit that came to me to work as a seer and to heal sicknesses. This man said, "I do not know what door you could pass through to recover your health without allowing this spirit to do its work. You must return to your mother's family. There you will find peace."

I responded, "My mother is dead, my grandmother is dead. I do not even know my maternal language. How could I do that?"

He responded, "We are in Africa, you will find someone to help you."

And so, several months after my Ndjèmbè initiation, I followed his advice and found myself in the village where my mother was born.

Despite the pain and our economic situation, my husband and I found a way to go to Port-Gentil, then take a boat to my mother's birthplace, a village called Inchonaybani. When I arrived, along a river, I saw my maternal relatives for the first time. Everyone cried a lot during this reunion. Mama had died; she left a child. And now they saw this child as a grown woman, with children of her own.

They welcomed us, they fed us with so much kindness; it was a grand party in the village. Everyone was happy. What a party! Africans do not have much, but they make the best with what they do have, with great heart.

My grand-uncle said, "We know you. Your mother presented you to us when you were an infant." I never knew that.

I was so thin, so sick. An old man received me. He said, "You will not die in this country." I believed it, without believing it.

He added, "Here, no one can heal you." I said, "What, must I return back home?" He replied, "No, you will not have to go home and come back another time. You are our child. No one here will heal you, but you will heal yourself."

One day passed, then two, then three, then four. I was still there, waiting. I went there to be healed, but no one was taking care of me. The hunters went out, captured the prey, and prepared the large cooking pots. I ate. Although I was still sick, the pain in my head began to diminish.

One day the old man came over to me and said, "This morning you'll go walking in the forest with the other women." So we left by canoe. I was afraid to go in this fragile boat. My uncle's wife told me to place a basket on my back.

Once we docked on the shore of the thick forest, we climbed up and arrived in a place full of shrubs and set our baskets down. "Each person must pull up a shrub," they told me. "No one will pull it up for you, you must do it yourself—even if it is hard and you fall." And so I began my efforts to uproot the plant. I pulled, I fell.

They asked me, "And why are you crying?"

Because everything hurt.

They didn't tell me that it was the *iboga* that I was uprooting.

When we returned, the whole village had changed. The temple was prepared. They put me alone next to the fire. "You will heal yourself. We will not heal you. Today you are your own doctor. Everyone will listen to you. No one will talk."

This was the beginning of my initiation into the iboga.

They performed the preparatory purification rituals. Then they initiated me. Five days in the forest. I was accompanied by a Lumbu master, a Mitsogo master, and a master sitarist, playing the sitar invested with a power that had been transmitted to him through his own initiatory path. These three masters initiated me in the iboga.

It was through this initiation that I encountered the spirit at the origin of my sickness. It was a spirit of a man with whom I had no ancestral ties. We call this type of spirit a genie. He spoke his name and then told me where he came from and why he had come.

Before I returned to Libreville, the pain in my head disappeared. I was no longer ill.

The spirit demanded his own temple. My maternal relatives came to accompany me here in Libreville and marked the location of my first temple. Later the temple was moved, enlarged, and modernized.

This spirit has taken a very important place in my life. It is a protector spirit, a healer who helps me teach a lot of things. He has ripened inside of me and has matured me as well. His presence has helped me to understand life and especially to understand human beings. He teaches me to be humble.

I thank this spirit because every time I encounter someone sick, he

Iboga plant. Oyenano Village, Libreville, Gabon, 2014

…the more
I have
practiced my
traditional
ways, the
more I have
understood
their universal
significance.

is present. He brings healing and relief when I lay my hands on the sick. He counsels me during treatments. In this way he's a spiritual helper for me, a gift from God.

Often I say that God gave me this guide, this protector to fill the void and the suffering left by the absence of my mother and her affections.

Today, through me, this protector serves not only myself and my children. He serves the world and all those who really need him. I was far from thinking that I could fulfill anything like this. I grew up in a religious community. I had no contact with traditional dance, with iboga. I do not know by what miracle I find myself here today, in a temple.

But the more I have practiced my traditional ways, the more I have understood their universal significance. These rites do not oppose my Catholic culture. This is why I continue to pray and commune. Even in my dreams. When I pray, when I fast, I receive help. And when I have difficult cases, sometimes I may even ask for a mass. So my traditions are united with one another.

The Gift of Divination

The gift that I have is a spiritual gift. Unlike teachings passed on by our family, gifts come to us without us having learned them. Today I am a grandmother. I can teach my children which plants heal which sicknesses. The day I am no longer here, you can pick it up and heal, because your mother or grandmother showed you. This is direct transmission.

Anniek and Geneviève preparing a purification bath for a woman's initiation. Oyenano Village, Libreville, Gabon, 2014

Bernadette's main temple. Oyenano Village, Libreville, Gabon, circa 1990s

Bernadette's main temple. Oyenano Village, Libreville, Gabon, 2014

Gifts are different, we do not learn them. They come upon you. The visions began when I was eight years old. I remember once I saw my father's friend in a dream. His name was Midis. In the dream, I saw him fall into the water and the fish ate his eyes. In the morning at breakfast I told my father. He told me to stop telling such stories. I stopped talking. But not long afterward, his friend died.

I continued to see while sleeping, but also with my eyes open. My father forbade me to talk about it. So I kept this all to myself.

Sometimes I did share certain visions with my school friends. I remember that in my dreams I would be shown the next day's lesson on the chalkboard. I would see it very clearly. In the morning, when I went to school, it was the same lesson I had seen in my dreams. And it became a game with the others. What did you see? I would say, "I saw that the lesson will be a dictation." And it would be true. So we would have fun with it, as if it were a game, without knowing that it was the sight that served me.

Divination is a spiritual gift. Sometimes it is hereditary, or it comes from a spirit. No one really knows. This is why I place myself first in the hands of God, the Supreme Being who is the master of all.

It is a heavy responsibility to predict, to do a consultation for someone you do not know, to foresee a sickness that someone may have had, may have, or may be getting in the future. It's important to utilize it in a constructive way to serve those in need.

We should never do harm with our gifts. I cannot change the content of what I see, the way God gives it to me. It is in service to humanity, to help others. The first level of responsibility is the way we say what we see. If I find that you have an internal illness but I cannot heal it, I must encourage you to see a doctor and not lead you to believe that traditional medicine can heal you. One should never give others false hope. We must speak the truth, but that does not mean we must tell all.

Some visions are best not brought forward in their raw form, so I don't alarm the person too much. I owe the truth to everyone, but remain careful to check which truths can be heard.

The other responsibility is humility. We must make ourselves very small. We say here in Africa, "He who knows does not speak." Silence is not a sign of stupidity. Silence is sacred. And so, I have the responsibility of one who listens and does not judge. People come to me to confide the most precious things of their lives. I must be deserving of this closeness. Humility is to recognize and to say what I can and cannot do. To accept that I cannot know everything. To recognize the times I do not have the experience to help.

Another important responsibility is what I owe to God. This is primary, elementary. Because He judges us, He knows what we are doing; even if we hide it from ourselves, we are accountable for the gift He has given to us. After our lives are complete, we have debts to repay for what has been given. We must justify how we have used these gifts. *I gave you these glasses; you wore them and used them. Yes or no?* Yes, I used the gift.

Even though I am not a businesswoman, all work deserves a salary. I pay everyone who works with me. Like hospital services, people who come for consultations pay for the visioning and their treatments. So what I ask for must be proportionate to the care I provide.

The gift that I have is a spiritual gift. Unlike teachings passed on by our family, gifts come to us without us having learned them.

Bernadette preparing a remedy for a patient. Oyenano Village, Libreville, Gabon, 2014

Another important responsibility is what I owe to God. This is primary, elementary. Because He judges us, He knows what we are doing; even if we hide it from ourselves, we are accountable for the gift He has given to us. After our lives are complete, we have debts to repay for what has been given.

Beyond the care we provide, solidarity is very important in our culture. If one of my adepts or one of their relatives has difficulties, it's our responsibility to do everything possible to support them physically, spiritually, and financially. Because we are here for one another in misfortune as well as in health.

Sometimes my assistant, Antonio, asks me, "Why do you continue to work?" I say, "It is my gift. It is my destiny. I have the pleasure of knowing that it is useful." In the end, I thank God from the depths of my heart for what I have received. Beyond the responsibility, it is an honor and a joy to help others.

Forces of Nature, Spirits and Rites

Antonio harvesting medicinal tree bark for a remedy

For us Africans, there are many forces in nature. Most of the time they are invisible, they are forces that command nature. The plants, the trees, the birds, the stones, these are the things we see. We can touch them. But there are other forces of nature that we do not see with our human eyes. In these invisible forces, there are spirits. And among these are several types of spirits.

We have tutelary spirits, that is to say, those that come from our ancestors who have passed on, who are a part of the beyond. There are also spirits we call genies. Among those, there are some that belong to the forest, and others are spirits of the water. And within the water, there are genies of the oceans, of the rivers, and of the little streams. You have spirits of air, like the birds; spirits of thunder. These are the forces we do not control but that have existed since the birth of time. Even after we die, these forces will continue forever. No one can stop them.

I myself am inhabited by a thunder spirit and other *Inkinda* (tutelary spirits).

Bernadette entering a space in the forest where a woman's initiation is taking place

In all of manifestation, there is also one spirit we call *Bumbaeyano*—that is to say, the spirit of birth. Each of us is born with this. Some call them guardian angels. There are many names for this spirit in all the languages of Gabon. There are ones that manifest and others that do not manifest. There are some who speak to you in dreams. There are some who come while you're working and ideas may come to you, all by themselves, as if you are guided. And all these are Bumbaeyano, the guiding spirit that never leaves you, because you were born with it.

I am a priestess of several rites in which the spirits manifest themselves: the women's rites; the mixed rites with women and men. I also initiate thunder spirits, water spirits, and forest spirits, which we call *Abandji*. I am also an initiated master of the iboga.

To initiate means to learn. It is a moment of connection with the spirits. These rites also provide the space for profound healing and help people to better know themselves, be guided, and understand life.

All this knowledge is usually transmitted orally, not written. Once someone dies, he or she leaves with the knowledge. Myself, I refuse to leave this world without transmitting my knowledge to the future generations. This is why I write and do recordings.

While I initiate, I try to do it with love. Why with love? Because first of all, it is a gift from God. I did not ask for it. I was chosen. And why again with love? Because I serve my brothers and sisters. This is why I do this, truly; with the little force I have left, I try to do what I know.

Human beings do not resemble one another. Each one of us is unique. Just like with a medicine, everyone's reaction to a plant or an initiation will be different. There are things that correspond to some people, whether physically or even spiritually, and not to others. The same plant will cause itching in one person and in the other, a deep healing. This is why it requires a lot of attention.

In this work, I have learned a lot. It has permitted me to understand human beings. Who are we? What are we? And what have we come to do here on earth? It has also helped me to understand universal suffering. Suffering does not choose a particular skin. Suffering does not choose a country. The suffering you feel, that suffering is universal.

Yet everyone suffers in their own way. There are people who speak up about their suffering, they can talk. There are people who suffer in silence.

I have accompanied some people at the end of their lives. Some have looked at me in silence. A tear on their cheek. You can sense they suffer, but they do not speak. Others will get enraged. The agony of the person who gets enraged manifests in their refusal to die. They hit. They cry. They make noise. "Why me?" Little by little, death being stronger, death takes them. I have even seen some leave singing. I once helped a woman who sang for a long time before dying.

Grandmother Maria Alice assisting Bernadette with an African American woman's initiation. Oyenano Village, Libreville, Gabon, 2014

No one gets past death. We must love and we must also forgive.

I do not heal; it comes from the spirits that work through me. Little by little in my experience through these rites I have gained another vision of life. Seeing another view of life, seeing in another way has allowed me to mature, to grow my wisdom. All the rest goes back to the spirits.

For us Africans, there are many forces in nature. Most of the time they are invisible, they are forces that command nature. The plants, the trees, the birds, the stones, these are the things we see. We can touch them. But there are other forces of nature that we do not see with our human eyes. In these invisible forces, there are spirits.

Advent of the Grandmothers Council Project

In 2002 I was in Paris for vacation with my children. One evening the telephone rang. At the other end of the line was a woman who spoke in English. Because I am not anglophone, I asked to the person next to me, who spoke a little English, to see who was calling me.

And so through both of our translators I spoke with Dayna, who wanted to meet me to be initiated in the iboga. She said that she had received my number from Jean Claude Cheyssial, a filmmaker who had come to Gabon to work with me on several projects. I asked her how she knew iboga and she said she had worked with Ibogaine, a product derived from iboga, converted into pill form, nothing at all to do with my work.

So I found it would be necessary for her to come to Africa, to Gabon. This is how we finished our call. In a few months, she called me to say she was ready to come to Gabon. I received Dayna; her husband, Scott; her mother-in-law, Jyoti; and Ann, her translator for the first time in my house in Libreville. I let them know that I did not work in the city, that my temple is in the forest.

We traveled to my temple at Oyenano Village and I began to take care of Dayna, offering her the initial treatments and visioning, to see exactly what I needed to do. In this way, I was able to diagnose that she had spirits and needed to be initiated because she absolutely needed to know where they came from, what they had come to do, and why they were there.

In this way I initiated Dayna in my temple in the presence of my family, my children, Jyoti, Ann, and Scott. This went very well. Dayna understood everything that had been bothering her.

During Dayna's initiation ceremony, Jyoti asked if I would accept to initiate her. I asked her what drew her to the iboga. She said that she had a certain sensibility that drew her toward that sacred plant. And so I initiated Jyoti in my temple. Jyoti had not come to Gabon to do this. Thanks to Dayna, Jyoti and I came to know each other.

During Jyoti's astral voyage she asked me, "Can I sing and dance?" I said, "Why?" Jyoti explained, "Because I see women around the fire who tell me that I must sing." I said, "Why dance?" She said, "Because the elder women around the fire are telling me to dance."

I was seated. I asked, "Do you know who these women are? Because you are in Africa, and my temple is very inhabited. I have my ancestors, and a lot of other spirits are present. These women, can you describe them, what do they look like?" She responded, "These women here, I have the impression they are old, but each one is very specific."

Our visions met. I told Jyoti that each time I light my fire I see these women. They talk. Some talk my language, some talk other languages, but it is as if they are all saying the same thing: the Grandmothers must rise up to speak.

I said, "The Grandmothers are the roots of all nations." Jyoti said, "It's true." I said, "I do not understand all the languages, but I know the Grandmothers at the sacred fire approve." I said, "I do not know if one day this vision might be realized." I had just returned from Peru, where I had signed a paper in defense of the earth with the Amazonians.

I continued, saying, "I hope I do not die before the Grandmothers can rise up and speak. I do not know where they will come from, but the moment has come for the Grandmothers of this world. Whether

they be Asian, African, or Indian, they have something to say. Because the next generations come from the wombs of the Grandmothers. Without the Grandmothers, there is no humanity, because it is these women who give and give and continue to nourish us all. Everything comes from somewhere. Every tree has its roots."

And this is how Jyoti left Gabon. She said, "I will see if we can concretize what we saw in the fire in Gabon." It's in this way that the Grandmothers Council project was born in the Oyenano temple.

Oyenano Village

Oyenano Village was founded on February 2, 1978. *Oyenano* is an Omyènè word meaning the reunion. I purchased this site from an old member of the original peoples of this area we call the Sékiani. This site is called Bayumba, the name of the river that flows there down to the ocean.

Oyenano Village is thirty kilometers from the capital of Libreville. It is first and foremost a part of the forest, an area dedicated to remain in the traditional ways. A place where everyone is free to come, whether they be national or international visitors; a place of reunion; a place of reflection; a place of meditation; and a place of the good life. There are also those who come to study, they come to calm themselves and prepare for their exams, because this is truly a place of retreat.

Oyenano is surrounded by mangrove trees on the left bank and an arm of the ocean.

Bernadette's daughter, Antoinette, leading the opening procession of the ECHOES OF THE GRANDMOTHERS: Roots of Humanity gathering, hosted by Grandmother Bernadette. Oyenano Village, Libreville, Gabon, 2015

"The Grandmothers are the roots of all nations."

Behind the river is the village; this river comes alongside the airport. I kept the vegetation for the oxygen and for the respect of the environment. I destroyed nothing, only the places where I raised the little houses around the temple. Otherwise, when you arrive at Oyenano, you feel that you are in the forest.

Before, we used to come on foot. Now we can arrive by car in a short time. We did not have drinkable water, we had a well for washing, but drinkable water came from the city. Back in the day, Oyenano was lit with torches and fire. Now we have electricity.

And so, little by little there has been progress and the space has become comfortable and welcoming; good food and conviviality have a home.

Many people belong to the village. I have my own children, the assistants, my spiritual children, friends—a beautiful family. It's a small community, in fact.

Oyenano Village is also a pharmacy. I have medicinal trees and medicinal plants here that help me to work, to heal others. It's a kind of small traditional hospital. People come to find relief for their difficulties, their illnesses, whether they be spiritual or physical.

Oyenano is also the Grandmothers' village. The cock sang for the Grandmothers for the first time here in Oyenano. The spirit of the council was born here through the original visions of the grandmother spirits around our ancestors' fire. Through our initiations, through our sacred fire, the Grandmothers Council's footprint is here and cannot be erased.

Now after all these years, we made our world tour together to each other's homelands. The last gathering was here in Oyenano, in the very place where the Grandmothers Council was born. Even those Grandmothers who could not join us for my gathering in Gabon were represented by their photos in the temple. And so whether in spirit or in flesh, we were all present to complete our journey around the world.

Members of the International Council of Thirteen Indigenous Grandmothers and Oyenano Village at a press conference in Libreville, Gabon, 2015

Oyenano Village is very dear to me. It is a part of my life. Now I live here permanently and I go to the city as a visitor, despite the fact that I have property I built in the city on ancestral land. There's even a tree there, planted by my grandmother.

The day that God calls me back, I want to be buried at Oyenano. For me it is the direct fruit of my actions and my spiritual life. My home in the city is the land of my ancestors. But Oyenano Village is my land.

Oyenano has seen the birth of generations of masters who have been trained, have been initiated, and now have become masters. I hope that Oyenano continues on after me. Because when we plant a tree, it is not the person who plants it who eats the fruit. It is those who remain who eat the fruit. Like my grandmother and my mother, who planted a garden before us, from which we have harvested for a long time after their deaths. I hope the mango trees I planted here in Oyenano continue to bear fruit. Like the trees, I hope that the spirit and the knowledge of the traditions continues on in perpetuity.

I want Oyenano Village to become modernized. I dream, I pray, and I implore God that traditional and modern medicine can coexist together in service to those in need.

I dream that Oyenano might become a grand village, continuing to receive brothers and sisters who come from abroad. Like I have been able to receive them in my life. What a pleasure it has been to receive them! They have traversed the oceans and come to our village. It is an honor. So I dream Oyenano can continue to house a unity of cultures and global health of body and spirit.

The Main Temple

In each temple there are symbols that talk. Each temple has its own type of pillar, and there is a central pillar. On the central pillar of my temple, my male and female guardians oversee everything. The male is on the top of the pillar; he is seated on the head of a woman. And this woman is seated on the earth. What does this signify? It means that all the weight of the temple, all the responsibility of the temple rests on the shoulders of the woman. It is this woman who is also the force of the temple. She gives life to it. In the same way that you and I gave birth to our children, she gives birth to the life of the temple. I saw this pillar in my initiation, just as it is. I invented nothing.

In my astral voyage, I was shown that these spirits wanted a temple. This is what I saw with the divinatory shells.[2] I asked the sculptor to carve it as it is. Even after me, my children know, there is no question about changing the column of the temple.

And then there is another weight-bearing foot in the rear of the temple. At the very back there are two statues and a parrot. All that is here is what I saw. There are two statues, one dressed in red, one dressed in white. For me these are the two colors of the life of the soul, red and white. And in the center, there is one fire that we light to give vitality to the temple. Then there are the traditional musical instruments, the drums, the sitar, the *umbanda*, way in the back. They are part of the life and the heritage of the temple. The master spirit of this temple did not

---

2. Cowrie-shell divination.

want any imported objects, only elements close to nature. There are the plants that we dry, that we weave. The ground is made of earth, so our feet are connected to her.

All these objects have their own reason for being, their own language. And during the rituals, during the grand ceremonies, these objects are alive. When one enters into the domain of the astral voyage, they will speak to you, as I am speaking to you now.

The torch, *okoumé*, is irreplaceable in our ceremonies. It is the spiritual presence. If it has not been lit, the ritual has no worth. Once the torch is lit and held in hand, the presence of the spirit of the temple, the spirits of the ancestors, the spirits of nature, can reveal themselves. The torch is made from a resin that we wrap in bark. It is that which enlightens us. It is like the candles in a church. It is the presence of the fire inside of us.

The instrument that I play, a rattle, we call the *tsokai*. This instrument addresses the spirits of the forest. We take seeds from the fruit of several trees to use in our tsokai. The men also use the same seeds for their *Bwiti* instruments.

The iboga that is around the temple was planted initially by necessity. Rather than going far into the forest, we have it at my door. We use the leaves and the root below. I planted them myself so that they would be close to the temple. It is a powerful plant. Sometimes it grows on its own, without me having to plant it. It serves the temple

(above) Central pillar of the main temple. Oyenano Village, Libreville, Gabon, 2014

(opposite page) Geneviève playing the *tsokai* at a *Bwiti* woman's initiation

Women singing and dancing in front of the main temple on their way to the sacred forest, as part of the Ndjèmbè initiations

because it is medicinal, and above all, it is sacred. Like all my plants, I do not cut them. They are irreplaceable and inseparable from the life of the temple.

Music—Sacred Helper and Healer

For every African, music takes a central place. Music is a healer because music is spiritual. Our babies are very sensitive; this is why we cradle our babies while singing. We accompany the dead with singing, with music. The woman who marries is accompanied by specific chants that her husband must listen to.

Sometimes I receive sick people who have intense psychic difficulties. While I'm treating them in their room I put on music, sweet music with words that touch their spirits. Because the content of the music increases its significance.

In almost all of the ceremonies, especially with the women, and also with the men, we begin the ceremony by a call: "Kia kia ohhhh." It is spoken, it is not sung. It is a message that we send, a spoken song.

Before entering the forest, we make a little chorus to alert the spirits that we are going in the next day. We don't want them to be surprised by our presence in the forest. Each morning when we are about to enter, we do the same thing. We let the forest and the spirits know, we give them notice that we are coming and ask for their help. Our ancestors guided us in these traditions.

You can pray while singing. Even at the foot of a tree. Pray as you are. I learned to sing my prayers by evoking the spirits. For example, before the initiates go into the forest I tell them to follow those who have gone into the forest before us. "Because you, our ancestors, have done this before us, and we are your apprentices. But as you are already in the other world, I know you will do it better than I." I say this, but in song.

Some things we cannot do in the temple without music. Music accompanies and attracts the spirits. Positive or negative. Special instruments are dedicated to our ceremonies, like the sitar, which resembles a little harp in human form; the *mumbango* (musical bow); and different types of drums and rattles, whistles, etc. Certain instruments actively contribute to the initiations, supporting the astral journey to connect with the spirits. Their uses vary according to needs that arise. The practice, accompanied by the human voice, is a very respected art.

Music is inseparable from Africa: even in misfortune, even in suffering, music consoles and heals. For us, music is sacred.

Types of Diseases Treated by Traditional Ways

There are several types of sickness that disturb humans. We begin by examining the source of sickness itself. Man is a being composed of different facets: the visible facet; the physical aspect, his body; and the invisible facet, that's to say his soul or spirit. Often sickness begins internally, that is to say, with the spirit. Over time, the sickness appears in the physical plane. It is possible for someone to suffer for years with a sickness for which the real cause is unknown. Why has the cause been unknown? With all the modern technology, often the doctors find nothing. Examinations come up negative, simply because the sickness is situated in an incorporeal aspect of the person, in her or his spirit. We call these spiritual sicknesses.

It is more difficult to heal spiritual sickness, one could say psychic illness, than to heal a purely physical illness. What doctors often cannot perceive with their instruments can be seen by the traditional therapist, who knows ways to heal the spirit. Perhaps it would be through plants, ritual, or many other ways. Here she or he attends to the soul, to the spirit that is suffering. This is why I insist, for the good of humanity, that modern medicine and traditional medicine need to be complementary—because humans have a double identity. If the physical body is sick, they will come automatically to modern medicine but could also be treated with traditional medicine. If someone has been bitten by a snake, for instance, there are traditional medicine plants that can heal the snake poison in the body, just as modern medicine has its remedies.

But when a person's spirit is sick, when the sickness has wounded the soul for a long time, things do not follow the same route. It is here where traditional medicine can provide specific, complementary care.

Dreams play a major role in the diagnosis of disease. The understanding of their scope and their message comes from the healer's knowledge and from a God-given gift.

Women's Initiation Rites

In Gabon, there are two fundamental types of initiation: the Bwiti (the rites with the iboga) and the feminine rites for the women that we call Ndjèmbè. This very ancient rite allows communication with the interior woman, the real woman. The African tradition, and most precisely the Gabonese traditions, call for the young girl to be initiated in the Ndjèmbè once she has her first menstrual cycle, around thirteen, fourteen, or fifteen years old. Nevertheless, there are women who initiate

Woman's Bwiti initiation at the main temple

later in life due to their studies or living abroad. They may be initiated at twenty, thirty, or even forty years old. Not all the Gabonese communities initiate in the Ndjèmbè. We find this rite among the Omyènè and with our sisters in the interior communities, the Eshira, Chogo, Dagomba, and Lumbu.

There are elements of the feminine rites that are strictly secret. Truly secret. In the Ndjèmbè rite, the girl follows an apprenticeship to prepare herself in her life as a woman. It is spiritual, psychological, physical, and sociological, because it offers a way to take care of oneself and live in society. It prepares the young girl in her duty as a woman: how to hold herself when she has children, how to behave in relation to her husband, how to live within the society of her community.

It is also a healing rite. Many women come to be initiated because they are sick. So it is possible to help her internally within the rite. She can find healing there. Men can also receive healing through this rite. They only need to ask the women who are gathering to help them.

We teach the initiates the language of the forest, the language of certain forces of the universe. Here today we call this a tree, but in the feminine rites the true name is not "tree." We will enter into the interior of the tree to give it the name of the energy of this tree. It is a coded language, a secret language. That is why we speak very little of it.

Our people respect the Ndjèmbè rite. Even those who are not initiated respect it. It is also a rite that can help bring peace, not only peace at home but also peace in the country.

From the beginning of time we performed these rites so that our country would not know war. It is fundamental for the women, to contribute to the tranquility and the unity of the country and all the people.

I am going to die, but I will return so this rite can continue for the women. Men have their own rituals as well and tend to them with as much care as the women take care of theirs.

Before Leaving This Earth

If there was a prayerful wish I would like to realize before leaving this earth, what would it be? I have been doing my spiritual work for sixty years. Now, at the end of my life, there is a project that is close to my heart. I would like to create a multidisciplinary health center.

As I mentioned before, man has two bodies, the physical and the subtle, astral body of the spirit. And the cause of most of our sickness is found in the spiritual plane. I want to build a place where I can call upon the two medicines. That is to say, a place where one relies on both scientific modern medicine and traditional medicine. When the sick person arrived, she or he would be treated by two people. That is to say, both the doctor and the traditional therapist would tend to him. This same person, then, would have two files: one scientific file, created by the doctor, that would be brought to the appropriate places, and another file created by the therapist who practices traditional medicine, close to nature with plants and rituals.

This project is something that could remain in service to man, not only in my own country but also on an international level. I look for the means to help complete this project. Because it requires funds and contributions from those who have the knowledge and interest. So I call out to the people of good will who might truly help me fulfill this vision. As a grandmother, I have faith in those people I see, and I pray to the Good God to help us with the realization of this project before I leave this earth.

There is also a project for the education of the young people, to study the plants. Because after me, there will be others who will continue the work. The study of plants is long. Plants are difficult to master. I envision the transformation of our herbal products to find a way of conservation.

So I am making a call again for help, for those who can accompany us—those who want to help the Grandmothers and those who want to help me.

For the well-being of everything and everyone.

ROSE BERNADETTE REBIENOT OWANSANGO

January 1, 1934–January 21, 2021

Grandmother Bernadette used to say: "After I die, I want everybody to speak of me using the present tense." She wanted to ensure that she remains vividly alive in our memories.

The announcement of her passing deeply affected the numerous members of her initiatory circle, especially the new initiates (*ingondjè* in the Omyènè language), who found themselves orphaned. But before departing, she had the will to "leave her traditional tools on the table," so that her knowledge could remain and continue to serve her work.

Every day, she was dedicated to transmitting and imparting words filled with wisdom. She bequeaths to us a treasure trove of proverbs and stories rich in teachings.

Her presence had something simple and powerful, very natural and reassuring, that words can barely describe. A mother's love for her children is so limitless that it has no form. Simplicity, acceptance, openness, happiness—a wisdom that transcends understanding—Grandmother Bernadette embodies all of this and much more.

To go straight to the essence, to observe and patiently contemplate the origin of things, to pay attention to the smallest details—her signature is distinctive, unique, and still very tangible. Her objective was to develop our spiritual potential so that it is adapted and in service to our lives and our community.

For Grandmother Bernadette, cultural equilibrium was indeed central to social equilibrium. That is why she dedicated her entire life to the promotion and preservation of her country's traditions.

As a mistress and priestess of numerous Gabonese rites, transmission was at the heart of her teachings. She always took care to pass on a portion of her knowledge to her biological family and to some of her children and grandchildren who chose to follow in her ways.

Regarding the Ndjèmbè, the ritual at the foundation of all female rites, she spent more than sixty years initiating young girls in her community and passing the torch to those on whom the future rests.

She used to emphasize that a traditional practitioner follows the truth because they are guided by their inner light. Accompanied by the spirit of her ancestor, she had the ability to diagnose a patient at a glance. There was no deceiving this master healer; she validated if the patient was accepted or not and decided on the appropriate treatments.

Foreseeing, she left behind invaluable manuscripts detailing the methodology of her science to precisely guide those who have taken up the mantle in the path she opened.

But it is primarily through pure oral tradition that her transmission occurred, especially through the practice of traditional songs. Holding an immense repertoire from her Ngwè-Myènè community, her voice still resonates and ensures the posterity of Ndjèmbè, Abandji, Ivanga, Ibo-Ikabo, Bwiti Disumba, Bwiti Akowa, ôlôgô, Igna, and Agombè-Nêrô rites. This knowledge comes alive whenever this heritage is awakened during healing sessions, initiations, vigils, and other traditional ceremonies, as well as special community offerings such as the Evandaganyè march.

Furthermore, Grandmother Bernadette greatly contributed to the life of her Mpongwè community. Indeed, she served the Eka zi Mpongwè chieftaincy for decades, actively participating in key stages of its history. A few months before her passing, she carried out her last community act, directly involved in the choice and enthronement of the current chief.

Today it's at the Village Oyenano, a place steeped in history, that the legacy of this great lady is perpetuated. Like her daughter Antoinette, who continues to welcome patients and ensure treatments and initiations, we have a duty to carry on Grandmother Bernadette's work. We must honor what she entrusted to us by keeping the flame that burns within each of us alive.

That is why we've created the Rose Bernadette Rebienot Owansango Foundation for the preservation of Gabonese culture, traditions, arts, and ancestral rites. It is a space that will facilitate the organization of cultural and traditional events dear to Grandmother Bernadette, ensuring that her invaluable legacy remains alive. This is how we wish to pay homage to this wonderful woman, who above all remains a mother. It's our way of saying, "Akewa!" (Thank you).

Serge ALEKA REBIENOT (her son)
and Charif Remy EL SHAFEY (her spiritual son)

ELEVEN

GRANDMOTHER MARIA ALICE CAMPOS FREIRE

MY NAME IS MARIA ALICE CAMPOS FREIRE. I was born in the city of Rio de Janeiro, Brazil. I am Brazilian. My parents were born in Brazil, and I have no recent ancestors from other countries.

My father's name was Eduardo Solón de Magalhães Freire. He was from the northeast of Brazil, from Ceará, a region where there have been various types of colonization. The Portuguese colonized everything, then the Dutch colonized as well. Then the colonizers warred with each other. The indigenous peoples of this region were massacred, practically exterminated.

My mother was born in Rio de Janeiro, but her family is Mineira, from the state of Minas Gerais (General Mines), a region where there was a lot of slavery in the past. A place full of memories of the black people, of Africa, of the slaves who worked in the mines.

I have sisters and brothers. We were six. Two of my brothers already passed. I still have one younger brother and two older sisters. I was the fourth child. We grew up in Rio de Janeiro in a neighborhood called Irajá. Back then it was like a little countryside town; there was a creek, a mountain, and a quarry. Nowadays it is part of the second most populous city in Brazil.

I'm not from the culture of the people who are considered Cariocas, people from Rio de Janeiro, who have roots from the colonizers. I'm from the culture of a small town in Rio de Janeiro, which is more related to festivities, dance, and other cultural practices. The people were friends and celebrated together on the streets. It wasn't like today where it's all separated, everyone inside their own homes, which happens in big cities.

My parents suffered within the institution of the Catholic religion. They left their home places to come study and live in the city. When they left the Catholic schools they became atheists, because they witnessed things that were so inhumane inside these institutions that they thought that was God. So they left without religion. So in our home there was neither religion nor spirituality, because for them it became the same thing. They rejected it.

In my family, no one was very spiritual, yet I had visions of the spiritual world. When I was a child I had a lot of visions, I was clairvoyant. Nobody knew what that was, so to them I was just an unusual child. I used to tell them about my visions, but they didn't understand. Since I was very sensitive, I absorbed many things from my father's karma. And I used to get sick.

I worked a lot with the spiritual world, and when I arrived at a certain age I was completely disconnected from the things of this world. I had no interest in the things that the other children were interested in. I lived in another world. I didn't even like to eat. I was completely different. I had my siblings, we were a family, and we played a lot too. My father did good things with us, like planting vegetables in the yard, reading stories to us; we had a family life like that. In my family, there was a strong culture of self-sufficiency. So we made everything in our home. We painted the walls, planted, took care of everything. My mother sewed, made clothes for all of us, so there our family dynamic was very cool. However, that was inside my home; in relation to the things of the world, to school, things like society, I was distant. Even though I was a great student and only had good grades, I didn't speak a word at school; I was always silent. I have this memory until today, because I didn't relate to that universe and although I would learn with ease everything they were teaching, I didn't have the courage to express my private life. I didn't feel at home.

I really enjoyed being with my mother. She planted flowers, planted the garden, sewed. So I learned everything she did. When I was about ten years old, my family got worried about me because I was different. I didn't sleep at night, as I kept having visions. They took me to the doctor, who prescribed medication to stop the visions, to dull my sensitivity. They called it a neurovegetative disorder, considered an anomaly. I suffered because I was already working with the spirits, but nobody understood that, not even I. They believed they were helping me, that this disorder was the source of my organic imbalances, but in reality, when they inhibited the symptoms, they inhibited the visionary aspect of my mediumship.

My father and my mother were communists. When the Second World War was over, it was also the period of the Russian revolution. There was a rising hope that socialism was going to save humanity. It was a utopian view, and they believed it. They were good people; they

Achiote (*Bixa orellana*). State of Amazonas, Brazil, 2011

were communists in the sense that they believed humanity could live without hierarchy and share things, without social classes, with equality. At my house when I was a child, there were Communist Party meetings. I liked to go to the meetings because I could see many things. In those days, through my sensibility I saw the auras of the people. I could identify those who were sincere, who were loving, who were fake, all based on the colors of their auras. I wasn't aware of anything; I was simply a channel for the manifestation of that perception.

My father was proud of me; he used to say, "Listen, when she grows up she's going to be a communist!" I was very small, about two or three years old. After I left the room where the meetings were, something inside me identified and decoded the visions that I had. There were those people I didn't like, who had those colors that I rejected. And there were others I liked. Afterward I started to understand it: some were sincere and others were not.

After this period, my father started to realize that most of his companions in that Communist Party did not have his same ideas and that he was living a utopian ideal, very distant from what they were practicing. He started to have disagreements in the Communist Party, to speak about what he considered wrong. When the Soviet Union invaded Czechoslovakia, he really could not handle it anymore, and he was finally expelled from the party. I didn't understand anything; I was a very little child. But I realized that my father was devastated when this happened to him because he was a social activist; his dream suddenly fell apart.

Still, he was a great professional engineer who started to travel a lot, dedicating himself entirely to his career. He went to the Amazon as an engineer building roads. Then he found out that while building these roads, the government destroyed indigenous peoples. He was a witness to human evil, to human falsehood, and in the end he became an alcoholic. He was an extreme alcoholic, and he kept drinking until the end of his life. I witnessed all of my father's history. It was overwhelming for me when he drank. I always had some connection with him, even with those obsessions that surrounded him; I always had this connection with his life story.

My mother was another kind of person. She was less worried, less cerebral. She was a good mother, a loving, good person. She didn't speak ill of anyone. She did not participate in my father's agony and an-

guish. When all of this was happening, she detached herself. When she was young she had been very daring, because she didn't fit the mold of her Catholic family. She became a communist—imagine, a woman of her age. She was political. Still, when she married my father and had kids, she committed herself to raising the kids.

My grandmother, the mother of my father, was what is called in Brazil a *sarará*, a person who has a mixture of black and white bloodlines. Their skin is fair with features and hair of blacks. Yet she was racist toward blacks and Indians. She was raised by the oppression of colonization. My grandfather, my father's father, had an issue with her when she spoke about racism. He would say: "Look at your hair!"

My grandmother was the typical person who denies her origin. This was a defining trait of the people who came mainly from the northeast, where the Indians were all decimated. To be accepted you could be neither Indian nor black. You had to be white. You had to look like something you were not. It's our history.

My parents were not racists. They followed the socialist path, being against oppression, but they were not aware of the memories that remained in their subconscious. They acted in accordance with these memories, but they were not aware of them. I was the only person in my family who woke up with this ancestral memory. I had a brother who like me walked this path. But he only got to a certain point and didn't go any further. He disincarnated before finishing it.

I was very successful in the structures of the world, but those things didn't fulfill me. I always had a lot of compassion in my heart, since I was a child. In my schools, those children who had a lot of suffering, who were poor, whose families had suffering, they were my best friends. They told me of their suffering, but at that time I didn't understand.

Activism

Then there was a dictatorship in my country. My father had already left the Communist Party when the dictatorship came and started persecuting activists. Despite that, he hid the fugitives in our home because he had feelings of fraternity. He harbored the fugitives, so we learned since childhood to share everything we had with other people. There were always many other people who ate at our home, other children who slept in our bedroom. We shared our fortune.

I couldn't tell anyone at school that we had those people at our place, because they were fugitives. So I grew up with this awareness of social and political conflict. The dominant spirit in my home was community oriented, of sharing, egalitarianism. When the dictatorship really came about, things started to happen at school. The best teachers we had vanished, disappeared, were arrested. It kept happening.

Things escalated when the dictatorship closed a restaurant, a gathering place for many students from all social origins, an environment that encouraged rebellion. The students gathered in protest outside to ask that the restaurant be reopened, and in this protest the police killed an innocent student.

The public response took on enormous proportions. The general population took to the streets and rebelled against the dictatorship. The dictatorship activated the police. Then began a very intense social and political conflict. Even my mother took to the streets. The families, the homemakers, the breadwinners took to the streets. Over one hundred thousand people gathered.

Most of the students who started the protest came from the northeast, from the place where people already shared a history of persecution. From these gatherings, the people organized to fight against the government. I left my parents' home and got involved in this movement. I became a guerrilla fighter. When I was seventeen years old I was linked to the groups who were fighting against the government. I was arrested, imprisoned, and tortured. I was tortured a lot.

In one of the torture sessions there was a very small man, a high-ranking military officer. He had tortured many people. At that time when I was going to be tortured he was already high-ranking, so he didn't apply the torture anymore. He was in command. He had the ideas, the guys followed his orders, and he kept laughing. During these torture sessions, something very special happened to me. I had an awakening of spiritual consciousness in the very moment this man was laughing and the guys were torturing me. It was me and two other men. We were all being tortured, all three. Then I looked at this high-ranking official and I had an awakening of my most profound compassion. I looked at him and thought: *How is this possible? What kind of being is this? How can he have been born as a baby like I was, a baby, and have become this, to be pouring all this hatred over me, since I have never done anything against him? And he is doing this to me.*

I can't have such hatred against him, like he has against me. In the moment that I had this feeling, I had a spiritual awakening. A superior

blessing fell on me, and I stopped listening, I stopped seeing, I stopped feeling, I stopped everything. I entered another dimension.

This was a milestone in my life, because from that moment on I realized I was a spirit who was living in a body, that I wasn't only a body. They beat me until I fainted and took me to a solitary confinement cell. They threw me into an area where they kept many people, each and every one alone, in a tiny cubicle. The guards would carry out inspections to make sure the prisoners were really there or see if they had escaped or what else was happening. When they passed by, the person had to stand up and say their name. When they approached my cell, I had fallen on the floor, unconscious, and they kept screaming at me to stand up and say my name.

And then I had an incredible experience. I realized I was standing, but my body was still lying on the floor. That's when I realized I was a spirit that inhabited a body. Because before I believed I was that body. And they kept screaming that I had to answer, that if I didn't answer they would open that door and beat me up more. I was tranquil, because I wasn't inside that body. Suddenly I heard a voice say: *Go ahead and stand your body up, because this body is still yours, you still have a long mission with this body.* So I stood myself up, said my name, and they left.

This was a milestone in my life. After this discovery, my life changed. I started to pay more attention to the spiritual signs, starting with the suffering. I still endured a lot of suffering. I was there for six months.

Grandmother Maria Alice leading a prayer vigil during her Grandmothers Gathering, at the administrative region of Brasilia, surrounded by government buildings. Brasilia, Brazil, 2011

My mother came after me, searching, because I was able to send a message through a woman who was leaving. My mother finally found me. She hired lawyers and then they rescued me. Because I was underage, they couldn't put me on trial in the military judicial court.

In those days, the government did whatever they wanted. If they wanted to do something against the law, they would issue a decree that would stand above the constitution and it became law. So they issued a decree saying that people over sixteen years of age, if they were arrested for activities against the government, would have to undergo a competency evaluation. And if it was proven that they were competent, they would be tried as adults. My lawyer gave me some instructions, sent through my mother because he couldn't see me. So I did very well in the sense that they believed I wasn't fit to stand trial, and they had to let me go because I was underage.

But when they released me from prison I ran away because they were going to arrest me again. I was about to turn eighteen, and they would arrest me again and try me as an adult, which is what they wanted.

Exile

Only my mother and one of my sisters knew I was running away. My mother was my accomplice, but I wrote a letter as if she didn't know about it and she gave me some time to escape. Later she showed the letter to the police. Now I can speak about this. She already lives in the world of the spirits, no one can arrest her. And I have already been given amnesty.

I ran away to Chile, which was granting political asylum to everyone who escaped dictatorships, because there were many dictatorships in South America at that time. There was Brazil, there was Argentina. They were the worst dictatorships. So Chile granted asylum.

My sister helped me escape to Chile; later she returned to Brazil. And there I got married to a man who was also a Brazilian in exile. We lived for some time in the city; later we went to an archipelago. I worked with the women weavers. I learned to spin yarn, to weave. My husband worked with the beekeepers. So we lived in the Chilean countryside with traditional people.

Then there was the coup d'état in Chile, and the dictatorship arrived. By then I was one month pregnant, expecting my daughter. My husband and I were arrested because we were exiled and couldn't flee. We stayed three months under arrest in Chile. We were brought to Santiago, where they imprisoned us in the Estádio Nacional (National stadium). The stadium housed eight thousand prisoners. And there they did many horrible things, they used torture. The Brazilian military went there to teach torture techniques to the Chilean military. My husband was tortured a lot, and they separated him to be executed.

When this all reached the level of international diplomacy, there were many conflicts. The ambassador from Sweden intervened and was shot. It was total chaos. Finally, the UN declared that the stadium was a concentration camp and they had to tear it down and set free all the foreign prisoners. But when the UN came to take me, another woman and I, whose husband had also vanished, got together and we said, "We will not leave until you release our husbands. Only if we see their dead bodies. We are going to stay here until they show up." Then our husbands showed up; they were both already sentenced to death. Then we went to a refuge, a nunnery with the UN flag.

We stayed in Chile, where various people from the embassies offered asylum. They would come to interview us and choose whom they would like to take. It wasn't up to us to choose; it was up to them. But my case was very serious, as I was six months pregnant and my weight was around only thirty-five kilos (seventy-seven pounds). I was just skin and bones. The nuns gave me food, treated me well.

Not long after that, my husband and I, and that woman with her husband, were put on a plane to Switzerland, exiled. I suffered a lot there because my husband went crazy. He couldn't handle all of the torture. I experienced a lot of suffering, and my daughter, Barbara, when she was born, she screamed a lot.

We were welcomed by the government, from a material and social point of view. They took care of everything. The social workers found us jobs and a home. They accompanied us until we were integrated in the daily life. But in truth, it was very difficult because there was a lot of racism. I remember when I was living there, there was a plebiscite to decide whether or not to send the foreigners away. So we faced hostilities in the streets, because just by our physical appearance, they could see we were not white. Culturally as well, because I used to sing in the street with my daughter. People were aggressive toward us because we sang. But we were also welcomed by many good people, we had many good friends who welcomed us there.

I was hired by the Swiss government and worked at an educational institution. I could bring my daughter because there was daycare. It was an educational institution for marginalized children and teenagers—children of inmates and drug addicts who had had run-ins with the law. I began working there as a cleaning woman, and after a while I started helping with the children. They had so much respect for me that when there was an opening for an educator they offered it to me. I got to be adjunct to the director. When she had vacations, I assumed the role of director. My daughter was growing up there. We learned how to speak French. French was my daughter's first language. From the time of her birth, my daughter screamed every night. She screamed every night for two and half years. Then one day I had a vision, I received an instruction. It said she would only stop screaming when she stepped on the ground in Africa.

I ended up separating from my husband because I couldn't handle him. He remained my friend. He lived in Switzerland until he died in 2016.

I went to visit some friends who lived in Geneva, Switzerland, the capital. Leaving the train station, I met a friend in the street. He was also a political refugee I had met upon my arrival in Switzerland. We started talking. He gave me a tip that the UN was hiring educators with Portuguese as their first language to go to Africa. And so I went to the UN and introduced myself, had an interview, and three months later, my daughter Barbara and I traveled to Africa.

When my daughter stepped on the ground in Africa, she didn't scream anymore. A new phase in my spiritual awakening began. On the day when I arrived in Africa, they took me to a reception, a celebration and theater play, all in the traditional language. And I understood everything. I felt, in that moment, I was home; my daughter too.

When we settled there, we didn't want to live where the white people lived; we chose to live in a house among people of the community. While we were living there, some people tried to break into our home. The following day I talked to my neighbor, an old man, and he said, "Don't worry, I'm going to take you to a session, then afterward never again will anything bad happen to you in Africa."

I went with him to this spiritual session. It was in a large wooden structure full of *atabaques*,[1] drums. Those guys hit those drums and some of them fell to the ground in trance. I was feeling great there, my daughter too, we were feeling at home. When we left, the old man said, "Well, now everything is okay with you. You can be at peace because never again will anything bad happen to you." In less than a month after arriving, my daughter stopped speaking French and began speaking Creole from Guinea-Bissau.

This was another phase of my awakening, because during the two and a half years that I lived there, I faced many challenges as well. Many things happened to me that were parallel to my normal life, my social life, my work. I was a functioning person. I worked a lot. I loved

---

1. A musical instrument brought to Brazil by African slaves.

Africa; I worked with orphans of the war. I trained teachers who were the orphans' teachers, because there had been thirteen years of war, civil war, the War of Liberation[2] from Portuguese colonization. They were undergoing a process of nation rebuilding when I arrived. I went to help the children to rescue their identity, their culture. In theory, we had to teach them Portuguese because it was the official language of the country. But I struck a deal with them, that we were going to learn Portuguese and would write Creole, which was a language that had no writing.

When my daughter was five years old there was a coup d'état in Guinea-Bissau, and the UN decided to leave and remove all of its personnel. We returned to Switzerland, and soon after that, amnesty was granted in Brazil. My daughter and I returned from exile, along with another Brazilian woman who had three children. When we arrived at the Brazilian airport there were the press, television, amnesty supporters, and lawyers—all waiting for us.

Return to My Roots

After eight years in exile I returned to Brazil, searching for a spiritual path. I got married again and had my second daughter, Julia. This daughter intensified my spiritual connection. When I was pregnant I had visions, and when she was born many people entered my life, people who pointed to a spiritual path. So each of my daughters marked a step in my re-encounter with myself, with my spiritual truth.

I got involved with social work in the city, with the people of the slums, always in the

2. The Portuguese Colonial War (Portuguese: Guerra Colonial Portuguesa), also known in Portugal as the Overseas War (Guerra do Ultramar) or in the former colonies as the War of Liberation (Guerra de Libertação), was fought between Portugal's military and the emerging nationalist movements in Portugal's African colonies between 1961 and 1974.

Altar dedicated to the *Pretos Velhos*. Céu do Mapiá, Brazilian Amazon, 2011

role of educator but also from a health perspective. That was my work. When I was pregnant with my second daughter, I walked in the middle of the slums with a big belly, climbed hills, faced the thugs, the criminals, drug traffickers. Everybody liked me because I would go there and do good. It's not that they liked me, but they didn't have the courage to attack me. Still, I had many disappointments with the professionals with whom I partnered—doctors, psychologists—who created the projects with the people. I always faced politics and power struggles, and that sort of thing. Then when I couldn't believe anymore in anything in the material world, I suffered a lot. I separated from my second husband because the relationship wasn't going anywhere.

It was then that I arrived in the Umbanda. My encounter with Umbanda was another milestone in my life, the beginning of my conscious re-encounter with myself, with my mission, with who I am, with my original traditions.

Umbanda

Umbanda is a spiritual line that works with the spirits of light, the ancestors of light who left the earth already enlightened, ancestors of the different lines of Brazilian roots. It's a syncretic spiritual line that brings together the African traditions that arrived in Brazil through the slaves with the Brazilian indigenous traditions and with pure Christianity— not the oppressive institutional Christianity but the Christianity of Christ himself, of the truth of Christ. Umbanda is founded on an alliance of spiritual traditions; thus, it also includes the spiritual contribution of all human ancestry.

I entered Umbanda through the heart, through the memory of my spiritual being manifested in the feeling of being home, of returning to my birthplace. To be in an Umbanda ceremony meant happiness. I progressed and developed very quickly. My guides arrived to work. All of those things I'd had when I was a child returned, my clairvoyance and my ability to communicate with other spiritual planes. When I arrived in the Umbanda, the doors of spiritual communication and guidance from other planes reopened.

I went to Africa, I had that direct spiritual experience. It wasn't until later in life that I became aware of its meaning. When I returned from Africa I was another person. My heart expanded. It weakened the defensiveness I had toward spirituality.

This was the first revelation I had in the Umbanda: that a significant part of my suffering in life was because I had been a medium since childhood. I was born with this mission. I was born with this gift, a tool with which to further my mission. But I didn't know much about my mission. I simply surrendered to spiritual charity and coexisted with the spirits.

For instance, the strongest thing that happened to me was my encounter with my African ancestor, who started to bring me the memory. I understood that my experience in Africa made this re-encounter possible, because when I arrived in Brazil I was almost ready for this. I started to receive the memory of the knowledge of nature, of the plants, of healing with plants through these entities who are called a phalanx in the Umbanda, the phalanx of the *Pretos Velhos*, the old black slave ancestors. I started then to work a lot with my *Preta Velha*, my *guia de frente* (front guide), and my main and most important guide of my crown. This is when I reencountered the identity of my being, of my soul. I also re-encountered other entities, indigenous spirits, who are called the phalanx of the *caboclos*,[3] who bring another kind of knowledge, also of the plants and the elements.

I also worked with the *mesa branca* (white table), which is part of the Umbanda line. This line is of a purer Umbanda, called the white line because it's the line of peace. Peace among all beings, the alliance among the beings of good. To unite all the ancestral knowledge to do good and to liberate souls from the spiritual entrapments they live in: from their karma, from their confusion, from their past. So I worked at this white table, which is a type of ritual where people are more concentrated and they open to receive communications from the spiritual plane. They came bringing me messages, dictating messages for me to write down. They sang, and I received those songs. For instance, I would be sitting in a circle around the table, but my spirit would project and I would encounter the ancestral spirits of light from various provenances, not only African, indigenous, Christian, but also beings of the orient—spirits who were chained, enslaved, suffering, rebellious—all kinds of spirits. So I started to work with the guides of light.

Being a medium is not only about your physical body (as a vessel)

but also about your consciousness. It's about being a mediator between different planes, different realities: between the light and the darkness; between the material plane and the spiritual plane; between the past and the present time; between different planes of various dimensions. I kept discovering this with practice, working and doing charity. I started to feel happiness and joy in my soul's realization.

The origin of Umbanda is in the history of Brazil, because when the white people arrived in Brazil, the colonizers came with a cross in one hand and with a weapon to kill and oppress in the other. They used the Catholic Church to oppress the culture of the people, to subjugate the indigenous peoples. But the indigenous people didn't let themselves be dominated by the colonizers. They left the shores where they lived, the coast, and sought refuge in the interior, in the forests. They possessed knowledge of nature, they had strength, and they were not exposed to the colonizers. The colonizers were unable to enter the forest. They didn't have the knowledge or confidence to go in, so they stayed on the coast. That's when the colonizers went to Africa to enslave the African people and bring them to Brazil. But the African slaves experienced so much suffering that they ended up knowing the truth of Christ through oppression. Christ experienced a similar thing: He died on the cross. The oppressors killed Christ, and just a short time afterward the oppressors were using His name to continue to oppress the people, just as He had been oppressed and killed. Spiritually, the slaves who died, who reached the light, they had the help of Christ. They had this understanding.

There came a time when many slaves managed to escape and flee

3. Evolved entities related to the spirits of the natives of the forest.

BEING A **MEDIUM** IS NOT ONLY ABOUT YOUR **PHYSICAL BODY** (AS A VESSEL) BUT ALSO ABOUT YOUR **CONSCIOUSNESS**. IT'S ABOUT BEING A **MEDIATOR** BETWEEN DIFFERENT **PLANES**, DIFFERENT **REALITIES**: BETWEEN THE **LIGHT** AND THE **DARKNESS**; BETWEEN THE **MATERIAL** PLANE AND THE **SPIRITUAL** PLANE; BETWEEN THE **PAST** AND THE **PRESENT** TIME; BETWEEN DIFFERENT PLANES OF VARIOUS **DIMENSIONS**.

into the forest. There they met the indigenous people and created communities. The indigenous people welcomed the runaway slaves, the Africans, and helped them create communities in the forest because they had knowledge of the region and of nature. The Africans also knew because they came from Africa, where there are also forests but a different environment. It was a very rich exchange, as they didn't know who the oppressors actually were. They didn't know anything about the people who arrived to oppress. They simply ran into the forest. And they also didn't know anything about Christ. But they formed a community, and there they shared their spiritual wisdom. These communities are called *quilombos.*

These types of communities still exist. Nowadays there are quilombola communities that preserve their tradition. But all of them had an indigenous component. It was the indigenous people in the forest who helped the African slaves survive. So the quilombola communities have at their origin this connection and the parallels between the indigenous people of Brazil and the African slaves, their identities, and their rituals.

The white people, the Portuguese, organized themselves. They were well established and fortified, and with their thirst for conquest, for domination, they entered the forests. These expeditions were called *Entradas e Bandeiras.*[4] The Portuguese ventured into the interior of Brazil to conquer the land and kill the indigenous people and the runaway African slaves. That was the greatest genocide of the indigenous people of Brazil.

In this process is when Umbanda was born, as a great number of people disincarnated in that war: indigenous people, Africans, and Europeans. Those who had good in their souls united, bringing the knowledge of their traditions. So the origin of Umbanda is in Brazilian history. It contains all the good things and all the bad things that happened in our history. After that it started to evolve, through the mediumship of the people who channeled these indigenous entities and opened this work. Then it started to syncretize with the entities from Spiritism opening then to other lines, the lines from the east. Spiritism was already opened to this line because it comes from another part of the world, closer to the east.

I evolved within this tradition. My first teacher was Baixinha, a very humble person. She's a descendant of indigenous people. Her father or grandfather was indigenous. So her ancestry was more recent, closer to the traditions of healing through the mysteries of nature. Then she became a master in Umbanda. We call them *Mãe,* a mother, a mother of Umbanda.

The first ceremony I attended was with her. Something very powerful happened then. She was channeling these indigenous ancestors and they talked to me, they talked about my life. No one there knew me or had any idea who I was or where I came from. Those entities coming through Baixinha's *aparelho*[5] talked to me about my life. I was very impressed with that, and when the people started to sing and dance in their ritual, they invited me to join. I didn't want to join in, my mind

---

4. *Entradas e Bandeiras* (Entries and Flags) were expeditions with strategic and economic purposes, carried out in the interior of the Brazil colony between the seventeenth and eighteenth centuries.

5. *Aparelho* (apparatus, instrument in English) refers to the body of a medium when it is being used to channel spirits.

Maria Alice with her teacher, Baixinha, in Lumiar, Nova Friburgo, State of Rio de Janeiro, Brazil, 2013

wouldn't allow it, but my heart was calling me. As soon as I joined in, my ancestors arrived for me. It was very sudden. When Baixinha was incorporating them, it was not her, it was the spirits who were guiding that ritual.

She invited the mediums to participate in a meeting for only those who were already working with her current (members of the group), but then she looked at me and said, "You are invited as well." So I quickly graduated there and I never left . . . until I found the Santo Daime. My encounter with the Santo Daime was another milestone in my life.

The Santo Daime

The Santo Daime came to me through my work in the Umbanda. I left the city and went to live in the forest, on a mountain in the Mata Atlantica, the Atlantic forest. There I joined a group of people who were Umbandistas (practitioners of Umbanda) who had formed a small community. I went to live there with my daughters. We were just a few people. We used to do a lot of spiritual works, three ceremonies per week: one in the *terreiro*,[6] one at the table, and another one in a circle.

One day during a table work I met the spirit of Mestre Irineu (Master Irineu). Raimundo Irineu Serra. Mestre Irineu was a man of African descent, a *maranhense*, from the state of Maranhão in the northeast of Brazil. He carried traditions that were not exactly Umbanda, that came from an even more pure African origin, from Ketu in West Africa.[7] He had this origin, but at the same time he was Christian. This mixture is typical of Brazil—almost everybody is part Christian, but they also have their origins.

So he was from Maranhão but went to the Amazon as a *seringueiro*, a rubber tapper or a "rubber soldier," which was a social phenomenon at the time, known as the Rubber Era. The rubber extracted from the *seringueira* (rubber tree) was used for the production of tires and shoe soles. There was a great upsurge of the industry when rubber became available in the world markets. The seringueira was considered the "gold of the forest."

It was there in the forest that Mestre encountered this sacred brew of the indigenous people of the Amazon. Not only of the Brazilian Amazon, but from the entire region: Peru, Bolivia, Colombia, and Venezuela. He encountered this beverage that is known worldwide as ayahuasca but has various names. Each ethnicity has its own name for it. It's called *uni, yagé, cambarambi*; it has many names.

Mestre received this brew from the hands of an indigenous *pajé* (shaman), a traditional healer, a pure origin. When he drank it he had an experience, a vision. He then followed a diet for many days that was prescribed to him in that vision. It required focus, as it's an extremely reduced nutritional fast. After this diet, he drank the brew again and received many revelations. Through these revelations he initiated the line of Santo Daime, using this brew of the indigenous people in a ritual, within a new Christianity. A Christianity not identified with the churches of the world, but centered on discovering the truth of Christ. What was it that He said? He preached that all people are brothers and sisters; all human beings, we are all brothers and sisters.

Raimundo Irineu became a master. He brought this truth and started to receive songs called hymns as well as a complete ritual, which is a syncretic ritual, because it has the *maracá* (rattle), an indigenous element; the *bailado* (dance), also indigenous; and the clothing with its symbols known as *fardamento*. There are also the colored ribbons that are related to Africa and the Brazilian culture, a syncretism present in our culture. Not religious or spiritual, but in culture, in dance, in the Brazilian popu-

---

6. Ceremonial grounds.

7. A historical region in what is now the Republic of Benin, in the area of the town of Ketu. It is one of the oldest capitals of the Yoruba-speaking people.

Raimundo Irineu Serra, also known as Mestre Irineu

lar culture of the northeast of Brazil. All of this is syncretized within the ritual of Santo Daime, and the clothing has various symbolisms. The colors of the clothes; the green represents the forest. The colors of the ribbons. The star comes from another line; it is the star of Solomon.

Mestre Irineu is the founder of the line of Santo Daime, developed in the city of Rio Branco, the state capital of Acre in the Brazilian Amazon. The Santo Daime is a line of healing. The people who drink Santo Daime, it doesn't matter if they're white, black, mestizo, oriental, Arab, or if they don't know their origins. They drink this brew and participate in the rituals and slowly begin to know themselves, start having visions and remembering and connecting with their origins, with their ancestors. Mestre Irineu's line of the Santo Daime is a line of open, eclectic devotion.

I met Mestre Irineu in spirit. When he arrived for me, I was working at the table in a circle of spiritual connection. I had never heard of Santo Daime; I didn't know Mestre Irineu, by name or otherwise. I was in this small ritual and he presented himself to me. I saw this black man. When he arrived, I felt great peace in my heart. I looked at him and asked who he was. He said, *I am the guide of all pretos velhos.* Through this he established a connection with me, and myself with him, as I already was part of that line. He was black and he had white hair, and he brought with him the highly elevated dimension in which he existed. He brought that peace to my being, to my heart. When he approached, I noticed the scent of flowers. My heart was filled with roses. I sensed the perfume, and he said to me, *I have a message for you to share with your companions.* He gave me the message and I wrote it down. He was about to leave when I said, *Aren't you going to sign the message?* So he signed it: *Mestre Irineu.* I didn't know who he was. I met him in spirit, not in the material world. At that time, he no longer had a material body.

After the end of the ritual, when we closed the connection with the other planes, we shared our experiences. When I read Mestre Irineu's message out loud for the circle, the leader of our group, who coordinated the works, said he knew of Mestre and the Santo Daime from seven years previously. He had been to Padrinho[8] Sebastião's church in Colônia Cinco Mil[9] in the state of Acre. He drank the Santo Daime and had a very strong experience. He received this instruction in the Santo Daime, for him to found this Umbanda community.

Padrinho Sebastião was a disciple of Mestre Irineu. Before Padrinho Sebastião met Mestre he was already a person of the Amazon forest. He was a Spiritist and a great healer, a medium who worked with healing guides. He went to Rio Branco to be healed from a serious illness. There he found Mestre Irineu and healed himself with that sacred brew, with the Santo Daime. From then on he followed Mestre.

After Mestre Irineu passed on, Padrinho created his own line, which was strongly identified with Saint John the Baptist. He gathered his people, the ones who wanted to follow him, and developed the study of living in community and being integrated with nature. They journeyed deep into the forest and practiced the Christian teachings in their material lives.

After I had the vision of Mestre Irineu for the first time, everything changed for me. I received many *pontos,*[10] and I would sing them in the rituals. After I met Mestre Irineu I started to receive another kind of song, another rhythm. I would sing them to this man who was my brother in that work, and one day he told me, "Do you know what it is that you're hearing? This is a Santo Daime hymn."[11] I didn't know what that was. The Santo Daime embraces all spiritual lines because each person has their own past, their trajectory, their ancestry. The objective of drinking Daime is to discover who you are.

This study is vast, because as you are discovering yourself you'll find that many things are in the light, but other things remain in darkness. These memories slowly return, and when they return you have to work a lot to be able to purify all of it.

To be in love, to be in peace, to be in union. Because in the end we are all one. This is Christian because it's the truth that Christ brought us, what we call *boa nova* (good news). That isn't the truth of the Catholic Church that persecuted the indigenous people and massacred the people of Africa. It is the truth that we are all brothers and sisters. This is the good news.

---

8. Literally "Godfather"; refers to the name for the male spiritual leaders in the Santo Daime tradition.

9. The place where Padrinho Sebastião created his first congregation after leaving Alto Santo and where the seeds of the community were planted.

10. Sacred chants of the Umbanda spiritual line.

11. Songs received by the initiated direct from the spirit world, each carrying a teaching. The hymns are sung during the works and can have different functions.

The person who receives this beverage with respect, they know where it came from. It came from the hands of the indigenous people, through the hands of Mestre Irineu. In my case, it also came through the hands of Padrinho Sebastião. When you drink this beverage this way, you only receive benefits and advancements in your spiritual mission. That's what happened to me. I only received benefits: the healing of my physical body, of the illnesses I carried. I was healed of everything. I also gained a deeper understanding of my work. I am of the line of Umbanda; this is my line that I carry with me. When I went to drink Daime I worked with the Umbanda within the Daime.

I was a *daimista*.[12] Right away I joined that *egregore*. But I was also an Umbandista. I couldn't deny my line. By then Padrinho Sebastião had moved to a reserve, a national forest land that was given to them by the federal government. That's where Céu do Mapiá[13] is, where Padrinho Sebastião built the community. It was there in Mapiá that he became very ill. The people who had already brought the Santo Daime to the city and had their churches and communities there brought him to the city to do

12. A practitioner of the Santo Daime religion.
13. Céu do Mapiá (Portuguese for "Heaven of Mapiá [river]") is a village founded in 1983 by Sebastião Mota de Melo. It is located within the Inauini-Pauini National Reserve in the western Brazilian Amazon.

Madrinha Rita Gregório de Melo and Padrinho Sebastião Mota de Melo traveling by boat on the Purus River in the Brazilian Amazon, 1987

Baixinha leading a spiritual work on her first trip to Céu do Mapiá. Padrinho Sebastião sitting and Padrinho Manoel Corrente behind him. Céu do Mapiá, Brazilian Amazon, 1989

Maria Alice clearing the *terreiro* before a spiritual forest work. Céu do Mapiá, Brazilian Amazon, 1989

some medical tests. They also wanted to bring him to the city because he was a man with great history, great light. He was a great spiritual guide and leader.

But he was ill, and Baixinha wanted to meet him to help. That's when that meeting happened and she drank Daime for the first time. She then introduced him to her line, her caboclos and Caboclo Tupinambá, who is the chief of a Brazilian indigenous nation.

She met him in a healing ceremony. Her indigenous ancestor from the Tupinambás manifested in her.

Caboclo Tupinambá talked to Padrinho Sebastião and they established an alliance. From this alliance Umbandaime was born. This is when the Umbanda officially became part of Padrinho Sebastião's line of Santo Daime. My mission was to go to the Amazon forest, to Céu do Mapiá, and establish the Umbandaime there. Baixinha brought the Santo Daime into the Umbanda. In turn, I brought the Umbanda into the Santo Daime.

When I arrived at Céu do Mapiá, Padrinho Sebastião asked me to teach Umbanda to his people. I lived there for twenty-four years doing that. We formed a great egregore of Umbandaime that is well established now. Baixinha promoted this connection. She brought Santo Daime to her people, who were a people of Umbanda, who didn't know the Santo Daime. She created another part of the Umbandaime. There are two parts: the Daime that received the Umbanda and the Umbanda that received the Daime. This is our difference. Actually, it's what unites us. Because she continues to be my teacher, and these teachings entered the line of Daime and have already been transmitted throughout the world.

A very important part of my history is related to the Amazon rain forest because I was called by the forest and by the Santo Daime. I compare my going to Africa to my going to the Amazon. In the Amazon, I had a very deep experience with the forest. The forest itself, all that it represents, all the knowledge it contains, all that life. All the teachings that are in the forest, they're not someone or in someone's head. They're in the forest itself, in that very important manifestation.

Within the teachings that the forest transmitted to me, I sealed my commitment to peace. This is related to a memory I understand as part of my ancestry, also connected to the forest. And that's why I went there, where everything became clear to me—my mission, what I had to do, work to heal the people, to help find in that forest all the resources so that people wouldn't have to leave it, wouldn't have to go find external resources. So that's where I developed this work with medicine, the work with the children, with the youth.

I spent a significant part of my life in the forest, building the community at Céu do Mapiá. All of that was weaving an experience of a tribal life from the past where there was no money, where social relationships were based on exchanges, cooperation, charity, and sharing. This was related to a cultural heritage I had in me that I re-encountered there and practiced with the people of Padrinho Sebastião.

I developed the Centro Medicina da Floresta (Forest Medicine Center, CMF), together with other women,

Maria Alice, Padrinho Sebastião, and Madrinha Rita on a special visit to a community by the Purus River shore. State of Amazonas, Brazil, 1989

Grandmothers from Céu do Mapiá after Umabanda work. Left to right: Maria, Francisca, Clara, Helena, Maria Alice, Raimunda, Ilma, Albertina, Dalvina

youth, and children. In this center, my task was to recover the traditional knowledge of medicinal plants, organize it, and teach it to the next generations.

I was called to another part of the Amazon to expand the Centro Medicina da Floresta experience around the Juruá River, right in the middle of the forest, in a wild and unexplored area. I took my daughter Júlia with me. There we had the opportunity to deepen our healing through our experience within the alliance of forest peoples, where we developed a relationship with the indigenous peoples of the Amazon. We worked hard for the preservation of our culture, of our knowledge, and for the construction of the schools of our lore. We made many commitments. We brought our experience, the systematization of the knowledge of traditional medicine, to share with other peoples of various indigenous ethnicities, with the people who lived along the banks of the rivers or deep in the forest. And for them this was a great awakening as well. It was a healing as well, a rediscovery of themselves. Therefore, this work was an unfolding.

We made commitments and established principles related to the preservation of our culture and our heritage. We focused on not only our cultural knowledge but also our material heritage such as lands, waters, and the forests. We signed a Statement of Principles with many healers and shamans in Brazil and became organized. As a mixed-race person, aware of my roots, I was completely committed and dedicated to cultivating and preserving this culture through my work with the children so that they could grow up with the preservation of that knowledge. So they could grow with love for their own culture, and later in life they would teach their children and perpetuate this knowledge.

This has always been my work. It was in this context that I became a member of the International Council of Thirteen Indigenous Grandmothers, because in my community, Céu do Mapiá, and through my work in the Amazon, many people came to me in search

Maria Alice preparing the altar for an Umbanda spiritual work at the Santa Casa in Céu do Mapiá, Brazilian Amazon, 2013

of healing, in search of knowledge, for the benefits this knowledge could bring them. People from various parts of the world, pilgrims, came in search of themselves, in search of truth, of their own truth. I helped many of them and became someone with that kind of connection, known by many throughout the world. It was in this context that I was invited to a gathering in New York in October 2004 in which we birthed the International Council of Thirteen Indigenous Grandmothers.

Grandmothers Council

When the Grandmothers from around the world met for the first time in New York, we didn't know each other; we didn't have a plan in mind. It evolved naturally. We somehow helped weave that gathering, because it was due to the work of each one of the thirteen women, and what we were doing in our lives. It was my Statement of Principles combined with the Statement of Principles of Grandmother Bernadette of Gabon, Africa, and the prophecies of Grandmother Rita Blumenstein from Alaska. It was our individual paths, the things we had accomplished, the healings we had performed, the battles we've fought, which were all interconnected and culminated with our presence in this event, the beginning of our alliance and of our journey.

Our pilgrimage throughout the world as a Council of Thirteen Grandmothers represented, and still represents, the alliance of the four directions of the world and of our dedication to the next generations; to the future generations. It is about planting the seed of our memory as a way of preservation.

The truth is that the Grandmothers Council was a continuation of my life, a crowning of my mission, the culmination of everything I've accomplished. Everything I went through, everything I did, everything I realized culminated in this alliance. I believe, when I look at my comrades, my sister Grandmothers, that this is their truth as well. Because many of the things we have been learning about ourselves and our missions, it is as if they are all part of a mosaic, putting the parts together and revealing this mosaic. I discovered things I didn't know about myself through the other Grandmothers, and other Grandmothers say the same happened to them. I saw the Lakota Grandmothers discover their relationship with Grandmother Julieta, the common origins of their people. They discovered that in the council. In the same way, my story with Grandmother Bernadette from Ga-

Maria Alice leading an administration meeting at the Centro Medicina da Floresta. Left to right: Ana Lúcia, Maria Rosa, Nívea Maria, Mariana, Maria de Nazaré. Céu do Mapiá, Brazilian Amazon, 2011

Centro Medicina da Floresta

bon became evident from the time of the creation of the council. I had signed a Statement of Principles with the Amazonian spiritual leaders, and she had also signed a statement with shamans from other parts of the Amazon. So, all of this was the foundation that generated this first meeting where the Grandmothers Council was born.

When I met Grandmother Bernadette, she recognized me immediately. When I offered my first ceremony at the Council Gathering, she said to me, "Ah, we are like this. When we work, it's beautiful." When she told me this, it was a very special validation because she embodied an African tradition. I have those roots. I found it so interesting that she

also had a revelation when she saw me work, when she recognized me. After I presented my prayer in the line of Umbanda, she shared with me the meaning of the word *umbanda* in her traditional lineage. She said that in Gabon, in Africa, *umbanda* was the name given to a horn that is used in her rituals.

She also said that every traditional spiritual leader has an *umbandeiro*, which is a ritual assistant. When he plays his umbanda all spirits, incarnated and disincarnated, present themselves. To me that made total sense, because in my trajectory it's another language, it's speaking Portuguese, but as it was translated by the entities of Umbanda them-

Maria Alice leading the medicine preparation team at the Centro Medicina da Floresta. Céu do Mapiá, Brazilian Amazon, 2013

selves, they said that *umbanda* means "a single band," where all are inside the same circle. So, it's a mystery. There's a great mystery and at the same time the meaning of the mystery is clear, completely clear. The mystery is like the turning of the world in order to unveil the mystery and to reveal it. I believe this is something very important. These words I am saying are related to the Grandmothers Council because that is what we are doing. We are going around the world as a single band.

In this turn around the world, the mysteries are revealing themselves for those who follow us, for those who witness or participate in our work, as much as for ourselves. The mystery is revealing itself

to them and at the same time it is revealing itself to us. We are grandmothers, we have traveled our own path, but this doesn't mean we are the final authority. We are instruments of the Creator, of life itself. We are part of the history of Creation, and our part was to do this. We are closer to the end of this cycle of travels we committed to, to realize the thirteen gatherings at each other's homelands. And now the seeds that we have sown are already germinating.

After this, it will be a new time. In this preparation for a new phase of the council, we trust that the seeds we have planted have formed a good seedbed and soon will sprout. Along our journey, some of our children and grandchildren formed the group of our youth ambassadors. We have hope in the harvest.

I have just returned from a journey of harvesting the seeds that I planted in my Amazonian community, Céu do Mapiá. I have not lived there the last few years, but I continue to work there and to cultivate everything I left. I went there recently for the harvesting, because everything I planted produced fruit. Today I'm handing the directorship of the medicine work I started to the new generation whom I taught in the past. Then I went to the Juruá Valley, where many seeds had also sprouted. In the past, together with my daughter Júlia, we gathered many people of different ethnicities to establish an alliance, and later they dispersed to spread the work. Today we see that they took with them the knowledge, awakening new action. In many instances because of the action of the preservation of knowledge, the traditional indigenous medicine is thriving. The movement is like this.

Antonio playing the *umbanda* horn at a spiritual work in the Oyenano Village in Libreville, Gabon, 2014

Grandmother Maria Alice and Grandmother Bernadette at the Oyenano Village in Libreville, Gabon, 2014

When I think about my life today, I can say I understand my mission, just as I understand the mission of the Grandmothers Council. I think this is a wonderful realization, and I consider myself a victorious person for understanding and continuing forward, continuing to live in the here and now. Because for me in this moment there isn't a plan anymore. I don't have any plans in my life, I simply keep moving forward, with the understanding that I have this mission of being a seed planter, a preservationist; accepting and surrendering myself to the flow of life. I don't have any plans; however, I don't stop, I never stop. I'm always in motion, working, with conviction in what I'm doing. I have no doubts, I keep going. And this is good. This is what I have to say, this is the teaching I bring to the people. To move forward, to surrender to your path. And to connect to your roots, because when you connect to your roots this become a reality. This is it, we're building a time of peace, a time of understanding, a time of healing.

When I first arrived I asked myself, *My God, why am I in this council? I'm not indigenous!* But then I would say *I'm not indigenous, but I also am indigenous. I'm not white, I'm not black, I'm not yellow . . . who am I?* The council brought this deepening in the process of rediscovering my identity, the understanding that nowadays the great majority of people are racially mixed. However, everybody has ancestors, everybody has roots, everybody has an original culture to be preserved, or more than one. Little by little, as we kept growing within the council I started to have this understanding of my role, because I already am the alliance itself for having these diverse roots. This helped the council.

In 2011 when it was my turn to host the gathering of the Grandmothers Council in Brazil, it was a very important validation of everything I'm sharing with you now, because we Brazilians represent the expression of various peoples and ethnicities. All the Brazilian Grandmothers who came together to host the Grandmothers Council with me were an example of what I represent within the council. When everybody came together and endorsed this work, it empowered me to continue. It was a wonderful experience. The theme of the gathering was "In the Flow of the Waters," and everything I said is exactly the flow of the waters, which is to continue to flow, overcoming obstacles, barriers; purifying, carrying, and clearing the memory of the times; continuing to move forward, continuing on this path.

Florais da Amazônia

I am deeply grateful for being one of the researchers and co-creator of the Amazon Flower Essences System: Florais da Amazônia, in partnership with Isabel Barsé. This is a therapeutic system that brings together seventy single flower essences and thirty-seven formulas. It is available in several countries around the world. There are

Everybody has ancestors, everybody has roots, everybody has an original culture to be preserved, or more than one.

books, teaching materials, and a deck of cards. Its therapeutic benefits reach many people. I travel around the world spreading this system, in the context of Instituto Floresta Mãe (Mothers Forest Institute), caretaker of this material and immaterial heritage. Its mother essences are produced within the Amazon rainforest through a partnership with the Centro Medicina da Floresta (CMF), where we are always training young people to produce the essences and care for their birthplace—the forest. It's been a few years since I stopped living in the community, but I'm always there, helping and teaching.

I have just arrived from Cruzeiro do Sul, which is the city in the Juruá Valley where there is also an expansion of the Florais da Amazônia. There, together with my daughter Júlia, we coordinated the research into a new arm of the system, which unfolded from the original research. A book has already been published: *Iapuna, Language of People, Language of Flower.* And there is a continuity project.

Grandmothers from Céu do Mapiá. Left to right, top to bottom: Vó Nogueira, Ilma, Regina, María Sebastiana, Marlene, Francisca, Maria, Madrinha Julia, Dalvina, Albertina, María Irene, Noemia, Maria Brilhante, Maria de Nazaré, Gecila

There are many types of flower essences. One for each situation. Each is from one kind of flower. How did we discover this? It's a gift, a skill that anyone can develop. This ability to listen to the plants comes from respect and love for nature. When you love nature, it is like loving a person. When you meet someone and you feel a connection with them, you start loving them, they start to reveal themselves to you, and you also slowly reveal yourself to them. It's mutual; it's not only one-way. It's not a magical thing like, "I have the gift of reading the plants," no. I love them. I admire them. Before wanting anything from them I revere them as beings, as creatures. Then they recognize me. They recognize my reverence when I manage to understand their revelation through their own behavior in nature: their shape, color, and fragrance. If it's a flower of a vine, if it grows high up, if it's facing down, if it's very delicate, if it's exuberant—all of this is part of this reading. When I make the remedy from the flower essence, when I develop this medicine, it also receives the energy of reverence.

We are in the transition of an era. There is an ancient system, based on the denial of the natural aspect of life. The political and economic system, all of that, which controls, dominates—this system created the

Maria Alice and Isabel Barsé at a Centro Medicina da Floresta meeting with other healers from the Juruá (Brazilian Amazon) region where they shared their knowledge on the medicine of the forest. Centro Medicina da Floresta, Céu do Mapiá State of Amazonas, Brazil, 2003

pharmaceutical industry, which generates enormous profits for some and very little help for the majority. This industry also did whatever it could to keep the medicine of the traditional peoples from being accepted. But the evidence is stronger than that. There was a time when Flower Therapy was denied and even considered charlatanism. Some of the health professional boards in Brazil have prohibited its prescription. For example, the Psychology Board has banned psychologists from prescribing them. However, science has a mind of its own. It is

This ability to listen to the plants comes from respect and love for nature. When you love nature, it is like loving a person. When you meet someone and you feel a connection with them, you start loving them, they start to reveal themselves to you, and you also slowly reveal yourself to them.

Rubiane preparing tinctures at the Centro Medicina da Floresta, Céu do Mapiá, State of Amazonas, Brazil, 2013

not just at the service of the industry. It is also at the service of the growth of humanity. Quantum physics provided the theoretical basis for Flower Therapy. Nowadays Floral Therapy is increasingly accepted. As it does not have biochemical active ingredients, it does not interfere with the body's biochemistry, therefore it does not pose any risks, making it more accessible to the public.

Floral Therapy works through interactions of consciousness fields. There are no devices that can measure its effects. However, a large number of people managed to abandon the use of controlled prescription drugs through treatment with Flower Therapy and subsequently no longer needed any medication. About two years ago, catastrophic heavy rains occurred in the mountainous regions of Rio de Janeiro and many lost their families. Doctors asked that victims be treated first by the Flower Therapy specialist, so that they would be calmer and easier to talk to, when they were seen by them. Thus, little by little Flower Therapy is being included in the government health system, Sistema Único de Saúde (SUS), in Brazil.

Centro Medicina da Floresta

I also have the great satisfaction of having coordinated the creation and organization of the Centro Medicina da Floresta (Forest Medicine Center), which works to produce many varieties of therapeutic products, originating from the traditional knowledge of the forest people.

The CMF has a medicinal garden. There is gardening work, reforestation work, because we also practice extractivism in the forest, so we have to replant these seeds so that the plants are never lost. In the traditional medicine sector, cooking and reductions for the preparation of *garrafadas*, made with roots, vines, and barks, is a great ritual, the highlight of forest medicine. People from the community take time off and come to participate. The activity of preparing powerful medicines that cure many types of illnesses is very important. We have a powerful antimalarial tonic that prevents and cures the disease. We have depurative remedies for various purposes, various types of tonics, regenerative and blood tonics. We have remedies for all types of afflictions.

I had several opportunities to talk to scientists and biochemists of Brazilian universities who wanted to establish a partnership with the Centro Medicina da Floresta to study the plants. But when we were about to sign the agreement, it became clear that all interest, all benefits, everything was just for them. We were never able to sign these agreements because they were not fair. When I was talking to the biochemist, he said: "This antimalaria remedy of yours, is it nine plants? Why so many plants? If we study it we will discover the active ingredient that kills the plasmodium parasite, the malaria protozoan, and we're done, we don't need this bunch of plants. We have just to synthesize this active ingredient and we're done." I said to him, "Brother, do you think you're smarter than the Creator? I'm a little more humble. I believe that in the composition of one plant there's an active principle that kills the bug, but it also has an active principle that protects the liver, another that enhances immunity, and others that together will harmonize and balance the health of the being. The plant offers a systemic balance to recover our systemic health. That's why we study the medicine in its entirety." I am completely in favor of science, of all studies. I have many friends in the science field who dedicate themselves to this type of study. What makes things difficult are institutions and power agreements.

There are other countries, Bolivia for instance, where traditional medicine is part of the government health system. There are the doctors with their specialties—cardiologists, gynecologists.

The CMF guidelines and regulations establish that the economic benefits generated there must return to the source, to the forest. They must be used to preserve the forest; the knowledge of the forest and the health of the people of the forest who receive very little assistance. It is difficult to find partners in the world who adopt these ideas, because the world functions for the most part in a win-lose perspective. I win, you lose. But we want to play the game of win-win.

Originally, the medicines produced at the Centro Medicina da Floresta were distributed free of charge to the local and regional population, and the resources from the sale of Florais da Amazônia provided financial support to the Centro Medicina da Floresta. But there was also an internal exchange system in the community, in the area of planting and species preservation. Today, the community finds itself interfered with by the global thinking of the capitalist system. Internal cooperative commitment is currently difficult. Then, the challenge grew. At the moment, it is about rescuing the concept of sustainability and the preservation of the forest, its waters, and its culture. The educational process continues to optimize resources to guarantee autonomy. We have this power; we just need to find good partners. Our partners, our allies in the world are not the industries, nor the capitalist system. They

Teaching the new generations is how we preserve the knowledge and tradition. Because if everything remains in the hands of the old people, they die and that's it, it's over.

are the world's alternative networks, which work to build a global solidarity economy. These are our allies.

The Centro Medicina da Floresta continues to evolve, within the demands of time. Today it has new facilities, with updated equipment, which favors the validation of its production process with ANVISA (Brazilian health surveillance agency). It also seeks to adapt to the requirements for official validation of its products. We are also empowering the youth to learn even more so that they become the keepers of this work, because I'm getting older. It is necessary to invest energy in training guardians because this is the process, and the path is teaching the younger generations. Teaching the new generations is how we preserve the knowledge and tradition. Because if everything remains in the hands of the old people, they die and that's it, it's over. So I feel that the Centro Medicina da Floresta is a successful venture.

At this moment, I'm really calling attention to this: *Let's have a look at our traditions, at our roots.* There isn't a single person in the world who doesn't have an ancestor. We all represent a line of tradition. Every tradition has an important knowledge, as much about nutrition as medicine, as well as social interactions and economic mutual support. This is why we cannot lose sight of returning to our roots and passing on the teachings that come from them to new generations. This is what I am doing at the CMF, and this is how I am planting a seed in the world that contains the multiplication of these principles for a future of unity between humanity and Mother Earth.

Maria Alice going to work at the Centro Medicina da Floresta.
Igarapé Mapiá, State of Amazonas, Brazil, 2013

TWELVE

GRANDMOTHER MONA POLACCA

GAM'YU, I GREET YOU. I'M MONA POLACCA. My name, Polacca, means butterfly in the Hopi language. I am Hopi, Havasupai, and Tewa. I am from the Colorado River Indian Tribe, in Parker, Arizona.

I was told that I was born under a special star, that I have a special star up there that watches over me. An elder told me that.

I love the stars. In the summertime our whole family would sleep outside the house. I would sleep out there under the night sky, lie there and watch the stars.

I know the Lakota have star nation teachings, and the Hopi also talk about certain stars, but certain people only speak about the knowledge at certain times. Everything has its place. If you talk about some things out of season, it creates an imbalance in your life. It's a power that has to be kept in place. I guess in a way, if it's not in balance that way it's breaking tradition, and that's not good to do.

My parents are Edna Yumtheska Polacca and Starlie Polacca Jr. My mother is from the Havasupai and my father is from the Hopi and Tewa. The Havasupai are the people of the blue-green water, and the Hopi people are the people of peace.

I had four brothers and three sisters. Eight children. I'm the third youngest.

Havasupai

Havasupai are the people of the blue-green water. *Havasu* means blue-green water and *pai* means people. Supai is the capital of the Havasupai Indian Reservation.

Supai is a very remote village at the bottom of the Grand Canyon. The only way into the village is by horseback, hiking, or helicopter. So the Havasupai contact with the outside world is somewhat guarded, very isolated. It is considered the most remote Indian reservation in the United States.

The whole Grand Canyon is home to the Havasupai. When the government established the Grand Canyon National Park, they relocated all of the Havasupai out of that area, out of the park. The Havasupai were restricted to only some of the land down in the canyon, although historically they had homes, land, and everything on what they call the South Rim of the Grand Canyon. They maintained their village there on the South Rim, but also down below in the canyon. There is evidence of where they used to live on the South Rim.

The area of Supai, where the reservation is now, was also part of their traditional lands. They still have their gardens down there where they grow their corn and squash, and they also have fruit trees, like peaches and apricots. They have these ancient irrigation systems where the water flows into their gardens.

Medicine People

My mom and her grandfather were medicine people. They were chiefs. They called my mother the "Real Havasupai Princess," because she came from the chief line. She could speak on behalf of the tribe. She could take a stand, which she did. She'd go to the government and chew them out, for the people, for the tribe. She had a voice.

She would take me with her and I would witness her ways. I witnessed how the tribe acknowledged her. If she had something to say, the tribe would acknowledge her and let her speak.

The U.S. government came in and created tribal councils made of elected officials. The councils restrained the traditional system of governance, overseen by chiefs and different people, certain families who had roles to fulfill, who knew how the village community operated. When the government established the governance of elected tribal council officials, the chiefs no longer had any authority. The traditional leaders were stripped of their authority. The U.S. government appointed their own

Havasu Falls, Supai, Arizona, United States, 2019

government, just like they still do, entering all of these countries to take control. They imposed that same strategy on our traditional leaders.

So in this way the tribe gets younger and younger as the old people are going. Their knowledge is leaving with them. It's not preserved as public knowledge because there's no written history. So this is what's happening to a lot of tribes.

Today, the elders acknowledge I'm from that traditional family line of chiefs. My mother's name was Edna Yumtheska Polacca. Yumtheska was her maiden name, but she also had an English last name that was given to her, and that was George.

When she went to the boarding school, they just gave them names. They'd have the kids line up and they'd say, *Okay, you're going to be Edna George.* Brothers and sisters, siblings could be standing in the line and they'd say, *Okay, you're Tom and you're something else,* a different name. They're brothers, but they now have different names. This created confusion in people's identity.

Mona's mother, Edna Yumtheska Polacca, riding her horse on the trail into the Grand Canyon going to Havasupai village. Supai, Arizona, United States, 1951

The government operated the boarding schools. Children were forcibly removed from their homes, from their villages, and from their people. This was part of the assimilation policy of the government, part of the genocide. The strategy was to remove the child from their culture, their language, their ways, their traditions, everything that represented their identity as a Havasupai. They had a saying: *Kill the Indian, save the man.*

They literally kidnapped the children. Forcibly, they took them away from their families, their villages, and their culture. They weren't allowed to speak their language. My

The remote village of Supai, located within Havasu Canyon, in Arizona, United States, 2010

Mona's mother, Edna Yumtheska Polacca, holding a Havasupai pottery vase she made, circa 1978

mother and father come from one of the several generations that went through that. Their generation was forcibly removed. They were punished for speaking their language or having anything to do with their culture. They were brainwashed, so to speak.

In my family, my parents are from two different tribes. They spoke the tribal language. Even though they went through boarding school, they were able to retain the language. But then when they had their children, they didn't teach us the language because they didn't want us to suffer the way they did. So I'm one of these children. I know a few words, but I don't speak the language fluently.

In our tribes it's very important to know who your relatives are. Part of knowing who your relatives are is being connected to the support system and caring for one another. The other part is that you have to know who your relatives are so you don't marry them. It's kind of funny. These entirely different tribesmen, they all have this joke. The guy will say, "Oh! I met this beautiful Indian woman. She was so nice and I just really fell in love with her. Then I went home to my mom and my grandma and told them about her and they told me: 'Oh no, you can't get involved with her, that's your relative.'" So they say, "Oh, pretty soon we can't marry anyone in our tribe anymore because we're related to almost everybody." So then they have to go outside of the tribe.

My mom was in boarding school all through twelfth grade. Once in a while she'd get to go back home, back to the canyon, for a little while during the summer. Or sometimes they'd place her with white families. Like up in Flagstaff, she stayed with this elderly white lady she worked for, housecleaning and things like that. I don't know if she got paid. She might have gotten paid, but she had room and board.

My grandmother passed away when my mom was a baby, so her grandparents raised her. Then her grandmother died and her grandfather raised her. Her father was around for a while, but then he died and her grandfather was raising her. One thing my mother always told us was that she never got to have the experience of saying "Mom." That was something that she really missed.

My maternal grandmother, Kaleen Watahomigie, was very present in my life as I was growing up. My mom's

Children were forcibly removed from their homes, from their villages, and from their people. This was part of the assimilation policy of the government, part of the genocide. The strategy was to remove the child from their culture, their language, their ways, their traditions, everything that represented their identity as a Havasupai. They had a saying: *Kill the Indian, save the man.*

strength, I believe, came from her, as well as from her grandparents. Being a mother was such an important responsibility for her. My mother would talk about her mother like she was always there with her.

I have a picture of my grandmother, and it's like she's watching over me all the time. I talk to her all the time. Especially when I'm praying with the water, I always call on her to help me and to be with me, guide me with my words. So that whatever I'm going to say, my thoughts are one with hers, and the spirit of the water is going to hear me. And the Creator and all the spirits of the four directions are going to hear me. I ask her to help me so that they might recognize me.

Whenever I go to the Grand Canyon, and this is something I follow from my mother, the first place where you could see the canyon from the road, we would pull off and stop there, and we would get out of the car and go to the rim, to the edge of the canyon. We would tell the Mother Canyon that we were there. *We're your children. We're your grandchildren. We're here. We're here to be at home with you, and to be with our relatives, our loved ones here.* My mother would make that prayer, and talk. And she would say to me, "You know, it's colorful. The Grand Canyon is colorful. It's alive." And sometimes you could feel the breeze come up from the canyon, and she would say, "That's the breath. That's the breath of the canyon, breathing on you and acknowledging your presence."

I never did get to know my grandmother or my grandfather. But

Grandmother Mona holding a photo of her Havasupai grandmother, Kaleen Watahomigie. Phoenix, Arizona, United States, 2009

through my mother, whenever she shared, it was in a spiritual manner. That's how I maintain this relationship. It guides me. And protects me. That's the way I believe, anyway.

Upbringing

My Hopi grandmother, Elsie Lomayesva Polacca, had a lot of influence on me too. My elders would tell me, "This is the Indian way." They would tell me how to do things and how to be. *This is the Indian way.* That was the way I was raised.

In the '40s our tribes were relocated to Parker, to the Colorado River. I'm an enrolled member of what was established as the Colorado River Indian Tribes, which includes four tribes—the Mohave, Chemehuevi, Hopi, and Navajo. So I was born and raised in Parker, Arizona.

That was during World War II, when the United States went to war with Japan. The Colorado River Indian Tribes reservation was the site of one of the United States' largest Japanese internment camps. My father was hired to go and work there, clearing the land so they could build those so-called internment camps. They were actually concentration camps that were built on various reservations, and they built three camps there, on the Colorado River Reservation.

As children we went swimming all the time in the river, playing in what we called the sand hills, an area with beachlike sand. In the summertime my father would take us all to stay with my Havasupai auntie in the village on the South Rim of the Grand Canyon.

The National Park Service never succeeded in removing the people from this village. Those were my family, my mother's family, the Watahomigie. They refused to leave.

During the summertime they would go down into the canyon, because that's where they had their gardens. That's where the water was, a creek and the river. Then in the wintertime they would come up on top. They had these little villages both up on top and down in the canyon. But once the Park Service was established, they put them into the canyon, at Supai, and they were told they couldn't leave. They were supposed to no longer walk, travel around, or stay within the national park boundaries. Still, we used to hike from the South Rim to the North Rim. My mother would take one of us at a time. She would take me down to Supai, to the village there.

Young Adulthood

I was about fourteen when my mother told me about my responsibility to the Native American people. When the American Indian Movement (AIM)[1] started, I realized that this was what she'd been talking about. These things are very real; we have to uphold them, take care of them, and practice them. That's when I became an activist, when I was a teenager.

I listened to my mother and other elders. I've always had a sense of pride about being who I am, about my Native American heritage. I've

---

1. A Native American civil rights activist organization, founded in 1968 to encourage self-determination among Native Americans and to establish international recognition of their treaty rights.

Mona's mother, Edna Yumtheska Polacca, sitting under a cottonwood tree with a visiting Havasupai relative, splitting willow to make baskets. Poston, Arizona, Colorado River Indian Tribes Reservation, 1969

Cotton plant. Cotton seed crop in Parker, Arizona, United States, 2010

always spoken about it. I've never wanted to be like anybody else or anything else other than what I am.

When I was in my teen years, our families created a coming out as being members of our tribes. We couldn't partake in the traditional ceremonies in our original homelands. So my mother dressed me in the traditional Havasupai dress and also my Hopi aunties dressed me in the traditional Hopi dress. And I made a public appearance. I was instructed on how to behave and to be proud of who I am.

So I've been dressed as a Hopi woman. I've been dressed as a Havasupai woman.

Water Woman

I have the honor of being a water woman in the Native American Church (NAC). I relate my being a water woman to being of the Havasupai people, the people of the blue-green water. Water is very sacred. It's life giving. There's a sacred responsibility for a woman to bring water into the ceremony and pray with it in the morning.

There's a certain time of the morning when you'll see the sky turn this beautiful blue color. I was told that it represents that moment when your life began, which is a very holy moment. I always like to look out at that time. Look out at the top of the tipi to see that, so pretty. At that sacred time, the water woman takes all of the thoughts and the prayers of everyone and put them into the final prayer that is offered with the water.

That's only one of the many, many places that I pray with water. I've been taught to pray anytime I come upon water. My mother instructed me that way. She told me, "When you approach the water, you must pray and acknowledge it as a living being, having power to give life and take life." She said, "Before I take any water or get into the water, I must always show my respect."

When you're drinking that water, you're drinking water for all of your relatives. You're drinking it with reverence and respect. There might be some loved one who is very sick or having a struggle in their life. You drink the water and keep them in mind so that they might receive that blessing.

As Havasupai people, we're not supposed to eat fish, because they're our relatives. That's the way I was raised. That's what I was taught. I don't question. I never questioned any of those teachings that were passed on to me. I accept them and recognize them as what we call the instructions, our instructions about how to live and relate with everything around us, including the animals in the water, animals on the land and in the air.

I was told that anytime you come around water you do a prayer and acknowledgment. There's not any real big ceremony. We go and feed the water by making an offering to the water and praying with it.

My mom said, "Water can give life but it also can take life." So if

Mona's Hopi grandmother, Elsie Lomayesva Polacca, with her father, Starlie Polacca Jr. (left), and uncle, Tony Polacca (right)

I'VE BEEN TAUGHT TO PRAY
ANYTIME I COME UPON WATER.
MY MOTHER INSTRUCTED
ME THAT WAY. SHE TOLD ME,
"WHEN YOU APPROACH THE
WATER, YOU MUST PRAY AND
ACKNOWLEDGE IT AS A LIVING
BEING, HAVING POWER TO
GIVE LIFE AND TAKE LIFE."

there's going to be activity on the water, like people going swimming, playing in the water, or being around the water, we make a prayer and make an offering so that there won't be any drowning. It's very seldom that you hear about Native Americans drowning in any of the bodies of water that they live around. It does happen, but it's very seldom. Usually when someone drowns it's a signal to the spiritual people that they have to pay attention and make that offering again.

One time I was really touched by this Havasupai man. He had come up from the canyon over to my office. He went to the water dispenser there, got his cup, and he got down on his knees. He let a little bit run on his hands and he sprinkled it on the floor. Then he patted his hair and patted his heart. Then he filled his cup and drank the water. That was the most precious moment, to witness this man being so humble to the water and being humble in front of the water. That's what we're doing in the tipi when we're praying with the water, we're being humble to the water. My mother told me, "You don't just go up to any body of water and jump right into it. You have to pay respects to it and introduce yourself to it. Let it know who you are."

I'm an Aquarian, which is the water bearer. The water is always making a way for me. And through my prayers and in my everyday life, I go with the flow of the water.

Sacred Medicines

The plants are out there for a purpose. In the Native American Church we use peyote as a sacred sacrament. We also use sage and cedar, which are sacred herbs. The use of cedar in ceremonies goes way back to the beginning of time when these different medicines presented themselves.

In one of the old stories about the way peyote came to the people, a woman was very sick, close to death. In the old times, a person close to death would go away from the village to die. So she did that, she went off to die. And while she was lying there, she heard a voice say: *Eat me.* She found the plant that was speaking to her and it was peyote, and she ate it and got well. Then it told her to take it back to her people. It told her that it would be their medicine.

That's the same way Quanah Parker[2] was introduced to the medicine. I believe he had been injured and had a severe infection and was close to death, and he found himself at the home of an elder woman. And that woman fed him medicine, and while he was under the influence he started having visions about how to use the medicine in ceremony.

Community Service

My work in community service began when I was about fifteen, sixteen years old. There was a program called the Community Development Program in which elders had activities for the youth of the community. We'd do activities like roller skating or making arts and crafts. Sometimes we would go to the river to go swimming. In the summertime they had summer camp. It was all focused toward having good socialization skills, learning to get along with each other. That brought all the

2. A Comanche leader of the Quahadi (Antelope) band of the Comanche people.

children together, youth from different families and different parts of the reservation.

Without this program the children would be at home, and it was too far to try to walk to your neighbor. So they would go through the valley community and pick up all of the children. We'd all get together and have playtime and activities together.

Eventually when I was in high school a youth leader program evolved. We would organize what we called Youth and Elder Conferences. The elders would talk to us about their experiences being youths. They would share some of their traditional songs or traditional games. We were developing our leadership skills by doing planning, and we did fundraising. Sometimes we'd go out and clean the yards of elders. It was community service oriented.

Sometimes we would run from the south end of the reservation and elders would come up there with us and they would make these special staffs with feathers on them. We'd meet out there early in the morning and they'd say a prayer and give the staff to the runners. The runners would do a relay run. They'd run all the way through the valley, all the way here to this mountain. When we'd arrive, the elders would be there to meet us. The people would bring food, and when we got there they'd sing some songs and we'd all eat together at the base of the mountain.

When I finished high school in the early '70s it was recognized that tribal communities were having problems with alcoholism. So I approached the Tribal Alcoholism Program and was hired as the youth services coordinator. I also continued work with the youth

leaders. These activities also created preventative alternatives to alcohol abuse.

Eventually I earned my master's degree in social work. I go into communities and help them develop programs to address their social problems, including alcohol and substance abuse, suicide, and domestic violence. The programs also help to strengthen their cultural ways within the youth population. That's how I started my life's work. I continue to do that today.

That all relates to what my mother told me when I became a young woman. She told me that I have a purpose in life, that what I do, what I say, how I conduct myself has an impact on others, especially my family. I have a responsibility to help our people. I listened to her. It went into me and became part of my being, of who I am.

All of my sisters followed this line of work too. Community service. My brothers also; they're always in service to others.

I worked in a community as a consultant family therapist. As we know, suicide is escalating. There are many cluster suicides happening right now. In Alaska recently there were a number of suicides. They call it group contagion. I think the most-documented case was in Wyoming. I believe it was the Arapaho. They had a number of youth suicides, one right after another. Right now in South Dakota in one month I believe they had around twenty-three. That was only in one month. It's continued to happen.

In some communities, three or four funerals take place in one day. What comes after that? There's unresolved grief attached to historical trauma. The deaths are occurring so close together, families and communities don't even have time to resolve the grief of the death that hap-

“Grandmothers Wisdom, Waterbird.” Gouache on paper by Angelina Nasso, 2019

(above) Mona's mother, Edna Yumtheska Polacca, on the shore of the Colorado River in Parker, Arizona, United States

(opposite page) Mona wearing a traditional Native American buckskin that belonged to Unci (Grandmother) Beatrice

pened maybe two weeks ago or last month. It's a continuous circle of grief, unresolved grief and despair.

We approach the school as a community, the school administrators, the counselors, teachers; they need to develop systems to address and intervene for the young people. Sudden, traumatic events produce psychological and physiological responses. Not only the immediate family is impacted. Even their friends are impacted. Many times the people in the extended community are overlooked. Throughout the community we encounter stress reactions: irritability, sleep disturbances, anxiety, startled reactions, nausea, headaches, difficulty concentrating, confusion, fear, guilt, withdrawal, and reactive depression.

It's very important to have an appropriate and meaningful intervention to respond to these children. Many times our response from within the schools may not include being connected with the adults. I would go into the home sometimes two days a month. Once when I went to visit a family, the wife of the deceased told me: "You're the first one who has come to visit me. There haven't been many visits." And here in these houses the children would be having a difficult time. The expectation of some service providers is that community members should present themselves for help. It's highly unlikely that that's going to happen. The tendency of a person who is reacting to a sudden traumatic event is to withdraw. They don't feel comfortable even coming out of the house.

Sometimes traumatized people seem to under-react. They can only tolerate intense feelings for a short period of time, these upsetting feelings we all feel when someone we know has committed suicide. What the parents need to do is to take advantage of opportunities to talk about the trauma when their children are present. Because of traumatic feelings, they may not continue to participate in certain activities, like being involved in holiday events. They may be disinterested in some of their usual activities. They may not even want to watch TV. They may become very frightened. Some may even get nauseated. Sometimes they're not prepared to deal with many things about parenting. And of course, dealing with trauma is not a parenting skill that's normal.

If we had it our way, we would probably want to protect our children from having to develop such skills to deal with trauma in their lives. Adults can serve as a cushion against the full impact of the tragedy that children might not be able to intellectually or emotionally process. It's very important to check in with a school counselor, because the child may be affected in certain ways in the classroom. They may not be able to concentrate, sitting at their desk and just kind of staring off, giving the appearance that they're daydreaming, but actually they're having a traumatic reaction.

Younger children may even laugh, as their sadness may appear with cheerfulness, which is a normal response to loss. They may act out and be angry, even toward the deceased. *Why did this happen to me?* Anger may be displaced on a person, the adult who is present. They may blame the surviving adult, wondering, *How could they let this happen to me?*

I worked with a little boy whose father passed away. He said to me: "Why did God take my father? I'm just a little boy, I'm only six years old, and I need my father." That was heartbreaking. But the little six-year-old was thinking about that. We have to hear what the children have to say. They might have anxiety about their own death or anxiety about the possible loss of a parent or other siblings. They may become more attached and insecure about where their parents are and things like that. For parents who have lost children, they become overprotective and worried about the children who are still alive.

Sometimes there's shame, not wanting even to be seen breathing. They might begin to think that they have caused the tragedy. They also worry about negative encounters they had with the deceased, prior to their death. They blame themselves, believing it's something they said or did.

It is alarming that children as young as six years old have committed suicide. They will say, *I'm going to commit suicide.* I'll give you an example. I have a little grandson and he must have been only about four years old and he was riding with me in the car. I told him, "Don't open the door, don't touch the handle. You're going to fall out." He got mad at me and he said, "I'm going to kill myself!" And I said, "Don't say that!" And he said, "I'm going to kill myself, Grandma." I said, "How do you think you're going to do that?" He said, "I'm going to open this door and jump out of the car."

I was so shocked and hurt. I asked him and his older brother, "Where did you hear that?" and he said, "Patrick said that." I said, "Patrick, who's Patrick?" He said, "Patrick, on SpongeBob." I didn't know which show that was, but that was where he heard it. He didn't know what it meant. But Patrick on SpongeBob said that and it stayed with him.

Suicides are a vicious cycle. What we have to do is to create hope to continue living beyond the unresolved grief. One of the things that Native people always say is that *you have to walk on*. You have to go on and continue to live life and continue to move forward and not step in that sadness and grief. These are some of the things you might hear them say in Native communities to someone who has lost a loved one.

In the way that we're socialized today (because of the way we have been institutionalized), we have been conditioned to depend on programs. These programs provide certainty. In response to this collective grief and trauma, some communities are connecting their elders with the youth to encourage a system of value and respect for one another and for life. Others are developing a community plan. You might call it suicide prevention, but it would focus on wellness. The intention would be to prevent suicide and to prevent alcohol and substance abuse. The overall approach is to practice a healthy lifestyle.

I usually tell my clients when they come in for outpatient counseling, "I can only spend this little bit of time in this day of your life, and that's all. You're going to walk out my door and get back out there." I'd say, "See that trash can by the door? As you're going out, all the work you just did with me, you can throw it in the trash. You can go back out there and pick up all the unhealthy stuff that you just let go of. Or you can go out there and pick up certain activities to grow a healthy lifestyle."

We can't implement a model of treatment that's based on sitting with the clinician in the office. We have to rethink this, how are we going to engage the community? Maybe throughout the week you have these different activities set up. It might include a women's night and we would do facials. We'd have the Avon lady or the Mary Kay lady come in and they would get to do their makeup.

Mona wearing her traditional Havasupai regalia, the last dress made by her late mother.
Havasu Falls, Supai, Arizona, United States, 2019

Someone might come in from the career development office and do a workshop with participants for their resume. Some people have never gotten their GED, so we have someone do an overview of what it is to get into a GED program. A lot of times, even if people graduate and get their GED, they really haven't been on the job market, they don't feel like they have any skills or experience. So we do these workshops and draw them out. "Okay, so say you're a homemaker. What kind of things do you do as a homemaker?" And then you take some things that they do as a homemaker and show them how they could be easily applied in the workforce. In this way these programs help begin creating this positive self-image.

We had an elder come in to work with a particular tribe. They made these finger weavings, these bands. They're like belts, but they use them to tie the baby up on the cradleboard. The people learned how to make the cradleboard. The elders taught them these basic things, like how to make moccasins.

We also had a movie night followed by discussion. In this way we were creating a social life in a clean, healthy, sober environment where there's no confrontation, no violence, no name-calling, no bullying, none of that. This is an approach to creating the healthy lifestyle among the adults.

The same thing is needed for the children and youth. Sometimes the youth write. Or they create little performances, like shadow shows. They stand behind a sheet and act out different things. So they can dance and move any way they want without feeling really inhibited.

We also use exercises for values clarification. We give them a little scenario to think about. For instance, there's a kid who needs to cross a little stream and a boat there that doesn't belong to him. He has to make the choice of whether to take the boat without asking permission or walk a distance to where the stream is narrowest and get across without the boat. In these scenarios they have to think about right and wrong, what's acceptable, and what are the consequences of their choices.

Another approach is guided imagery. I always love to see those kids during the guided imagery exercise, sitting there with their eyes closed. The music begins kind of slowly, they go on their journey, and when they come back they've left something that they've been carrying, that they don't need anymore. It could be sadness or even a message that they wanted to give to someone on the other side. As they're coming back, the music is more lighthearted. Then they take some deep breaths, stand up, and stretch out their bodies. This all grows self-awareness toward a healthy outlook on life.

To bring health into the community, I pick out certain people, the natural leaders, the natural helpers, and talk to them and ask them, "What do you think about doing something like this? Could you help me? Would you be there? Could you be there and bring along some other people?"

Recently, I was at this gathering up in British Columbia with people from all over the world. I saw no children involved in the big circle. So I went out to where the kids were all playing. I went over and I talked to one and I said, "I'm going to do something with water and I really could use your help; would you help me?" "Oh yeah, sure, I could help you." The other kids saw him talking to me and so they all rushed over, they asked, "What are you talking about? What are you going to do?" I said, "Well, I'm going to be doing this thing with water; would you help me?" "Oh yeah, sure."

And they did. When they came up to me I said, "It's really important for you to pray and to respect the water. Respect this water. Respect and take care of it. It's really important for you to sing the songs when the people sing. Sing with them." I said, "If you feel like dancing, it's really important for you to move and dance, and even if you don't dance, at least move."

When it came time for me to be out there in the circle, these children, they all just came out. And when the drummers started singing I was in tears, because their mouths were wide open and they were singing and moving, and some of them were dancing. It sounds simple enough, and it is. It's that simple.

Our tendency, and I've heard this a lot even from people at the state government level when we talk about services for the people, they say, "Well, we tried already, we tried to engage the tribe to be part of this and participate, we tried, but you know, it's really hard to get them to do it. They didn't want to. They're not interested." And I look at them and I tell them, "You know what? You still have to keep trying. You can't give up on them. You still have to open that opportunity."

And I'm not just talking about state programs and their funding. I'm talking about within the communities, the tribal communities. One of the teachings that we have is that *you extend your open hand*.

One of the Hopi elders told us, "You know, there's that stereotype

of Indian tribes: How!" Well, he said, "When we meet someone, we greet him or her with an open hand. We're saying, *I'm coming to you in peace. I don't have my hand in a fist and I'm not hiding anything. I come with an open hand.*"

That is a practice that I believe really needs to be strengthened. It hasn't disappeared, but it does need to be strengthened. To embrace people with that open hand, acknowledge their presence, and allow them to participate and share their own ideas and perspectives about how things could be done.

Moving forward in life, so people have hope, so they have the four principles of life: love, faith, hope, and charity. If we come to life with those principles within us, it creates a better life experience. When we're going through these challenging situations such as suicide, it's very important to embrace hope. Sometimes it may not feel that way for the people and their families stuck in such a traumatic event. At the same time, the community, the providers, the immediate family, the extended family, might support them to embrace that hope.

The Beauty Way

Throughout Turtle Island [3] there is a diverse group of Native Americans, and we all come from different geographical locations with rituals and ceremonies, spiritual practices, and beliefs that may not all be the

---

3. The name of North America according to some indigenous tribes.

Grandmothers Rita and Mona praying over a water hole at Prophecy Rock, an ancient site in the Hopi Reservation, near Oraibi, Arizona, United States, 2009

same. So when I talk about the *Beauty Way*, this is from my perspective and experience in my culture. I'm not necessarily speaking for all of the indigenous nations. When we join together, we often recognize our similarities rather than the differences, and that's one of the key pieces of the Beauty Way.

There is a very simple, basic Beauty Way practice. It's one of the ways of acknowledging the foundations of life: the water, the air, the fire, and the earth.

Every morning, the first thing we do is come to the water. We use the water. And so we acknowledge the water as we're washing our face or drinking our first glass. We acknowledge and give thanks and ask for a blessing from it. In that way, we're being respectful to the water.

The second step we take is to honor the second foundation. We walk outside our home place, our doorway. When we walk out there, maybe we're not conscious of it, maybe we are, but one of the first things most people do when they walk outside is take a deep breath. We take that deep breath of air and it's full of life and energy for us. So we think of it as being a blessing and give thanks for the air.

Then there is the third step, the third foundation. We reach with our hands out in front of us and see the sun for the day, Grandfather fire. The great one we see is right here before us again, greeting us. And we reach out and put our hands toward it and bring the light to ourselves. Blessing ourselves with the light of the sun.

And then we move into the fourth foundation. We reach down and touch the earth, and then we touch our heart and our mind. We bless ourselves with all of these four foundations. It only takes a couple of seconds sometimes. That puts the Beauty Way into practice.

These foundations teach us how to live in this world. We're constantly consuming these sacred foundations, but it's not very often that we stop and give thanks to them. That's all part of reciprocity, to give and to take. Being the receiver and being the giver. These foundations never ask anything of us. They're there, and it's a good practice to give

thanks for them. In that way we have balance in our life, we have the foundations of nature.

My elders say that when you drink, the water is going to visit with you because it's going to go inside your body and it's going to touch every bit of your being: the cells and tissue, everything, all of the little spaces in there.

It's a wonderful feeling to go to the water to look at it. I can feel the spirit. It's like the spirit of the water rises and comes up and I'm looking at it and it's looking at me, and it's like it smiles at me and I smile back at it and it's a good feeling, almost like I can hug it. The spirit of the water will rise up, it will look like a wave. To me, when the water rises up it's acknowledging me and I'm feeling its love. That's the way it's been all of my life. No matter where I am.

I say, *I'm your child and grandchild.*

It's the same with the fire, the sunlight. One time I worked with a medical doctor, part of Doctors Without Borders. They provide medical services, usually in third world countries. He returned from Africa and showed me pictures of this African village. There was a fire out there. He said, "This is a village fire, and they keep this fire burning all the time." Long ago most of the indigenous people had a sacred fire they kept burning all of the time. It wasn't a huge, blazing bonfire, just a little fire. It's like a spirit that watches over the village. Also whenever the people in the village needed to light their fire in their homes to cook or whatever, they would take from that central fire, to light the fire at their homes. So this is how it was. And then they have certain people watch it. Taking care of it and watching over the fire. Having that sacred fire around is pretty universal.

It's the source or sustenance for each family. They can go to that source to feed themselves and warm themselves. That's what I saw when I was in India. They also have sacred fires that have been burning for thousands of years. Just amazing! I looked over into their little tent and would go there. Then the swami or the baba or the yogi would go and get that ash and put it on my forehead so I received the blessing of the fire.

The same thing with the earth, how we consume what has grown from the earth and how we touch the earth. So it's all incorporated, even in that one motion of going out and greeting the day through that prayer. Some of the old teachings have stories about the time when the animals spoke. The ones that live on the earth and in the earth, we learn from them, they give us songs. Sometimes they give us visions, or they visit us when we're out on a spiritual path somewhere. We recognize the animals as being far more intelligent than we are. We learn from them, we are respectful of their space. Some of the foods that we eat are foods that they eat. We saw how they eat it and so we still collect, as you say, *in the wild*. We learn from them.

As a child, I was told how to treat the other creatures that coexist on Mother Earth. I was told never to disturb the anthills, where the ants lived. We were told that the ant people help us. As children when we were out playing in nature, we were told that if we saw a snake track that crossed our path we had to turn around and go another direction. We were not allowed to cross a snake path. We were taught to pay attention to these things. Like the birds—I was told by an elder, "The eagles will come and see you, and when you see them you know that that's my spirit looking out for you, and I'm giving you the signal that wherever you're going, there will be a really good blessing, a good spirit." Sure enough, that's how it's been for me.

So that's the first part of walking in the Beauty Way. Then the other part is, once you establish that relationship as an individual person, then you come to acknowledge yourself as a person who represents your bloodlines and your ancestry. Acknowledging those ones who have made you who you are. In that way you have a better sense of your well-being, which is again part of the Beauty Way.

When you're in this Beauty Way, it is very important how you're being toward your relatives, your immediate family, your extended family, your community, your nation, the world, and all the way up to the universe. You bring awareness to your connection with everything and how you are being respectful of the ways they contribute to your existence.

Another really important practice is acknowledging each other's needs and greeting each other in the day. When you see relatives or family members, go greet them. When we meet our relatives, the first thing we do is either go give them a hug or else shake their hand. That's extending the beauty of being a good relative, being in good harmony with others.

Oftentimes we're being treated as if people are invisible, rather than warm human beings. It's important to revive that concept, that we're warm human beings. We're not invisible, we're not enemies. We have to begin to relate to one another, having good relations.

When you're walking in the Beauty Way, even the way you look at a

If you're going to take the time to pray, then why not have faith in your prayer?

person, even the way you pass by them has an effect on them. They can feel your energy. If you have a negative shield around you as you pass someone, they're going to feel it. They may even move away or feel like they were pushed away without you even touching them.

You can take the water and talk with it about whatever concerns you. You can ask that there be a shift in your inner energy to be positive. You can drink water with that kind of thinking. Or you can use the air you take in, and as you breathe out you're blowing this negative energy away from you. You can light a candle and sit with the fire and talk or meditate about whatever it is that's creating this negative energy in you. Or you might even just go out and touch the earth. What I do is I touch the earth and make a washing motion of my hands. I do that with the air, I make a washing motion with the fire and the earth to cleanse myself, to release what is not useful to me.

When negative things start happening in my day I stop and I say, *Let's see, what's going on here?* I pause, and usually when that's happening I realize that I didn't do my prayer for the morning, I didn't give thanks for the day. So I take time out to do that because in my belief, if you make your prayer, you've put your whole day in the hands of the Creator to take care of things. So if things come up, little barriers, little negative things cross your path, what I say is, *It's going to be all right because I prayed about it.*

I keep that in my mind. I get other people frustrated sometimes because they want me to get mad or they can't understand how could I be so optimistic about things. But you know, if you're going to take the time to pray, then why not have faith in your prayer?

The Grandmothers' work is to revive the concept that we are all related and to extend a basic consciousness about our self and our relationships. That's our work. Through prayer, ceremony, and spiritual practices, through the earth-based medicines. If you read the mission statement of the Grandmothers Council, it incorporates all of these things that I'm talking about as the Beauty Way.

It's not limited to any specific group or practice. All of the Grandmothers come from different parts of the world and have different spiritual practices. But we have taken a step beyond that and have joined together and grown this relationship as Grandmother sisters. All this is connected to living the Beauty Way.

As women, it's very important for us to practice the Beauty Way.

It's not just how you walk and talk but how you acknowledge and accept your existence in this world. The way I was told, when we were born into this world, we became connected to everything that's on Mother Earth and all of these four sacred foundations of life and all the way clear into the universe. Our existence extends all the way to the universe.

The Circle of Life

My mother and my grandmother told me that we have four stages in life: the child, the youth, the adult, and the elder. Our life is in a circle, our life cycle. Each stage or each part of the circle has very significant teachings for the development of yourself as a person.

One of the best ways for a person to absorb, to retain, to learn, is by using their own senses. So when I'm sharing this teaching I have people draw a circle. It becomes a visceral experience. The paper should be big enough that you might be able to write some words in and around the circle. Then you draw the four directions, a cross in the circle. This is your circle of life. Up in the center where 12 would be on the clock, to your right in the outside of that first piece you would write "Child." On the second piece just below there you would write "Youth." And then on the third piece (moving in a clockwise direction) from 6:00 to 9:00, you would write "Adult." And then on the fourth piece, 9:00 to 12:00, on that part of the pie you would write "Elder."

What you're seeing is the four stages of life, or sometimes what we call the *four hills of life*. I guess that's where they got that saying, "Being

over the hill." You've got the four stages of life in front of you, and that's the life cycle.

I do this with all age groups. My greatest joy is doing it with the children. They get excited about their childhood. They're happy about being a child, having fun, playing. You know, swimming, fishing, or playing with their dog. They can verbalize it and put their thoughts, their feelings all together to describe it.

So then I say, "What's the next level of growth?" And it's youth. So they say, "Well, when I'm thirteen these are some things I'll do. I'll be in high school." Or if they're connected to their traditions, they would say, "I'll have my manhood ceremony, or my womanhood ceremony." Those young ones look at their life that way. Their siblings or maybe others in their community, what are they doing? What are the experiences they want to embrace?

And then they look at being an adult. Okay, when I'm an adult, usually somewhere in between youth and adult, they're talking about college, education. They're talking about their goal of becoming a doctor or whatever kind of job they want to have. And then they say, "Well, maybe I'll have a family. I'll have children or have a wife."

Then for the elder part, they look at their grandparents and talk about their grandparents and things that their grandparents do with them. "I like to go fishing with my grandpa." Or "Sometimes my grandpa takes me walking by the river or hiking up whatever mountains

Mona at a waterfall along the Colorado River, Arizona, United States, 2010

Mona leading a presentation about the Circle of Life. Arizona, United States, 2010

around here." They talk about what the elder, or the grandfather or grandmother, does with them. And maybe they will be that way when they become an elder.

So that's how I use it to work with children as well as adults. It lifts up their spirits.

By doing this exercise with adults, they acknowledge the beauty of each stage of life they've already passed. So going back to the child and the youth, those people who are not yet elders, they identify their aspirations. This exercise is a way of putting into practice what we call *to aspire* in the Hopi way.

There's a prayer that's made for the infant that says: *May this child aspire to live a long life, to reach old age.* So using this exercise creates a kind of a map and some direction for your journey in the circle of life. It's like the prayer that's made for the baby in Hopi. That prayer is the road map for that child's life.

Positive Aging

I've had a job as the aging specialist at the University of Arizona Center on Aging. I produced a film on Native American aging. I also produced a training curriculum on working with Native American elders. My video received an award for quality and effectiveness from the Aging Society of America.

Our eldest Grandmother, Agnes Baker Pilgrim, says, "Being an elder isn't for wimps." She then asks how many people out in the crowd are grandmothers or grandparents. People raise their hands. Then she says to the rest of the crowd, "If you're not a grandparent now, you're a grandparent-in-training or you're an elder-in-training."

If aging is not an issue for you, it soon will be. There's a tendency in Western society to not even consider the fact that everyone is in the process of aging. Also, there are both myths and realities about aging. There's a tendency to believe that the myths are the truths and the realities are some fantasy. I've produced an educational curriculum on mental health issues among the Native American aging population. I traveled to different tribes and interviewed them. One of the questions I asked was, "When you were a child, what were you told about aging or being an elder?"

One elderly grandmother said, "When I was a child we were taught to treat our elders as if they were so precious. That's the way that we were told we should treat them. We were told that those who reach that stage of life are very precious and special."

Another elder told me that a person in their elderhood has experienced so much of life, they have a wide, long view of life. They can tell you things. You could seek them out and ask them for their advice about certain situations in your life. You could ask them about situations involving your community. Do you hear what they have to say? The people in this elder stage of life have seen more, they have seen all of the rapid change of our society and our culture.

Many of the changes have been to do with technology. Our elders have gone through all of this change. Our indigenous elders have seen some changes that they were told were going to happen. Their elders, those we call the Old Ones, told them these things.

Those in the elder stage of life have knowledge and much wisdom. That stage of life is one of beauty. One of the prayers is to aspire to that stage of life, of elderhood. Another teaching I was given is that as an elder, our body goes through different changes. One of the myths of aging is that people attribute memory loss to aging, but it it's not necessarily so. Many elders continue to function very well mentally. Part of maintaining that function is by their activity; for a Native elder, they may continue doing their beadwork, they may continue doing their weaving. They may still go out to tend their gardens.

And in the case of the Navajo, elders may still go out to herd their sheep and tend to the livestock. Those kinds of things keep them functioning. My Hopi grandmother lived to be 102 years old. She was fully functioning. The thing that got her was she had fallen and broke her hip and went into the hospital. In the hospital she developed pneumonia, and that's what took her.

In my teaching, aging is beautiful.

I don't really want to attach attitudes about aging as being Native or indigenous. It's a human quality. Acknowledging aging as part of the cycle of life needs to be revived. When we're talking about the cycle of life, the old gives way to new and the new gives way to old. That's the cycle of life.

When we have to send our elder to a nursing home, it's very disturbing, it interrupts our family life. But that's the society we now live in. To me it's a shame that these senior adults live in these gated communities where their grandchildren can't come and spend a week with them. I wonder what in their life experience made it so necessary for them, to feel like they needed to live in this gated community. Maybe they do have a good relationship with their families, but it gives that kind of impression to me, that they feel like they have to go isolate themselves that way.

but for our future generations yet to come, the ones we will not see. We want them to have a future, so we are doing what we can to uphold that and to make a contribution toward the future.

It's also important to understand that our relationship isn't only with human beings, it includes all life forms on Mother Earth. We all equally have a place in this world, we all have this interconnectedness of interdependence with all of the life forms on Mother Earth. That's what the Grandmothers are upholding, and passing this message on.

We all rely on the same things. There's no difference. For our own survival as well as the survival of all our relations. We are connected to Mother Earth, from the ground all the way up. My people, the Havasupai, we're creating just a little bit of connection outside the body of the Grand Canyon. I feel really good that my people are willing to step out of their sacred home place down in the canyon to come out and greet others, people of different nations. To share their sacred knowledge with others so there might be one word, one song, and one movement. Maybe just through that, we might create a new awareness within all of us. Maybe it creates another little bit of understanding about the ways of being of the indigenous people of the Grand Canyon.

I was told that whenever sounds are made, like the vibration of the drum, the rattle, or the movement of the dance, they are sent out. We are not just sending them out to those who are present. We're also sending this vibration to our ancestors. They're looking at us and they're rejoicing and feeling so happy. They are filled with joy to look at their children, grandchildren, the generations that are after them continuing to walk this path and continuing on with the teachings.

The songs, the dance, the stories have come to us through the generations. Our ancestors made a prayer for us that we would be doing this. They made these prayers for the generations to come, the grandchildren, the great-great grandchildren that I will not see. *Creator, bless them; I want them to live, be strong, continue being our people. We want to see our people continue on.* They make prayers like that. That is why we are here today. They continue to be here and continue to hold on to these things as precious reminders of our connections to Mother Earth and our ancestors.

World Water Forum

I belong to an international body of indigenous people who have been organizing and planning what we call the Indigenous World Forum for Water and Peace. It came from a call from elders, a call to address water issues of indigenous people because the United Nations was not including indigenous people in their forum, the World Water Forum.

The indigenous elders called for this in 1999 at the World Indigenous Peoples' Conference on Education, which was held in Hawaii. One of my colleagues, Darlene Sanderson, took that to heart. So in 2006 indigenous people went to the World Water Forum in Mexico and voiced their issues. Again, they weren't allowed inside. They weren't included in that forum. So Darlene approached me, I believe it was in 2010; I was at the World Peace Conference in Vancouver, British Columbia.

She said, "What we need to do is, we need to have an indigenous

World Water Forum." I felt called to support it, so I told her I felt it was important, that it needed to be done.

We went to the United Nations and presented what was called an intervention. It was a statement that we delivered to the United Nations Permanent Forum on Indigenous Issues in 2007, calling for the United Nations Permanent Forum to have a Indigenous World Forum on Water and Peace.

We had no money. We didn't have a place to stay. We just had enough money to get us there by airplane, but everything worked out. At the United Nations we had to lobby. We had to get other indigenous organizations to support this concept of having an Indigenous World Forum on Water and Peace. So we stood by the food court in the United Nations. As indigenous people came walking by, we would approach them and tell them about it. And they'd say, "Yes, we need this, we need to have this."

They signed on, supporting it. And they would say, "You need to talk to so-and-so"; then we would seek out that person and tell them that so-and-so told us that you would want to hear about this. So all together, we ended up having more than thirty-six indigenous organizations at the UN Permanent Forum on Indigenous Issues signing on, supporting this initiative, this intervention. Then we presented the intervention to the forum, the Assembly.

This was the first time we were at the UN Permanent Forum for Indigenous Issues. After that, we started going every year, connecting with other people doing work for the protection of water. We have a working group of people. We have a hereditary chief from Vanuatu, in Oceania; a person from the Cook Islands. Unfortunately, she has passed away. We have a lady from Kenya, Africa, who founded the Indigenous Information Network. We have Huirangi Waikerepuru, a Mâori elder from New Zealand, from Aotearoa, and we have a man from the indigenous tribes of northeast India. And then from Canada, British Columbia, is Darlene Sanderson, the cofounder of this initiative. We also have people from the Indigenous Environmental Network, which is based in Minnesota, and myself.

So we have this working group that has been doing this work ever since that time, that beginning. We represent all of this range of both poor countries and what some call "developed" countries like the United States, who have safe and clean drinking water. Of course, we're finding out that's not true. There are also people throughout the world, indigenous people, who lack clean drinking water for their communities. And today, with climate change, we're also facing water scarcity and extreme flooding.

These issues that we've been talking about as part of the Indigenous World Forum on Water and Peace are in full swing; they are major issues, major problems, not only for indigenous people but for all people. This year (2018), the World Water Forum is in Brasília, Brazil. This year our working group was able to submit a proposal seeking funding to bring a delegation of indigenous people from seven regions of the world, and we were fortunate to have received the funding. So we have a delegation of indigenous people who've got sponsorship by the World Water Forum to attend and to be speakers on various panels about their water issues.

As far as the International Council of Thirteen Indigenous Grandmothers is concerned, we are extending a basic call to consciousness. And the basic call to consciousness is that we are all related. We are all related. We all have this life force within us. We all rely on the basic foundations of life: the water, the air, the fire, and the Mother Earth.

One of the most important issues is the impact of building dams on the rivers. The indigenous people rely on the water from rivers, lakes, and streams for their livelihood. It's also where their medicines are. The waters are their sacred places.

In the case of a dam, it holds back the water and interferes with the regeneration of the water life, the fish and the various animals that live in those waters. And of course, those are also food sources for the people. They have traditional ways of fishing. When the water is held back, it interrupts the traditional ways of fishing. If they hold that water when the fish are hatching, the water temperatures change so the fish and the animals in the water can't survive. Then when they release water, the water is flowing at speeds that aren't natural to the riverbed. So it washes away the fish. So dams have huge impacts. The waters become contaminated by industrial waste along the rivers, including the mining operations spilling into the rivers. All this has huge impacts not only for the people but also environmentally. These are some of our concerns.

Often the indigenous people are the last ones to be informed by the water corporations or by the nation-states setting their policies and determining what to do with the waters. This affects not only surface waters but also the aquifers, the underground waters. So these are huge impacts on the indigenous people. The indigenous people are basically the first ones to feel the impacts of water shortage or climate change and the last ones to know about policies and changes. All of these various issues interfere with continued existence. Literally.

Our intention is to create awareness of these impacts and build communications with the governmental agencies as well as the corporations, as well as the UN agencies.

All of the people are taking a stand, making efforts, giving voice for the protection of the water. It's a responsibility that all of us should embrace. Many of the people involved in this work recognize their roots to all of the elements. We understand and recognize that we don't have life if we don't have water.

If we don't have safe and clean water, we will not have safe and clean food. We will not have good health. It's very important to understand that *water is life*.

THIRTEEN

GRANDMOTHER AGNES BAKER PILGRIM

MY NATIVE NAME IS *TAOWHYWEE*, which means morning star, and my English name is Agnes Emma Baker Pilgrim. While visiting the Kainai Nation (Blood Tribe) in southern Alberta, Canada, I was given the name *Naibigwan*, which means dragonfly in their language.

I was born in a little place called Logsden, Oregon, on a tribal allotment at the headwaters of the Siletz River on September 11, 1924. My mother's maiden name was Eveline Lydia Harney and her married name was Eveline Lydia Harney Baker. My father's name was George Wentworth Baker. He was a Coos Indian, and my mother was a full-blooded Takelma. The Coos people are from southern Oregon, down on the coast. My father was from the oceanside and my mother was from inland in southern Oregon.

I had eight other siblings, nine of us total. I was the third from the end, but they are all gone except me now.

We all grew up in Logsden, Oregon, until my brothers and my dad had to move out to log. Being loggers was the only way they had to make money at that time. They had to go to logging camps. They would come home and my dad would work on his nets and our boats because we had to keep them going for our livelihood. They also had gardens to plow and hay fields to plant. Gardening and gathering was a constant thing. We had our own orchards and we hunted and fished. We had chickens, we had sheep, we had longhorn cattle, and we had horses and milk cows. So we were always busy from the time that we were old enough to do chores. We all had our work to do. Every single one of us.

If we wanted any buckskins, my dad had to tan the hides. We had a smokehouse to take care of, wood to get, fishing lines to prepare. So the work was a constant. We had to learn how to run the smokehouse. We were always doing something when the fruit season was on. We would go berry picking and gather apples. They had us girls learn how to can. There was wood to be cut and the fires to be kept, chickens to feed, cows to milk; and so we all had our job.

Mom and we girls didn't move, the men moved. We stayed in our home place, an allotment from my grandfather, chief George Harney. My grandfather was the chief of the Confederated Tribes of Siletz, Oregon. He traveled to Washington, D.C., to fight for the allotments that we had, not just for us, but for other people in the tribe too.

An allotment is land that is given to us to live on by the government. It was supposed to be for us forever, but it didn't end up that way. The government took it away from us. We had to pay taxes to stay on it and we couldn't afford the taxes, so it reverted to the state. That happened all over our reservation. All over where I grew up.

Even my grandfather, when he died, he left land to my mom and his wife, my grandma, Elizabeth. She got to live on eighty acres and my aunt Margie got to live below us on another eighty acres. My aunt Agnes had her allotment as well.

In Lincoln County, where I was born, there were signs printed and put on businesses stating "Indians and dogs not allowed."

In Lincoln County, where I was born, there were signs printed and put on businesses stating "Indians and dogs not allowed." I was a young kid when the priests and the nuns came to my mom and dad and told us to stop wearing our buckskins and to stop speaking our language. They said if they loved us, when we went out into the dominant society it would be easier for us if we didn't do those things. So they convinced them. They agreed to comply with that order for our people to stop learning and speaking our language.

Even when my grandma took us to work in the Catholic Church we got slapped around if we spoke our language at all. People watched over us so we would not speak our language. It was hard for us kids. My brothers were altar boys, and we were really treated mean. We were beaten with sticks, and our hair was pulled and our ears pulled. It's a wonder that I don't have bare spots on my scalp from them pulling on my hair.

Speaking our language was natural to us, it was a habit. We'd drive down to the church on Sundays with my gram, who worked in the church. She helped the priest to clean. So when we went into the church we'd talk to each other that way. Then we'd be slapped around. All of my brothers and sisters were in the Catholic Church there. We were into communion and everything. They made us go. If we didn't, then we got slapped around again.

My mother and my aunt Frances spoke our language. Yeah, we all spoke it for a long time. We were forced to stop. If you don't use your language you lose it, and that's what happened to all of us on the reservation. They wouldn't let us speak our language, none of us—not just my family, all of us, everywhere. The government forbade us.

I loved both my mother and my father, but the Bureau of Indian Af-

Nurse holding Agnes; her mother, Eveline Baker; sister Marion; Great-Aunt Frances; brothers Lloyd and Charles; with brother Terry and sister Evelyn in front, 1927

fairs wouldn't let us go along on the roll of both parents. If your father belongs to one tribe and your mother belongs to another, you can't join both tribes. They wouldn't let you do that, and it is still that way today. My daughters, my kids, they can't belong to both tribes, the tribe of their father too, you know.

My daughter Nadine took care of her dad, who was a Yurok. So she joined the Yurok tribe. She's still on the Yurok roll. Her daughter is part of that tribe, and her grandsons too. Her other daughter is in my tribe, and her daughter's kids are also with my tribe, Chantele, Jasper, Nisha, and Kymarii. And it's that way in every tribe; you can't belong to both tribes, anywhere in the United States.

My mom and that generation prayed in the old ways. That was the way her father did, in our native way of praying to Creator. Then she had to stop letting us do that. And we would have to kneel down to pray and read the catechisms. Grandma would see to it that we read the catechisms all the time.

Tribal Relocation

In 1856 my people were taken forcibly from southern Oregon more than 200 miles over rough terrain, rain, snow, everything. The only thing they were allowed to take at that time was the clothes on their backs and whatever food they could carry in a buckskin bag. The people in southern Oregon, my grandfather and all of the old ones, were marched out to the two reservations. Some were taken to Grand Rounds Indian Reservation, some to the

Siletz. Their families were separated. It was a hard time. Grandma said that they wore some of their moccasins out—they walked over rocks, their feet were sore, and they didn't have any way to be allowed to make anything to cover their feet. Some of the elders fell, and then when the young went to pick them up they were beaten and told that if they did that again they would leave the old ones back there for the animals to eat them. It was horrible. Then when they arrived at the reservations, the agent who had been given money by the government for their food, shelter, and blankets had used up a lot of the money. So a lot of my people died from exposure and lack of food. It was really a terrible time for them, and many of them perished.

My mom's father was the chief. They said that she was an Indian princess, but they didn't call her that because there was no word in her language for it.

Schooling

I was taken to the Chemawa Indian School near Salem, Oregon, when I was eight years old. Many of us were taken from home. Before taking us to school they took us to the hospital to have our adenoids and tonsils taken out. They sent us to the schools to stop the bonding process between parents and their children. These schools were like military schools: the students had to march to meals, march to classes. It was hard for a lot of them.

Soon after I began school, my mother refused to send me to Chemawa. She said, "That's it. They just teach those girls how to drink and smoke." So I stayed home. It was a good thing too, because my mother fell ill and I was the only one there to take care of her. I was nine years old. And that's when she taught me how to cook standing on a box.

So instead, I went to a public school called the Logsden School, a one-room schoolhouse. My younger brother Terry—his given name was Tharold—and my brother Gilbert went there too. A lot of Indian kids went there. To this day I'm glad I did, because I wasn't in boarding school; I got to stay home and I was there to help my mother. Since my father was gone, we were the only ones at home at that time. I was glad that I stayed. They were good to me in that little school.

Mother's Illness

Then my mother got sick and I took care of her at nighttime too. It was hard. I would fall asleep in class. My grandma talked to the superintendent of the county to let them know that I was taking care of my mom at night. So they made it possible for me to go to school and take care of my mom. It was really a wonderful gesture. They moved me from sixth grade to eighth grade, which made my brother Terry very angry. It made him really upset because I caught up with him. They moved all of my classes to the morning so that I could get my class work done early. I'd have lunch, and then they'd let me sleep in the teachers' lounge. Then we took the bus back home to Logsden, so I could take care of my mom.

My mom had cancer. They didn't name it like that at the time. A Chinese doctor gave her herbal medicine so she could hold things down. He told us to shave around the area where the cysts were on top of her head, to keep the hair away from it. I had to do that before I went to school too. I'd take the scissors and cut around her head and keep the hair from growing back in that area, and use gauze with the ointment that the doctor gave us to put on it and leave it that way until I came home at night. And then I had to bathe that and sponge it before she went to bed.

Not too long after my mom got sick, my father left us. He went to logging camps in different places, and he stayed away so long that, I guess, he got used to it. Then he didn't come back. He finally divorced my mom and married a Grand Ronde Indian woman. Then he went to work in northern Oregon. We got to see them once in a while. It was okay for me because he drank too, and I didn't want him coming around my mom with his breath, acting the way he used to. My brothers kind of kept him away.

I was around thirteen years old when my mom passed.

There was a woman I used to call Mother Pearl. I asked her to help me bathe my mom. I was very upset because I had read somewhere that if the legs or hands were crooked when you died, they would break them with a wooden hammer to straighten them out. I didn't want that to happen to my mom. So I cut some gauze and tied my mom's hands together. I tied her ankles and her knees too. We put a new gown on her and brushed her teeth. Then I took cotton and stuffed her cheeks so they weren't sunken in. I bathed her head and put new gauze on before they came to take her to Toledo, to the mortuary.

When it came time for the services, they brought her home. They don't dig the grave until the morning of the burial, so my brothers carried her out and we had a service there for her. We wrapped her up in a blanket. A lot of this was blanked out to me because I kept blacking out, they said. I was screaming and crying.

Great-Aunt "Quis-quas-hum" (Chipmunk Face), Frances Harney Johnson (1844–1934), with mother, Eveline Baker, at the opening ceremony for the Salmon River Cutoff Highway near Lincoln City, Oregon, United States, 1926

I don't remember too much about the service, but they said they circled around the house and took her out through the largest window. They don't go out the door the last time when someone passes. They did that to make sure that her spirit would be all right with all of us, to be sure her spirit would stay with us with a good feeling.

I don't remember too much about it, but they said I tried to jump on top of her casket and the boys and my brothers were trying to hold me back.

It was very hard after Mom died. I went to live with my oldest brother and his wife in a little place called Taft, which is called Lincoln City today. I went to high school there. There were only two Indians in that school, another young man and me. They treated us okay. When I graduated I was crying because my mother always said, "You go ahead, you go to school and you get your degrees." I was crying, holding up my diploma thinking: *I got it, Mom, I got it, Mom!* I could always hear her voice in the wind saying: *Go to school, keep on going to school.*

I met a doctor and his wife in Portland and he said that when I graduated I could come work for him. And so I did. I went to work with Dr. Robert Greene at the Greene Mangel Clinic, in Portland. They had this beautiful home way up high in the hills. After his wife gave birth to Robert Junior I moved into their house and took care of him. Today he's a doctor in Salem, Oregon, and delivers babies. I helped him that way.

Then I went to work part time in Vancouver, Washington, at the Barnes General Hospital for injured veterans. I sterilized operating room instruments. Then I worked helping a lady in a convalescent home.

I worked all the time, so I didn't have much time to meet anyone.

But once I went to a skating rink in Portland and met a man named Robert Taylor. He was an ice skater. I couldn't seem to get the knack of ice skating, and he'd just laugh at me. I told him, "You better just get me a mattress then, because I'm going to be all banged up if I continue this." So I just quit trying. He was a musician and would play at the church with his mother. She was an evangelist in a full gospel church. Robert seemed to treat me pretty nice. He was German. When I was young it was against the law for an Indian to marry a white person. So I thought of that, but it was kind of gone with the wind, like a lot of things. He was good to be with at the time.

When his father died, they sent two tickets to take his body back to Arkansas, so I was an escort with Robert to take his father's body back home. Once we were back there we got married at the church. Robert and I stayed living back there. We had three kids, Robert Lloyd Taylor, Lewis Keith Taylor, and Sonja Rose Taylor, my oldest girl.

Sonja is a grandmother now; she lives in Encino, California, and Keith lives out in California too. Robert Jr. passed away in 1996. I lost my son from my second marriage, Tony Junior, in 2003. He was fifty-one years old. So those two boys are gone. Now I just have one biological son living, Keith. But I have other adopted sons.

Robert went to Fort Benning, Georgia, and I was there with the kids. Then he was sent to Camp McCall, North Carolina, and that's where Robert Jr. was born. We lived on the East Coast for some time. When Robert left the service we went back to Portland. We were back there when Sonja was born.

Robert's mother sang in the church, and he and I played instruments.

Around that time, nobody wanted to be Indian because no one liked the Indians. You had to learn to fight or you would get beaten. I didn't ever let anyone put me down because of my native ways. I always identified with my native heritage.

even when she was walking. And it was always like that. And it kind of bothered Tony Junior. And it was that way for a long time.

Things went from bad to worse. I was tired of arguing and fighting. I shot at him once. It was good that I was shaking, because I missed him. But I shot at him. There were a lot of alcohol problems on the reservation. One time I cut him with a knife and he went over to his folks and told them. I tried cutting him with a knife because he was pulling my hair and stuff. I tried to keep out of his way. I drank with him at times, but I really didn't drink because I had the children to take care of. But he liked it when I drank with him.

Around that time, nobody wanted to be Indian because no one liked the Indians. You had to learn to fight or you would get beaten. I didn't ever let anyone put me down because of my native ways. I always identified with my native heritage. I was dark then. I had black hair and dark skin. I was Indian, all right. I am the only one of all of us nine kids who ran around in my buckskins. And I danced when I was in school. I danced at our native Feather Dances in Siletz.

The government wanted to put us down as caucasian, and I thought, *My God, my mother would turn over in her grave!* I said, I don't want to be white on my birth certificate. I guess they wanted to do that so they wouldn't have to be concerned about us Indians. I didn't want that. Then the government terminated our tribal recognition. That was a really awful time too, not just for me, for all of our tribe. One good thing about our tribe was that they kept the tribal council going. Even though we weren't recognized. My brother George was on the tribal council.

My brothers always loved me because I took care of my mom and them, so when she was gone I became like the little mother at home. The boys were always good to me.

I eventually divorced Tony. I moved to Tillamook, Oregon, where I raised my two kids. I went to work and I lived alone. I liked the country up there. My gram was part Tillamook. I got acquainted with people. I used to sing in a nightclub. I was also working in a hospital. Tony begged me to come back to him, and I just couldn't do it, because he had not yet corrected his life. I didn't want to be subjected to any more abuse. I just couldn't do it.

So I stayed there in Tillamook. My kids went to school there. It was a great school. I think Nadine was in about seventh or eighth grade, and they went all the way to high school there. From fourth grade to eleventh grade Nadine and Tony Junior played in the school band. I worked, I worked back and forth. I worked at Tillamook Cheese, a restaurant. The kids had an open ticket to eat anything they wanted there, and I used to always laugh because they could have gotten steaks or salmon, but they always got hamburgers and french fries. That tickled all of us, you know. I also worked for a nightclub, the Workman's Club. I was bartending there. I was a bartender and a bouncer.

I liked to drive. I would put the kids in the car and drive. I've always had a car. So if I was worried or upset, I liked to go for a drive. It kind of unwound me. I still like to do that nowadays.

These people who had these nightclubs wanted me to be a race car driver. They got these Chevy cars with a Jimmy motor and they would take me out on the racetrack and teach me how to drive, to take the corners, at what speed, what time. They timed me in, and they really gave

Everything that comes from Mother Earth we have to use with gratitude. You walk on Her face every day, and through Her we have all these things. I teach this to kids in schools and colleges and everywhere. I always remind them to just take a little spot on Her face and to always give thanks for the nourishment, for everything you have. Give thanks in that way, because She takes care of us.

Gold Mining

Years and years ago, back in the 1800s, the Chinese people found out that there was gold in this area in Oregon. So the mining started, and it created a lot of problems. Our people used to call it the "shiny rock," but they had no use for it.

But miners would go after other miners and kill for this gold. A lot of that occurred when the Chinese people came. It created a lot of problems in sacred grounds. Many people protested because our sacred grounds were being dug up for gold.

A lot of people got killed along the way. Some of our people would get killed just for walking close to the mining camps. Even the non-natives were killing each other over the gold mines. It was sad what happened at this place called Gold Hill, near Grants Pass. The "yellow rock," as my people called it, was never picked up from the river; they had no need for the yellow rock.

I am glad now that things have stopped that way. It caused a lot of havoc. Like I said, our tribal people, my people, they had no need for the yellow rock.

Grandfather "Olhatha" (Forehead with Hair), George Harney (Takelma), 1837–1900. Elected first Chief, Confederated Tribes of Siletz, 1870. Photo taken in Washington, D.C., circa 1875–1877

My grandfather, the first elected chief of my tribe, the Siletz Nation, learned how to use it. He used some yellow rock to pay for his own trips to Washington, D.C., to fight for our people's land allotments. They used it to trade too. But other than that, our people had not much use for gold.

Cancer

In 1973 they found cancer in me. I went to the doctor and they took some x-rays. I had to have a mastectomy. In December of the same year, they said it is very rare, but they found another cancer in my colon. So I had to go back to the hospital and they took out a foot and a half of my colon.

My daughter Nadine started taking care of me when this cancer started. I was living in Crescent City, California. I then went to Eureka, California, to have my surgery. She took care of me through all of that, my chemo and radiation treatments.

So every few years I have to have a colonoscopy done to see if I'm still all right. That was a sad year. They called me a "miracle patient" because they don't usually have patients who have two major cancers detected and two major surgeries in one year. But I've had that. I did a lot of chemo and radiation, and my hair nearly all came out. It's still real thin, but I don't complain, because I'm alive.

I'm always thankful, all the time thanking my God for not letting it come back. So I'm very grateful to be sitting here now, available to help others. I now tell others to watch what they eat and to be positive.

When Creator came to me years ago and told me, *I don't want you to get mad at what you see, what you hear, or what you read . . . you got other things to do*, I said, *Yes, God!* So I really follow God's orders. I don't get mad at anybody anymore. You can't change somebody else, but you can change yourself. So I changed myself to do a better thing, and if I could do it, others can do it.

Spiritual Awakening

At the time of what I now understand as my spiritual awakening, I kept on feeling Creator coming to me. It kept coming to me and I would be up in the middle of the night hearing this voice saying, *I want you to do this, I want you to do that.* And I kept saying, *I'm not worthy, I'm not good enough, you give it to somebody else.*

But the voice just kept coming and kept coming, so finally I said, *Yes, God. I'll do it.*

So since then I've been walking a spiritual path. That's how I got into being one of the International Council of Thirteen Indigenous Grandmothers, because people heard of my walk and watched my walk right here in this valley. Right now, I think I am the oldest living member of the Takelma people, my people who have lived here in this valley for 22,000 years.

I feel really good about this and about following Creator's orders and how He helps me every day. I'm so grateful to wake up every morning and have another day. You know, God is good, and He could do this for anybody. Anybody can do what I've done, if you listen to God. Because of God, this is how I think that the world came about. For us people here. I'm so thankful that I'm still alive and able to do what I'm doing, and I keep on keeping on.

Restoration of the Salmon Ceremony

For thousands of years, my people, the older ones, did the gathering of the salmon and had a big feast and all types of people came. They did the gathering before anybody started fishing, to honor the salmon so that Creator would bless them and the salmon would come home.

They hadn't done this gathering for a very long time, and in 1993 the spirit told me to bring it back. Now, for over twenty years, the Creator has helped bring the yearlings back up the river.

Four dams were here for nearly ninety years, and they're all off now. We cleaned up tires, batteries, plastic, and things that were all jammed up in these dams and along the river. The year 2012, we celebrated the removal of all of these dams and all the junk so that the swimmers in the water, the salmon, all can run free.

I feel the presence of the old ones who guided me through all these things. My people have a legend that says that fish look like us humans and live in beautiful cities below the ocean floor. Every spring and fall they choose to put on the shape of the salmon and come back upriver to feed us.

We are the voice of the waters, we are the voice of the salmon, because they have no voice except ours.

In 1994 we restored the Sacred Salmon Ceremony for the first time in the history of southern Oregon. In 1995, a person from the state fish and game department came and said, "I don't know what you've done over here, but there's more fish than we've seen in that river for a long time." I said, "When you teach reciprocity, then the Creator blesses." "What does that mean?" they asked. And I said, "Well, I do the Salmon Ceremony like the old ones did for thousands of years."

Our divers do a purification sweat lodge. I have salmon cooked and give a taste to everybody there, elders down to the little people. I have a beautiful big fish bowl. Everybody, the little children and all, bring all the skin and bones back to me to put in the bowl. When the divers come out of the purification sweat with the cedar boughs in their hands, I place the skin and bones on top of the boughs, and then the drum starts. It drums the divers back to the river. They stand on the river's edge, and they pray to the Salmon Nation.

Then they dive in the water and they place these remains underneath some rocks. They continue to pray as they swim underwater with these offerings for the Salmon Nation. When they come out, the young men are warriors. They receive an eagle feather because they've earned it. The older ones always help the young people in the sweat lodges. This is quietly done the evening before the big day of the Salmon Ceremony.

In 2012, I got to sit where my great-aunt and my dad sat, where all the elder Indians sat when they came there and did their Salmon Ceremony. I was sitting up there on that rock, crying and holding up my eagle fan, looking up and telling my dad, *Here I am, Dad! I've come full*

circle. And I am sitting where you sat, and I pray that you watch over me, all of you up there.

Ancient Ways Carried On

The red-headed woodpecker is the only bird my people in southern Oregon shoot. It's very sacred to our people. They take the scalp of the woodpecker and dry it and use it in their headdresses. They also use the scalps on a banner over their shoulders that hangs down from the left side to the right side. They use them on their sacred dance clothes and regalia.

On my spiritual caps I have the woodpecker scalps in honor not only to the woodpecker but also to the ancient ones of my people who would use them. On my spiritual caps I also have the shell beads, the Indian *wampum*. It's a dentalium seashell gathered on the south side of Vancouver Island, about four feet down in the water. When you gather them, you have to take out the little inside. Sometimes they are lying around where you can just pick them up. There are all sizes; some of them are smooth, some are rough, according to their age. You can find them from a half inch to maybe four or five inches long. I have some of that length in some of my jewelry.

We call the wampum, the shell beads, "money beads" because the Hudson's Bay fur traders who came with their ships along the

Salmon Ceremony by the Rogue River, Gold Hill, Oregon, United States

(left) Agnes with her daughter Mona Hudson and son Keith Taylor, filleting and preparing salmon; (middle) Agnes's daughter Nadine Martin preparing salmon; (right) Agnes sharing cooked salmon with the Salmon Ceremony participants

West Coast taught the native people how to use the dentalium shells for money to buy things on their ships. They would buy iron, blankets, beads, pots or pans, anything else that they could use. If a man had a lot of dentalium strands, he could even buy a wife. That's how these shells were used by my people way back. We used them as money.

They are sacred to us today as native people. We wear them on our regalia, necklaces, earrings, or caps. And it is very sacred, very special. Even today we honor these things. The ancient ones handed down these things to us. I am very proud to say that our tribe's cultural camp teaches all these things to young kids to keep our cultural traditions going in this way.

The youth are taught basket making, gathering, clamming, fishing, eeling. They are taught to check to see if the eels are coming to certain rivers, streams—how to protect these swimmers in the water. They are taught all kinds of culture, plus the language is coming back. Our tribal members are slowly doing it. They have different places where they are teaching throughout the eleven counties of our tribal people.

The things I wear with my regalia were also worn by our ancient tribal people. It's really good to see our youth

(opposite page) Agnes's great-grandson, Tyee Rilatos, praying with the fish skin and bones at the Rogue River's edge

(top) Agnes river rafting on the Rogue River

(bottom) Agnes being helped to the rock where her great-aunt, father, and ancestors sat and did the Salmon Ceremony

learning how to make the beads, size them up, cut them to make them fit, how to clean them, sandpaper them to make sure they are the same size when they string them on a necklace or on a dress or something.

Everything we use from our Mother Earth, handed down from our people's generations, is being preserved by our tribe. We're teaching these cultural ways to our young people. I want some of their things to be put in our museum so that when they grow old, they can look back and see what they made.

Our basket-making ways are being carried on. Sometimes our tribal people take a group of people where the bear grass is and where they can harvest hazelnut sticks. They teach about how they burn, where they grow. It is a lot easier now than it was a long time ago, when the forest service would not let us into areas where we needed to go. But they are more flexible now; we can go and gather in different places and they know we are in there. So it is good that we do these things.

To make baskets, you have to burn along the creeks and some shady places for two years before harvesting the shoots. Then when the little hazelnut shoots come up in the second year, they are straight, and there are no little limbs coming out of them. Around May, June, and July, these are cut and picked. Then we bring them in and right away they are peeled, the little bark is taken off them.

My people used to peel them with their teeth. But you cannot do that now, because people have done aerial spraying in many areas all over the state. We don't use our teeth anymore to peel the little bark off the little limbs. We pick little short ones for finer things, like the barrettes and things like that for your hair.

There are bigger sticks for baskets. And we have burden baskets, heavier sticks for papoose baskets for carrying babies. After the sticks are gathered, you can bundle them and put them away and keep them from year to year. When you want to use them, you have to soak them in water so that they will be flexible and not break. You can soak them in the morning and start making baskets in the afternoon. It doesn't take long for the small sticks to absorb the water and be flexible enough to bend. A lot of people keep them in water day after day if they are going to be working most of the week. The hazelnut tree is a tree that has a little nut on it, with a little green

(top left) Agnes's father, George Baker, photographed in the "story chair" by linguist John Harrington in 1933; (bottom left) Agnes's brothers at the Rogue River, 1933; (top right) Agnes Baker Pilgrim photographed in the "story chair" by Marisol Villanueva in 2012; (bottom right) Rogue River, 2012

Agnes's great-granddaughter Chantele Rilatos beading a dance regalia

burl-like thing around it. We used to always pick and dry the hazelnuts and eat the meat inside the nut. The shoots were then used for basketwork.

There are ways to gather spruce roots too. Sometimes spruce hangs down a bank toward the water, and those are really nice roots to get. You gather the spruce roots and you bring them home. If they are wide and thick, you split them. Some of the roots can be used in the shape that you gather them. But they have to be small for the weaving. We use these to weave the basket together or make any basket.

Then there's bear grass up on the mountains. You pick the clump of bear grass from the center. And again it's gathered around May, June, July. That too has to be burned and then picked. It's green in color when you pick the middle of the bear grass, and you can bring the clumps home and hang them upside down, on your patio or wherever in your house, until they bleach out to kind of a light egg color, kind of an off-white. These are then also soaked to be woven, to hold baskets together or sew them to make designs. A lot of people used moss or the inside of the alder bark to dye bear grass. I have a cap dyed from the inside of an old tree's bark.

The basket-weaving gathering goes on year after year, and I know that there are sticks up there, but my hands are crippled now. Still, I would like to get some sticks and try to make some small baskets.

We're even teaching our young people how to gather the food, how to run a smokehouse, where to go to get the clams and the mussels that we eat from the ocean. They are being taught about our berries and our fruits that are in season, how to gather, prepare, and store them for winter.

When I was young, we could get very big berries because of the burning. Back then the wild berries had smaller leaves and bigger berries. Nowadays, you go to these patches of berries and the leaves are too big and the berries are too small. So it is sad that in some of these places you can't burn to keep it that way for our seasonal wild fruit picking. But there are still places where we have done that out in the valley, where we have done the cool burnings.

They are being taught how to dry our fish and eels. And we are fighting for the rivers and streams to keep them pristine, so that we can continue to help the swimmers in the waters, so that we can have these kind of traditional foods. So I thank our tribal people for all that they do to carry on our traditions and culture.

Another thing we gather is the ocean tea, a tall stalk—green—that doesn't grow just anywhere. When I lived in Crescent City, California, it grew close to the airport, close to the beach. That's why they call it "ocean tea." You pick its green leaves and dry them. Takes about two leaves to make a cup of tea. It is good for anyone who drinks it. We used to gather it from many places. And now we have to go farther out to get it.

The blue camus bulb is another staple that our people used to use. We still have places where we can gather the bulbs. We show our young how they can plow and dig around so the bulbs underneath will be big. Then we can cook them. You don't cook them for very long. If you cook them too much then they get sweet.

We used to gather the acorns and bring them home. We would have to look at each one to be sure there weren't any worms in it. Otherwise the worms would get into your bag of acorns and ruin it all. So you have to look at each one to be sure that there isn't a hole in it. This happens in the fall, when the wind blows. The wind blows them down and you gotta be there to pick them up. And then you take them home and dry them. When they are dried you crack them and take the nut out. I used to put mine in a paper sack and dry it by my fireplace and stir them around all the time. We had a grinder that kind of looked like a meat grinder that makes hamburgers. And then we made it into like a thin soup. Our Yurok people called it *kegoh*, and they ate it with their fish and their deer meat. It is very healthy, a lot of protein, very good for anybody's body. So the old ones relied on this for their strength, and it helped them to get well.

There are many things we gathered from our Earth Mother that would come up in season year by year. There were different varieties of apples that we don't even see anymore. There are a lot of things now that we can rely on for our foods. We used to can and preserve our food. I think I still have my canner. I was always canning things, fruits and meats, deer meat, all the time. Now it is too hard, I am getting old. It is so much easier for me to have someone bring it to me.

Like I said, when I was a little kid, the priest would come to my mom and dad and in front of all of us, tell them, "If you love your children, you won't let them speak your language." Sometimes when we were on the bus some of us kids would use native words and some kids would tell the bus driver and afterward we would get spanked. The Catholic Church told everybody that we could not speak our language, so we couldn't use it. So it just withered away then. But the Siletz tribe restored it a few years ago, and now they have a language program and are teaching classes.

Agnes at Table Rock

Table Rock

Upper Table Rock in Oregon, near the town of Medford, is a protected area of critical environmental concern because of rare species that grow there. There's a plant called the dwarf woolly meadowfoam that grows there at the edge of the vernal pools and nowhere else in the world. Vernal means spring. They form in spring because this rock is mostly made up of very porous lava, so the pools form and the water doesn't really have anywhere to go.

There's also a fairy shrimp (*Branchinecta lynchi*) that lives in the vernal pools. It's very tiny, almost microscopic. As the pools dry up, the shrimp go dormant until the water comes again in the fall.

One theory claims that many thousands of years ago, lava flowed through a fissure crack near Crater Lake and flowed down through this area, filling the ancient riverbed with lava. Table Rock, actually everything around there is weathered away to leave this reminiscence of Table Rock. These are probably the deeper parts of the riverbeds. Lava filled the riverbeds, the river hardened, and then everything around eroded away.

It's such a unique and special area, because of the geology and the plants and the history.

The Pit House

My old people in southern Oregon used to make these pit houses. The pit house is a little house made of planks split with hand tools. The roof is very close to the ground, and there's not a nail in it. They used willow. They'd soak it and wrap the vines around the connections to hold it together. In the center they'd dig a hole down in the ground about eighteen inches, and they had their fire down there. They would cook anything around that fire: fish, meat, whatever. So it served them very well.

We have a replica of a pit house here behind the Kerbyville Museum in Kerby, Oregon. It was done in 1999. The grant money came in from my adopted son, George Fence. In this little replica pit house, I asked them to make the door a little bigger so I could get in. But they didn't usually have doors in them. They just had a blanket to cover the doorway. My ancestors would just crawl in there on their hands and knees. This is what they did when a tree fell; they would cut it and make their pit houses.

This little replica pit house isn't authentic because we had to bring in a portable mill to make the lumber for it. There were so many knots in it, they couldn't split it by hand. But still, it is a very wonderful replica of the pit houses of my people.

We Are Here

There was nothing here in Ashland to honor the native peoples of this land. Once, when an ancient alder tree died by the creek near Matthew Haine's home, he asked a local artist, Russell Beebe, to come over to carve it. Russell had never done anything like that before.

They called me, and I came over and blessed the tree. We thought a new sculpture would be a good way to honor the native heritage here. We all talked to the city council and they said that the tree could come out.

Russell began to talk with the tree, then took it to his property, stood it up, braced it and cabled it up good, and built a scaffold. And over the scaffold he built a kind of frame to hold and protect the tree during rainy weather, snow and hail, and everything. It took him a year and a half to do this.

When the sculpture was done, we were all amazed.

We met with David West, a professor here at the university, and a lot of the native people and told them that we wanted to place the

I tell people that we are all water babies, born in the amniotic sac. And when we come out we are followed by a big gush of water. People don't really think about water being the first medicine, but it is.

My dad used to say, "When you come to the table, it is not a war zone. So if you kids have been fighting with each other, don't carry it to the table." We were given a lot of orders. My brothers were not allowed to hit us girls, not even playing. They gave us a lot of instructions from very young. We all had our chores too. We had been working since we were three years old. My dad got a can and put a bell on it and some wire, and I had to go down to the creek and get water for the plants. I had to get up in the morning before I went to school and water all those plants. My brothers had chores. All of us had to do something.

Nowadays, when I travel, a lot of the elders ask me, "What can we do, now that we are old?" And I say, "You have a voice. You can still teach, you can sit and talk to the children. Help them with some of this knowledge. Talk to them about water. Talk to them about the rain. Talk to them about pollution." All these things grandmas can do. Elders can do a lot of stuff. I always tell the elders, "You got knowledge, and that needs to be given to the little ones. To the ones that will carry on after you go. So you give your knowledge to your children and your children's children." I'm the oldest of five generations and they know, because I passed down all of these things.

Grandmothers Council

There was a lady from California who knew a friend of mine over here in Williams, Oregon. This woman had heard and watched my walk for four and a half years here. That's how my name came up to them and the Center for Sacred Studies. My name came up to them and I was called.

It took a few months to ponder upon that and pray about it. But anyway, I went to New York with them in October 2004 and sat with them at the table. After they found out I was the oldest, they selected me as their chairperson. That's how I got involved with the International Grandmothers. They came from all over the world.

As I look back now, I see how Spirit works and how God called each and every one of us.

Take for example the Grandma from Alaska, Rita Blumenstein. When she answered the call, she came with us to New York and she brought a gift that was given to her by her great-grandmother. Her great-grandmother told her to hang on to these things because one day she would sit with a council of grandmothers. So she gave each of us one of those thirteen stones that her great-grandmother gave to her. It was a prophecy fulfilled. When Rita came in and validated that, we all knew we were doing the right thing.

It was meant to be for us to do what we're doing. I feel that all the time. Every day I thank God that I've been able to do the things I do as one of the International Council of Thirteen Indigenous Grandmothers, and to walk my talk. I tell people, "Do it right, because you only got one time to walk this earth. Make it good, make it a good thing."

When I took the spiritual walk, I began to read the history of my people. I went back in history to the seventeenth century and found my great-great-grandfather Jack Harney and my great-uncles. So I found out a lot of things about my ancestors.

I'm the only one left of my generation, of my brothers and sisters. My brothers' and sisters' kids, some of them call me auntie-grandma. I'm the elder of five generations. Some of them call me the 5Gs, which stands for great-great-great-great-great-grandma. So I'm very proud that I am still here to be able to help my children and teach them that love is all there is. And not to be biased about the color of people, because we are all from the same God, we just walk different paths. And so I teach them about acceptance. God is good to all of us.

As humans we need to do a better job. Our job is to keep on doing good, not only for those who are alive on the planet but also for the seven generations ahead.

We need to guard our water. I keep talking to the youth around the world, in schools and to my kids, about it because when I'm gone they need to ripple it out. We've taken for granted our Mother Earth; we have to start giving back to Her our love and respect. Our ways of caretaking Her have got to change. We have to do better things for our Mother Earth.

AGNES EMMA BAKER PILGRIM

September 11, 1924–November 27, 2019

When I was a young girl my great-grandmother Aggie would tell me the story about her mother's passing. I learned from Grandma's story how to prepare the body for burial and many other traditions we have around death. This story taught me about grief. How to carry and deal with grief, how to face it, and then how to live on. My great-grandmother, whom I called GG, lived a full and rich ninety-five years here. When Creator called her home, I had the honor of joining my Grandmother Nadine, my Great-Aunt Mona, and my mother, Tanya, in preparing her body. I thought of all those teachings from Grandma that had prepared me for that very moment. We took her to Siletz, Oregon, where we had a traditional wake ceremony for her at our longhouse, followed the next day by the burial, where she was laid to rest by her ancestors and family.

My siblings and I were blessed kids to be raised closely with our great-grandma. When she moved to Grants Pass, Oregon, in the nineties, my mom followed her. A year later, my mother birthed me at home here, in my Takelma homelands. From the very beginning of my life, my grandmother played a major role in making sure I grew up to know who I am and where I come from. Being born and raised in my homeland is a privilege, considering my ancestors were forcibly removed from here to the Siletz reservation. Being a Takelma Indigenous person comes with responsibility. Grandma taught her family that it is our responsibility to keep Mother Earth in balance and to always honor our ancestors. To be a voice for the voiceless. These teachings have shaped our lives in the way we view and live in this world. Grandma wanted us to learn and carry on our traditional ways for the future generations to come.

In Grandma's home she had lots of old Indian baskets. She would tell me about these baskets, the plants used, and how and when to gather them. There had not been a basket weaver in our family for many generations and there are not too many basket weavers left in our tribe. I started learning to make baskets after Grandma's passing, and I feel it has become my responsibility to my family and community to carry on these practices. When I'm out gathering materials or working on a basket I always think of Grandma. I give thanks for the plants I am taking, and have good thoughts and intentions every time I make a basket. It has become a common practice of mine to ask my ancestors to guide my hands when I begin. I have no doubt Grandma is guiding me.

I am a mother of two boys, Jasper and Hoxie. Grandma's teachings are now living on through my children. She lived during a time when being Indian was forbidden; however, my children get to grow up proudly speaking and learning their language. They know the significance of Table Rocks and that we go there to pray. My boys dance in our world-renewal ceremonies and sing our songs. We eat our traditional foods. We make our regalia. My sons know where we come from, who they are; and they know Grandma and Grandma's teachings.

Our grandma was very proud to have five living generations. Today her descendents continue to be involved members in our tribal community and the areas where we reside. Many of her grandchildren and great-grandchildren sit on the same tribal committees as she once did. In our family we have regalia makers, beaders, basket weavers, singers, dancers, scholars, and teachers. The women in our family have carried on our ceremonial ways and many now carry our traditional chin tattoos, like Grandma. In our tribal community, her teachings are still being passed down to the children. Our tribe has implemented a curriculum that is taught in the Oregon schools, where some of Grandma's teachings are used. I know she is proud of us for carrying on our traditions like she taught us.

To say Grandma's work has only continued through her family and community is an understatement. My grandma touched the world. Everywhere she went she made a difference and impacted many from all walks of life. There is still of course so much work for us to do. She lived her life with kindness and love. She was beyond generous in sharing our sacred ways with all. Some of them have been exploited or used in hurtful ways. But Grandma's teachings cannot be sold. Grandma's teachings are as old as time, passed down to her from her grandmother, and from hers since time immemorial. The love of our grandmother and the devotion she had to me, her family, our people, and the world lives on through us all. We miss her physical spirit dearly but know she is always with us.

Chantele Rilatos, great-great granddaughter

October 2010—**Council Gathering: Grandmother Clara Shinobu Iura, Kirishima, Japan. Hosted by Brazilian/Japanese Grandmother Clara, the theme of this gathering is *Novo Tempo, Nova Vida, Novo Mundo, Novo Povo, Novo Sistema* (New Time, New Life, New World, New People, New System). The Grandmothers establish relations with the indigenous peoples of Japan in Kirishima.**

October 2010—Grandmothers visit Nagasaki. After the Council Gathering, a delegation of Grandmothers travels to Nagasaki to lay down prayers at the site of the atomic bomb blast.

2011

May 2011—**Council Gathering: Grandmother Rita Pitka Blumenstein, Alaska, U.S. The Grandmothers gather at the Dena'ina Center, hosted by Yup'ik Grandmother Rita, with the theme *Healing the Spirit from the Light Within*. Public council topics include the role of women and motherhood, restoring your foundation and peace, healing Mother Earth, and balancing life with laughter, tears, and healing.**

June 2011—Council of All Beings, Vermont, U.S.

June 2011—Omega Institute, New York, U.S. The Grandmothers return to Omega for their third year of teachings.

October 2011—**Council Gathering: Grandmother Maria Alice Campos Freire, Brasilia, Brazil. The Grandmothers gather at UNIPAZ (University of Peace), hosted by Brazilian Grandmother Maria Alice. The theme of the gathering is *Grandmothers' Voice: In the Flow of the Water*. During the course of the gathering, indigenous elders from across Brazil and South America discuss issues related to water.**

2012

May 2012—Global Justice Award. The Grandmothers receive an award from the Partnership for Global Justice for their efforts to approach the Vatican to rescind the fifteenth-century papal bulls.

June 2012—Compassion Award. The Grandmothers receive the Humanity4Water Compassion Award, previously awarded by Humanity4Water to President Obama, Vice President Al Gore, Archbishop Desmond Tutu, and the Dalai Lama.

June 2012—Omega Institute, New York, U.S. The Grandmothers return to Omega for their fourth year of teachings and prayers.

June 2012—Niagara Falls, New York, U.S. A delegation of Grandmothers offers prayers at the falls in a crosscultural gathering.

July 2012—**Council Gathering: Grandmother Margaret Behan, Montana, U.S. The Grandmothers gather at the Northern Cheyenne reservation in Lame Deer, hosted by Cheyenne Grandmother Margaret. The theme of the gathering is *Gratitude Brings Freedom*. Thirteen tipis, one for each grandmother, encircle the sacred arbor where prayers and teachings take place.**

November 2012—**Council Gathering: Grandmother Aama Bombo, Kathmandu, Nepal. Hosted by Tamang Grandmother Aama, the theme of the gathering is *Praying for Peace in the Land of the Buddha*. Grandmother Aama shares with the people that we are now moving out of the tumultuous Kali Yuga into the Sattvic Age, where only truth will be spoken.**

2013

July 2013—European Tour:

Stockholm, Sweden—Grandmothers Gathering: "We Cherish the Earth We Have Inherited," invited by Aurora's Ring in honor of the Sami people.

Karlsruhe, Germany—Grandmothers Gathering: "Be the Change." The Grandmothers convene with an audience of almost 1,000 people each day.

October 2013—Schweitzer Institute, New York, U.S. Five Grandmothers gather for teachings, ceremony, and a public gathering in which they receive the International Pfeffer Peace Award from the Fellowship for Reconciliation.

October 2013—The Path Open House, New Mexico, U.S. Five Grandmothers gather for teachings, ceremony, and a public gathering at Grandmother Flordemayo's Seed Temple.

December 2013—Grandmothers Gathering: Gisborne, New Zealand (Aotearoa). Hosted by Maori Ambassador Pauline Tangiora.

2014

March 2014—In the Name of the Mother, Arizona, U.S. The Grandmothers come together in a women's gathering to pass their wisdom and ways of connecting through prayer and ceremony to our Mother Earth. On World Water Day, the Grandmothers make a pilgrimage to Montezuma Well and hold a water blessing.

September 2014—**Council Gathering: Grandmother Rita Long Visitor Holy Dance, South Dakota, U.S.** The Grandmothers gather in the ancestral lands of the Lakota Nation, hosted by Oglala Lakota Grandmother Rita. The theme of the gathering is *Wowahuala Na Wowaunsila Ta Cangleska Wakan Ki* (The Sacred Hoop of Peace and Compassion).

2015

July 2015—**Council Gathering: Grandmother Bernadette Rebienot, Gabon, Africa.** The Grandmothers meet for their thirteenth Council Gathering, hosted by Omyènè Grandmother Bernadette in her home temple of Oyenano. The theme is *Echoes of the Grandmothers: Roots of Humanity.* Gathering topics include women, spirituality, and the environment.

2016

August 2016—Grandmothers Gathering: Creation to Completion, New York, U.S. Upon completing a full cycle that began at Menla in 2004 with the creation of the International Council of Thirteen Indigenous Grandmothers, the Grandmothers Council comes together to complete their circle of prayer around the planet.

2017

June 2017—Ninth International Indigenous Leadership Gathering, "Honouring Our Grandmothers—Full Circle," British Columbia, Canada. Grandmother delegates participate as honored guests in the St'át'imc Territory community of the P'egp'ig'lha.

2019

April 2019—Grandmothers' Earth Day Celebration, Arizona, U.S. Grandmothers in attendance were Agnes Baker Pilgrim, Rita Long Visitor Holy Dance, Rita Pitka Blumenstein, and, hosting, Grandmother Mona Polacca. The Grandmothers shared teachings and ceremony on the sacred relation with Mother Earth. Earth Day was celebrated at the ancient water of Montezuma's Well.

2019

September 2019—*Grandmothers Wisdom: Reverence for All Creation* book launch, New York, U.S.

September 2019—**Grandmothers Gathering: Lift the Earth: Bringing Peace to Our Ancestors, New York, U.S.** A four-day event that included the participation of the International Council of Thirteen Indigenous Grandmothers, Dr. Henrietta Mann, Mother Maya, Chief Phil Lane, Dr. Robert Thurman, and other spiritual leaders and activists from around the world.

2020

June 2020—**Online Event: Summit of the Rose: For Living and Dying.** A four-day online retreat and ceremonial gathering, with the International Council of Thirteen Indigenous Grandmothers, Dr. Henrietta Mann, Loretta Afraid of Bear Cook, and special guests.

July 2020 to May 2021—**Online Event Series: Listen to the Grandmothers Wisdom: Meeting Challenging Times.** An online book reading and dialogue with the International Council of Thirteen Indigenous Grandmothers, relatives, and collaborators. The Grandmothers read and expanded on their life stories portrayed in *Grandmothers Wisdom: Reverence for All Creation.*

2021

October 2021—**Online Event: The Way of the Mother: Embracing the Infinite.** A four-day online event with the participation of the International Council of Thirteen Indigenous Grandmothers, the Oyenano Village Grandmothers, Mother Maya, and other spiritual leaders and activists from around the world.

2022

April 2022—**Online Event: Grand Mä Offering: A Circle of Support.** A two-day online free fundraising event taking place around Earth Day, with the participation of founding members of the International Council of Thirteen Indigenous Grandmothers, their families, and special guests. The Grandmothers and guests shared and presented projects and causes close to their hearts.

Image Credits

Angelina Nasso: cover, ii, 13, 77, 229, 411, 468

Diana García: xviii, 38, 78, 114, 148, 186, 218, 250, 288, 322, 356, 396, 436

Marisol Villanueva Méndez, courtesy of the Grandmothers Wisdom project: 3, 5, 22, 25, 26, 28, 29, 30, 33, 35, 37, 41, 42, 43, 54, 61, 65, 66, 69, 70, 71, 75, 82, 83, 86, 89, 90, 91, 93, 94, 101, 106, 107, 109, 113, 118, 123, 124, 125, 126, 127, 130, 132, 133, 136, 138, 145, 147, 152, 156, 157, 158, 159, 162, 167, 172, 174, 177, 180, 183, 185, 189, 191, 196, 198, 200, 201, 204, 205, 209, 210, 211, 212, 217, 224, 226, 230, 232, 239, 240, 241, 242, 245, 258, 260, 267, 270, 271, 274, 275, 276, 278, 279, 281, 287, 295, 298, 299, 308, 310, 311, 314, 316, 318, 319, 321, 327, 329, 331, 332, 334, 335, 337, 338, 339, 346, 347, 348, 350, 351, 359, 366, 372, 379, 381, 383, 384, 385, 386, 388, 392, 395, 399, 400, 406, 413, 416, 417, 425, 426, 430, 431, 445, 453, 454, 455, 456, 457, 459, 460, 464, 471

Courtesy of Tsering Dolma Gyaltong's family archive: 10, 14, 19, 22, 23, 24

Mya Pagán: 12, 64

Tibetan Women's Association: 17

Marisol Villanueva Méndez, courtesy of the International Council of Thirteen Indigenous Grandmothers: 32, 45, 52, 102, 119, 190, 215, 248, 249, 342, 344, 355, 362, 404, 420, 429, 469

Courtesy of Clara Shinobu Iura's family archive: 49, 62

Courtesy of Alex Polari de Alverga: 57, 376

Courtesy of Iberê Périssé: 64

Courtesy of Beatrice Long Visitor Holy Dance's family archive: 81

Courtesy Red Cloud Indian School and Marquette University. Holy Rosary Mission—Red Cloud Indian School Records: MUA_HRM_rcis_02868, Immaculate Conception Sodality, 1945, 84; MUA_HRM_RCIS_02199, Student Actors and Adults by tipi, n.d. (1940-1950), 85; MUA_HRM_RCIS_02565, Fr. Steinmetz, S. J. with pipe pointed upwards 1975, 100; MUA_HRM_RCIS_03185, Elementary School Girls and Franciscan Sister 1939, 293; MUA_HRM_RCIS_02563, Fr. Steinmetz, S. J. Praying with Pipe 1975, 304

Courtesy of Bob Boyll: 97

Courtesy of Loretta Afraid of Bear Cook's family archive: 103

Courtesy of Julieta Casimiro's family archive: 117, 124, 125, 142

Courtesy of Antonio Aquino: 141

Courtesy of Rita Pitka Blumenstein's family archive: 151, 153

Courtesy of Nadema Agard: 182

Courtesy of Aama Bombo's family archive: 193, 206

Courtesy of Margaret Behan's family archive: 221, 222, 223, 238

Courtesy of Elise Chehowski: 247

Courtesy of Flordemayo's family archive: 253, 256, 263, 265, 268

Courtesy of Rita Long Visitor Holy Dance's family archive: 291

Courtesy of Nathaniel Blindman: 313

Courtesy of Bernadette Rebienot's family archive: 325, 326, 332

Courtesy of Jean-Claude Cheyssial: 355

Courtesy of Maria Alice Campos Freire's family archive: 374, 377, 379, 390

Courtesy of Mona Polacca's family archive: 401, 402, 406, 407, 412

Courtesy of Agnes Baker Pilgrim's family archive: 440, 442, 459

Courtesy National Anthropological Archives, Smithsonian Institution: NAA INV 10070900, OI-ha-the or George Harney before 1877, 450